D0902026

LET JUSTICE BE DONE

A NEW YORK TRIAL LAWYER'S ODYSSEY THROUGH THE LAST HALF OF THE 20TH CENTURY

PETER E. DEBLASIO

Kindle Direct Publishing
Let Justice Be Done
A New York Trial Lawyer's Odyssey
Through the Last Half of the 20th Century
ISBN: 978-1-7351563-0-9
Author Peter E. DeBlasio

DISCLAIMER: This is a work of non-fiction but in some instances names, characters, businesses, places, events and incidents are used in a fictitious manner. The contents of this book do not constitute legal advice; should you need legal advice you should contact a professional.

ATTRIBUTIONS

Cover design:	Alessandra DeBlasio; Allan Haynes, Jr.; Bruce Hall; Debbie Burke
Cover by:	Donna Lynn Designs, rarequality@hotmail.com
Sketches:	CC BY Images courtesy of The Courtroom Sketches of Ida Libby Dengrove, University of Virginia Law Library (originals in color)
Photos:	Author's personal collection
Photo restorations:	Phil Cantor Photography, www.philcantor.com
Author photo:	Phil Cantor Photography, www.philcantor.com
Proofreading:	Debbie Burke, www.debbieburkeauthor.com
Preparation for publication:	Debbie Burke, www.debbieburkeauthor.com

For My Wife Joy

For My Daughters
Alessandra and Caralee

For My Grandson Allan

CONTENTS

ILLUSTRATIONS

The Overture

Maestro Arturo Toscanini, the world-renowned conductor of operas and symphonies, is quoted in an exchange with a fan in his dressing room, after one of his concerts, as follows:

> The Fan – Maestro, your music comes from the soul, you must love what you are doing.
>
> The Maestro – Madam, do you love dying each and every night?

I do not compare myself to Toscanini, but his answer struck a chord with me. Before I read what he said to that fan, I never thought of the effect that my being a trial lawyer from age 25 had on me, or even if it had any effect at all. However, think about it I did, at that time, and I realized sadly that I too felt I died with each and every trial, especially during those dreadful minutes, hours and sometimes days while I was waiting for the jury's verdict.

I began to analyze myself to learn why that was happening to me. I always knew that with each case I felt that if I could just win one more time, just win that one case, I would achieve my dreams of being successful and happy. It never happened. No matter how many times I won, the next case was just like the last one, I had to win it or else. I did know that trials were taking a toll on me, so much so that my blood pressure reached extremely high limits from age 30 on. I knew that Toscanini's blood pressure was also at the highest levels throughout his career, but it was little comfort to me that he lived well into his eighties because I often felt that I would not reach my next birthday. Fortunately, even after more than fifty years as a trial lawyer, I joined Toscanini in that group of octogenarians, and have since surpassed him, as I am now 90.

Why then, after all these years, do I, shy by nature, have the temerity, or *chutzpah* as an appellate judge said about me to my then-partner when I was representing one of the alleged kidnappers in the Samuel Bronfman kidnapping case in the 1970s – and he didn't say it in a complimentary tone – why do I write what I will call memoirs of some of the more than 600 trials, mostly civil, that I tried in my lifetime?

Is it for my wife Joyce, who back in 1982 – when she was still Joyce

Marruso and had been my office manager and administrator since the early 1960s – was so elated when I called the office after the record verdict of $10,000,000 in the Crabbe case, the first eight-figure verdict in New York State history, that she jumped for joy (the name she prefers) and broke off the heel from her shoe? I think the best insight to who I am, or who I was and who Joy is, was encapsulated in what my great friend from Illinois, Jack Mullen (whom I met when we were both admitted to the Inner Circle of Advocates in 1973) wrote to the International Academy of Trial Lawyers in support of my nomination to that body:

> I recommend heartily that Peter join us because although you may not like him, you'll love his wife.

Is it for my daughters Alessandra and Caralee, of whom I am so proud? Brains, beauty, accomplished at everything they have pursued, sports, music, languages, art, photography, and the list goes on. Do I write these trial memoirs so that they can be proud of their daddy, understand a little bit more about his life and career?

Is it for my only grandchild, my daughter Alessandra's son Allan Haynes, Jr.? He is so smart, good-looking, well-behaved, always smiling and a great athlete. I couldn't be prouder, and yet a part of me wishes he was more like his grandpa. For example, when I was eight years old, my life's dream was to be a major league baseball player and to take over center field for the Yankees when my idol Joe DiMaggio retired. Allan, however, does not have such lofty ideals. When he filled out a questionnaire for his third-grade class, when he too was eight years old, in answer to the question of what he intended his life work to be, his one-word answer was "inventor."

Is it because of myself that I write this book? I don't know, or as I like to say, but we never said in Brooklyn when I was growing up and at my happiest, "je ne sais pas" ("shay pa," as I liked to pronounce it). That was my explanation in my summation to the jury in the DeVito federal criminal trial in Brooklyn for not being able to explain why DeVito's good friend and co-defendant, who pled guilty to possessing stolen goods, testified that Paul (DeVito) was also guilty when in fact he was innocent. "You must have done it with mirrors," Chief Judge Jacob Mishler said to me after the *not guilty* verdict.

So as I now think of it, I guess the answer to why I am writing this book is "I don't know," and the reason I don't know is because I'm a trial lawyer and not a writer. I don't know why writers write books.

Although I would like to think I am writing it to help young trial lawyers be the best they can be, that sadly is not completely true. The reason I say this is because one of my strongest beliefs is that to be a great trial lawyer, one has to be born to it. It must be within you. You must be independent – you must be fearless – you must be competitive – you must be innovative. You must know and understand the psyche of those to whom you are talking and dealing with, you must be sincere and most of all you must think for yourself – think of things which no one has thought of or done before and then do them without fear of the consequences.

But I say to myself, why should a young trial lawyer want to read such a book when the author says it won't help him? To begin with, the author hasn't won every case he has tried and hasn't always been right, so maybe he's wrong here too. In addition, there are things to learn both good and bad in reading about another's life in the courtroom, and perhaps someday very deep in your unconscious a thought will surface that you will add to, modify, or improve on, which will be a turning factor in achieving what you are meant to achieve. In any event, hopefully at least my loved ones in reading the following pages will know that I always tried to have justice be done, and as such set an example for them, and for as many others as dare to venture with us into the book.

Frankly, I don't believe many people will read this book, but yet I persist. Why? First, I'm stubborn and I don't like to give up. But that's not enough and I know it. Second, it may do some good or be of benefit to someone. That is what I tried to achieve throughout my career. Third, and finally, I believe I am writing this book because of what the Staten Island jury said to me in December 2004 after the verdict in the Murray case, which was the last case I ever tried:

> We wanted to applaud after your summation. We felt that we deserved college credit for all we learned.

They then all asked for my business card, little knowing it would no longer be of any use.

If I really did enlighten some about the mysteries of law and medicine, and if it made them feel good about themselves and knowledgeable to deal with whatever came along, then maybe my odyssey through our legal system will help others and better their futures. For as I said in the Avula case: "Hindsight is the pathway that leads to foresight."

Happy reading.

Part I

Picking the Jury

Mr. DeBlas – the Dott – he has a diplome?

–Prospective Juror (1960s)

CHAPTER 1

"Mr. DeBlas – the Dott – He Has a Diplome?"

I always loved picking juries – a process known as voir dire – because I learned so much from the prospective jurors, their thoughts, ideas and beliefs. Some of my best memories are of comments made during voir dire. In the voir dire I used to tell the jurors that I wanted it to be as informal as possible and that they should feel free to interrupt me anytime they wanted and ask me any question they had. I said that I'd answer any of their questions as long as the rules governing the voir dire permitted me to do so.

One day in the 1960s I had a prospective juror whose name I have forgotten but whom I will call Mr. Bacciagalupo because I do remember he was Italian-born and spoke with a thick Italian accent, like the Bacciagalupo character in Abbott and Costello. He asked me a question I have never forgotten partly because I never expected the question and partly because, with it, Mr. Bacciagalupo expressed the innocence of a child.

I have forgotten the name and subject matter of the case but the question tells me it was a malpractice case where we were suing a doctor. The dialogue between Mr. Bacciagalupo and me was as follows:

Bacciagalupo - Mr. DeBlas, can I ask a quesch?

DeBlasio - Sure you can ask a question Mr. Bacciagalupo.

Bacciagalupo - Mr. DeBlas, the dott, he has a diplome?

DeBlasio - Yes Mr. Bacciagalupo the doctor has a diploma.

Bacciagalupo - Oh.

DeBlasio - Mr. Bacciagalupo may I ask why you ask if the doctor has a diploma?

Bacciagalupo - How can he make a mistake?

I am still stunned by Mr. Bacciagalupo's words, but I should not be. He was expressing a belief widely embraced by many in the Italian culture in which I grew up. That belief was that doctors were infallible, authoritative and to be blindly followed.

I am sure that Mr. Bacciagalupo did not realize it but the beliefs that led to his question were the reason why trial lawyers had just recently embarked on a new field in the practice of law, namely the malpractice lawsuit. I am also sure that Mr. Bacciagalupo did not realize that these new malpractice lawsuits were not confined to medical doctors but also included lawyers, engineers, architects, dentists and the like.

Trial lawyers therefore had to become trailblazers to serve the Public Good (or as was said in the English Common Law which begat our legal system, the "Public Weal") and help educate our citizenry to the fact that no one is infallible, we all can and do err. From those early years on, I tried to fulfill my function and purpose in my legal work to not only "Do No Harm" (allegedly per Hippocrates to the doctors), but to "Do Good," the "Good" being to help as many as I could to right a wrong and achieve justice regardless of whether the wrongdoer had a diploma or not.

CHAPTER 2

"I'LL LISTEN TO HIM"

I liked Mr. Bacciagalupo. Although he was naïve, he was innocent and honest. He was true to the voir dire.

In 1972, a few years after my meeting with Mr. Bacciagalupo, I questioned a juror whom I did not like because he was not true to the voir dire. The case was Komoroff v. Nowak, tried in Supreme Court, Kings County, before Judge Harold Kelly.

The facts of the lawsuit were simple. Mr. Komoroff underwent surgery performed by Dr. Nowak, an orthopedist. The surgery was not successful. Mr. Komoroff sued the surgeon.

The legal basis for the lawsuit was not so straightforward. This was not the usual malpractice case where we sued a surgeon for departing from accepted practice in the operative procedure. (The orthopedists who reviewed the medical records for us all said the surgery was done in accordance with accepted procedures and that the bad result Mr. Komoroff suffered was simply a well-known risk of that particular surgery.) Instead, we sued the surgeon for failing to inform Mr. Komoroff of the well-known risks of the elective surgery and to get his consent to proceed despite the risks.

The issue for the jury to decide was therefore going to be a simple one: Did the doctor tell or did he not tell the patient of the risks to the surgery? Both parties to the lawsuit had been questioned under oath by each other's lawyers in what are known as Examinations Before Trial, or depositions. Doctor Nowak said that prior to surgery he informed Mr. Komoroff of the risks and hazards; Mr. Komoroff said Dr. Nowak told him he would have a good result, and that had he been informed of serious risks, he would not have gone ahead with the elective surgery.

And now to the voir dire, and the juror I did not like.

I told the prospective jurors that they would hear testimony about a conversation between two men. At this time the subject matter of that conversation was not important; what was important was that the two men totally disagreed about what had been said. The disagreement was so sharp that only one of them could be truthful. It would be the jury's task after seeing and hearing the two men on the witness stand to decide who was telling the truth and who was not.

I then, as per my custom, questioned the juror who was sitting in the first seat, known as the foreman:

DeBlasio -	Mr. Foreman, one of the two men who took part in the conversation and who will testify is a doctor. May I ask, how do you feel about doctors?
Foreman -	I respect doctors.
DeBlasio -	The other man who took part in the conversation and who will testify to what was said is a lawyer. May I ask, how do you feel about lawyers?
Foreman -	I'll listen to him.

To me, here was the voir dire in all its glory. When he gave his first answer, the foreman was truthful. When he gave his second answer he was not. The truth in response to my second question, which he did not say, was "I don't respect lawyers."

Maybe he would have answered the second question truthfully if he were talking to a friend and not me. I understand that he may not have wanted to hurt my feelings, and those of the defense lawyers, but such niceties have no place in a voir dire setting. You cannot be true to another if you are not true to yourself.

I did not want to use one of my "peremptory challenges" on him, so it took me a few minutes of questioning him before he reluctantly agreed that he should excuse himself from the jury because he would not be fair and impartial. (A peremptory challenge is a veto that lawyers may use to excuse a prospective juror without stating a reason for doing so. In civil cases in New York each side is permitted three peremptories when picking a six-person jury, and six peremptories for a twelve-person jury.)

The questions I asked this prospective juror when I wanted to convince him that he should voluntarily excuse himself all dealt with the word "respect." For example: Why did you *not* use the word respect for the lawyer? What does it mean for you to respect one person, or one class of people, or one class of professionals? What other people, or class of people, do you respect and why? When you respect someone such as a doctor, before even seeing or hearing him testify, does that mean to you that he is more likely to be truthful than others, including lawyers?

When he agreed to leave us, a victory for me? Unfortunately not. The final jury voted for the doctor. I believe that the professions of the two antagonists played the major part in the jury's decision, or as they might have said in Socrates's time: "It is better to be respected than listened to."

CHAPTER 3

THE VOIR DIRE

Most people who have ever received a jury summons have experienced a voir dire. While they may not ever have sat on a jury, they probably went through the initial screening process – what we call the voir dire.

"Voir dire" simply means "to tell the truth." The term derives from the Latin – "veritas dictum" – meaning "truthfully said." The Latin made its way into French as "vouloir dire" – literally "to want to say" but colloquially "to mean" (i.e., to speak one's truth). The French, difficult for so many to pronounce, made its way into English legal parlance by dropping a few letters and becoming simply "voir dire." When the early Americans then borrowed from the English legal system, they kept their voir dire.

I have been present when some lawyers have mistakenly told jurors voir dire means "to see" (voir) and "to say" (dire). Not so. Voir dire means that prospective jurors are to say what they mean, that is to speak *truthfully* about their beliefs, feelings, biases and prejudices when questioned by a judge or a lawyer during the selection process, to allow the judge and lawyers to determine if that prospective juror can be fair and impartial in deciding the facts of the case and thereby render a just verdict.

The prime function of a juror is as a fact finder. And as a fact is a truth, a juror is a "truth finder" and says so by his verdict. Not surprisingly our term "verdict" like "voir dire" derives from the same Latin "veritas dictum." Thus, the voir dire begins the legal process with the jurors telling us the truth about themselves, and the verdict ends it with the jurors telling us the truth about the case.

So how do we get to this truth? How do we as trial lawyers ensure through our voir dire that our jurors will be fair and impartial in finding the truth and stating it in their verdict?

The voir dire in New York state court, in civil cases, has always been handled by the lawyers. The judge plays no part. The plaintiff's and defendant's lawyers meet with a roomful of prospective jurors and ask them almost anything they want to elicit information that enables the lawyer to judge whether they can be fair and impartial to their particular client. (There are some limitations on what a lawyer may ask, and among excluded topics are questions about religious practice, political party affiliation and ethnic background.)

The plaintiff's lawyer is first to address the prospective jurors. I usually explained to them how and why the voir dire is so important in our system of justice, that it is the only means to try to determine who among them, as the triers of the facts, would be fair and impartial. I would let them know that the purpose was for them to tell us about themselves generally, and that at this juncture I was not going to tell them everything about the case, but just enough for them to be able to give us their thoughts and their beliefs as they related to the subject matter of the case. It is only when we learn the truth from the jurors at this stage that all concerned can be satisfied that a true and just verdict will follow.

To me, in New York in the second half of the 20th century, fairness and impartiality turned on ethnicity, race, religion and gender, and sometimes on profession (as in Komoroff), education and socio-economic status. One of my goals was to discover a potential juror's biases and prejudices and then decide whether to retain or remove that juror *not* on the basis of *the juror's* own ethnicity, race, religion, gender, profession, education, or socio-economic status, but on whether the juror was likely to hold *my client's* ethnicity, race, religion, gender, profession, education, or socio-economic status against him or her. Conversely, my other goal in selecting a jury was to end up with jurors who would identify with my client and not with my opponent's client. It was an art.

I, like everyone, am a product of my time and place. I believe what I believe, and what I have always believed is that "blood is thicker than water." I believe that people unconsciously identify with – and more often than not will give the benefit of the doubt in a lawsuit to – those most like themselves or those whom they love unconditionally. And I believe that people unconsciously deny the benefit of the doubt to those against whom they hold some (usually irrational) bias or animus.

To be a great trial lawyer, you must know both the questions to ask to get at these concealed prejudices, and the follow-up questions to convince those jurors to remove themselves because they cannot be fair (as I did in Komoroff). I could spend hours, days, even weeks picking a jury, and in my 600 trials I asked jurors thousands of questions – varying them according to the nature of the case – but in every voir dire I ever did I always asked each juror the same three questions:

1) What are you proudest of?

2) Have you ever had any major disappointments?

3) What do you like to do most in life?

Everybody – almost everyone is the same – everybody who has children is proudest of their children. Disappointments, on the other hand, were never one's children, and very often jurors would say they didn't have a disappointment they could think of, but I liked the question, it could be very revealing. I asked what people liked most in life because I wanted to know who was in front of me, who they were, if they loved to read, travel, go to the theater, play sports. Sometimes I would add a fourth question to this trilogy: "Who is the most important person in your life?" But I really didn't have to ask it, and toward the end of my career I rarely did anymore, because the answer never varied: "My mother." Children and mothers, certain answers are always the same.

When I was allowed free rein to ask what I liked and for as long as I liked, I was usually able to pick a jury that I thought would be 100% for me. Sometimes though, it doesn't matter what you do, you will just end up with a jury that appears to be 100% in favor of your adversary (the dog, for example, in the next story about the Greenspans), or 100% against your client (a McCarthy in front of an all-Italian jury), in which case you have to be creative enough to find some commonality, some way to bridge the gap and get these jurors to see beyond their inherent prejudices.

I couldn't overcome the jury's bias to win Greenspan, but by the time I took my client Mr. McCarthy's case to trial I had learned how to spin that straw into gold. And then there are times when you simply have to make a leap of faith and go without a jury altogether and try the case before a judge alone, as I would do in Rabbi Nitzlich's case.

CHAPTER 4

"Those Collies Are Mean Dogs"

When selecting a jury it's not just the parties' professions or expertise you have to take into account – like whether they're a doctor or a lawyer – it's also the jurors'. I learned this the hard way, but lucky for me, it was still early in my career.

In 1965 I selected a jury in the Greenspan case in White Plains. I had joined a plaintiff's firm as a partner in 1963 – Kramer, Dillof, Duhan & DeBlasio – and cases that the firm had started before I became a member were still pending. Why some of them were accepted I will never know and this was one of them. I assume it was as a favor to Dr. Greenspan, a prominent orthopedist who had reviewed cases for the firm and rendered opinions regarding malpractice cases and the like. In any event, it was a case involving a dog, but not a dog bite case.

The basic facts were that Dr. Greenspan's 11-year-old daughter was playing with her 11-year-old friend at the latter's home in Scarsdale one day when, while running up and down the stairs, indoors, the family collie joined in the fun, brushed against little Miss Greenspan and caused her to fall down the stairs and break her arm. Fortunately, there were no permanent damages.

The claim of negligence was against the parents of little Miss Greenspan's friend because they were the dog's owners, and it was claimed that they knowingly kept a collie with known vicious propensities and, therefore, should not have permitted it free rein with a young guest in the house. The case was tried in Westchester County and I, therefore, had to deal with a Westchester jury and then a Westchester judge, both well known in the profession as quite defense-oriented.

I learned a number of lessons from picking that jury, one being that if people like someone or something, they are comfortable in serving on a jury involving that person or thing and are confident they can be fair and impartial to both sides; whereas if one does not like someone or something, they do not believe they can be fair and impartial when it comes to judging that person or thing. For example even I, with all of my experience in the law and objectivity, would have a hard time being fair and impartial if I had to judge between lasagna and liver. I love to eat lasagna; I can't stand liver. It is hard for me to see how liver could win out.

I decided that a bad jury for me would be one that consisted of dog lovers; a good jury would be one without dog lovers. It is always hard to get a good jury in Westchester and when a dog is concerned, it's even harder because most people living there are homeowners and most homeowners own dogs, and you don't own what you don't like, unless it cannot be helped.

True to form, most of the prospective jurors owned dogs. I, on the other hand, had lived in apartments all of my life – first in Brooklyn, then in Manhattan – and never had a dog until my two daughters were born (in 1964 and 1965, respectively). I knew very little about dogs and had no love for dogs, possibly because of my mother's lifelong fear of dogs. In this case, I would have been a good juror for myself.

I went into as much detail as I could in questioning the prospective jurors about dogs, their dogs, their experiences with them and the like. Each and every juror who had a dog – most of them since they were children – loved their dog and dogs in general and each one said that he or she would be willing to sit on the case and judge it fairly and impartially. Try as I might, I could not get any of them to excuse themselves from the case.

Some prospective jurors never had a dog and never wanted a dog and most of them did not like or trust dogs. Each of them asked to be excused from the jury because they felt they could not be fair and impartial toward dogs and thus to the dog's owners. Try as I might, I was not able to have any of them change their minds about jury duty.

I used five of my six peremptory challenges and still had 12 dog-owning, dog-loving jurors in the box. I figured it could get no worse and, since I particularly did not like the juror sitting in the foreman seat, I used my sixth and last peremptory on him.

Onto the jury came a very sweet looking older woman who would now be our forelady. "Yes," she responded, "I have owned dogs all my life." "Yes," she said, "I loved all of my dogs." "Yes," she answered, "I can be totally fair and impartial in such a case as this." And so on.

A final question I always asked prospective jurors was: "Although we have covered a lot of subjects and matters in this voir dire, please tell me if there is anything which we have not covered but which pertains to you and which you think it would be fair to let us know." I don't remember if it was that question which brought out the fact that the dog she had at home and would be returning to at the end of each trial day was a collie, or if I had asked her directly about collies – I must have asked all of the jurors about them because I knew none of the other 11 ever had a collie – but for me, this was the last straw. No more challenges left and our forelady had a collie at home. I did everything I could to persuade her to leave, even bringing up Lassie, the movie, etc. She would not budge; she would be fair. (Naturally I knew after the word "fair" she omitted the words – "to the dog.")

When I first started trying cases, if I believed I had 11 but not all 12 jurors on my side when I finished picking the jury, I was upset even though I only needed 10 of the 12 to win. I remember one time asking one of the young lawyers working for me what kind of a jury he had after he returned to the office from a day in court picking a jury and his answer was: "Looks like a good jury, I think there are three for me and three against." Sadly I realized right then that he would never be a good trial lawyer, and he had already lost that case. Both turned out to be true.

With 12 jurors against me from the start in Greenspan – nothing even close to it had ever happened to me before – although I didn't throw in the towel, I knew that the trial was going to be a mere formality. So when the verdict came in and the jury was asked "how do you find," the answer was "for the dog." Was I surprised? Answer: No. Was the verdict expected? Answer: Yes. Did something unusual happen after that? Answer: Yes. What was that? Answer: I asked to have the jury polled. (Following a verdict, the losing lawyer has the right to have the jury polled wherein the Clerk of the Court asks each juror individually if that is his or her verdict, Yes or No. If three of the 12 answer No, then there is no verdict and they are sent back to continue deliberations. Only once in a blue moon will it turn out that it is not a true verdict, but it is worth the try.)

So the collie woman, meaning the juror in seat No. 1, the forelady, was the first one whom the Clerk asked if that was her verdict and her answer was "No." I was stunned. I even thought that the verdict could have been for us and the jury had misspoken when it said for the dog's owners. This hope was quickly put to rest when the other 11 jurors answered "Yes" it was their verdict.

Whenever I lost a case I always liked to talk to the jurors who voted for me because it gave me some consolation, but more importantly I wanted to learn why I lost and why they did not agree with the majority.

So I went over privately to juror No. 1 and asked her, "Why did you of all people, a collie owner, vote as you did?" Answer: "I know those collies, they're mean dogs."

What did I take away with me from that response?

1. I should make sure I know more about the subject matter of my cases in the future.

2. Things are not always what they seem - skim milk masquerades as cream.

3. When a juror has some expertise in the subject matter of the case and knows more about it than does the ordinary person, his or her view and perspective may be unusual and different from the views of the rest of us.

CHAPTER 5

"Do You All Know What Giambotta Is?"

In 1971 I was on trial in Staten Island before Judge Vito Titone, a great judge who was later elevated to the Court of Appeals (New York State's highest court), and a jury of 12 Italian men. Judge Titone, like the jurors and like 40% of the 450,000 people living in Staten Island, was also Italian. Unfortunately, my client Patrick McCarthy was Irish.

It may not be well known by many that going back to the early 1900s the Italians and Irish did not always get along well together. So here I was again, just like in Greenspan, with 12 against me. Somehow, someway, I felt that I would have to bridge the gap and let my Italian jurors know that Mr. McCarthy was really a nice, likeable guy. In fact he was so likeable that a nice Italian girl married him, and had half-Italian children with him.

The problem for me however was how was I going to inform the jury of this? I am bold on trial but I could not just come out and say: "Hey, he's one of us – he married an Italian." Not only is it bad form, it is much too obvious. I had to think of another approach. It came about as follows.

The lawsuit was a simple dental malpractice case. Mr. McCarthy had a toothache. He went to a dentist who said the tooth had to be pulled. Mr. McCarthy agreed to it and the dentist started to extract the tooth. Unfortunately for Mr. McCarthy while the tooth was being extracted, so too was part of his jaw. When the dentist realized what was happening, he stopped everything, rushed Mr. McCarthy to his car and drove him straight away to the office of an oral surgeon, who successfully extracted the tooth and left the jaw in place. But Mr. McCarthy's jaw had to be wired shut and kept that way for six months. During all that time Mr. McCarthy did not speak, or eat solid food.

By the time of the trial Mr. McCarthy had no problem speaking. While he was on the stand I asked him to describe how he felt being wired up as he had been for the six months. He said it was bad – pain – confinement – couldn't play with his kids – couldn't work – couldn't eat solid food.

I asked what he missed most about not eating. He said – "Giambott." I asked what he meant by "Giambott." He answered: "My wife's mother, Mrs. Bellavita, who was born in the old country, made the best Giambott and it was my favorite dish and I loved it and I missed it."

Judge Titone, always a wit, interrupted and asked the jury: "Do you all know what giambotta is and if so raise your hands." They all raised their hands and yelled out: "Sure we know Giambott and we love it too."

After that love fest the defense lawyer decided that it would be best to settle the case and we did for $22,500. This might not seem like much money, but it is recognized in the field that Staten Islanders, although they like to eat their food, they do not like to give too much money away.

POSTSCRIPT: Giambotta is basically a Monday dish of combined leftovers from a big Italian Sunday dinner. My mother made it on occasion and I loved it too.

CHAPTER 6

"I Don't Believe in Awarding More Than a Certain Amount of Money"

Rules are meant to be broken and mine are no exception. For me, when I represented the *defendant* in the 1950s, Irish, Germans, Scandinavians and Italians were good jurors, and Jews and Blacks were bad jurors. From the 1960s on when I represented the *plaintiff*, Jews, Blacks and Italians were good jurors for me, and Irish, Germans and Scandinavians were bad jurors.

One day when I was selecting a jury for the plaintiff in the 1960s or 70s in New York County, a man I will call Patrick O'Toole took a seat in the jury box. He was stern looking and he was Irish born. Foreign-born people were also a no-no as jurors because they grew up in countries where their laws were such that it was very difficult for plaintiffs to succeed, if they were even allowed to sue in the first place.

However, when I first saw Mr. O'Toole I decided that I was going to make an exception to my rule that the Irish were bad for plaintiffs because of my belief that "blood is thicker than water." I forget the name of my client, but I remember he too was Irish born.

When, in answer to one of my questions during voir dire about money damages Mr. O'Toole said, "I want you to know I don't believe in awarding more than a certain amount of money in any case," I ignored his comment because this wasn't just any case. This was a case where a hard-working Irishman was injured while he was driving his car at 5:30 a.m. on a Sunday morning on Park Avenue in New York (Manhattan) to go to work for the Long Island Railroad, when he was struck at an intersection by a car that went through a red traffic light. Not only would our client testify with a brogue similar to Mr. O'Toole's but our main witness – a priest who had gone to his aide – was also Irish and would testify with an Irish brogue. The defendant driver was not Irish and was a kind of playboy who had been partying all night.

The trial proceeded, it went well and we settled just before summation. Why did I settle? Because the defendant had a $50,000 automobile liability insurance policy and I knew that if we got a jury verdict in excess of that amount the only way we could get more than the $50,000 would be for the defendant to pay it out of his own pocket. I was always loath to, and never did, take money from an individual no matter who he was, and that included doctors in malpractice cases, primarily because they weren't committing crimes with intent to do harm, but instead had accidents due to negligent conduct.

I settled the case for $47,500. I agreed to accept less than the $50,000 policy - even though the injuries were worth about $50,000 - because taking a little less than the maximum was the usual custom and courtesy awarded to a fellow trial lawyer who was beaten.

After the settlement I went over to Mr. O'Toole and talked to him because I had been intrigued by his statement of only believing in awarding a limited amount of money as damages and I wanted to know if I was right or wrong in not excusing him from the jury, and how my theory of "blood is thicker than water" held up. I learned in no uncertain terms that I had been wrong.

I first asked him if he would have found for the plaintiff and he said yes. When I asked him how much he would have voted for he said $10,000. I guess I should have asked him why so little but I did not. I think the reason I did not ask him that question was because I knew, and I believed he knew, that at that time most automobile liability policies were for $10,000 and he was against having people pay out of their own pocket.

I was convinced from then on that my jury rules were not infallible.

Naturally, I was not the only lawyer who had strong viewpoints on who would be good and bad jurors for plaintiffs and defendants based on ethnicity and the like, and some lawyers were very obvious in their prejudices. I remember a case I was trying in Queens representing a plaintiff against the Transit Authority. We had about 50 prospective jurors in the room - all men except for one woman. (In those days, in the 1960s, women had an automatic exemption from serving on juries, I think based on the old days when a woman's place was considered to be at home, taking care of the children.) When the Clerk of Court called the name of the woman juror who was seated in the back of the room to take the place of an excused juror, the defense lawyer who was Irish rudely told the woman, who was Jewish: "Don't bother even getting up, you're excused." Sadly, he got chuckles from many of the male jurors.

Long after the days I have been writing about, determining who is likely to be a good or bad juror has become a thriving business. Lawyers now pay substantial fees to people who call themselves "jury consultants" to provide their "expert" opinions on how people's biases and prejudices play such a vital part in why they vote for one side or the other. These jury consultants remain popular today among trial lawyers nationwide.

Nor is it only trial lawyers – and jury consultants – who think about this subject; so too do ordinary people. That became clear to me in a later case when, after I picked a jury in Queens, my German-American client asked me about the make-up of our jury. I told him we had a couple of Frenchmen, a couple of Jews, a couple of Greeks, a Russian, a Dane, a few other Scandinavians and an Englishman. He then said, evidently upset: "You've got all my enemies on the jury." I answered: "Who was I supposed to get, your Axis allies?" (N.B.: During World War II the three Axis powers fighting the free world were Germany, Italy and Japan.)

In my beginning years, ethnicity even divided which lawyers were on which sides. Plaintiff's lawyers were Jewish; defense lawyers were Irish; Wall Street lawyers were WASPS (Ivy League lawyers); African-American lawyers were almost nonexistent and the poor Italian lawyers picked up the crumbs and were on whatever side would have them.

To me, the best trial lawyers I knew were the Irish. Why that was so I do not know. Maybe because they seemed to have a gift in telling a story, because that's what a trial is, a story about past events. Maybe because they kissed that Blarney Stone. Maybe because they knew how and when to use humor to keep the jurors interested and involved, because trials can be very boring.

The next best trial lawyers were, in my opinion, the Jews. The reason for that is easy – they were the smartest. (When I was a kid it was a common thing to hear – even from Italians – "if you want a smart lawyer, get a Jew.") Alas, the poor Italians followed. Why they were lower in my estimation, I don't know. Perhaps because there weren't too many of them trying cases in those days. (As for the Wall Street lawyers, I didn't consider them trial lawyers, and African-American lawyers I rarely saw.)

The best trial lawyer I ever knew was John G. Reilly, my boss from 1958 to 1961. Second best was my friend Peter Johnson. Both were born in Ireland and both were defense lawyers and both told me that I made a mistake with Mr. O'Toole because "Irishmen are independent cusses and they don't believe that blood is thicker than water." The best plaintiff's lawyer I ever knew is my good friend Tom Moore. He was also born in Ireland, but I don't think he would agree with Mr. Reilly and Peter about the Irish being cusses, because he was trained in Jesuit schools to be very proper. I am sure though that plenty of Irish defense lawyers cussed Tom, because he beat them so badly.

CHAPTER 7

"YES, WE CAN BRIDGE THE GAP"

Not all jury selection is about uncovering latent bias and prejudice. Sometimes it is just about discovering which prospective jurors can take a leap of faith. Such was my task in the personal injury case Morales v. Kiamesha Concord, which I tried in 1973 before a Queens County jury.

On the day of his injury, my client Antonio Morales was the sparring partner of a boxer about to compete for a heavyweight title. Thus, his accident, injury and lawsuit made the major newspapers. The facts of the case were basically as stated in the April 4, 1973 article "Morales, Ex-Boxer, Wins $1.75 Million Jury Award" in THE NEW YORK TIMES:

> A negligence award of $1.75 million, said to be one of the highest in the history of New York State, was handed up yesterday in State Supreme Court, Queens, in favor of Antonio Morales, a former prize fighter.
>
> The defendant in the case was the Concord Hotel of Kiamesha Lake, New York where on May 26, 1966 Morales was a sparring partner for Doug Jones, who was training to fight Ernie Terrell for the World Boxing Association version of the heavy weight title.
>
> Peter E. DeBlasio, of the law firm of DeBlasio & Meagher of 233 Broadway, who was trial counsel for Morales, said that Morales had sparred for five rounds with Jones before going into a hotel dressing room to change his clothes.
>
> Fifteen minutes later, when he did not reappear, Morales was found unconscious on the dressing room floor, one of his legs lying over the foot of a bench. Counsel for the plaintiff contended that Morales had tripped over the bench, which it was claimed, was an outdoor type that should not have been in a dressing room. According to DeBlasio, Morales suffered a brain injury as a result of his fall, is almost completely paralyzed, is confined to a wheelchair with no control over his physical functions and was

> unable to testify. Morales who is now 33 years old . . . has nursing service around the clock.
>
> A jury of six men handed up the negligence award after two days of deliberation. Defense motions to set aside the verdict, first on the ground that it was against the weight of credible evidence and second on the ground that it was excessive were denied by J. William G. Giaccio.

The DAILY NEWS reported the same day:

> Witnesses testified during the week-long trial that Morales . . . was being groomed as a possible heavy weight contender.
>
> . . . [T]he dressing room was a men's lavatory converted for the fighter's use. The conversion included several wood park-type benches which had protruding slats on their legs to keep them from tipping over. Morales apparently tripped over one of these slats and fell striking his head. Morales' manager entered the dressing room about fifteen minutes later and found the fighter unconscious on the floor. He was rushed to Monticello Hospital where he underwent surgery for a subdural hemorrhage.

The LONG ISLAND PRESS also had an article about the case:

> A former boxer living a permanent second infancy won $1.75 million in what is believed to be the largest damage judgment ever awarded in Queens, possibly in the state.
>
> Although Morales briefly visited the four-day trial . . . his attorney Peter DeBlasio said Morales was basically unaware of the suit. . . . The Puerto Rican born Morales was six feet, 209 lbs. and had won his only professional fight in a one round knockout after turning professional in 1965. . . . DeBlasio said the suit was based on circumstantial evidence because Morales never remembered what happened and no witnesses were present. The evidence was testimony that Morales' foot was discovered lying over the bottom protruding section of a wood bench designed for outdoor use. "Benches like that are a trap," DeBlasio charged apparently convincing the jury.

To clarify the facts in one aspect – there are outdoor benches and indoor benches and while both have legs, they differ in style. The legs on outdoor benches, unlike indoor benches, fit into slats, which are flat pieces of wood that protrude about four inches in front of the bench. When outdoors, these slats lie in the earth; but when inside, they sit on top of the floor and can be tripped over.

Our claim was that the hotel did not use reasonable care and was negligent in placing an outdoor bench in an indoor space, especially in the circumstances where a boxer has to use the dressing room after sparring and obviously with his being sweaty, and having sweat go into his eyes, he would have difficulty seeing where he was going.

The problem I faced was to select a jury that could find for the plaintiff even though such a finding would be based solely on "circumstantial evidence" (i.e., inferring an unknown fact that reasonably follows from a known fact or a known set of facts). The way I successfully overcame the problem was as follows:

> I outlined the case to the prospective jurors. I told them we would produce witnesses, including the famous heavyweight Doug Jones, who would take us up to the point when the five rounds of sparring ended and Morales, sweating, left the ring to go to the locker room. Then there would be a gap of no testimony for 15 minutes while he was alone changing out of his boxing trunks. Then testimony would resume when his manager found him on the floor in the locker room, unconscious and with one foot on one of the slats of the bench.
>
> I concentrated my voir dire on this 15-minute gap, explaining to the prospective jurors how certain people would be unable to sit on a case such as this because "seeing is believing" – or "I'm from Missouri, the 'show me' State" – and without an eyewitness to testify to how the accident occurred, they would think it pure speculation to try to reconstruct the events. People who felt that way agreed with me that they couldn't be fair, and they excused themselves. On the other hand, those who could use their common sense about what must have happened during that 15-minute gap, if given enough detailed testimony before and after it, believed they could be fair and would be able to render a just verdict.

In that manner, I was able to have about 20 people decline to sit in judgment and ended up with a group, to a man, who could "bridge the gap." It was then easy to show that Morales tripped over a slat that should not have been in that room and, as a result, his life was tragically altered.

This was my first million dollar verdict and since the first million dollar verdict ever in New York was awarded just 13 years before in 1960, it was still considered quite a feat. (That 1960 case was tried by Jacob Fuchsberg, who was later elevated to the New York Court of Appeals and, a few years after the Morales case, he wrote the opinion when we appealed the Bronfman verdict.)

In fact, as a result of the Morales trial, I was invited into The Inner Circle of Advocates, an organization of the top plaintiff's trial lawyers in America, which back then in 1973 had only 33 members, one of whom not surprisingly was Fuchsberg. The Inner Circle is now limited to 100 members, plus Emeritus Members, of which I am one. One of the requirements for entry was and is that a lawyer had to have tried at least 50 cases and had to have received a verdict of one million dollars or more. (My good friend and the great plaintiff's attorney Tom Moore, who joined Kramer Dillof a while after I left the firm, was invited into The Inner Circle a few years later, as was his wife Judy Livingston, the first woman to become a member. The first African-American to become a member of The Inner Circle was Johnnie Cochran of O.J. Simpson fame, among many other cases. Another recognizable member was former Senator and vice-presidential candidate John Edwards of North Carolina.)

In any event, it's a good thing that membership in The Inner Circle is not revoked if your million-dollar case is reversed, because that is what the Appellate Division, Second Department, did one year later.

Five appellate judges unanimously decided that there were a number of possible reasons why Morales fell, including a convulsion due to blows received sparring, and thus it would only be a remote possibility and speculation that the bench was the cause of his fall. (Had I realized that the Appellate Division judges would think that Doug Jones's "held-back" sparring punches could cause a convulsion, I would have reminded them that his "all-out" punches against Ernie Terrell a few weeks later were ineffective in causing injury because he lost that title fight.)

The take-away? I only won the Morales case because of the voir dire. Knowing how to pick the right jury is often the decisive factor between victory and defeat at trial. But a great jury does not guarantee success on appeal. Appeals, as evidenced here, are a whole different ballgame. As one might suspect, when a litigant appears before an appellate panel – or before a single judge on a bench trial – he does not have the right to voir dire the judges in regard to how they feel about "bridging the gap" when there is no eyewitness testimony nor direct evidence to the actual occurrence. And judges are not known to take a leap of faith.

CHAPTER 8

"MUTTEL MY FATHER'S NAME IS"

There are cases where no good jury can be had, and in such instances it is the trial lawyer who has to take the leap of faith and try the matter before a judge alone. Nitzlich was just such a case.

In 1972, my client Rabbi Mordechai Nitzlich brought a wrongful death lawsuit in Supreme Court, Brooklyn, for the death of his 10-year-old son. I tried the case before Judge Abraham Multer without a jury. It may seem odd to include a non-jury case in a section on picking the jury. So, why do I include it here? Because in a "bench trial" as they are called, the judge takes on the jury's role of factfinder and when deciding whether to take the leap of faith to forsake a jury in favor of a judge, I applied my same voir dire rules. But more than anything, I include this case because it is an example of what to me makes a trial lawyer a trial lawyer: innovation, thinking of doing that which others would not dare to do and, of course, being right and being lucky.

The decision I made in this case to try it non-jury was one that most lawyers would not have made, let alone even thought of making. They would have been right most of the time because Brooklyn jurors were known to be "plaintiff's jurors" (i.e., they most often preferred and voted for the plaintiff), and Judge Abraham Multer was well known to be a "defendant's judge" (i.e., he did not look favorably on plaintiffs' cases).

Why then did I waive a jury and try the case before a defendant's judge when I always loved juries and believed that selecting juries was the most important part of any case? The reason was simple – I thought I had a much better chance to win it non-jury than with a jury.

To better understand my reasoning we must consider three things, namely: 1) the facts of the accident; 2) the facts relating to the parties involved in the accident; and 3) the fact that a trial is a kind of war fought in a courtroom where one side ends up victorious and the other ends up defeated. To be a successful trial lawyer, you cannot afford to lose too many wars.

1) The Accident – This was what was known as a simple automobile accident case. Young Nitzlich while on his way to school started to cross a Brooklyn street, at the corner, when he was struck by a truck as it was making a left turn. There were no traffic signals controlling traffic at that intersection. Nitzlich died instantly. Our claim was that since the boy was in the crosswalk he had the right of way and the driver was negligent in striking him. The defendant's claim was that the boy was running across the street and, therefore, he was contributorily negligent in causing the accident.

2) The Parties – The Nitzlichs were Hasidic Jews. The defendant truck driver was an African-American man.

3) The War – Thus, we had two peoples of different cultures and backgrounds opposing each other.

The goal in selecting a jury is to end up with jurors who identify with your client and not with your opponent's client. The more one is of the same culture – the same background – as your client, the more he will identify with and understand him and be receptive to him. Thus, all things being equal, a jury consisting of mainly Jewish jurors would identify with the Nitzlichs, whereas a jury made up of mostly African-American jurors would, all things being equal, identify with the truck driver. One reason being that when a group of people, or a tribe, or a race, has been oppressed, as both the Jews and African-Americans have been, they tend to close ranks and unify with their own. In Brooklyn where we were trying the case, there would be a big mix of both, so the chances of an all-Jewish jury were slim.

In addition, contrary to common thinking, wrongful death lawsuits are usually difficult for plaintiffs to win in front of a jury, especially when a deceased child is involved, because: a) jurors are reluctant to declare a defendant responsible for the death of a fellow human being; b) jurors will only see and hear from the defendant, not the deceased; and c) a number of prospective jurors when questioned during jury selection declare that they do not believe one should seek "blood money" for the death of a child.

To further complicate this case for the Nitzlichs, I noticed while waiting a full day to select my jury that the majority of the prospective jury panel members were African-Americans and it was obvious that our jury would have much more in common with the defendant driver than with the Nitzlichs. Thus, I faced a dilemma – to have or not to have a jury.

As I stated, Judge Multer was known as a defendant's judge. With my background as an Assistant U.S. Attorney for four years prosecuting those accused of committing federal crimes, and then my three years representing defendants in automobile cases while at Mr. Reilly's firm, I felt quite comfortable trying jury cases presided over by defendant-leaning judges. I found them to be strict, no-nonsense and completely in control of their courtrooms, but since I had been trained to conduct myself in the same manner when trying a case, we usually got along very well. But by far, one other factor convinced me to waive the jury in this case, namely the culture, the history and the identification of Judge Multer: I knew he was Jewish.

To waive a jury is perhaps a misnomer because although it is true that the case is then tried by a judge and not a jury of twelve, there is still a jury – albeit a jury of one, the judge. A jury's function is to weigh the credible evidence and determine the facts. The facts and the truth are the same; that which is fact is true; that which is true is fact. In a non-jury case, the judge rules on questions of law as is his function in a jury case, but he also takes on another duty when the jury is waived, which is to determine the facts – to determine the truth.

One difference, however, between a judge deciding the facts as opposed to a jury deciding them is that the lawyer does not get to voir dire the judge. In this case, I was willing to waive my voir dire of Judge Multer because of my life-long belief in the adage "blood is thicker than water."

I still had a serious problem to overcome and that was to convince the defendant's lawyer that it was in his best interest and the best interest of his client (the insurance company for the truck driver) to agree to try the case non-jury. The defense lawyer was shrewd and capable and his bailiwick was the Brooklyn Supreme Court. He had tried many cases before Judge Multer and I am sure with great success. I had one additional thing going for me, however, and that was that he had to think I had lost my senses in wanting to try the case before Judge Multer. I was right, he had no trouble in obtaining the consent of the insurance carrier.

And so we come to the trial. The first part related to the liability question, and the second part of the trial was to determine the damages if the judge found the defendant liable. A word about damages.

Under New York law, if a plaintiff is successful in proving liability and causality in the death of a loved one (in this case the son), the damages to be awarded are limited solely to the pecuniary loss of the deceased's next of kin (in this case the father and mother, Rabbi and Mrs. Nitzlich). "Pecuniary loss" means monetary loss, and monetary loss means how much money the son would have given or provided to his mother and father had he lived. Ten-year-olds rarely are able to give money to their parents at that age. Naturally the opposite is true – the parents provide for their child. The law, therefore, enters into a legal fiction to correct or modify what would normally be an unjust result, namely no damages for the death of a ten-year-old.

That fiction is as follows: the law permits the plaintiff parents to offer evidence of the good character and good habits and intelligence of their child, and then assuming and concluding that the child would have grown up to be industrious and earn a good living – and that as the parents grew older the child would have provided for them – a reasonable sum of money can be awarded for that child's death.

To provide the basis of an award for damages, Rabbi Nitzlich was therefore permitted by law to testify at trial as to his son's excellent grades, and to read some of what he wrote in school, to establish his intelligence and future prospects. Thus, we introduced into evidence one of the child's school books and Rabbi Nitzlich started to read from a page that detailed the boy's family history. Rabbi Nitzlich, known by his family and friends as Muttel, got no farther than reading the first sentence, translating from the Hebrew into English "Muttel my father's name is," when Judge Multer interjected "my father's name was also Muttel."

Then and there I knew that we had won. There is no better identification with a plaintiff than that, and I realized what I had learned as a boy growing up in Brooklyn about blood and water was true. Judge Multer's verdict was for the plaintiff in the sum of $50,000. In today's world it does not sound like much, but in 1972 it was quite substantial for the death of a child.

POSTSCRIPT: When Judge Multer announced his verdict, the Rabbi, Mrs. Nitzlich and I all shook hands. I was later told by one of their male relatives that under Hasidic custom or law what I had done in shaking hands with Mrs. Nitzlich was not permitted. I felt bad and when I next met with Mrs. Nitzlich, I apologized and asked her why she had permitted me to do that. I remember she was very gracious about it and said, "I knew you did not know and so no apology is necessary."

Rabbi Edgar Gluck (the public relations representative for the Hasidic community at City Hall), together with Attorney Gene Rossides (the great Columbia football quarterback and former teammate of mine), had referred the Nitzlichs to me. Before making the referral, however, they had to discuss it and obtain permission from the Grand Rebbe David Twersky, who was the leader of the Hasidim in Spring Valley, New York. All Hasidim in the Grand Rebbe's flock, including Rabbi Nitzlich, always sought counsel from their Grand Rebbe when they had to make decisions on matters of great importance.

From that time on until my retirement, the Grand Rebbe invariably referred his people to me when it related to legal matters in my field. I have always been most grateful to Grand Rebbe Twersky for his kindness to me.

CHAPTER 9

A Very Smart Jury

There is one case that sticks out in my mind only because, in hindsight, I should have done what I did in Nitzlich and just tried it before the judge. I no longer remember the client's name, or even the decade, but on account of the jury and its verdict, I do remember that I tried it in New York County and that it was early summer.

When you try a case in New York County (that is, with jurors who are Manhattan residents), you often get a jury with very smart jurors, especially if the case is tried in June and July, after the school year has ended. In early summer, those who have deferred their jury duty during the year because of their employment, notably professors at the local colleges, now fulfill it.

What little I recall of the case is that it was a motor vehicle accident and I represented the plaintiff, and the lawyer who represented the defendant was young and inexperienced. But what remains as clear as a bell is that the jurors voted against me and I was stunned.

As I liked to do when I lost, I went to speak with the jurors and I asked them why they voted as they did. Their answer went something like this:

> The defendant's lawyer was so ineffective that we asked ourselves: "What would DeBlasio have done if he represented the defendant? What questions would he have asked?" So we put ourselves in your place and we asked the questions we thought you would have asked. In that way, we were able to figure out what the facts really were, and we're sorry, but they were against you.

I guess the lessons learned are: Don't over-try your case and don't select a jury that is smarter than you.

Judge George Beisheim, Jr., addressing the jury panel during voir dire, State of New York v. Lynch and Byrne (Bronfman kidnapping trial), Westchester, NY, 1976.

Bronfman jury: the coal miner's daughter is center; the Israeli-born juror is to the far right and next to him is the Italian-American man; one of the two Irish women jurors is front left.

CHAPTER 10

THE COAL MINER'S DAUGHTER

The greatest jury I ever picked was for the greatest case I ever tried, State of New York v. Lynch and Byrne, widely known as the Bronfman kidnapping trial. (In August 1975, two men, a fireman and a limousine driver, abducted Samuel Bronfman II, the 21-year-old heir apparent of the Seagram liquor empire; they held him for nine days and collected $2.3 million in ransom.) I was able to convince a jury of 12 that my client, caught red-handed in a Brooklyn apartment with his victim bound and blindfolded, was not guilty of kidnapping. I knew the moment jury selection was complete that the case was won. All because of the voir dire.

I was able to select the greatest jury ever assembled only because of the immeasurable - though unwitting - help of the Westchester County judge presiding over the case, the Honorable George Beisheim, Jr. But for the fullest free-range Judge Beisheim gave me, I could not and would not have won the case.

Judge Beisheim was selected by the powers that be to try this case, which was in the national spotlight, because he was what's known as "a hanging judge." He was all for law and order (the government - the prosecutor) and not for the defense.

Even though I was appearing before him on behalf of the defense, I liked Judge Beisheim. I found him to be fair. That description cannot be said of many of the more than a thousand judges before whom I have appeared. Judges are human, they have their biases and prejudices like so many of us do, but he was able to keep his in check. Although a prosecutor's judge, I did not see any evidence of it during the trial.

Judge Beisheim's aim and function was to see that justice was done. Justice in this case was obvious and known to all for the year between the 1975 kidnapping and the 1976 trial: a guilty verdict for the kidnapping and a sentence of life imprisonment for the defendants.

The case was so "open and shut" that no other verdict was conceivable. The facts regarding guilt were overwhelming and irrefutable:

1. The defendant Dominic Byrne (my client) contacted the NYPD just after midnight on Sunday August 17, 1975 and told them he knew where Sam Bronfman was being held. He then met with the FBI chiefs in charge of the search and rescue operation and told them that he and his friend Mel Patrick Lynch had abducted Sam Bronfman nine days earlier, and that they were holding him at Mel's apartment, which was around the corner from his own, in the Flatbush section of Brooklyn.

2. At 3:30 a.m. that Sunday morning, Byrne led the FBI and NYPD to Lynch's apartment and opened the door for them with his key.

3. The FBI and NYPD rushed in and found Sam bound and blindfolded, with Lynch sitting nearby guarding him.

4. Lynch's loaded gun was on a table near where he and Sam were seated.

5. Byrne and Lynch were arrested and taken to FBI headquarters where they immediately confessed to the kidnapping. On that Sunday August 17, after approximately 14 hours of questioning by FBI agents, Byrne signed a 17-page confession and Lynch initialed a 16-page confession.

6. During the course of their confessions, both Byrne and Lynch independently told the FBI agents where Lynch had hidden the $2.3 million in ransom money – under the bed in the apartment of a friend of Byrne's who was then in the hospital.

7. The FBI went to the friend's apartment, which was two blocks from Lynch's apartment, and recovered all of the ransom money, just where they were told they would find it.

8. During their confessions, Byrne and Lynch also told the FBI agents that the typewriter and tape recorder they had used during the previous nine days were both at Byrne's apartment. The FBI went and retrieved them.

9. Sam also gave a statement on that Sunday to the FBI, identifying Lynch ("the big man") as the one who abducted him at gunpoint from outside his mother's Westchester estate home; and identifying Byrne ("the little man") as the driver and the one who stayed at the apartment with him when the big man went out. He told the FBI that he was bound and blindfolded the entire time.

10. Further, at the time of the ransom delivery, about 24 hours before the rescue, over 100 FBI agents had been on surveillance – by car, taxi, van, truck, motorcycle, bicycle and helicopter, as well as on foot – as Sam's father Edgar Bronfman met the kidnapper to deliver the ransom money; and some of the agents had watched as the kidnapper (Lynch) transferred it from Edgar's car to his own. The license plate of the kidnapper's car, which two agents had managed to get close enough to read, showed the car was registered to Mel Patrick Lynch. A follow-up inquiry showed that the car had not been reported stolen.

Judge Beisheim's role, therefore, was to conduct the trial so that the defendants received a fair trial and just as importantly that no legal errors were made so that a guilty verdict could not be reversed on appeal.

To that end of conducting an error-free trial, Judge Beisheim was fully committed. That total commitment, however, backfired because it gave so much leeway to the defense in what it was permitted to do, that it was a major factor in bringing about the result which was inconceivable to almost everyone – there was no kidnapping, it had all been a hoax.

At no stage was the judge's lenience more devastating to the government than during jury selection. The judge permitted a voir dire that I had never seen or heard of before. There were basically no limits on what we, the three lawyers, were permitted to do. In fact, he permitted the defense (me) such untold leeway that I was able to whittle down a panel of 300 prospective jurors to the only 12 people in New York State – seven women and five men who resided in Westchester County – who might defy truth and common sense to find red-handed kidnappers not guilty.

It came about as follows. Due to the intense media coverage around the Bronfman kidnapping in our newspapers, magazines and television newscasts in August 1975, and because of the projected length of the trial – about three months to get through the anticipated 60 witnesses – nearly 1,000 people were summoned for jury duty at the Supreme Court building in White Plains, Westchester County, in September 1976.

The first order of business was for Judge Beisheim to address them in a very large makeshift courtroom and tell them what was expected of them as American citizens, and then for him to listen to those who would have hardships in performing their duty. Judge Beisheim excused about 700 people after he decided that their requests for not serving were legitimate.

The next step Judge Beisheim took was, I thought, quite unusual. He directed that we continue the voir dire in his chambers. His plan? Each one of the remaining 300 or so panel members was to be brought, one at a time, to chambers and questioned individually.

In the judge's chambers were ten people: the judge, his law clerk, a court stenographer, the three lawyers, the two prisoners accused of the kidnapping and the two officers guarding them.

The judge did not set forth any ground rules for the lawyers. The procedure we followed was that a prospective juror was brought into the room and given a seat. The judge spoke first, basically and briefly asking some background questions (employment, family members and the like), telling them what was expected from a juror, and primarily asking if they felt they could sit on the case fairly and impartially.

After a juror said he or she could be impartial, the lawyers were permitted to ask questions. As per procedure, the prosecuting Assistant District Attorney, Geoffrey K. Orlando, went first because he had the burden of proving the case. Defense counsel Walter J. Higgins, Jr. followed because he represented Mel Patrick Lynch, who was the first named defendant in the indictment. I was last because my client, Dominic Byrne, was the second named defendant.

At first, I had no idea about what the prohibitions on my role and questioning would be. When the judge finished with what he had to say to a prospective juror, Orlando and Higgins either said nothing or very little. I then tested the ground slowly and innocuously with the first few prospective jurors, and soon realized that no matter what I said or asked there was no objection, there was no cutting me off, there was no restriction. It was as though I was alone in the room with the prospective juror and could do, say and ask anything I wished, provided I kept within the bounds of polite society, good manners and respectfulness.

There are two jurors I would like to tell about to give the flavor of what followed for the next three days as we continued in chambers picking the jury. But first, I should make clear about the purpose of this stage of voir dire.

There are two ways a lawyer can keep a juror off a criminal jury. He can use a "challenge for cause" or a "peremptory challenge." A "challenge for cause" is made to and decided by the judge. The lawyer has to state a reason why that person is unfit or unqualified to serve as a juror. It usually has to deal with a bias or prejudice – either known or unknown to the person being questioned – which bias or prejudice would most likely interfere with a defendant's receiving a fair and just trial if that person were to sit on the jury.

Scenarios where a lawyer might ask the judge for a "challenge for cause" arise more than one might think. For example, in a civil case I have heard a prospective juror say: "I believe that whenever a person is injured in an accident, he had to be negligent, no matter what he says." And in a criminal case I have heard a prospective juror say: "I believe that police officers, FBI agents and all law enforcement people are always truthful, whereas people accused of a crime are likely to lie." In such instances, I asked the judge for a "challenge for cause." If the judge grants a challenge, that person does not sit on the jury; if the judge denies it, the lawyer then has to be skillful enough to continue talking to and questioning the juror to have him finally realize that he cannot be fair sitting on this kind of case.

If all that fails we have the "peremptory challenge." In civil cases with juries of 12, each lawyer is allowed six peremptories; and with juries of six, the lawyer has three peremptories. In criminal cases, which usually have juries of 12, the number of peremptories may vary, but it is often six. In the Bronfman case, each defendant was permitted ten peremptories, which meant that the defense had 20 peremptories total, and so the prosecution too was given 20 peremptories. Higgins and I used all 20 of our peremptories; Orlando did not use most of his.

A "peremptory challenge" simply means that a lawyer can excuse a juror without giving any reason for doing so. There are a number of reasons why I use a peremptory in a particular instance, but the common thread is that I think a particular juror will not be receptive to our case and will vote for us to lose.

Now to return to Judge Beisheim's chambers and the questioning of two jurors who, I still remember, played such an important part in our eventual verdict.

The first juror in one sense played no part in our verdict because, at my request, she was excused by the judge "for cause." However, in another sense, in my mind, she did play a big part because had she sat, I know she would have voted with the prosecution and not only that, I believe that she was of such a character (strong, immutable) that she would not have changed her mind and joined in with the majority, so that we would have ended up with a hung jury and a mistrial. (In a criminal trial, unlike a civil trial, the only verdict that is permitted is a unanimous one.[1])

I do not remember the prospective juror's name. She was middle-aged, married to a Wall Street lawyer, and lived in Scarsdale, which I and almost everyone else knew was home to many wealthy people.

The following occurred. She had passed the questioning of Judge Beisheim and Orlando and Higgins with flying colors; that is, she had heard about the Bronfman story a year earlier and she would serve as a fair and impartial juror.

Next, it was my turn and I started to question her as politely and respectfully as had the others. I told her to go back in her mind to August 1975 and the time of the kidnapping, and I asked and *she answered* as follows:

> Did you watch TV?
>
> *Yes.*
>
> Did you read the newspapers?
>
> *Yes.*
>
> Do you remember much of what you read about the events relating to Sam Bronfman?
>
> *Yes.*
>
> Did you discuss some of these events with your husband, on occasion?

---

[1] Up until April 20, 2020, in 48 states and the federal courts, a jury had to be unanimous in order to convict a criminal defendant; in other words, a single juror's vote to acquit was enough to prevent a conviction. There were two states, Louisiana and Oregon, however, that permitted convictions based on 10-to-2 verdicts, which would have resulted in mistrials everywhere else. On April 20, 2020 in the case Ramos v. Louisiana, the U.S. Supreme Court issued an opinion of monumental importance deciding that *in all states*, for all "serious" criminal offenses (defined as "non-petty"), "the Sixth Amendment right to a jury trial – as incorporated against the States by way of the Fourteenth Amendment – requires a unanimous verdict to convict a defendant."

Yes.

Did you realize that Sam Bronfman had been kidnapped?

Yes.

Did you know the FBI was searching for him for nine days?

Yes.

Do you remember that there were ransom demands?

Yes.

Do you remember that the ransom – in the millions – was paid?

Yes.

Do you remember that finally the FBI rescued him?

Yes.

Before the rescue, how did you feel about Sam Bronfman and the Bronfman family?

What do you mean, Mr. DeBlasio?

Were you anxious for them?

Yes.

Were you fearful of what might happen to Sam?

Very.

Whether he was alive or dead?

Yes.

How did you feel when you saw him on TV and saw pictures of him and his family in the newspapers at the time he was rescued?

What do you mean Mr. DeBlasio?

Were you happy?

Of course.

Were you relieved?

Of course.

Were you glad he was alive?

Naturally.

Do you remember that the FBI caught and arrested the two men who they said kidnapped him?

Yes.

How did you feel when you heard about the arrests?

What do you mean Mr. DeBlasio?

Were you relieved?

Of course.

Were you happy?

Yes.

Now, would you please look behind me. Do you see the two men seated in the chairs?

Yes.

Do you know who they are?

No.

They are the two men whom one year ago you were happy about because they were arrested at the rescue scene for the kidnapping of Sam Bronfman.

Oh.

Do you, in all fairness and honesty and truthfulness, still want to tell His Honor and us that you can put everything you have just told us about the Sam Bronfman events of one year ago completely out of your mind, so that these two men can get a just and fair trial?

Well, I really didn't mean --

I interrupted her, faced the judge and asked for a challenge for cause. He forthwith excused her.

At a Columbia Law School Alumni event after the trial was over, I was seated at a table with a man who told me that his wife had been called for jury duty in the Bronfman case and she was quite upset when I had her excused. He described her to me and I remembered that she was the Wall Street lawyer's wife whom I had questioned thoroughly in the early stage of our voir dire in the judge's chambers. I told him I was sorry.

He then asked me why I had let her go when she so wanted to sit and would have been a good juror. I asked him how she would have voted. "Guilty, of course," he answered. My obvious reply: "That's why I excused her."

Back to the jury selection.

From that time on, whenever a prospective juror took his or her seat in chambers and I sized them up and decided that they would favor the prosecution and identify with the Bronfmans – and not Byrne and Lynch – due to their upbringing, social status, professional life, intelligence and the like, I repeated the same procedure with each one of them: How much did you follow the events? How interested were you? How did you feel when Sam was freed? Were you happy when you heard that two men, the two defendants sitting here, were arrested? About 90 percent of the time, Judge Beisheim removed them for cause.

On to the second juror we questioned in chambers of whom I have a vivid memory.

When it was my turn to question her, I started with my usual background questions: Where were you born? Where were you raised? What was your maiden name? What were the professions or occupations of your parents and brothers and sisters? Who is in your family at present? With whom do you reside? And so on.

She said she was a coal miner's daughter from Pennsylvania and she was married to a construction worker and spent her time raising her four young children and keeping house and all that goes with it.

When I went through my routine about the newspaper and TV coverage of the Bronfman events in 1975, she firmly and bluntly said: "I had no time to waste on any of that – I was too busy taking care of the house, myself, my husband and my kids." Nobody challenged her for cause. To me she was exactly the juror I was searching for – there was no possible way that I could imagine that she would identify and side with the billionaire Bronfmans.

When we had completed our in-chambers voir dire of the 300 prospective jurors, we returned to the judge's courtroom for the next phase of our jury selection. The judge had excused about 175 of the 300 for cause, leaving us 125 from whom to select the final 16 who would sit on the jury - 12 regular jurors and four alternate jurors. (If at any time up to the verdict, one of the 12 regulars could not continue, an alternate would replace them; but as it turned out, our original 12 remained throughout the entire three-month trial.)

Sixteen names were selected at random by the Clerk of the Court from the "drum" and they took seats in the jury box. Among them was the coal miner's daughter.

When the judge addressed them and asked if anything had arisen since we last met that might prevent them from judging the case fairly and impartially, I received a terrible blow. The coal miner's daughter raised her hand, stood up, and told the judge that she was sorry but her health issues would prevent her from being a juror on a case such as this.

Judge Beisheim said he was sorry and he would grant her wish to be excused provided that none of the lawyers wished to be heard. He then according to protocol first asked Mr. Orlando if he wished to be heard. "No." Mr. Higgins? "No." Mr. DeBlasio? "Yes, Your Honor, if I may, I would like to ask Juror No. 9 some questions." He said I might.

In response to my questions, she told us she had high blood pressure; she was under a doctor's care; she was on medication; she became very nervous when under stress; when under stress her blood pressure went sky high; from what she had already heard she was sure this would be a long and stressful trial; she had to think of her husband's and kids' welfare. She could not sit.

I then did something I almost never did in jury selection, I told her about my personal life. Once again, Judge Beisheim gave me all the leeway in the world.

I said: I have high blood pressure which is off the charts and which the doctors are having a hard time keeping under control; I've had it for about 20 years; I'm a trial lawyer, which is a very stressful job; I'm different from you, however, in that I have voluntarily chosen to place myself under this stress because I believe it serves a purpose in seeing to it that I do all I can to fit into our democratic society and do my duty. "So should you," I told her, "as a proud American citizen, proudly and selflessly serve when called to sit on a jury and do justice to all our fellow citizens who are in need of justice, as countless numbers of people with all kinds of ailments have done for hundreds of years. I cannot promise you, but I will do all in my power to make this trial stress-less and even, on occasion, add some humor and I am even more certain that you will learn a lot and receive an education in how our legal and jury system works and has lasted for so long, due to people like you and your neighbors."

Will you stay with us? – *Yes.*

To move forward three months to December 10, 1976, after our verdict, one of the women jurors came over to me, said some kind words and asked if I remembered her. "Of course I do," I said. "You are the coal miner's daughter and my favorite juror."

Back to jury selection. Higgins and I used all 20 of our peremptories. Some attorneys are against using up the last peremptory challenge. Sometimes they are right. In this case, much to my chagrin, that was so.

Once we used that last peremptory, there was a vacant seat to fill. The Clerk drew the card from the drum and it was the last one I wanted to see.

The Clerk called a young, educated, successful businessman who was born in Israel. He was, what we called in Brooklyn when I was a boy, "the spitting image" of a young Edgar Bronfman – or even Sam Bronfman – both of whom were going to testify for the prosecution.

My concern was that as an Israeli he would identify with the Bronfmans because it was well known that Edgar Bronfman, and even his father before him, had made multi-million-dollar contributions to the State of Israel for years. Without a peremptory left, I did everything under the sun to question this potential juror so that he would agree to excuse himself. I failed.

The young Israeli was seated and with him our jury was set. When I added the 20 peremptory challenges that we used to strike jurors, to the 175 challenges for cause that the judge had granted in chambers, I figured we had rid ourselves of almost 200 people who would have rendered a guilty verdict. I was very happy with our jury and was sure that they would never convict my client Dominic.

It turned out that I was not only correct about our jury, but I was also correct about the Israeli-born juror. The jury deliberations had taken three days on account of two jurors holding out for a guilty verdict: the young Israeli man and an Italian-American man seated next to him. Just as in the Nitzlich case, what I learned as a boy growing up in Brooklyn about one's blood and one's kin again held true, although I have to admit my disappointment that the Italian-American man was not in my camp all along. (Italian-American women were always my best jurors, but not so the men; sometimes they were strong for me, but sometimes their innate conservatism trumped our common ancestry.)

I have believed that blood is thicker than water – which I recognize is its own form of prejudice – since before I was even born. It was a truism instilled in me by my parents, who had it instilled in them by their parents, immigrants who left a desolate Italian village and upon arrival in the world's greatest metropolis sought out – and found camaraderie among – those like themselves. I saw examples of the preference for one's own "blood" – and the ethnic, racial and religious bias, and sexism and elitism, which this at times engendered – throughout my childhood, then in the Navy, later at my Ivy League law school, and even after graduation as I tried to get my first job.

I am the lawyer I am, I picked the juries I picked, and I had the greatest successes with those juries that a plaintiff's attorney and a criminal defense attorney could ever hope to have, because of where and when and how I grew up. And so I digress to spend a few pages to tell a few stories about my life before the law.

PART II

LIFE BEFORE THE LAW

There's Peter's father, again.

–Classmate, J.H.S. 128
Bensonhurst, Brooklyn (ca. 1937)

If you join the Service be sure you get a good clean and warm bed to sleep in at night, and that's the Navy.

–My Father Amerigo DeBlasio
U.S. Army, PFC 1917-1919
Bensonhurst, Brooklyn (ca. 1948)

You'll earn one-third the salary and have to register as a Republican. Will that be a problem for you?

–Leonard Page Moore
U.S. Attorney, EDNY (1954)

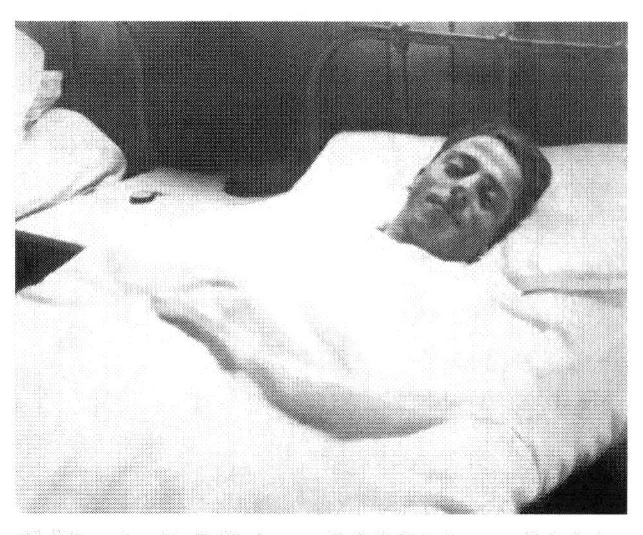

My father, Amerigo DeBlasio, age 18, PFC, U.S. Army 107th Infantry Regiment, Company E, recovering from WWI injuries sustained on the front lines in France, at a hospital in England, November 1918.

My father and mother, Amerigo DeBlasio and Lena Rubertone, on their wedding day, New York, September 16, 1923.

Me on the right (as you look at the photo), with my mother and my brother Eddie in Crooning Pines, New York, summer 1938.

CHAPTER 11

How I Became a Lawyer

A BROOKLYN BOY BORN AND BRED

As in so many of my trials the answer to how I became a lawyer is both complex and simple. It is simple because there is one reason and one person responsible - my father. It is complex because some other factors played a part - my brother, the bass violin and my not being the athlete I hoped I would become.

When I was born in Brooklyn, on August 20, 1929, I figure the odds were one million to one, or higher, against me being a lawyer or anything like it. No one in my family, which included a couple hundred cousins (almost all of my relatives had families of 12 to 14 children), was a lawyer. We never knew a lawyer. We never hired a lawyer. No one in my extended family had ever gone to college; they were lucky if they had graduated from high school.

I was proud that both my mother and father were born in the United States, as opposed to many of my friends' parents who were born in Italy, Russia, Poland and the like. All of my grandparents though were born in Italy, and the only one I ever really knew (my mother's mother) was illiterate, not only in English but also in Italian.

My mother's mother, Maria Rubertone (née Spera), came to this country in 1901 from Craco, an ancient town of cave-like dwellings built into the arid hills of Basilicata at the arch of the boot of Italy. She was 17, an orphan, and was following her only sibling, her older brother Vincenzo, who had emigrated to New York the year before. She soon met and married Pietro, who was also from Craco. In 1920, after 18 years of marriage he left her a widow, three months pregnant with their sixth child. She never remarried. Instead, she went to work cleaning office buildings in lower Manhattan in the nighttime, and lived with her young children in a railroad flat in Little Italy. (One of the buildings I believe she cleaned was the Woolworth Building, which opened in 1913 and was the world's tallest building until 1930. Some fifty or so years after she worked there, and sometime after she died, my law firm took over the entire 43rd floor of the Woolworth Building, one of just two floors with a wrap-around balcony and a 360-degree view of the city and beyond.)

Of my mother's father Pietro little is known except that he had been a shoemaker in Italy, he arrived in New York around 1896 at age 23, and he had a flourishing moustache and was a kind and gentle man adored by his children. He made a meager living gathering paper and rags for resale – a trade common in those days among recent immigrants from Craco – collecting them from office buildings in lower Manhattan.

My mother Lena, the first of my grandmother's children, was born in August 1903 in Manhattan. When she was six, she moved with her parents back to their ancestral home – either because of nostalgia or squalid living conditions in New York – but within four years, shortly before the outbreak of World War I, they were again in America, life simply too harsh in Craco. Her father Pietro returned to his menial job, but when the United States entered the War a few years later, his income as well as his status rose dramatically as he and his fellow immigrant "gatherers" supplied badly needed paper to the U.S. government, their trade now crucial to the war effort.

When my mother was 16 and in the eighth grade – her schooling delayed on account of the move to Italy – her beloved father died from the Spanish flu, one of the last to succumb in February 1920 to the worldwide pandemic. (To honor her father Pietro's memory, when she married three and a half years later, she chose his birthday September 16 as her wedding date, and six years after that, she gave me his name.) Following his death, my mother never again had any formal education, leaving school to help support her mother and younger siblings. She started as a pieceworker making gloves at Richelieu Pearls, but within the year she was promoted to factory forelady, a feat of which she was always very proud.

My father's father Pasquale Di Blasio, born in 1868 in Torre del Greco, near Naples, arrived in New York together with his wife Lucia (née Colamarino) in 1899. Pasquale sang opera and popular Neapolitan folk songs in the many Italian vaudeville music halls then all over New York, and he also travelled the vaudeville circuit performing in cities as far away as Pittsburgh. He was rarely at home with Lucia in Little Italy and when he was, the dynamic was said to have been explosive. Pasquale unfortunately had what was known as "the Italian man's curse" – a violent temper – and as family lore had it, when Lucia was pregnant with what would have been her eighth child, he shoved her, she fell down a flight of steps, and she died. All I remember of my grandfather was his buying me candy at a store in Brooklyn a few days before he sailed to Naples on the S/S Vulcania in November 1934, when I was barely five years old. My father, together with his brothers and sisters, had bought their 66-year-old father a one-way ticket back to Italy and no one ever saw him again.

My father Amerigo was born in January 1900 in Manhattan, his parents' third child but their first one born in America. Like my mother, he spent several years living in Italy when he was young, in his case either because his father could not afford to keep all the children in New York as the family grew, or because his mother could not manage them all virtually on her own in a city that was foreign to her. In Italy, my father lived with his mother's family in Torre del Greco, and there is a single photo remaining from this period, of him with five of his siblings, his maternal grandfather Giovanni Colamarino, two aunts and an uncle in 1907. By 1913, my father was back in New York and had just started to attend DeWitt Clinton High School, when in late September his mother died from her fall down the stairs. He had worked as a newspaper boy to earn the five-cent trolley fare to and from the high school, but with his mother's death, he had to quit to get full-time work to help support his younger siblings. Like my mother, he never again had any formal education.

How, then, with this background could I, an ordinary Brooklyn boy born and bred, be admitted to one of the great colleges in this country (Columbia) at age 16, and then be admitted to one of the great law schools (Columbia) in the world? The answer: my father. It was due to my father's foresight and his being 50 years ahead of his time.

WORLD WAR I

In a way, my father was a hero to me in my childhood, although I did not then appreciate it, nor think about it. My life was playing ball – all kinds of ball – since I was five years old: baseball, football, basketball, punch ball. My dream was to take over center field for the New York Yankees when Joe DiMaggio's playing days were over.

Why was my father a hero? Because when he was 17, in 1917, America entered World War I and he enlisted in the Army. There was one problem. He was not old enough to legitimately do so because the minimum enlistment age was 18 years of age. So he did what I call "the good lie," and somehow and someway he convinced the government that he was 18 years old. Even though he told a falsehood for a patriotic reason, he was worried for the rest of his life that it would be found out and he would be punished; this even up to the time when he was eligible for Social Security benefits in his 60s.

In any event, at age 18 he was sent to France, a Private First-Class in the 107th Infantry Regiment, Company E, assigned to the 27th Division at the front lines, living in what had to be a muddy trench. As part of the Somme Offensive, at dawn on September 29, 1918, the 27th Division was ordered into battle and participated in the heaviest fighting on the Hindenburg Line – my father's Company suffering a very large number of dead from machine gun fire. But their drawing the Germans' fire power upon themselves allowed the 30th Division on their right flank to break through the Line, which led the Germans to surrender and brought about the Armistice and end of the war six weeks later. My father celebrated Armistice day, November 11, 1918, in a hospital bed in England. When he went over the top of the trenches on September 29, charging forward with two of his buddies, one on each side of him – artillery fire killing his buddy on the left and severing the leg of his buddy on the right – my father was sprayed with shrapnel all about his body. He was carried off to an Army hospital, designated "severely wounded," and moved to England to recuperate, after which he presumably was to be returned to his Company, but for the end of the war intervening.

As a boy, I used to feel proud holding and looking at his damaged and indented helmet, but I never thought about how scared this boy had to be during those times and the permanent emotional scars he had to be bearing when I knew him. I do remember that he rarely smiled and at times threatened to commit suicide by jumping off the roof of our Brooklyn apartment building; and that at times he hit my mother and that I at the ages of 8, 9 and 10 had to rush to her aid because I was strong and could hold my father off until he regained his senses. I remember going out to the movies with my mother and brother many Friday nights to avoid him, and then all of us slipping back into the apartment quietly so as not to wake the sleeping monster. I never tried to find out why he acted the way he did. I guess I know now it was post-traumatic stress disorder.

AMERICANIZATION

My father's prime employment when we were boys was with the Post Office in Manhattan as a clerk, and he finally retired after 40 years. He worked the midnight to 8:00 a.m. shift so that he could also work as a waiter during lunch hour at Fusco's, a by-gone Italian restaurant in lower Manhattan and, during baseball season, a third job as an usher at Yankee Stadium in the Bronx for home games. (He was well able to get by with three to four hours of sleep at home.) On many days, after his Post Office shift and before heading over to Fusco's, he liked to attend trials at the nearby lower Manhattan courthouses.

I have wondered if my father went so often to watch the trials because he wanted to understand the law in order to steer me into the field, or because he already recognized the trial lawyer in me and wanted to understand who his son would become, perhaps hoping I would surpass even his idol, Bill Fallon, the "Great Mouthpiece."

One of the sorriest moments in my long trial career is the fact that my father died three months before the Bronfman kidnapping trial began in 1976, perhaps my most famous trial and one that might have given Fallon a run for his money. My father would have been there every day, and I believe he would have been quietly proud.

My mother and father had two children – my brother Edward, born in 1926, and me, born in 1929, exactly two years, ten months and one day after Edward, as he never let me forget. We were both born at home in Brooklyn, delivered by one of our great-aunts, a midwife, Zia Giulietta.

I find it interesting how my brother got the name Edward. In Italy there was a strict custom in the naming of children. The first-born son was named after the father's father; the second-born son was named after the mother's father. The first-born daughter was named after the father's mother; the second-born daughter was named after the mother's mother.

Ordinarily, there should have been no problem or controversy in naming my brother, but these were not ordinary times. We were in America, not Italy, plus my mother hated my father's father's name "Pasquale." She hated the name, which happened to be her name too, the female version Pasqualina (which means *little Easter* in English), and never could stand it when she heard it called out in her grade school classes. As soon as she could, when she went to work at the age of 16, she decided she wanted to be called Lena and from that time forward, she was Lena or Lee for short.

When my mother came through the birthing process there in our apartment, the first words she supposedly said were: "No son of mine in this country is going to be named Pasquale." (Even had she wanted to follow tradition, my father would have prevented it in this instance. He and all his brothers and sisters broke with centuries of Italian tradition by refusing to name any of their sons after their father Pasquale, holding him responsible for the premature death of their mother. When it came to their daughters, however, the tradition held fast and all named their oldest Lucille, American for *Lucia*, in their mother's honor.) There was then a discussion amongst the relatives who were present at the birth and, as the talk on the radio at that instant was about the English monarchy and Edward the Prince of Wales, everyone agreed that "Edward" was a good and appropriate name for my brother. When it came my turn to be born, my mother had no problem naming me. Her father's name had been Pietro and everyone agreed that "Peter" (American for *Pietro*) was a good and appropriate name. When my brother was confirmed in the Catholic Church in his teens, he had to choose a middle name. To honor me, he chose Peter. When I was confirmed, I honored him, so I am Peter Edward DeBlasio. Years later, I honored my mother by naming one of my daughters Caralee, which in Italian means *beloved Lee*.

My father's name also has an interesting derivation. He, as the second-born son, was supposed to be named John because his *mother*'s father's name was Giovanni (*John* in English). But the Italian custom was sometimes flawed because his *father*'s father's name was also Giovanni and so my father's older brother had already been named John, and two brothers could not have the same first name. The family was probably more Americanized than I would have thought because they settled on the name Amerigo for my father, as he was their first child born in America and America was named after the Italian explorer of the 1500s, Amerigo Vespucci. Then, as soon as he was able, my father went a step farther, Americanizing our last name from Di Blasio to DeBlasio on account of pronunciation difficulties. (People still mispronounce my name as *DeBlayzio*, instead of our preferred pronunciation *DeBlahzio*.)

THE BASS VIOLIN

Edward, born as I said two years, ten months and one day before me, was the boss. He was strong-willed; he was independent; he was adventurous. When I was not yet 10 years old, and he still just 12, he would take me with him to the Metropolitan Opera House in Manhattan at 4:00 p.m. on a Saturday afternoon, so that we could stand in line to get tickets for the night's performance at 8:00 p.m. in the standing-room section for the admission price of 50 cents. I remember always hoping that it would be a nice Italian opera, rather than one of those German Wagnerian operas, which lasted so long that I usually got so tired before the final act that I had to lie down on the carpeted floor and sleep. Then we had to take the train (subway) for an hour to get home. How I miss my brother and those days in the 1930s.

Everything about my father was education for Edward and me – education in school and education in music. I well remember that when I was in the lower grades, we had parent-teacher days. Usually, only five or so parents came to visit us during school hours, four women and a man. The women were Jewish and the man was my father. In those grades we were divided into four classes of 40 students each. In third grade, for example, the classes were 3A, 3B, 3C and 3D. The "A" class consisted of the 40 smartest pupils based on our second-grade final report card; the "B" class had the next 40, and so on. Also, the pupils sat in columns based on the highest grades in the class. For example, the student sitting in the first column, first seat had the highest marks in the class; the student sitting in the first column, second seat had the second highest marks, and so on.

Our school was evenly divided ethnicity-wise – 50% Jewish and 50% Italian – and also gender-wise, 50% girls, 50% boys. Sadly, the split was not 50%-50% in the "A," "B," "C" and "D" classes. In the "A" class, we usually had 36 Jews and 4 Italians. In the "D" class, we usually had 36 Italians and 4 Jews. I was always in the "A" class, first column, usually in seat 4 or 5. My brother was always in the first column, seat number 1.

Every time my father came to the classroom, the kids made fun of me. "There's Peter's father, again." But as Shakespeare might have said "'twould serve me well," because my father's appearance brought about immediate positive benefits for me. I was sometimes a naughty boy at school. For example, when there was a girl sitting in the seat directly in front of me, which was usually the case, I would dip her pigtails in my inkwell, though it was of course meant only to dip my pen into. Also, I have always had a loud and resonant voice. So when our teacher left our room for a few minutes and we kids were having fun, as she was coming back to the room, she heard and identified one voice above the din – Peter's. I was appropriately chastised by her for my wrongdoings. All of that changed immediately after she met and spoke with my father. I was suddenly given the highest honor – "monitor of the class."

It may seem that I think the Jews are smarter than the Italians. Not necessarily so. I believe that Jewish parents stress study and education more than most others do. Had the Italian parents, or any others, realized the benefits of hard study and learning, then I believe that their children's marks and accomplishments would have evened out. Even little things mattered. I still remember the record my father bought for Edward and me to improve our speaking and pronunciation, to rid us of our Brooklyn accent. The first four words were: abacus, abaft, abalone and abattoir.

My father's father had come to America to sing opera and so naturally my father grew up surrounded by music, and he happened to be very musical himself, playing the trumpet (the cornet), the saxophone and the bass violin. He, in turn, raised us to be musical and found us an excellent piano teacher, Professor Rafael Saumell, originally from Venezuela, who from the time Edward and I were very young taught us once every two weeks at his studio in Manhattan.

At 12 years of age, my brother graduated from the eighth grade of our local public school P.S. 200 in Bensonhurst, Brooklyn. (In those days, the school system for some reason unknown to me permitted the teacher to have a pupil skip the next grade; both my brother and I skipped twice – I at the end of the third and seventh grades – and so we were two years ahead of our time when we entered high school.) My father, always thinking ahead, had Edward apply to the prestigious High School of Music and Art, then in upper Manhattan.

To be admitted to Music and Art, the prospective student had to be tested in a musical instrument he already played proficiently, as well as in school studies. My brother played the piano to satisfy that requirement. He passed the academic tests as well and thus spent the next four years leaving our house – we lived in an apartment but everyone who lived in an apartment called it their "house" – at 7:00 a.m. and returning at 6:00 p.m., travelling by subway, naturally. We did not have a car (or telephone) in those days.

At Music and Art, each student in the music department was required to study a second instrument. It was there and then that my father's brilliance shone through and his brain-child was born. His master stroke? Having Edward learn the bass violin. But it was not enough for my father that he merely learn to play it, he had to excel, that was my father's genius. So my father arranged for my brother to take additional bass violin lessons outside of Music and Art with Professor Frederick Zimmermann, the principal bass player at the New York Philharmonic Symphony Orchestra from the 1930s onward. And it was this stroke of genius, having my brother learn the bass violin, that directly paved the way for me to become a lawyer.

Why the bass? Because one thing instilled in us by my father was that "you must always be in demand, people must need you and not the other way around." I cannot think of a less fun instrument to play than the bass

– my father also had me study the bass violin (and the cornet) – and if most people thought about it, I am sure they would agree, which is exactly why my father had my brother learn it, because no one else wanted to. With so few bassists, my father reasoned, they would always be in demand because they were needed in symphonic halls, opera houses, etc. And so it turned out to be in my brother's case.

Naturally, and within short order, Edward rose to become the first bassist at Music and Art. Meanwhile, the United States had just joined in World War II and at Columbia, about one mile south of Music and Art, the NROTC Program (Naval Reserve Officer's Training Corps) was in effect. It was a 90-day program of studies and training for Columbia students, who at the end of the 90 days were commissioned as ensigns in the Navy and left school to join the fleet.

Columbia had a school orchestra with a single bass violin player. That student also happened to be in the NROTC Program. The Columbia school schedule was two five-month semesters each year. The NROTC students, however, were there for only part of a semester (three months out of five months); thus, there came a time when that bass player graduated with his NROTC class and Columbia's orchestra was left without a bass violinist.

To fix the problem of an orchestra without a bassist, a Columbia Administrator spoke with a Music and Art Administrator and asked if the high school could send a bass player to join the Columbia orchestra for its final performances. Music and Art complied and thus, while still a high school student, Edward was selected and sent to Columbia's aid.

Columbia returned the favor by admitting my brother to Columbia College when he graduated from high school. Columbia went one giant step farther when, three years later, in 1946, it admitted me into its freshman class.

COLUMBIA COLLEGE

My father had been ahead of his time, certainly within the world he came from. His total focus on education was what led me and Edward to be the very first of our family, out of hundreds of cousins not to mention thousands of ancestors, to go to college. His insight into the psychology and economy of "demand," his resourcefulness in getting us the top piano and bass violin teachers, and then his encouraging Edward to attend Music and Art are what enabled me to be admitted to one of the best colleges in the United States, which directly led to my being admitted to one of the premier law schools (Columbia) in the country. I am sure I never would have become a Columbia student otherwise and I say so for basically two reasons.

First, I was turned down by every other Ivy League school I applied to: Dartmouth, Yale, Princeton, Harvard. Dartmouth and its beautiful surroundings in New Hampshire was my first choice. I wanted to be in the fresh air and be free, up at Dartmouth and away from the city. But I too well remember my interview for admission to Dartmouth, held in the home of a Dartmouth alumnus in a wealthy section of Brooklyn. Even I, at 15 years of age, naïve as I then was, knew that my admission to Dartmouth was doomed five minutes after I met my prosecutor. Most if not all of what happened back then was my fault, but I do think that the ridicule and sarcasm heaped on me by an allegedly intelligent man was on the cruel side.

The backdrop to the interview had to do with the Dartmouth application and its request for the candidate's photo to be attached. I thought that this was the least important matter in the application, so I never thought of asking my parents for the money to go to a photographer's studio for a formal picture. Instead, I looked for a recent snapshot of myself. I found one where I was on the roof of our apartment building, wearing a non-collared sleeveless t-shirt, my arm muscles in full view, and with enough distance from the camera so that my facial pimples would not be prominent. I sent this photo to all the Ivy schools. At least Dartmouth gave me an interview; the others did not.

After shaking hands with the Dartmouth interviewer, he took out my application picture and said, "Let me feel your muscles." I reluctantly complied. After doing so he said, "Dartmouth is not looking for musclemen." That was it, the interview was over.

I have thought of this incident all my life. It certainly came back to me when I met my law school roommate, Aldan Markson, in our dorm a day or two before the beginning of our first semester, about six years after the Dartmouth interview. Aldan had just graduated from Dartmouth and my first sight of him made me think that maybe the Dartmouth representative was telling the truth. Aldan, weighing about 125 pounds, was far from being a muscleman. (Aldan quickly became one of my best friends and was as smart a lawyer as I ever knew.)

The second reason I felt that I would not have been accepted to Columbia College but for my father's great foresight was because I had a Jewish friend who graduated from Lafayette High School with me, and applied to Columbia for admission as his first choice. He had an average of 96 (out of a 100) for his four years in high school, and I was below him with a 95 average. He was turned down. Perhaps there was a Jewish quota, which was already filled, I do not know. However, I always felt it to be the bass violin that swung the tide in my favor.

Columbia College is what got me into Columbia Law School, but not without a lot of hard work. After a rather mediocre first year at Columbia College, I made the Dean's List the next six semesters, played on four teams (varsity football and golf; junior varsity baseball; and freshman basketball), and won the University-wide handball championship. But my sports career was not quite as glorious as I would have liked.

I wanted to be a professional ball player, but starting college as a 16-year-old, I was always one of the youngest and smallest players on all the teams. For example, my first year playing football, on the freshman team, I played all the time, but once on the varsity in my second year, 1947-1948, I found myself competing against mammoth 25-year-old classmates just back from the War and attending Columbia on the G.I. Bill. I did not get in the football games at all – no sophomore did that year. (I did, however, continue to receive a $200 scholarship for each semester that second year, which covered one-third of my tuition, purely on account of being on the football team.) In any event, because of football and my grades that first year, I did not go out for baseball – my favorite sport – until later on in college, by which time it was somehow too late.

Be that as it may, there is one story worth telling from my time as a college athlete that was seared into my memory. In the fall of 1947, one of the first football games on our schedule was against Yale. Levi Jackson, Yale's star running back, reportedly had sore knees coming into the game. The morning of the game, our highly-lauded Columbia football coach Lou Little (born with the Italian name Luigi Piccolo) – who used to wine and dine the local sportswriters who in turn then wrote of him as a "maker of men" – gave us his pep talk. It was short, but not so sweet: "Jackson's hurting and I want you to go out there and hit that Black bastard in the knees and get him out of the game fast." (In those days of earliest integration, the Ivy League football teams each had a single African-American player and on the day of the Yale game, our lone Black teammate Al Cannon was out with a broken leg, so Coach Little felt he could speak freely to the rest of us, mistaking our spirit as kindred.) Well, not a man among us listened to that Italian-American bastard. Jackson finished out the game unbroken, and Yale beat us – one of only two losses for us that championship year. (Our teammate Al Cannon, by the way, not only recovered from his own broken leg, but he went on to study at

Columbia Physicians & Surgeons Medical School and became a psychiatrist.)

Lou Little could not have been more different than my father. That same year, my old Willys car that I parked on campus was stolen. The police recovered it and wanted me to sign a complaint to prosecute the teenager they arrested for the offense. My father counseled me otherwise: "Peter, I spoke with the mother of the young man arrested, she pleaded with me to give her son a second chance. They live in Harlem, they're Negroes, she said he really is a good young man. Peter, you must realize he didn't grow up with all of the schooling and privileges you have had. Give him a second chance." I listened to and obeyed my father. I refused to prosecute and, although the police weren't happy, I am glad that I refused. My father was as unbiased and unprejudiced a person about race and similar matters as I ever knew.

But my education was just the first factor in my becoming a lawyer; it was the "how." Finishing up my second year at Columbia College I did not know that I was about to stumble into the "why" of life, but stumble I did.

CHAPTER 12

Why I Became a Lawyer

I joined up and served in the U.S. Navy for one year: July 29, 1948 until July 28, 1949. In 1948, World War II had been over for three years, but there was still a two-year draft in effect for 18-year-olds and older. I was 18 by then, but had not been drafted because I was in college, which qualified me for a deferment until graduation. In April 1948, however, Congress passed a law permitting boys of 18, and only 18, to satisfy their two-year military obligation if they volunteered for one year's active service and followed it with either four years in the active reserves or six years in the inactive reserves.

When this providential law came into effect, not only was I still 18, but I was just finishing up my second year of college and wanted to become bigger and stronger so I could play football and actually get into the games during my junior and senior years. When I was a sophomore on the championship team in 1947, I was 5 feet 9 inches tall and weighed 166 pounds, whereas about half of our 36-man team were World War II veterans, on average about 24 years old and well over 200 pounds and six feet tall. (Upon their graduation, five of them played professional football, something that was unheard of at Columbia.)

Thus, I calculated that under the new program, if I enlisted in the Navy in the end of July 1948 – I was not turning 19 until August – I would be discharged the end of July 1949, just days before our football pre-season summer practice started and my third year of college began. It seemed perfect for me.

I joined the Navy rather than the Marines or the Army because my father told me and my brother: "If you join the Service be sure you get a good clean and warm bed to sleep in at night, and that's the Navy." My brother took his advice when he volunteered for the Navy during the War when he was 17, then the minimum age for enlistment. And so did I, in 1948.

Me (#42) with my good friend Gene Rossides (#21), Columbia's great quarter-back, in 1947, the season we beat #1-ranked Army 21-20, breaking Army's four-year undefeated streak.

In my Navy whites, just turned 19, before we shipped out on the USS Midway, August 1948 (posing in front of a backdrop).

I also picked the Navy because since we were young boys, my brother and I always wanted to see the world. My brother used to take me and our mother to the piers in New York where the ocean liners docked and, for 50 cents each, we could go aboard and imagine ourselves going to Europe. Also, since I was born and lived in sight of the Atlantic Ocean, I thought I would be immune to seasickness.

When I took the test to get into the Navy, I scored in the 6% range (out of 100%). I say the reason for that abysmal result was because all of the questions were about mechanical things, like how to fix car engines and the like and I had barely ridden in a car up to that time. Even my beloved mother called me "clumsy Ike" because when it came to mechanical things, I was hopeless. What was worse, the test was taken at the federal building at 90 Church Street in New York where my father worked at the Post Office, and when the scores came out and were publicly posted, he was roundly razzed. I guess he had bragged to his co-workers how smart his college son was.

In any event, at 6% I passed – I guess the Navy would take anybody – and was sent to the Great Lakes Naval Station in Illinois for my 90-day boot camp training with my fellow 18-year-olds. Then to Norfolk, Virginia, where I was assigned to the USS Midway, an aircraft carrier and the largest ship in the fleet with a 5000-man crew.

While I was still in boot camp, however, Congress repealed the one-year service law for 18-year-olds because it made no economic sense to train someone for three months and have them spend only nine months on active duty. It was then when all hell broke loose for me. The Navy did everything it could to have me and my friends sign up for two years. None of us did so. As punishment, we were given the worst jobs possible – with the longest hours – such as pushing fighter planes on the carrier for the officer pilots' take-off and landing training, night and day.

I was an "Airman Apprentice" (the lowest position in the Navy) and my troubles really began when I talked back to an ignorant Petty Officer, who was a Navy lifer. I was ordered to wax down some handles on doors aboard the Midway. He criticized my cleaning abilities. I disagreed with him. He reported me and that night I was ordered to stand the midnight to 4:00 a.m. watch for man overboard at the back of the ship, and to report to the Bridge by telephone every half hour. Unfortunately at that time, December 1948, we were in the North Atlantic and the waves were 60-feet high and accordingly the ship rose and fell like an elevator going up to the sixth floor and dropping to the ground floor.

The man overboard watch was a ridiculous and outdated practice. First, if someone fell overboard you would not be able to see him, especially at night, he would be swallowed by the sea in an instant. Second, the ship was going the opposite direction from the way he would be carried by the waves, if he had not already sunk under the waves. Third, it would take miles for the ship to turn around. Fourth, it was not possible to throw him a life-belt from the deck one hundred feet higher than the water, particularly in that weather, and have him catch it. Fifth, almost no sailor was up and about between midnight and 4:00 a.m., especially outdoors to fall overboard.

I, however, had been an obedient boy all of my life and so I foolishly did my duty and looked intently and constantly at the dark and raging sea. At the end of my first half hour on watch, I vomited, but I kept looking. One half hour later, I vomited again, but I kept looking. I vomited a total of seven times, until there was nothing left to throw up.

I was now as sick as a dog. At 4:00 a.m., I managed to walk my way to my bunk, which was at the very front of the ship, one thousand feet from my look-out post. I slept for two hours, when I was awakened by my buddies for our regular day of pushing airplanes. The planes were F4Us, fighter planes with propellers. Our crew consisted of six 18-year-olds, and we moved the planes (with the pilots in their seats, but the engines not yet engaged) by pushing against the backs of the wings, three men on each side of the body of the plane.

The planes were kept overnight in the hangar deck, one deck (i.e., one floor) below the flight deck. In the morning, we moved them to an elevator, which carried them to the flight deck. Then we moved them to their take-off positions, all side-by-side (about ten in a row) and all one behind the other (about ten to a column). Then we placed wooden chocks at the two wheels and waited there beside the chocks until the engines were started and, naturally, the propellers began to turn. The winds that blew back to us from the propellers must have been 75 to 100 miles per hour. When it was time for our plane to take off, two of us removed the chocks and we six crouched and crawled our way to the sides of the ship, between the tails of the planes to our sides and the propellers of the planes in line behind us. We then did regular chores until the planes came back and landed.

When the planes came back it was a beautiful sight to see. They approached the back of the ship, one behind the other, a few hundred feet apart. A plane would fly over the back of the ship heading toward the front at about one hundred feet above the deck, when it would suddenly drop down and its tail hook would take hold of a ship-cable and the plane would come to an abrupt stop. When the tail hook was released and the cable barriers were lowered, the plane then moved forward. (The cable barriers, which were amidships in front of the plane, were there to stop any plane that crashed from traveling toward the front of the ship.) At that point, my crew went out to our assigned plane and once it stopped, we moved it to an elevator and brought it down to the hangar deck.

One thing about the Navy, they never alerted us to any dangers until after the event happened, although they did have printed on the side of the conning tower "beware of propellers." Such was the case one day when we were landing planes. My crew and I were pushing a plane that had just landed to an elevator on the flight deck, when I heard a sound that I had never heard before. It was broadcast over a loudspeaker and it had an eerie sound like "eee-aww eee-aww eee-aww." I turned and looked to the back of the ship and did not see anything unusual. Just a plane making a normal approach landing. While still watching it, I suddenly noticed that it did not drop down but was flying over the crash barriers. I then saw it clear the barriers, land and proceed straight to our plane, which was about 200 feet ahead of it. It was then obvious to me that unless it turned, it was going to crash into the back of our plane within a couple of seconds. And it was just as obvious to me that it wasn't going to turn because if it turned in either direction, it would have gone over the side of the ship and into the sea.

My crew and I ran to safety to the catwalks on both sides of the ship. (The catwalks were passageways from the front to the back of the ship, with their floors about three feet below the flight deck.) At about the same instant that I jumped into the catwalk, the plane crashed into our stationary plane with the pilot seated in the cockpit. Metal parts of the planes flew all over. Almost miraculously, the out-of-control plane and its propellers came to a full stop against the back of the pilot's seat of our stationary plane. Both pilots were safe and uninjured. But one of my fellow 18-year-old crew members, Joe Johnson, a farm boy from Missouri, was not so lucky and lost a leg at the scene. He was just what I always imagined a farm boy from the Midwest would be when I was growing up. What we would call the "salt of the earth," friendly, always with a smile, always helpful.

It was only after the fact that we were told by our officers that the "eee-aww" meant danger – an emergency – a crash about to happen – and that we should take action accordingly.

Thus, being an airplane pusher was not the safest of jobs on the ship. To do it after being up on watch all night and vomiting as much as I did obviously made it much worse. To add to it all, the seas were still raging, the ship was still rocking, I was not eating for five days after my watch and so it finally got to the point where I left my job and tried to find a place to lie down to stop my seasickness. My absence was quickly discovered, and just as quickly I was punished by being ordered to stand the same watch from 12:00 midnight to 4:00 a.m. for 14 days in a row, while continuing with my plane pushing duties. I was surprised they did not put me in the Brig, but I guess they thought standing watch was a worse form of punishment, and it was. I think I could have at least slept while I was in the Brig.

This was physical punishment meted out to me in the North Atlantic in December and January 1948-1949. The emotional punishment, which I did not expect and which was even worse, I experienced shortly thereafter when we entered the Mediterranean Sea at Gibraltar. And it continued the farther in we sailed.

When I was a boy, I had heard that the Atlantic Ocean was stormy in winter, but I thought that a sea like the Mediterranean was always calm like the "Narrows" (that is, the body of water from the Atlantic to New York harbor, which was just blocks from my home in Brooklyn). I was wrong. The sea was just as bad as the ocean and I was just as sick. Naturally, we kept on with our mission of training our pilots to land and take off on a carrier. In fact, it was when we were in the Mediterranean that for the first time our Captain spoke to the entire crew by loudspeaker and told us: "We are here for war." I was shocked. I thought the war had just ended and we had won and that all we were doing was being cautious and prepared in case the unthinkable happened again. No one I knew at that time ever dreamed that a little over a year later, in 1950, we would be at war in Korea; and certainly I could never have imagined that one of my buddies from the freshman football team, Tom McVeigh, an ROTC student who upon graduation became a Lieutenant in the Marines, would be killed in action there.

When we landed at Gibraltar, it was announced that we would remain anchored there for four days and that one quarter of the crew would be granted 24-hour liberty each day. I was ecstatic. Not only did it mean I would be on dry land and not subject to seasickness for a day, but my dream of being in Europe would be fulfilled.

It was not to be. When the list was posted with the day each sailor was given shore leave, my name was nowhere to be found. I did not even dream of questioning my superiors about this. I did know we had a number of other stops scheduled and I was hopeful and optimistic.

In the meantime, on several occasions during this period, I was called into the quarters of an officer recently graduated from the Naval Academy at Annapolis. Our talks went this way: "You're a college student, you're smart. Why don't you sign up for another two years? You can pick any job you want, you can be in Intelligence, you can become an officer, you can even transfer to the Academy. Why go on like this? Who's benefitting? Why not think it over?" Instead of telling him that from what I had experienced during the last few months, the last thing I'd want to do was to remain in the Navy, I simply thanked him for the advice and concern.

Our next stop was Oran, North Africa. Another four days, another list, another time my name was missing. We continued on with our flight exercises for a week or so until we stopped at Siracusa, a seaport at the southern part of Sicily. Hope is eternal and I was hopeful to be allowed off the ship at Siracusa. But once again my name was left off the list for liberty. I remained on the ship for those four days as well. At least I was seeing these cities and countryside from my ship. Another week of pushing planes and then we would go to Naples.

Naples was the home of my ancestors. I had heard about it, Vesuvius, Pompeii and Torre del Greco, all my life. Torre del Greco, a part of Naples like Brooklyn is to Manhattan, was the actual birthplace of my father's parents. I longed to see it and the people. I am not much of a "miracle believer," but many Italians do believe in them, and since we were approaching Italy, maybe what next occurred was not one, not two, but three possible miracle-like events.

The first occurred as we entered the straits of Messina, which is a waterway two miles wide, between Sicily and the Italian mainland. Suddenly, the water became as calm as a lake. No more waves and no more seasickness. At lunch, I ate a hearty plateful of macaroni, which tasted almost as good as my mother's.

The second "miracle" followed in short order when a day later we anchored off the city and port of Naples for our four-day stay. I do not remember how I learned of it, but I was granted one day's shore leave. I could not be happier, though somewhat bewildered. At about 6:00 p.m., I went to shore with my 18-year-old good buddy Ernie Buonocuore, a Bronx native of Italian ancestry. We first took a bus for the short ride to Torre del Greco and that is when what I had heard over and over when I was growing up came true, that the Italian people are as polite and kind as anyone in the world.

Ernie and I were going to meet one of my father's first cousins at his friend's pensione (hotel) in Torre del Greco. This cousin, whose last name was Lo Freddo, was to make arrangements for us to sleep there overnight. On the bus, I asked a passenger if he knew the location of the street where we had been told to get off and walk to the pensione. He said he recognized the street name and knew where it was. And when we asked him to tell us when we reached it, he said he would. When we got off the bus, so did he. He then walked in the same direction to the pensione that we went. During the five-minute walk I figured that it was the route he took to get home. When we arrived safely at the pensione, we thanked him for his courtesy and said good-bye. (I did not realize until years later, when I went back to Torre, that it was fairly notorious as a dangerous place to be, especially at nighttime.) About 20 minutes after our arrival and meeting with my cousin, I was surprised to see our bus passenger friend enter the pensione. He came over to us, asked if we needed him anymore, we said we did not, and he then asked for permission to leave.

My cousin spoke to him in Italian and then told us that the place where he got off the bus was not his stop and that he had to go back there to take another bus to his home, about one half hour away. He had accompanied us and waited outside to be sure that we arrived there safely. We all thanked him profusely for his kindness and gave him two packs of cigarettes for his trouble. I obviously have never forgotten it, or him, even though 70 years have gone by.

When Lo Freddo introduced us to the owner of the pensione, I found that not all Italians were so kind. But I understood the reason why and naturally felt very sorry for him. At first, the owner refused to let us sleep there. He told Lo Freddo that three years before, our Navy warships had bombed the pensione and his young son died during the shelling. He could not allow American sailors to stay in the place where they killed his son. Lo Freddo then told him, "He's not an American, he's my cousin." The innkeeper relented.

When Ernie and I slept in bed that night, it was in our heavy pea coats because what I had heard all my life about "sunny Italy" was not always true. I had never been colder, partly due to the fact that as a result of the Naval bombardment, some of the pensione's roof and part of the walls were missing.

The next morning, we took the train to Avellino, a city 40 miles from Naples so that Ernie could visit his great-uncle. I remember two things about the trip. The first is that we (Ernie, his uncle and I), had breakfast in the kitchen of a small farmhouse, which had dirt floors. The great-uncle wore a hat during the meal and spit on the floor at times. None of that mattered because I had the most delicious and largest fried egg I ever saw. It was probably five times larger than the ones I had eaten back home.

Second, while we were eating, and all during our stay, four teenage girl cousins of Ernie's were standing at an open door that led into the kitchen, looking at us intently. We were not introduced to them and no words were spoken. I thought it unusual, but I guess that the local custom was to protect the girls from strange boys and men, even if one of them was a cousin.

When we had left the ship, we had gone ashore with two cartons of cigarettes. They cost 10 cents a pack, one dollar a carton. Ernie and I did not smoke and we knew Italians longed for American cigarettes, so we gave them out as tips. When we said our good-byes to the great-uncle, we gave him half a carton. He was overjoyed. Too bad we did not give him his gift earlier, maybe he would have introduced us to the girls and let us talk to them.

We then went back to our ship, both happy and sad. Happy because we had been on our ancestors' soil and met the people; sad because of their poverty and not having had any of the advantages we had being born and raised in America.

The third "miracle" occurred after we left Naples and were on our way to our final stay-over in the Mediterranean, at Cannes on the French Riviera. It started with an announcement to the entire crew that a special four-day leave would be granted to 30 men who signed up for a trip from Cannes to Paris and back again; otherwise, everyone else would get the usual 24-hour shore leave. There was a caveat, however. And it was that selection for the trip would be according to rank. There were 5,000 officers and sailors on the ship and I, and my 18-year-old shipmate buddies, all Airmen Apprentices, were of the lowest rank. It was impossible some believed that out of the 4,900 officers and sailors above us, all would turn down a four-day trip to Paris to spend one day drinking in Cannes.

Hope is eternal and we lost nothing by signing up to put our names on the list, so that is exactly what we did. The "miracle" was that when the sign-up period ended, I and four or five buddies were on the list with about two dozen pilots. We left Cannes by train and 16 hours later we were in Paris. The city was as beautiful as I imagined and we saw almost all of its famous sites and landmarks, and I had a fine time practicing my French.

I well remember one night of relaxation at a dance hall named "Pigalle" (the Americans called it Pig Alley). There I met a very pretty 19-year-old dancer. Her name was Myrtille Salles and she was from the Pyrenees. She spoke very little English and none of my friends spoke French, so when she sat with us at our table (when she was not on stage), she and I became very chummy and we all had a great time. She was probably sent over to us by the management to encourage us to stay and drink, but no matter, I was starving for some time spent with a girl, especially a foreign one.

When we left Cannes, we sailed back to the United States. Finally, July 28, 1949 arrived. I received my discharge papers, returned home to Brooklyn and then, four days later, I was at Baker Field – Columbia's football field and camp in Manhattan – for 30 days of football practice, from 9:00 a.m. to 6:00 p.m., until my third year of college started. But there was one last glitch. My four years of active reserve duty started right up and would require me to miss one full day of football practice every two weeks. So I went to Coach Little and told him of my reserve-duty conflict and, as luck would have it, he managed to have my remaining four years of active duty changed to six years of inactive reserve duty, so as not to get in the way of football practice.

Thus, I missed being called up into service during the Korean War. True, Coach Little was powerful and persuasive, but I prefer to think that the debt of gratitude I owe for the change in my status was due instead to the President of Columbia University – who happened to be a strong advocate of our football program – General Dwight D. Eisenhower.

*****

My one year in the Navy, that's why I became a lawyer.

True, the one day in Naples and the four-day trip and stay in Paris were great, but they could not possibly make up for how I was otherwise treated. I do not mean to compare in any way my troubles with those of my 18-year-old father in the trenches in World War I, or with those of all of the many other soldiers, sailors and marines who suffered in like manner. I am only talking about myself and, although what happened to me pales in comparison to the suffering of those others – my 14 days of continuous man-overboard watch with barely four hours of sleep followed by 12 to 14 hours a day pushing planes – it was pretty bad.

As Shakespeare wrote of Mercutio's reply to Romeo, who sought to encourage him after he (Mercutio) was stabbed: "No, 'tis not so deep as a well, nor so wide as a church door; but 'tis enough, 'twill serve. Ask for me tomorrow, and you shall find me a grave man." That was how I felt. My suffering might not have measured up to that of others, but to me it was enough to direct the course of my life.

My great college friend and golf teammate, Robert Pinckert, was a Shakespeare scholar (and future college professor of English literature) and a bit of his enthusiasm rubbed off on me because I liked to quote Shakespeare's Mercutio story to juries, particularly in slip-and-fall cases when the hole that caused the trip and fall was minuscule. And that's just what I did in my summation in the Kaye v. City of New York trial, which involved a half-inch-deep, half-inch-wide hole on steps leading up to a school building. After the appellate decision in Kaye came down affirming our verdict, I bumped into one of the appellate judges, Sybil Kooper, and thought that she might let me have it for bringing such a de minimis lawsuit in the first place, but she merely said as a teacher to a favorite student with a bit of disappointment in her voice: "Peter, it's okay to quote Shakespeare in your summations, but next time be sure you do it accurately."

My favorite quote of all, sadly reserved for wrongful death cases, was from a poetic sermon by John Donne, beginning with the line "No man is an island" and ending with "for whom the bell tolls," which Ernest Hemingway adopted as a title for a novel. I recited it many times, always adapting it a bit to fit the situation. Such was the case in Aldycki v. Staten Island Hospital, which involved the very unfortunate death of a 44-year-old woman in the hospital following the delivery of her fifth child. In my summation, in effect I told the jury that although Staten Island where the malpractice took place was an island, we had the right to be treated with the same good and accepted medical practice as on the mainland. I won the trial and the defendant appealed, challenging only my summation. After the appellate decision in Aldycki came down affirming the verdict, I again bumped into one of the appellate judges, again Sybil Kooper, and again she let me know that I had mangled some of the lines. This time, however, they were the lines of her favorite poem and she told me in no uncertain terms to get it right next time.

Back to my disillusionment with the Navy. When I volunteered, I believed what my father had pounded into me and my brother: "Always remember that no one is better than you." Unfortunately, that was not true in the Navy. Everyone thought they were better than I, a mere "Airman Apprentice," and they acted with the regulations on their side. There was no appeal from anything they did to me, including punishment.

I had no rights, no hearing, no trial, no judge, no jury. The only right they could not take away from me was to complain as loudly as I wished to the roaring 60-foot waves while I was standing watch and throwing up.

It was during that time, thinking hopefully I had a long life in front of me, that I decided I had better learn how to protect myself from arbitrary and authoritarian rule, which promoted injustice. The only way I could think of to accomplish this was to study the law and become a lawyer.

For the next 60 years, not only did I learn how to protect myself, but just as importantly, I strove to aid, protect and represent as many people as I could seeking justice. Accordingly, my final words in all of my summations never varied, no matter if I was the federal prosecutor, the criminal defense attorney, the defendant's lawyer in a civil case, or the plaintiff's lawyer bringing the civil lawsuit (which was 90% of the time): "Let justice be done." Robert Donat, a British actor playing the part of a lawyer, said these words at the end of a film I saw when I was a boy. I have forgotten the name of the film, but I was so impressed with the words that when I became a trial lawyer I realized they would apply to any case I tried.

So, when I was a prosecutor, I never asked a jury to convict a defendant of the crime charged. I was not God. I could be wrong. I was usually the youngest person in the courtroom. It was my obligation to present the facts and prove the case as best I could. It was the jurors' duty to determine guilt or innocence, to do justice, and so that was what I asked of them. So, too, in the Bronfman kidnapping case, at the end of my summation, I did not ask the jury to find my client Dominic Byrne not guilty, I relied on the plain but powerful "Let justice be done."

CHAPTER 13

Luck and the Law

AFTER LAW SCHOOL

I learned long ago that there is incredible luck involved in winning a lawsuit. But this should come as no surprise to anyone, as it has taken incredible luck to get each and every one of us here. If my 18-year-old father had come out of the bunker on the left side, where his buddy came out, he would have been the one to die in World War I. Had my mother's mother not become an orphan, she a simple illiterate peasant girl would not have left Craco to start a new life with her brother in New York. If Columbia University President Dwight D. Eisenhower had not commuted my active Navy status to inactive on account of football practice, I would have been called into the Korean War and undoubtedly come back, if I came back at all, a different man.

Life is full of good luck and bad luck, the haves and have-nots, and the practice of law is no different than life. I realized this the first year of law school, the first day even. And I learned that while sometimes bad luck would change on its own, if it didn't, I'd have to come up with some way to change it, both in life and on trial.

On the first day of my first-year law school classes, and every day thereafter, we sat in alphabetical order. To my left sat Thomas Debevoise and to my right Al Ehrenclou.

Thomas Debevoise's many illustrious ancestors included the first public school teacher in the American Colonies, the inventor of the cotton gin (Eli Whitney), and the founder of one of Wall Street's premier law firms, which still bears his family's name today. Tom was known for earning what was then called "a gentleman's C" in most of his courses. No matter. Upon our graduation from law school in 1954, Tom went straight away to the prestigious U.S. Attorney's Office for the Southern District of New York; he later defended the Russian spy Rudolf Abel, who was convicted and subsequently exchanged for Gary Powers, the U-2 pilot shot down over Russia; and thereafter, Thomas Debevoise became dean of the Vermont Law School.

Al Ehrenclou's many illustrious ancestors included one of the founders of Yale University and, hundreds of years on, the banking magnate and America's foremost financier John Pierpont Morgan, who was Al's great uncle. Al and I spent a great deal of time together, side by side in class and then every single afternoon together at the gym. I was disappointed when, near the end of our first year, he told me that he would not be returning to Columbia Law. The school was more academically demanding than he had imagined. Al ended up transferring to another law school and, upon graduation, he and a friend opened a simple two-man law firm. When I first heard about this downturn in fortune, I felt sorry for my friend. When I met up with him a while later, and he told me their firm had just one client, I expressed my regret. He waved the sentiment aside, telling me that his client was the Morgan Guaranty Trust Company.

I, no Debevoise nor Whitney, no Ehrenclou nor Morgan, searched for a job for six months after graduation with no fortune or luck.

Other than my first year in college, my marks had been good the next six years: Dean's List from my sophomore to senior years at college; and a Harlan Fiske Stone Scholar my second and third years at the law school. Even so, when I applied to about 30 Wall Street law firms, I was not accepted by any of them. I remember that after I would introduce myself to the receptionist and wait to be interviewed by a member of the firm, I would look at and read the names of the firm's partners, which were prominently displayed on reception-area walls. What stood out to me, as clear as a bell, was that no last name ended in a vowel. It seemed to me that no Italian except for Columbus (*Cristoforo Colombo*, in Italian) and Vespucci must have come to America. I knew right then, as well as I knew anything, that my name was never going to be added to any Wall Street wall.

Back then in 1954, even in such a metropolis as New York City, Italians, Jews and African-Americans all had a terrible time getting a job in the legal profession. The established Wall Street law firms almost exclusively hired white Protestant men like most of my Columbia classmates, so much so that virtually the only law firms where Jewish men could work were ones that they started up for themselves. African- and Italian-American men were not so lucky, as they attended law school in far smaller numbers than the Jews and they simply did not have the manpower or economic opportunity to start Wall Street firms to hire their own. Nor were state District Attorney's Offices or federal U.S. Attorney's

Offices hiring Italian, Jewish and African-American men. And women, forget about it, I almost never came across a woman lawyer.

I was, after six months since graduation, beside myself. My father was right again. I was not "in demand." No one needed me. But then luck struck and I thought to call on the only professor in either college or law school to have befriended me, Professor George Hibbett, professor of speech at the college. He would give me sound advice.

I think he liked me so much because he did for me what Henry Higgins did for Eliza Doolittle in My Fair Lady. Our friendship came about as follows. In my freshman year at the college, I started out playing quarterback on the freshman football team. I was soon reassigned to the left halfback position because the quarterback calls the plays and none of my Pennsylvania and Massachusetts teammates could make sense of what I was saying. My coach strongly advised me to sign up for Professor Hibbett's speech class, to tone down my "Brooklynese" and I, always an obedient boy, listened to him.

Prof. Hibbett helped me immeasurably and I have been immeasurably grateful to him my entire life. We became friends, we played handball together, I dined at his home. I always wanted to play a joke on him in class, but never dared to do so. It would have been that after he said something to us, I would have asked him: "What was that? I didn't get it." It might have ruined the friendship.

When I met with him again in late 1954, I told him of my plight, that I could not get a job, and he said that he would see what he could do. He soon telephoned me with a bit of good news and good luck – he had scheduled a meeting for me with an old Columbia acquaintance of his, Nicholas Kelley, the senior partner of a prominent Wall Street law firm that would eventually become the legendary firm Kelley Drye.

As more luck would have it, my girlfriend at the time, Jo Warner, a pretty, fair-skinned, red-headed young woman from Idaho whom I had met at a Columbia Law School party in February 1954, just happened to then be studying at the Art Students League in Manhattan and was quite friendly with a classmate about 40 years her senior who went by the last name Kelley. A day or two after I told Jo about my upcoming meeting, as they were painting side by side, Jo mentioned to her older classmate Augusta that I was interviewing for jobs and was about to meet with a lawyer who coincidentally had the same last name she did. When I subsequently met with Mr. Kelley, he could not have been nicer. I am sure it did not hurt that Augusta was his wife and that she was quite friendly with Jo, my future wife.

Mr. Kelley did not have an open position in his firm, but he did better. He spoke with a friend of his, a fellow alumnus of Columbia Law School, Leonard Page Moore, who had recently been appointed as the United States Attorney for the Eastern District of New York (home base – Brooklyn). An appointment was set up for me to meet with Mr. Moore to see if I could qualify for a position in the office as an Assistant United States Attorney. Mr. Kelley told me that he had recommended me highly to Mr. Moore. Naturally, I thanked Mr. Kelley.

Years later, I in a way returned the favor when three lawyers from Mr. Kelley's firm came to my office with a prospective client for me to represent in a products liability case. She was a German-born executive at Deutsche Bank who had sustained a bad skin reaction to a pharmaceutical company's skin product. I well remember her because she was one of the most beautiful clients I ever had. Her name was Ms. Walter. We settled the case without a trial for $300,000, which was quite a good recovery in those days for injuries that were not extensive nor permanent.

THE GREATEST JOB, EVEN AT ONE-THIRD THE PAY

I met Leonard Page Moore soon after Mr. Kelley referred me. Mr. Moore's career had been as an appellate lawyer at the Wall Street firm of Chadbourne, Parke, Whiteside & Wolff, but more to the point, he had been an Amherst classmate of Herbert Brownell, whom the recently elected Republican President Dwight D. Eisenhower had just appointed as Attorney General of the United States.

As Attorney General, Brownell was responsible for replacing all of the U.S. Attorneys around the country. (When following a presidential election there was a change from a Democratic administration to a Republican one, or vice versa, the new administration customarily cleared out all of the U.S. Attorney's Offices and appointed a new batch of lawyers who were members of the same party as the president. The Republicans had been waiting 20 years – from the time of Franklin Delano Roosevelt's 1933 swearing-in as president until Dwight David Eisenhower's 1953 swearing-in – for just such a change in political affiliation.) Brownell wasted no time in appointing his good friend and Amherst classmate Leonard Page Moore to be the new U.S. Attorney in charge of the Eastern District of New York.

As to the appointment of the many *Assistant* U.S. Attorneys – the prosecutors who actually went into court and tried the cases – the new

U.S. Attorney had a large say in whom to hire, but so too did the politically powerful local leaders. This was especially true in Brooklyn, where the Republican County leader John Crewes, a former professional prize-fighter, had played a major part in turning out a strong vote for Eisenhower.

Johnny Crewes now had favors he had to return, and one of the plum appointments he was planning to make was to put in someone as an Assistant U.S. Attorney. Leonard Page Moore, however, had his own ideas about staffing his office.

At my interview, Mr. Moore told me that instead of taking one of Johnny Crewes's cronies, he planned to hire three recent Columbia Law School graduates for that single slot. The salary for Assistant U.S. Attorneys nationwide was $6,000 per year. The three Columbia men would split that sum, earning $2,000 a year each. He also said that they would have to be members of the local Republican District Club. He then asked me how I felt about these caveats.

I told him that the salary was no problem because first and foremost I wanted the chance to try cases and become a trial lawyer. I also said that since I had been in school right up to that time, I had not joined a political party. I did admit to him that I had voted for Adlai Stevenson, the Democratic nominee against Eisenhower for president, but I was ready, willing and able to be a member of my district's local Republican Club and attend its meetings.

Mr. Moore congratulated me, telling me that as soon as I became a registered Republican, I would be sworn in together with two of my classmates, Guy Linker and Don Jaffen. I went directly to the Republican Club near my home in Brooklyn, met its leader Joe Parisi and told him I was a recent law school graduate and wanted to join. He was delighted. When he asked me if I had a job and I told him I was about to become an Assistant U.S. Attorney, he was shocked. One of the reasons was that he had heard there was already a candidate lined up for that position, Bob Kreindler – coincidentally the older brother of one of my Columbia Law classmates – who had been waiting for years having been promised the job by Johnny Crewes. (My good luck was of course Bob's bad luck, but Bob did eventually become a state court judge.) But Joe's shock was short-lived, his delight quickly restored, and he signed me up.

Not long thereafter, Guy, Don and I, now all Republicans, were sworn in as Assistant U.S. Attorneys, splitting $6,000 a year three ways.

Annual Christmas Party, U.S. Attorney's Office, E.D.N.Y., Henri Ferrer's Restaurant, December 22, 1954, Brooklyn (my first year at the office) Attending are lawyers and secretaries: I am seated in the front row farthest to the right (as you look at the photo); U.S. Attorney Leonard Page Moore is seated at the center of the table, the fifth person behind me; Frances Thaddeus Wolff, my officemate and great friend, is in the seat of honor just at Mr. Moore's right-hand side; Marie McCann, Frances's very good friend and the only other female attorney in the office, is standing in the back row toward the right with hands crossed in front; Thomas C. Platt, Jr., future judge in the Eastern District of New York, is standing in the back row five from the left; Henry Bramwell, future judge in the Eastern District of New York, and the only African-American attorney in the office, is seated at the table in the second row five from the left; and Don Jaffen, one of the two fellows who joined the office when I did in 1954 (like me, at one-third the salary), is seated behind Bramwell, second to the right of the front pillar. Guy Linker, who joined the office together with me and Jaffen, does not appear to be in the photo.

The next four years were without a doubt the most fun I had in my entire trial career. I had no worries at all. My cases came to me ready-made, impeccably prepared by the FBI. To a T, the FBI agents were magnificent. Smart, well-spoken, well-dressed, they were born to their role and were uniformly ideal witnesses who could follow my instructions exactly, responding expansively to my questions during direct examination and turning markedly reserved on cross. When the day for trial would arrive, not only were they set, but my lead case agent would have all my expert and civilian witnesses present and accounted for in the courthouse first thing in the morning, prepared to stay there all day until it was their time to take the stand. The way I remember it, all I had to do was show up for trial.

FAIR TO A LADY?

There was only ever one Assistant U.S. Attorney I knew in our office who earned less than Guy, Don and I did. And it should surprise few to learn that she was a she. Frances Thaddeus Wolff was her name, and she and I shared a small office for years. She was one of just two female Assistant U.S. Attorneys there at the time. (The other was her great pal Marie McCann.)

Frances had been a USO Showgirl during World War II and, after the war, she married and then went to law school. Frances's husband Henry Wolff, several decades older than she, was a name partner at the Wall Street law firm where our boss Mr. Moore had been a partner. The fact that her husband made a partner's salary I suppose was what led Mr. Moore to believe it was fair to Frances to pay her just $300 *a year*, not even enough to cover the salary of her chauffeur, who drove her back and forth to work every day from her home at the exclusive Sherry Netherland Hotel on Fifth Avenue. I guess I can't really say "poor," but poor Frances to have been so underpaid. A nicer, more generous person in those days you just couldn't find. I was lucky to have her as my officemate.

For a long while after I left the U.S. Attorney's Office, Frances and I continued to stay in touch and she remained very generous, on more than one occasion giving me and my wife Jo gifts from Tiffany. I was able to reciprocate somewhat when, in 1965, she came to me after she was a passenger in a car accident and was left with a scar on her nose. We took the case to trial, but midway through, the judge forced a settlement. (Elsie Reilly, the daughter of my former boss, represented the defendant.) We accepted just under $30,000, which wasn't bad for a scar.

Sadly, in 1971 Frances died of cancer, before she reached her 50th birthday. Far too young for such a wonderful person.

BAD LUCK, GOOD LUCK

After two years at the U.S. Attorney's Office, my salary was increased so that I was earning the same as other third-year Assistants, but within another two years it was already time to move on. Even though it was the job I loved most in my life, back in those days after four years it was considered time to leave.

I still had no luck landing a position with a Wall Street law firm, despite my now impeccable credentials. But no matter, because what I really wanted was to keep trying cases and that was not what these exclusive Wall Street firms were about. So I went to the Columbia Law School Placement Office and put in an ad for a job. Mr. Reilly, as savvy an employer as any, periodically checked the Columbia classifieds, saw the ad and called me in for an interview. He hired me straightaway.

Mr. Hibbett and Mr. Reilly, the two greatest mentors a person could ever have.

POSTSCRIPT: When I left the U.S. Attorney's Office in 1958, I made one other change – I switched my voter registration to Democrat. I had not made a promise to *remain* a Republican, or even to vote Republican for that matter. In fact, in the 1956 presidential election – despite my debt of gratitude to President Eisenhower for having extricated me from further Navy service – I again voted against him and for his opponent Adlai Stevenson. And always thereafter, I voted for the Democratic nominee, whoever he or *she* happened to be.

PART III

EARLY TRIAL YEARS

While driving along, Mr. Goodhue saw, as did the man from Samaria, a stricken fellow lying on the ground pleading for help.
"Help me, help me!"
"Hold on, hold on, I am here to help you!"

–Peter James Johnson, Esq.
Leahey & Johnson
New York (1965)

I want you to represent Dominic Byrne. Do not concern yourself with a fee. This case will make you internationally famous.

–John Gabriel Reilly, Esq.
Reilly & Reilly
New York (1975)

Me and Mr. Reilly, at our office in the Woolworth Building, about 1959.

CHAPTER 14

A Fly Could Tell Its Tale

Humor is an important part of any trial, and I almost always had the jury laughing at some point, no matter how serious the case. I didn't tell jokes per se, but often I questioned witnesses in a way to bring out some absurdity in their testimony.

This happened often during the three-month Bronfman kidnapping trial. There was always some moment of comedy each day, something I did or said to relieve the tension. The New York papers, which were covering the trial daily, often reported it. For example, on November 15, 1976, the journalist M.A. Farber wrote in The New York Times:

> The 47-year-old former federal prosecutor, who generally handles negligence and other civil cases, seems to have almost endeared himself to four to six jurors who regularly resound with smiles and laughter to his gibes at prosecution witnesses.
>
> "Not yet, not yet," Mr. DeBlasio said the other day as he turned his back on an FBI agent who had mistakenly referred to Mr. DeBlasio as "Your Honor." Everyone, including the customarily dour Judge Beisheim, thought that was pretty funny.

But the funniest line I ever heard in a court of law during a trial came in my earliest years, and it didn't come from me. It was made by a man I represented in a minor automobile accident case in 1960, when I was with the defense firm Reilly & Reilly.

As in so many of my trials, the facts of this case were simple. They were indeed so simple that we conceded liability before trial, admitting that the accident was all the defendant's fault. The trial then would be about damages and whether this type of accident could have caused the extent of injuries that the plaintiffs alleged. Simply put, it all came down to which driver the jurors were going to believe.

The Facts: Plaintiffs' car, driven by Plaintiff #1 (Mr. Contomdrinos) with his father Plaintiff #2 as a passenger, was on an entrance ramp to the Long Island Expressway when it stopped at a stop sign. Defendant's car, driven by my client Mr. Dorsey, was immediately behind it and also stopped. Plaintiffs' car started forward to enter the highway and defendant's car followed suit. While rolling forward at a very slow speed, the defendant driver looked to his left through his left-front mirror to be sure that no vehicle traveling in the right lane of the Expressway was too close for him to safely enter the highway.

Unbeknownst to Mr. Dorsey who was looking left, plaintiffs' car again stopped on the entrance ramp thinking it unsafe to proceed. Mr. Dorsey's car struck the Contomdrinos car.

This was a classic hit-in-the-rear, which in those days was a plaintiff's lawyer's dream case. Better still, since I conceded liability, all the plaintiffs' lawyer here had to prove up to the jury was the pain and suffering it was alleged his clients had sustained on account of the accident.

Cases such as these rarely went to trial; they were settled. The Reilly firm, however, was known as a non-settling defense firm. It would offer $500 or $1,000 or the like on a case, but rarely any more than that. The plaintiffs here, however, had asked for an exorbitant amount of money in settlement discussions with the judge, and so the case went to trial in Supreme Court, Nassau County, before Justice Bernard Meyer (later elevated to New York's highest court, the Court of Appeals) and a 12-man jury.

At trial, the son testified about going to the doctor on 65 occasions over two years for the neck and back pain he suffered solely as a result of the accident. The father testified about minor injuries to his face and about his dentures, which were smashed to smithereens and had to be replaced, all on account of the accident. (Our expert dentist testified that it looked more like he had taken the dentures out of his mouth and smashed them with a baseball bat.)

The jury might have believed them had my client not caught us all off guard with the funniest line I ever heard on trial. It came about as follows.

After the father and son plaintiffs testified about the gravity of the accident, the defendant took the stand to testify that this was a minor accident, known in the trade as a fender-bender. I asked him to describe in simple terms for the judge and the jurors the nature of the impact between the front of his car and the rear of the plaintiffs' car. His response to my question, which is still vivid in my mind, now 60 years later, was simple:

> "The best way I can put it is, if a fly was on his bumper, it'd be alive to tell the tale today."

The jury laughed uproariously and their verdict followed suit. As we had conceded liability, the jury was required to award some amount in damages. They awarded the son just $650, the exact amount of his medical bills (65 visits at $10 a visit, which in those days was the standard), and the father $830, the precise amount he spent to replace his dentures.

The judge, who was very smart as evidenced by his elevation to our highest court, decided that an award simply in the amount of the medical expenses was insufficient under law because even if the jury didn't want to, it had to award some fair and reasonable money damages for "pain and suffering" above and beyond the bills.

Therefore, the judge set aside the verdict and said he would order a new trial on damages, unless the defendant would pay $3,000 in total. We agreed to do so, the plaintiffs accepted that sum, and I made a telephone call to Mr. Reilly, which was my custom following each and every verdict, and told him: "Justice was done."

CHAPTER 15

My Early Years

My very first trial I no longer remember, but I know it was in Brooklyn, the borough where I grew up, because my first job after I graduated from Columbia Law School in 1954 was trying cases as a federal prosecutor in the Eastern District of New York and, more precisely, in Brooklyn. I worked at the U.S. Attorney's Office there from 1954 to 1958, and tried 25 federal criminal jury trials. I was the only prosecutor on those cases - these days they try cases in teams - and all but one resulted in the conviction of the defendants.

When I left the U.S. Attorney's Office after four years, which was the typical tenure back then, I went to work in Manhattan for the greatest trial lawyer I ever knew, John Gabriel Reilly, "Jack" to his wife and "Mr. Reilly" to all others. He was a large burly and imposing man, over six feet tall, with red hair and untameably bushy eyebrows. Behind his back, he was known to all and sundry as "Eyebrows Reilly." He was impatient, intolerant and irascible. When he and I would step into the elevator in federal court, where we went together quite often, the elevator operator would welcome him by name and ask all others - the lawyers - to step out. He was in equal measure feared and revered. He and I got along just fine.

Growing up, my father used to tell me stories about his favorite lawyer, Bill Fallon, known far and wide as "The Great Mouthpiece." My father would attend his trials in lower Manhattan after his night-shift at the Post Office ended and before his lunch-shift as a waiter at Fusco's began. But I cannot believe that "The Great Mouthpiece," considered by so many at the time to be the greatest American trial lawyer of the first half of the Twentieth Century, could ever have bested Mr. Reilly, or Peter James Johnson, the second-best trial lawyer I ever knew.

I worked for Mr. Reilly at his firm Reilly & Reilly from October 1958 through October 1961. I tried 74 cases to verdict, representing defendants (insurance companies) in civil lawsuits, mainly automobile accident cases. Mr. Reilly didn't like to settle cases, so I was on trial constantly. While I might have a jury out deciding a verdict in one case, I was already picking a jury in the next case. I won virtually all of my trials, but after three years, it was not what I wanted, beating the injured and often indigent to save insurance companies money. So I switched sides.

When I left Mr. Reilly in 1961, I opened my own one-man practice. Mr. Reilly was not happy about my leaving and he asked me to move to another building. I obeyed Mr. Reilly in everything, and so I moved out of the historic and magnificent Woolworth Building at 233 Broadway, and took a one-room office in a building across the street at 225 Broadway. I bought two desks and four chairs, and my wife Jo hung as many of her paintings as would fit. Two months later, in mid-December, we celebrated the opening of my new firm by throwing a party at our house with 36 of my relatives and, a week later, another party with 27 of our friends.

For a time, I shared this new office space with my brother Edward, who was also in the early stages of his career, and this arrangement gave us a rare opportunity to collaborate. Edward had started as a magazine journalist, but when he began writing for TV crime dramas, such as "East Side/West Side" (with Cicely Tyson and George C. Scott), I lent a hand on matters of criminal law and courtroom scenes. Over the next few years, when he wrote episodes for "The Defenders" (with E.G. Marshall, Robert Reed, and Ossie Davis making guest appearances as the District Attorney), though no longer sharing office space, I continued to advise him. Our collaboration came to an end in 1971, when Edward moved his family to Los Angeles, his career having taken off. There he wrote for "Ironside," "Owen Marshall, Counselor at Law," "Marcus Welby, M.D.," and "Police Woman," before becoming a lead writer-producer for the first eight years of "Dynasty," which for a long stretch was rated the number one show viewed worldwide.

As for Mr. Reilly, he quickly got over his displeasure at my departure and gave me my first three trials. Over the next two years he, and plaintiff's attorneys against whom I had tried cases while at Mr. Reilly's, referred trials and depositions to me to handle. In late 1962 one of these plaintiff's attorneys, Charlie Kramer, asked me to join his firm. It was then and is today New York's premier personal injury law firm, known now as Kramer, Dillof, Livingston & Moore. I turned Charlie down.

Six months later, after I had won his cousin Mrs. Tulchin's case, Charlie asked again. This time I agreed, and I started in April 1963 as a partner, and was told I could expect to earn $25,000 a year, which was

12.5% of the firm's net. (When I left Mr. Reilly's firm, I was earning an annual salary of $10,000.) The timing was auspicious because within two months, Jo and I learned that she was pregnant with our first child.

Mr. Reilly also relented on my working in the Woolworth building, and so in 1965 I convinced Charlie to move our offices there. I remained with Kramer, Dillof, Duhan & DeBlasio (and then Kramer, Dillof, DeBlasio & Meagher) until 1968, when Tom Meagher and I left to open our own practice in the Woolworth Building. Thereafter, from 1968 until I retired in 2006, I continuously ran my own plaintiff's personal injury law firm.

In all, from 1961 until 2006, I tried about 500 cases as a plaintiff's attorney. Apart from those, I tried five criminal cases where I represented the defendants. Two were tried in the U.S. District Court in Brooklyn where I had worked as a federal prosecutor: U.S. v. Zito, a counterfeiting case in 1962; and U.S. v. DeVito, an interstate hijacking case of Squibb Pharmaceuticals in 1967. Two were tried in Brooklyn Criminal Court, one of them for vehicular homicide. All four trials resulted in not guilty verdicts on all counts.

I tried my fifth and final criminal case in 1976 in Westchester County. It was, perhaps, the greatest trial victory of my career and it came to me from Mr. Reilly, who called me on August 17, 1975, while I was away on vacation in New Hampshire with my family. Earlier that morning, the FBI had rescued the 21-year-old son of Edgar Bronfman – the billionaire magnate of the Seagram liquor empire – who had been kidnapped and held captive a total of nine days. The son Sam had been feared dead when, after Edgar paid the ransom on the eighth day, he remained missing. Like the other infamous kidnappings of the century – the Lindbergh baby, Patty Hearst and J.P. Getty III – the Bronfman kidnapping dominated the national news and captured the country's attention. All were riveted.

Hours after the rescue, Mr. Reilly was calling me not to rejoice in the news of young Sam's release, but because a sometime-chauffeur of his, Dominic Byrne, had been arrested for the kidnapping. "Peter," he said to me, "I want you to represent him. Do not concern yourself with a fee. This case will make you internationally famous."

I'd always known Mr. Reilly to be right about everything, so I did not hesitate in my decision to represent the chauffer. This time, however, Mr. Reilly was only partly right. He was right about the money, as I didn't earn a nickel, but he was wrong about the fame, which never did come my way. But I am getting ahead of myself.

CHAPTER 16

A FATAL MISTAKE FOR A TRIAL LAWYER

In January 1961, when I was with Reilly & Reilly, I tried a sad case involving a woman who, while walking on a sidewalk in Brooklyn, was struck on the head by a board that fell from the 14th floor of a building. It was quickly determined that the board, which was used to unfurl the building's flag, had broken free of the flagpole. The case, Sarokin v. 805 Fifth Avenue, was tried in Brooklyn Supreme Court.

The woman, who was represented by one of the leading plaintiff's firms in the city, brought suit against the building, which was owned by a real estate magnate named Louis Glickman. We represented Glickman.

I forget most of the details of the case, but I do remember that there was a question as to who was responsible for, and who had control over, the flagpole. That the pole was negligently maintained and thus was the cause of the accident was clear. But unless and until it became clear that, as owner of the building, Glickman was the party responsible for the flagpole's maintenance, he could not be held liable.

For some reason, the plaintiff's law firm had not established that fact in pre-trial discovery and so the case went to trial without that vital evidence nailed down.

I also remember that there was a certain document having to do with the flagpole and its maintenance, which bore the initials of a person of authority, but again for some reason unknown to me, the plaintiff's firm had not been able to identify who that person was.

In this light, the trial started. The plaintiff's lawyer called Glickman as a witness. He wanted, and needed, Glickman to tell him the name of the person whose initials were on the document.

The questioning went something like this:

> Q – On the date of the accident was there a man in your company with the initials D.E.B.?

A – No.

Q – Did you *ever* employ a man with the initials D.E.B.?

A – No.

Q – Do you know him?

A – No.

Q – Do you know how we can find him?

A – No.

On and on it went with no success for the plaintiff's lawyer. Without sufficient evidence of ownership and control over the flagpole, and its near-lethal board, the jury could not reach a verdict and the judge dismissed the case against Glickman.

When the case was over, I asked Glickman if he knew whose initials they were. He said sure he knew, and told me they were the initials of his top aide, a woman.

I told Glickman that most people would have volunteered to the plaintiff's lawyer that the document was signed by a woman and would have named her. I asked him why he didn't. His answer? "I've been on the witness stand before."

The plaintiff's lawyer's fatal mistake was *assuming*. He assumed that a person so high up in Glickman's organization had to be a man – could only be a man – and he was so blinded by his tunnel vision that he couldn't and didn't ask, "Did you ever employ *anyone* with the initials D.E.B.?"

I never learned if the plaintiff sued the law firm that represented her for malpractice. I doubt she did. But she should have.

I always remembered from that day on – never to assume. But that is easier said than done.

CHAPTER 17

"STOP THAT TRUCK, STOP THAT TRUCK"

The case of Fishman v. Motor Freight, a car accident case I tried in June 1960 when I was with Reilly & Reilly, is still of interest to me because of three factors. One, I was blindsided at trial on account of Mr. Reilly's rules that we not have a doctor of our choice examine the plaintiff ahead of time, and that we not question the plaintiff at a deposition before trial. Mr. Reilly was against physical examinations because he never wished to make an issue of the injuries - he believed plaintiffs always exaggerated and if we had them examined and then put a defense doctor on the stand, it could lend credence to their claim. With regard to not deposing the plaintiff in this case, Mr. Reilly felt we had nothing to gain because the facts of the accident were already so clear.

Two, the Fishman case was based on "the last clear chance" doctrine, which always made an accident case more interesting.

Three, Mr. Reilly ended up being sued by his client Motor Freight's insurance company, because it claimed that his fee for my trial services was not only excessive but unheard of.

THE FACTS

This as usual was a simple automobile accident case. The plaintiff, Mr. Fishman, a young college student, was driving on the Pennsylvania Turnpike when he was struck by a tractor-trailer. He was on his way to his home in Queens during a school break. It was morning, a clear day, the roads were dry, when his car was struck. Unfortunately for him, he had a major problem. He was facing the wrong way on the Turnpike at the time of the collision.

The plaintiff's claim was that he had lost control of his car and crossed the divider that separated the three eastbound lanes from the three westbound lanes of the Turnpike. His car, which had come to a stop, remained in the middle lane of westbound traffic for what he said was about 30 seconds. He was in shock, while seated there, and did not attempt to exit the car. Amongst the injuries claimed was a speech defect.

The truck driver's defense was that the plaintiff's car created an emergency that was too sudden for him to avoid.

The plaintiff brought the case to court in his home county of Queens, and we tried it before Judge Henry Latham and a jury of 12. Herman Glaser, a well-known plaintiff's lawyer, represented him and I represented the trucking company.

THE TRIAL

We selected the jury in one day and tried the case in four days. I sat at the defense table alone as usual; Glaser sat at the plaintiff's table and seated next to him was a well-dressed, good-looking young man, who I assumed was one of his trial associates.

Following our openings, when Glaser called his first witness, I was surprised to see the young man, who had been seated next to him, rise and walk to the witness stand. My surprise turned to one of shock when I heard him take the oath; it sounded something like this: *I - I - I s - s - swear t - t - to tell th - th - the t - t - truth*, etc. And that's the way it continued during his entire testimony. Only then did I realize that what the jury and I were hearing was what the plaintiff's attorney had simply claimed in his Bill of Particulars to be "a speech defect." (A Bill of Particulars is a pre-trial document that plaintiffs are required to give to defense counsel detailing particular information about the accident or malpractice claimed, including the extent of the injuries suffered.)

In his direct testimony, the plaintiff Mr. Fishman said that he was a good student and had planned to become a lawyer, but following the accident, he changed to a business major for obvious reasons of speech. He also said that he did not have any speech defect until after the accident.

In regard to the accident itself, he testified that he suddenly lost control of his car and was in shock while he was stopped on the wrong side of the Turnpike for about 30 seconds, hoping and praying not to be struck. It was the shortest cross-exam I ever conducted, and I am not even sure if I asked him one question. (And for obvious reasons, I was annoyed we had adhered to Mr. Reilly's rule of foregoing both physical examination and deposition of the plaintiff before trial.)

In any event, the law was on our side. In 1960, to win his case, the plaintiff had to prove that the defendant was 100% negligent in causing the accident and that he, the plaintiff, was totally free from contributory negligence. Seemingly impossible here, as his car was on the wrong side of the Turnpike, except there was a caveat. If the plaintiff could prove that, even though he might have been negligent in crossing to the wrong side, the defendant still had plenty of time – a last chance – to avoid hitting him, then the plaintiff might win. It would be up to the defendant truck driver to then prove that he did *not* in fact have enough time to avoid the accident, in which case the plaintiff couldn't win, his negligence having contributed to, or caused, the collision.

The amount of time the plaintiff's car was stopped in the wrong lane therefore became a major issue in the trial. Was it as long as 30 seconds as the plaintiff claimed? Or if less, was there still sufficient time to give the defendant the "last clear chance" to avoid striking the stopped car?

The defendant truck driver said that he saw the plaintiff's vehicle while it was crossing the divide and entering into his lane, and that although he tried to avoid it, there was no time for him to be able to do so. He also testified that if the plaintiff's vehicle did stop before the collision, it was only for a second or two. After listening to the lawyers sum up the case, the jurors would have to decide whose version was closer to the truth.

On summation, something occurred which I am not proud of: I interrupted my opponent's summation, for possibly the only time in my career. It happened as follows. Glaser was describing something that had not been testified to by the plaintiff and was not in evidence. He, in re-enacting the scene, sat in a chair at counsel table, yelling at the top of his lungs: "Stop that truck, stop that truck, stop that truck." As he continued doing so, at the 15 to 20 second mark, I stood up from my seat and yelled: "Stop that man, stop that man, stop that man." There were no objections, and there was no recrimination by the judge against either one of us.

THE AFTERMATH

The jury voted in favor of the defendant 10 to 2 – two older women jurors found for young Mr. Fishman – which was enough for a verdict in our favor. (Unanimous verdicts were not required, just five-sixths for one party or the other was sufficient; any less would have been declared a mistrial.) The truck's insurance carrier, Pennsylvania Thresherman's, was pleased with the verdict until, that is, it received Mr. Reilly's bill for $5,865.

The insurance carrier objected to the bill as excessive; tried to no avail to get Mr. Reilly to reduce it (he could be very stubborn when it came to parting with money); and as a last resort brought a lawsuit against him in New York County, where we had our office.

The insurance company's major claim was that a charge of $500 *a day* for a five-day trial was too much, even for New York City. The Pennsylvania-based company was savvy and knew that other leading defense attorneys in the city were only charging $50 a day; furthermore, they knew that I had only graduated from law school six years before the trial and so I couldn't possibly be costing Mr. Reilly anything close to $500 a day. (If they only knew how little I was actually costing him! Mr. Reilly was paying me $9,000 a year in 1960, which was $175 a week, which was just $35 a day.)

But Mr. Reilly was too smart for Pennsylvania Thresherman's. He asked the legendary Harry Gair – then considered by all to be New York's top plaintiff's attorney – to testify as an expert witness on legal fees. After Mr. Gair interviewed me at his office, he agreed that Mr. Reilly's billing $500 a day for my services was fair and reasonable.

At the 1962 trial of Thresherman's v. Reilly, both Mr. Gair and I testified. The jury voted in favor of Mr. Reilly, upholding his full bill, all except for a single line-item expense, a $25 charge for a court appearance that was adjourned because we had arrived too late.

Nobody got the better of Mr. Reilly.

POSTSCRIPT: I left Reilly & Reilly in October 1961, a little more than a year after the Fishman case, but before the case against Mr. Reilly came to trial. Even though I didn't know back then that the discrepancy between what Mr. Reilly was billing for me and what he was paying me was more than ten to one, I knew that I was earning too little. I also knew that my salary would continue to increase only by $1,000 a year (I started at $7,000 in 1958 and was up to $10,000 in 1961), and that I would never become a partner – Reilly & Reilly was a family firm, just Mr. Reilly and his daughter Elsie. But more than anything, what made me break from Mr. Reilly was that I wanted to help people like Mr. Fishman, not oppose them. I wanted to help people who had seen their life's ambitions taken away, or at least altered, on account of negligence.

Mr. Reilly must have sensed this ambition or quality in me, because he once told me: "There comes a day when little birds must fly on their own." As I always did, I listened attentively and did exactly what Mr. Reilly told me to do.

CHAPTER 18

"Is the Mixture 1/4 Wax and 3/4 Water, or 3/4 Wax and 1/4 Water?"

When I left Mr. Reilly to go on my own, I left without one client, without one case, and without one nickel in the bank. I became a solo practitioner, and when I say solo I mean solo. I had no one assisting me, not even a secretary. I had no telephone answering service. I used to time myself so that I made it to the bathroom and back to my one-room office within 30 seconds, so that I would not miss a telephone call about a possible case for me to try.

The cases I was trying at the time were known in the profession as "dogs." Mr. Reilly fed me some trials representing defendants, but the bulk of my work was trying the "dogs" for plaintiff's lawyers. A "dog" was a case that for one reason or another a plaintiff's lawyer did not want to try because he knew it was a loser, and he was looking and waiting for a newcomer who would take it over - for half of the fee - to rid him of his headache. In me they found the answer to their problems. I loved it; I was as free as a bird.

One of these "dogs" was Tulchin v. Bloomingdale Bros., the defendant company then a well-known department store in Manhattan. Ruth Tulchin, 43 years of age in 1958, was a cousin of Charlie Kramer, the senior partner at the plaintiff's firm Kramer Dillof. She had slipped and fallen and fractured her ankle when she was working as a saleslady for a concessionaire tenant at Bloomingdale's. I guess Charlie took the case because she was family, but after four and a half years of working it up he knew it was a losing cause and so, having tried against me when I was at Mr. Reilly's, he asked if I would help him out and try it.

I met with and interviewed Mrs. Tulchin on a Thursday in January 1963. I liked her. Unfortunately, that was the only thing I liked about the case.

Just as I always had done at Mr. Reilly's, I looked at the case from the defendant's point of view, and this one was a sure winner – for the defendant. Why did I think this?

1. It was an undramatic "slip and fall" case where the only witness to the accident was the plaintiff.

2. The slip was allegedly due to a dangerous accumulation of wax on an excessively and improperly waxed floor where customers walked to enter a dressing room, but it was not known when, how or by which of the department store's porters the wax was most recently placed on the floor.

3. The custom was to do a full waxing three times a year: once just before Christmas; once just before Thanksgiving; and once in midsummer. Mrs. Tulchin's fall occurred 24 days before Thanksgiving.

4. Apart from full waxing, spot waxing was done as needed, but always before 8:00 a.m. and Mrs. Tulchin fell at 7:30 p.m. What's more, if waxing had been done that morning, which we didn't know, many customers would have walked on that floor that day prior to her fall and apparently nobody else had been caused to fall.

5. There were no records of anyone ever slipping and falling because of excessively waxed floors at Bloomingdale's at any time before November 3, 1958; nor had Mrs. Tulchin or her co-workers ever complained about excessive wax. Notice of the dangerous condition would therefore be difficult to establish.

6. Mrs. Tulchin said that she knew it was wax that caused her to slip and fall, because she left a two-foot scuff mark on the floor and she had wax stuck to her shoe following her fall. Unfortunately, there was no photograph of the scuff mark, and the shoe with the wax on it had been discarded.

Knowing all of the above, why did I accept the case? Because I needed work and I needed money. But more than that, at no time before or after this case did I ever refuse to try a case that a lawyer asked me to try, whether it was at the U.S. Attorney's office, Mr. Reilly's office, Charlie Kramer's office, or when I had my own firm. My reason was simple: How could I become known as a great trial lawyer unless I did that which other lawyers could not do – namely, win the losing cases?

Why, though, do I include this relatively minor fall-down case in my memoirs? My answer is simple. I am fond of it.

First, it is an example of *do's and don'ts* for a lawyer and in this instance, my opponent's don'ts ended up in a very large verdict for my client.

Second, my winning this losing "dog" case for Charlie Kramer's cousin was one of the reasons he offered me a partnership three months later.

Third, when reviewing the transcript of the trial recently, I was reminded of how different trials were in those days. The trial lasted only four days, not months like many of my later cases. The 12 members and 2 alternates of the Queens jury were all men; women were routinely excused by the judges. And Judge Harold Crawford gave the jury breaks to "go up and have a smoke," and I always smoked cigars in the courthouse during breaks and while awaiting a jury's verdict.

Fourth, I did something in the Tulchin trial that I had never done before, never did again, and doubt that anyone else had ever done. I moved to *reduce* the amount we had demanded in the Complaint from $85,000 to $45,000 for Mrs. Tulchin and from $15,000 to $7,500 for Mr. Tulchin, which meant that the jury could not award more than $45,000 and $7,500 respectively. (Mr. Tulchin was allowed to sue for the loss *to him* of his wife's services – such as housework – while she was injured.) The judge and opposing lawyer must have thought I was crazy.

Why do such a thing? Because when I represented defendants, very often in summation I attacked the plaintiff, his lawyer and his case because of the outrageous, exorbitant and excessive amounts of money they demanded in their Complaints. For example, if the injuries were legitimately worth about $2,500, I would inform the jury during my summation that the plaintiff was suing us for $100,000 or $200,000. I equated it to a ransom demand – "pay us or else" – and explained to the jury that's why we were fighting the case. "Justice is one thing, extortion is another," I would tell the jury, "and we would not submit to it and so neither should you." Half of the time, the plaintiffs' lawyers would then have to spend time in their summations, which followed mine, futilely trying to explain away the vast discrepancy. Most of the time, the jury gave their clients nothing. So in Tulchin, even though $85,000 for her and $15,000 for her husband were not that outlandish, I determined not to take any chances and not have it as an issue. My motion to reduce the Complaint's *ad damnum* clause was, not surprisingly, granted on the defendant's consent.

TO THE TRIAL

From the time I first heard of Mrs. Tulchin's case on Thursday January 24, 1963, until the trial was over and the verdict in, only one week passed. I spent part of one day interviewing Mrs. Tulchin and reading the file; one day selecting the jury; and three days trying the case.

In regard to the case and how it was won, Mrs. Tulchin was an excellent witness and the defense lawyer Joseph Driscoll made several mistakes.

Mrs. Tulchin testified in a plain, simple manner, no exaggeration, no making the injury and disability any worse than it was. She testified as to liability, telling the jury that she slipped on wax at Bloomingdale's where she was a saleslady; and as to her injury, she told of the fractured ankle that required hospitalization for 21 days. She testified as to her medical expenses, that the total hospital bill was $476.22 (this was 1958, remember), and that the total bill for the orthopedic surgeon who performed the closed reduction under general anesthesia, and who examined her on 66 occasions during the six months following the accident, was $500.00. Finally, as to lost wages, she testified that in 1957, the year before the accident, her total wages were $3,864.00, but that in 1958, on account of the accident, she earned less.

Mr. Driscoll, for his part, committed at least two of the don'ts for a trial lawyer. His first mistake was that he should have rested without putting in a case, by which I mean he should not have called any witnesses to the stand after I finished with my witnesses. When I was with Mr. Reilly, we rarely put in any defense. We attacked the plaintiff and his witnesses, and then called no witnesses of our own, because when a jury hears inconsistencies, exaggerations and falsehoods from only one side (the plaintiff's), it will most often find against that side.

But most defense lawyers are afraid to rest without calling a witness, worried they'll be criticized if they lose, so they take what they think is the safe course and call witnesses, with the result that often their witnesses make the plaintiff's case. And Mr. Driscoll was no exception.

Mr. Driscoll called two porters who did waxing at Bloomingdale's. And, as luck or prediction would have it, they told conflicting stories and made my case.

The first porter said that the wax he put on the rubber tile flooring was mixed with water in the proportion 1/4 wax, 3/4 water. Upon my cross examination, he explained that the reason for only 25% wax was because the flooring was 11 years old and hardened, and wax would remain on its surface and be slippery. So, the less wax the better.

The second porter, who had not been in the courtroom to hear the first witness testify – because I had asked for non-party witnesses to be excluded – got up to the stand and told the jury the exact opposite. He said that the wax mixture he put on the floor was 3/4 wax, 1/4 water. On cross examination, he explained that the age of the tile made no difference in the wax-water ratio.

Each porter said that he did it the right way. And each said his way was the only proper way. Never mind that we still didn't know if either of them had even spot waxed the floor that day, their diametrically opposed stories made a mockery of the defendant's case.

Mr. Driscoll's second mistake was that he was fresh and disrespectful to his opponent (me) in front of the jury, sarcastically saying, "You are right there, my *boy*," and "Your cross examination was *inane*." He dug the hole deeper when, after criticizing me, he turned to the judge for help:

> Driscoll (to me) - You don't understand your own questions. That's your trouble.
>
> DeBlasio (to Driscoll) - You are the *smart* one.
>
> Driscoll - I object to that, Your Honor, will you please caution him about saying I am "the *smart* one." In fact, if he pleads he is dumb, that's his business. We will know tomorrow when the jury has it.

Well, the next day, the jury surely let him know. The jury took little time in finding Bloomingdale Bros. responsible for Mrs. Tulchin's fall and they awarded $39,023.78 *more* than the $976.22 she paid in total hospital and doctor's bills. Although this $40,000 award sounds modest today, in 1963 it was considered a very large verdict for a fractured ankle. At that time, the pain and suffering for such an injury was valued in the $3,500 range, and when added to her nearly $1,000 in medical expenses, one would have expected a verdict between $4,500 and $5,000. To further put the $40,000 in perspective, in the three years I tried defendants' cases at Mr. Reilly's, out of my 74 trial verdicts, the total damages won by plaintiffs combined was just $60,000, and the highest award to any one person was $10,000.

But, the incredibly high award for Mrs. Tulchin was far less a reflection of my skill than it was a reflection of the very low esteem in which the jury held Mr. Driscoll.

No one objects when a lawyer fights hard for his client and for what he believes in, but in the courtroom he must be civil and courteous to all. Otherwise, the jury likely will turn against that lawyer, and worse still, hold it against his client. I always tried to keep that in mind.

<u>POSTSCRIPT</u>: Our $40,000 award was reduced, which was typical when defendants appealed in the Appellate Division, Second Department, as Bloomingdale's did in this case. The Second Department in those days was notorious for reducing verdicts, and the presiding judge on the <u>Tulchin</u> five-judge panel was Judge Henry Ughetta, who was well known to be very defendant-oriented.

Given that a reduction was a foregone conclusion, I was pleasantly surprised when I read the opinion and discovered that the appellate judges let as much as $28,000 stand ($25,000 for Mrs. Tulchin and $3,000 for Mr. Tulchin), since the general thought was that the award would be reduced to about $7,500.

It may not have hurt my cause that Judge Ughetta was a bosom buddy of my former boss Mr. Reilly – so much so that they dined together every Friday night at a Manhattan restaurant on John Street – and not only did Judge Ughetta know me from my time at Mr. Reilly's firm, but he was the person who in 1959 sponsored me for membership in the New York Athletic Club, of which I am still a member.

CHAPTER 19

"WE WANTED YOU TO GET A FEE"

Most plaintiff's lawyers viewed a trial in Riverhead, Suffolk County, as being the equivalent of being sent to Siberia. On one occasion, I did not.

In December 1965 I spent four days on trial in one of my least memorable cases and yet I enjoyed myself because of the jurors' kind words to me after they returned their verdict.

The case was a total loser that I tried when I was with Kramer, Dillof, DeBlasio & Meagher. The plaintiff, our client Mr. Surburg, sued a local bar that he frequented most evenings because one night he sustained an injury there, which caused him to go blind in one eye.

The question for trial was how he was injured, but when I first read our Complaint the night before I drove out to Riverhead to pick the jury, I couldn't tell. The reason I could not tell was because in our Complaint we had listed two diametrically opposed reasons for the injury: 1) he fell down the defective steps that led to the basement of the bar and injured his eye; and 2) the bartender punched him in the eye.

Upon reading the rest of the file it became clear that the claim of defective steps was a total fabrication in order to bring into play the bar's liability insurance policy, because an assault by a bartender against a customer would not be covered by insurance. So, the first thing I did when I arrived at court the next morning was to meet with the Clerk of the Trial Part and tell him that I had to make a motion to amend and correct our Complaint, to remove the defective stair claim and proceed with the assault.

He told me that would be no problem and that it probably would not matter much because there had been 97 straight jury verdicts for the defendant in this Part (i.e., in this judge's courtroom). Suffolk County jurors, mostly made up of hard-working Polish potato farmers, were notoriously conservative-thinking people and they did not look kindly on those who brought lawsuits.

The facts that came out at trial were simple. The plaintiff, a married ne'er-do-well, had impregnated the 17-year-old niece of the bartender, thus leading up to the punch in the eye (and $11,000 in unpaid medical bills, for which there was a lien).

Each of the jurors probably would have reacted as did the bartender, but on the third day of trial, the jury rendered its verdict for the plaintiff in the amount of $11,000.

Following the verdict, the jury and I talked. They explained how they reached their decision. They said they hated the plaintiff and did not want him to receive any money, but they wanted me to get paid. They also said they knew that by awarding just $11,000 the plaintiff would not receive a nickel because of the medical lien, but that I would get my fee.

I guess we all went home happy, except for Mr. Surburg.

POSTSCRIPT: I remember this case fondly because in ensuring that I would get a fee, the jurors regarded me in a far kinder way than the general public tends to regard plaintiff's personal injury lawyers. Indeed, there seem to be few lawyers as widely derided as those in the personal injury field, the so-called "ambulance-chasers."

I have always seen our practice quite differently, as one that opens the courtroom doors to all. By taking cases on a contingency fee basis, without consultation fees, without a nickel of the client's money up front, earning a fee only if we win the case, the personal injury plaintiff's lawyer is able to represent anyone who is injured without regard to their ability to pay. It is law for the people by the people, "common law" in its truest sense. I like to believe that the Surburg jury understood this need for free access to the courts, even for those we might despise, and that it also understood I was a working man, trying to help others and earn a living at the same time.

CHAPTER 20

The Inimitable Peter James Johnson and His Man from Samaria

I include the 1965 Mensick case in this, my memoirs, even though I do not want to. Why don't I want to? Because anything I say will sound like an excuse and I am violently against making excuses. This was an impossible case to win. I tried many an impossible case, but this one was really impossible. I still do not understand why it was not dismissed at the end of my evidence, when I rested, for lack of proof of liability, but it wasn't.

One might think I would have forgotten some of the facts because, after all, it is more than 50 years ago that it was tried. Not so. I remember some of the events of the trial as though they happened yesterday.

THE FACTS

My client, Mr. Mensick, was driving a van that he used in his work when it broke down in the middle of the street in White Plains. He was alone and he exited his vehicle and started to put flares in the street behind it. The next thing he remembered was waking up in the hospital.

He was told that he had been driven to the hospital by a stranger who had seen him lying on the ground near one of the flares. Mr. Mensick's injuries were consistent with his having been struck by a vehicle. No witness to the events was ever found, and Mr. Mensick had amnesia about the accident.

Somehow, someway, someone in the firm Kramer, Dillof, Duhan & DeBlasio - which I had joined two years earlier - for whatever reason I have no recollection took the case and decided to name the man who drove Mr. Mensick to the hospital as the defendant. The theory being, I guess, why else would he have done so unless he caused the accident.

The case was tried; the case was lost; and some would say justice was done. Why memorialize it? I do so for one reason and one reason alone. I have always believed that to be a great trial lawyer one must stand above the crowd; one must think of and do things that no one else thinks of or dares to do. One of the rare few who filled the bill was my opponent in this case, the late Peter James Johnson.

In Mensick, Peter did something that I had never seen done before and never heard of being done since. That something was sheer theater – unforgettable – and ingenious. To him I dedicate this chapter.

First, a few words of introduction: Peter was primarily a defense lawyer, although he did try some plaintiffs' cases. He was extremely well thought of in the field. Either at the time of the trial, or shortly thereafter, he was the personal attorney to New York's Governor Mario Cuomo and he was an advisor to Mayor David Dinkins and Senator Alphonse D'Amato. He always dressed in a six-button jacket and wore his hair with flowing locks on both sides with a bald patch in the middle. He had been a New York City police officer, and he had been wounded when he served as a Marine in the World War II battle of Iwo Jima. He tried to and did terrorize most of the lawyers he faced.

At the time of the trial, I did not know Peter. Later on, we became dear friends. He eventually had me try all of the plaintiff malpractice cases referred to his office, because the insurance carriers he represented did not want him trying cases against them.

Why he tried this minor case against me I do not know and never asked him. But try it he did.

Our judge was John Dillon who, like Peter, was Irish. My former boss Mr. Reilly, whom Peter in a way modeled himself after, had told me that the Irish were the only people who did not stick together and, as with my juror O'Toole, in this instance Mr. Reilly was once again right.

Judge Dillon, like most of the Westchester County judges, was strongly defense-oriented and yet he and Peter continuously fought during the trial. I remember on the morning before summations we were in the judge's chambers when they had a furious argument – it might have had to do with the judge's failure to dismiss my case – which led to the judge's ordering Peter out of chambers because he could no longer tolerate his yelling. Peter responded by saying that he could not help it, he had lost much of his hearing when he was wounded at Iwo Jima.

We then summed up, Peter first and then I. Afterward we went to lunch, all at Schrafft's, across the street from the courthouse in White Plains, but separately. When the judge entered with his staff, I sitting alone as my custom was pleasantly surprised when the judge, very much out of character, whispered – "brilliant summation."

Those most unexpected words gave me a ray of hope, because the judge had yet to charge the jury. (To "charge the jury" is to instruct the jurors on the law applicable to the particular case, and while the jury charge is supposed to be neutral it often ends up favoring one party more than the other.) I thought that with the judge's anger and dislike towards Peter, and his apparent feelings for me, he might charge Peter out of court. Alas, no such luck. The charge was a tried and true one, totally favoring the defendant.

THE DENOUEMENT

Peter's summation – which could only have been thought of and been performed by him – was magnificent. I forget now the name of his client so I will simply refer to him as Mr. Goodhue here in my inadequate paraphrase of the summation:

> While driving along, Mr. Goodhue saw, as did the man from Samaria, a stricken fellow lying on the ground pleading for help.
>
> > (Peter, then six feet in front of the jury box, lay down on his back with hands and arms outstretched, and cried out)
>
> "Help me, help me!"
>
> > (Peter then stood up and imitated Mr. Goodhue's stopping his car, getting out of it and running over to Mr. Mensick, as did the Good Samaritan to comfort the helpless soul)
>
> "Hold on, hold on, I am here to help you!"
>
> > (Peter then resumed his position on the courtroom floor)
>
> "Help me, help me!"
>
> > (Peter stood up and in pantomime carried Mr. Mensick away to safety and to help)

I no longer remember his exact closing words, but I can imagine they were about how now, when out of danger, the plaintiff was ungrateful to the man from Samaria. But his final words did not matter. The damage was done, there was no need to say: "Et tu, Brute?" The bell had been rung; the jury was awestruck; the scene was implanted in their memories, as it still is in mine.

My summation followed Peter's. I have no memory of it, but knowing myself and how I would react after hearing and seeing such a magnificent summation, all I can say is I know I would not have taken it lying down.

CHAPTER 21

WHEN LEFT IS RIGHT AND RIGHT IS LEFT

The case of Kaye v. City of New York, tried in Manhattan in New York Supreme Court in 1966, the year after Mensick, is one of interest because of the number of lessons - do's and don'ts - for a trial lawyer.

Kaye was what is called in the trade a "slip and fall," or more accurately a *trip* and fall case. Such a case has never been one of my favorites.

One, there is rarely much drama in such a lawsuit.

Two, there is often a strong defense that the plaintiff contributed to the accident. (As in Fishman v. Motor Freight, before 1975 in order for a plaintiff to win a negligence suit he had to prove that he was free from any and all negligence in the occurrence of the accident. If he were found to be even 1% negligent, he lost.)

In a trip and fall, one is usually walking or in motion and the usual defense is that the person should have been looking where he was going. In this regard, I am reminded of a prospective juror I once questioned in Westchester County. He said he believed that a person injured when he was doing some activity always had to be at least partially at fault and thus partially negligent. I remember being so dumb-founded by such reasoning that I did not even bother giving him examples of when that did not follow, such as:

> Suppose in this jury room, while you were walking to take your seat, a slab from the ceiling fell on your head. How would you be negligent?
>
> Or suppose you were walking on the sidewalk and a drunk driver lost control of his car and struck you. How would you be negligent?

But I realize that where there is smoke there is fire, and so there must be others who think as he did, and thus the defense of contributory negligence is often effective.

Three, slip and fall cases mostly relate to defects, such as holes on sidewalks or on premises, and they are usually against a municipality or property owner. In such cases, the plaintiff must prove that the defendant knew or should have known of the defect before the accident – i.e., had "notice" – and had sufficient time to repair it. Failure to repair a defect upon notice is negligence.

Notice may be had in two ways: 1) written notice, for example when a citizen writes a letter to the city about a dangerous hole on the sidewalk; and 2) "constructive notice," for example when a hole has existed for a long while and timely inspections of the area by the property owner would have revealed it. Good "notice" witnesses for a plaintiff would be a mailman or a policeman (I am using 1960s terms) because they daily visit areas where holes and defects are located. But if the mailmen and policemen went to court for every slip and fall case, they would not be able to carry out their work and duties. So, a good notice witness is rare and hard to find, and has been the subject of abuse in many cases.

In any event, I ended up trying Mrs. Kaye's case while with Kramer Dillof. As usual, the facts were simple.

It was election night. Mr. and Mrs. Kaye, an immigrant husband and wife in their 70s, went on foot to a local school to vote. The school was about a block away from their apartment in Manhattan. When they arrived at the school, it was near the time when the polls were to close. To get into the school building so that they could reach the polling booths, they had to go up a great many steps that led from the sidewalk to the doors giving ingress to the building.

The steps were unusual, somewhat in the shape of a pyramid. There were about 30 steps, initially about 120 feet wide at the bottom, and gradually narrowing in width to about 60 feet at the top. When Mr. and Mrs. Kaye finally reached the polling area, it was too late. The polls had just closed. Thus, they turned around, left the building, and when they were about ten steps from the bottom, Mrs. Kaye fell and broke her hip.

While she was lying on the steps, she and Mr. Kaye saw what it was that caused her to trip and fall – a hole at the edge of a step – which was about one-half inch long, one-half inch wide and one-half inch deep. A young man, who had just voted and was coming down the steps, stopped, helped Mrs. Kaye up, and helped her down the remainder of the steps to the sidewalk.

He told them his name and address, and said if they ever needed him as a witness he would gladly help. The Kayes took a taxi to their home, then went to a hospital, and within 90 days filed a Notice of Claim with the city stating that they intended to sue.

Because the city would be the responsible party in the lawsuit, due to the fact that the school and its steps were city property, the law required notification to the city within 90 days of the occurrence, so that it could timely investigate. Thereafter, a lawsuit was filed.

The case was not without its problems.

THE CONS FOR THE PLAINTIFFS' CASE

1. The defect – the hole – was quite small. In law there is a Latin phrase "de minimis non curat lex," which means that the law does not consider nor take notice of trifles. Some defense attorneys might argue and not be laughed out of court if they said that a half-inch hole is a trifle.

2. There was the question of notice. What witness could be found who had seen this hole for at least a month before the accident – which would have given the city time to repair it – and would be willing to testify?

3. No police report, nor ambulance report, existed evidencing the fact that Mrs. Kaye fell on the school steps. Thus, credibility was an issue. Some people are known to fall and injure themselves, for example in their kitchen, and then fake a lawsuit by finding a hole someplace else and claiming that's where they fell.

4. There was no voter registration record showing that the Kayes were even at the school, because they had been too late to vote.

THE PROS FOR THE PLAINTIFFS' CASE

1. The Kayes were hard-working, honest citizens. They were credible.

2. There was the witness, the young man who could place them at the scene and who was willing to help.

3. Mr. Kaye said that he was the notice witness. He used to take

a daily walk to keep fit during his retirement from his job, and he passed that school and its steps daily, and he had seen that hole for months before election night.

4. We had a photographer photograph the steps and the hole, and while it was not a "defect" that would knock your socks off, especially in regard to a young agile student, it could be dangerous enough to an elderly person not in the best of health or shape, especially a woman wearing heels, to cause her to trip and fall. Or as Mercutio replied to Romeo in Shakespeare's Romeo and Juliet, when asked how bad the knife wound was that he had suffered at the hands of Tybalt: "'Tis not so deep as a well, nor so wide as a church door, but 'tis enough. 'Twill serve."

THE TRIAL

We were up against a tough, experienced, crusty Irish Assistant Corporation Counsel, who tried the case for the City. His trial strategy was to brand the Kayes as money-hungry fabricators. He was tough on cross-examination with Mrs. Kaye, whom I called as a witness one morning early in the trial. As I questioned Mr. Kaye right afterward, with my emphasis on the notice issue and his seeing the hole on his daily walks, I knew that the City's lawyer would be merciless with him on cross. However, before he could cross-examine Mr. Kaye, we had our luncheon recess.

During that recess, the first of the do's and don'ts for a trial lawyer cropped up. Don't tell a jury you have an eyewitness, or put an eyewitness on the stand, unless you have interviewed him before trial. This one was on me. I, in my opening, told the jury all about the young eyewitness and what he would say to prove where the accident happened, but I had never spoken with him.

Our office investigator had seen him prior to trial and reported he would make an excellent witness, but I had never met him, let alone heard his version of the facts or prepared him to testify. It was not until the luncheon recess that we discussed what his testimony would be.

He said that at the time of the accident he was a 19-year-old college student, and that night was the first time he had voted in a national election. It was late, he hurried up the steps, he passed an elderly couple who were slowly ascending the steps, and he remembered feeling bad that he did not stop and wait for them and hold the door open for them. He did not stop because he knew the polls were about to close. He went inside and made it just in time. In fact, he was the last one they allowed to vote. On his way out of the school, while descending the steps, he saw Mrs. Kaye lying on the ground, about ten steps from the sidewalk, and Mr. Kaye was tending to her. The witness helped her to the sidewalk and into a taxi, and gave her his name and address.

A great story, until the nightmare came, when I showed him the photographs.

We made light of the small size of the hole, but we recognized that it would not be such for an elderly woman like Mrs. Kaye. However, that was not our problem. He calmly and matter-of-factly told me that's not where she fell. "She fell about 50 feet away from that spot," he said, "on the other side of the steps." I said, "What do you mean that's not where she fell? Both she and her husband said she fell on the left side of the steps, and you told our investigator she fell on the left side of the steps." "Yes," he said, "but I was talking about the left side of the steps as you look down when leaving the school, as I was, not as it is in these photographs, on the left side as you look up from the sidewalk."

The way Mrs. Kaye had described it, what she was calling the left side would have been my eyewitness's right side.

I then tried to reason with my eyewitness, with all of the powers of persuasion I could muster: "Look, this happened years ago, it was a very major event in their lives. They're sure where she fell. To you, as a Good Samaritan, it was a passing thing. Of course you remember her on the ground, and helping her up, and the taxi, but certainly the exact place where she fell could easily be forgotten, or you could be mistaken. In fact, there are well-recognized studies which reveal that within 24 hours of an accident a witness forgets 90% of the details. Imagine what he forgets years later. Couldn't you be mistaken?" Answer: "No. These photos do not show the place where she fell."

I was at my wit's end. How could I go forward and put him on the witness stand and he says that's not where she fell, it was 50 feet from there. Because then it goes without saying that the hole is out of the picture, literally. What's more, he would be telling the jury that the Kayes were lying, or to be charitable, mistaken. That would be the death knell.

On the other hand, how could I face the jury, having told them I had a witness who would prove Mrs. Kaye was on those steps that night, and not put him on the stand? Without him, there's no evidence the accident happened at the school except for the testimony of the Kayes and obviously they in legal terms were "interested witnesses."

It seemed bad either way, so I decided I would put him on the stand.

I instructed him as follows: "I need you to show to the jury the Kayes were at the school on those steps that night. That you can truthfully testify to. I do not need you to point out where she fell. I am not obligated to do that. I therefore ask you to carefully listen to my questions, answer them directly, do not volunteer, but beyond that, you must realize that when I finish with you, the City's lawyer will question you. You must answer his questions truthfully, as I know you will, but you are not required to, not even allowed to, volunteer. Just listen to the questions and answer them directly. You will have to do what you have to do, and I will have to do what I have to do. Is that okay with you?" Answer: "Yes."

Fortunately for the Kayes, the defendant's lawyer had not asked that all non-party witnesses be excluded from the courtroom, so when the afternoon session got underway, our young eyewitness, of his own accord, took a seat in the audience section of the courtroom and listened to the defense attorney's cross-examination of Mr. Kaye.

That's when two more of the do's and don'ts came into play. First, don't needlessly and perhaps mercilessly attack, and hammer away at, and insult a witness to and beyond the point of no return. It may and often will work to your detriment with the jury, as well as with those persons in the courtroom listening to you and watching you do this.

Second, never assume. Never assume to such an extent that you become blinded to reason and believe that a witness called by your opponent is always called because he is going to be helpful to your opponent's case. Sometimes, your opponent is just dumb, and does dumb things. Sometimes, that witness can be helpful to your opponent with regard to one aspect of the case, and be harmful to him in another aspect of it.

With regard to the first "don't," the City's lawyer true to his calling hammered away at Mr. Kaye and his "cock and bull" story in such a crude and disrespectful manner that it infuriated our young eyewitness present in the courtroom and awaiting his turn. Not so much that he would lie under oath, which he did not do, but enough so that he did not volunteer to help the defense lawyer to see the error of his tunnel vision when he could have.

The scene – and along with it the second "don't" – went as follows. When the City's lawyer finished with Mr. Kaye, the young eyewitness took the stand. His testimony upon my direct examination went as I outlined above: he voted, he saw the Kayes, Mrs. Kaye was lying on the steps, he helped her, and he gave them his name and address. Then the City's lawyer cross-examined him:

Q – You spoke to Mr. DeBlasio?

A – Yes.

Q – He showed you the photos?

A – Yes.

Q – He told you what the plaintiffs said about the accident and where and how she fell?

A – Yes.

Q – He told you they said she fell on the left side of the steps?

A – Yes.

Q – And if I ask you where she fell, you're going to tell me it was the left side of the steps?

A – Yes.

Q – And that's not because Mr. DeBlasio told you that the claim is that it was on the left side of the steps?

A – No. I told him it was the left side of the steps.

Q – No more questions.

After he finished testifying, I asked our witness why he testified as he did. Answer: "After I heard and saw how he humiliated Mr. Kaye, I decided I was not going to help him, and I didn't. And I didn't lie. If he had asked me, 'When you say *left* side, which way is that, looking at the school, or looking out from the school?' it would have been a different story."

THE VERDICT

The jury awarded $72,500, a not-insubstantial sum in the 1960s. The case went on appeal to the Appellate Division, First Department, and they surprised me when they affirmed the verdict and did not say "de minimis non curat lex." As I remember it now, more than 50 years later, I am pretty sure they never mentioned the size of the hole in their opinion, quite possibly because they did not want a half-inch hole to be precedent for future cases.

POSTSCRIPT: Another lesson from the Kaye case, one which I think I knew beforehand: Do not be afraid to do something, like I did in putting the Good Samaritan eyewitness on the stand, because of how the opposing lawyer might respond or react if you were to do it. The reason? Most of the time, if not always, the opposing lawyer will do nothing, due to the fact that he or she will not know or think of what to do.

Years later, in the Bronfman kidnapping trial, a similar witness dilemma arose. It took all my powers of persuasion at that time to convince the co-defendant's lawyer that he had to go ahead and put his eyewitness on the stand - a doorman from the kidnapper's apartment building - and not fear what the prosecutor might do in response. As in Kaye, it worked to our advantage.

CHAPTER 22

"What Do Ten Drug Convictions Have to Do with Anything?"

Back in 1968, at cocktail parties, to break the ice, I would sometimes tell the story of a case I had recently tried. It was about a young man who stole a bicycle and rode it on the wrong side of the road and collided with a car head on. The cyclist, Mr. Ortiz, who already had ten convictions for drug possession in his young life, was at the time of the accident, not surprisingly, under the influence of drugs. The details of this stolen bike accident case, when related by me at those cocktail parties, served their purpose: all kinds of philosophical discussions followed relating to our legal system, our lawyers, drugs, justice and the like.

The story went like this. Mr. Ortiz stole a bicycle that had been left just outside of Central Park at West 65th Street in Manhattan. It was 4:00 a.m. on a summer's night, and he rode the bicycle into the park heading west to east on the two-lane road. The bicycle did not have a light, and Mr. Ortiz rode it in the left lane against oncoming traffic.

About halfway through the park, the bicycle going east collided head on with a car going west in its correct lane. The police investigation, which included measurements of the car's skid marks at the time of impact and prior to it, showed that the car was being driven about 50 mph. The speed limit in effect on that road in the park was 30 mph.

Mr. Ortiz, surprisingly, was not seriously injured and somehow ended up at the law offices of Kramer Dillof. They commenced a lawsuit, accusing the driver of speeding and negligently causing the collision, while claiming that Mr. Ortiz had not contributed one iota to the accident. (At that time, it was still the law that the plaintiff had to prove that the defendant was 100% negligent and the plaintiff totally free of any negligence.)

Like so many of my cases, I wonder why I tried it in the first place. By the time of the 1968 trial, Tom Meagher and I had just left Kramer

Dillof to open our own firm, and I guess I tried it as a favor to Charlie Kramer. Looking back on it now, though, two things fascinate me about the case, which I tried in Manhattan before Judge Thomas Chimera, both of which occurred during the jury selection process.

First, I was worried about Mr. Ortiz's ten drug convictions and how the jurors would react to them. So during the voir dire the first question I asked of each juror individually, starting with juror number one, the foreman, who was a Black man in his 30s, was: "Would you afford the same legal rights to Mr. Ortiz as you would give to anyone else who was in an accident and brought a lawsuit against another person, or would you be unable to do so and would you hold it against him because he had ten convictions for drug possession prior to the accident?" The foreman's answer: "What's that got to do with anything?"

I then questioned juror number two, who also happened to be a young Black man. I repeated the question. His answer: "You heard the man. What's that got to do with anything?"

Naturally, I accepted their answers without evidencing any surprise, and without feeling obligated to instruct them on the law – which was the judge's province and not mine – that the convictions may have legal consequences in regard to the credibility of such a witness.

I then questioned juror number three, who was a white man born in Poland. I asked him the same question and his answer was: "He vass on a trip." I questioned him about what he meant by a "trip" and other subjects, and after a while he agreed that he could not be a fair and impartial juror in such a case, and thus could not sit on our jury.

I then questioned juror number four, another white man who I remember was a professor at my Alma Mater, Columbia University, and I asked him about his thoughts in regard to the drug convictions. He answered that he would have to hold the convictions, and more, against my client Mr. Ortiz. So, too, did he disqualify himself.

After all the jurors were questioned, and after a good number decided that they could not fairly sit in judgment on such a case, we ended up with a jury of 12 men which, if not accepting Mr. Ortiz's way of life, at least would not hold it against him in this a *civil* lawsuit. (This became particularly evident when, during the trial, the defendant's lawyer cross-examined Mr. Ortiz about the date, place and nature of each and every one of his ten convictions – one conviction at a time. The jurors appeared bored out of their minds and couldn't wait for him to finish.)

Second, I was worried about Mr. Ortiz's riding on the wrong side of the road and how the jurors would react to this. So during the voir dire I asked each juror individually: "Do you know if there is a correct side of the roadway a bicycle is to use and, if so, which side is it? The side going in the same direction as the cars, or the side going in the opposite direction as the cars?" Their answers, which were mixed, surprised me, and made my task an easier one.

About half of the jurors thought that it was proper to ride a bicycle against traffic, and about half thought that it was proper to ride in the same direction as the traffic was going. Thus, even though the law was and is that a bicyclist is to travel with the flow and in the same direction as traffic, half of the jurors thought it safer to see the traffic coming towards them, and they, like Mr. Ortiz, would have ridden on the wrong side of the road.

With jurors who apparently would not hold Mr. Ortiz's convictions or drug use against him, and who themselves would have ridden on the same side as Mr. Ortiz, we proceeded to trial on the theory that: 1) the convictions and his being under the influence at the time had nothing to do with the cause of the accident; 2) the stealing of the bike had nothing to do with the accident; and 3) the riding of the bike on the wrong side of the road had nothing to do with the accident.

What did have to do with the accident, I argued to the jury, was that the defendant was driving about five times as fast as the bicycle was traveling. Thus, *even had they been traveling in the same direction*, the car would still have struck the bicycle, all because the driver was speeding.

If the car was going about 50 mph (as reasonably inferred by the trial testimony and skid marks), by mathematical formula it would have traveled 75 feet in a second; if the bicycle was traveling about 10 mph (as reasonably inferred by the trial testimony), it would have traveled about 15 feet in a second. Since I was a boy I always loved math, and I used it whenever I could at trial to make things simple for the jury.

Assuming then that both were traveling in the same direction, the car would have gained 60 feet on the bicycle *each second*. In two seconds, it would have gained 120 feet on the bicycle, and because that particular car's headlights on that particular section of road only shone 100 feet in front of it, the bicycle would have come into the driver's view with *less* than two seconds to avert striking it, which was impossible.

However, had the defendant been driving within the speed limit, at 30 mph, he would have traveled only 45 feet in a second and, with that same 100 feet of visibility, he would have had *more* than two seconds to swerve to avoid the accident. Thus, the cause of the accident was the excessive speed at which the defendant drove his car.

Sleight of hand? Mirrors? Perhaps. But the jury agreed and rendered a plaintiff's verdict in the sum of $12,500.

If I had tried the case at my cocktail parties, I think I would have lost. But perhaps that could be because at the cocktail parties I would have a drink or two. I never drank at lunch during a trial, or as they used to say in Brooklyn: "Don't drink and try."

CHAPTER 23

Be Sure to See the Original Records, Not Just Photostats

I tried the malpractice case Ferdon v. Stamm and Schwartz in Monticello Supreme Court, Sullivan County on two occasions. First in 1967, and the second time in 1969. Both times against Bob Bell of Martin Clearwater & Bell, a very fine lawyer and a good friend of mine.

I learned a very important lesson in Ferdon – and fortunately for me and Mrs. Ferdon (née DeBlasio, though no known relation) it was not too late. It was, once again, a very simple case.

Mr. Ferdon, 30 years old, was a farm laborer in Sullivan County. One day while working in a chicken coop, he stepped on a board that broke and he fell about four feet to the dirt floor and badly bruised his ribs and chest. He immediately went to the emergency room at Monticello Hospital because of severe pain, and was treated by two doctors, Stamm and Schwartz, who were partners. They gave him three injections of the pain killer Lidocaine, in three of his ribs.

When he got off the treatment table, Mr. Ferdon collapsed and died then and there.

An autopsy was performed and cause of death was listed as cardiac arrest following the Lidocaine injections. A malpractice lawsuit was brought on behalf of his widow.

The plaintiff's claim was twofold: 1) Lidocaine should not have been given because it was a dangerous anesthetic and the injury was a minor one; and 2) too much Lidocaine was given. The defense was twofold: a) each of the three injections was 7.5 cc, which was the normal dose; and b) there were no reported cases of Lidocaine given in these doses causing death.

There were several things of note in the first trial. Number one, it was a hung jury, seven to five in favor of the defendants. The jury happened to be composed of seven women and five men: the seven women voted in favor of the defendant-doctors; the five men voted for the widow. One lesson I learned was that women are especially partial to doctors, among other reasons I'd guess because they take their children to them to be cared for and cured. Men on the other hand don't prefer doctors over others – unless, of course, the others are lawyers – but they *are* partial to widows.

Number two, our expert pathologist testified that when he was a medical examiner in the Office of the New York City Medical Examiner, he personally reviewed a number of cases involving Lidocaine overdoses and it had been his opinion that the Lidocaine caused these patients to die. In support of his expert opinion, he relied on an anesthesiology textbook authored by Dr. Valentino Mazzia, which he referred to as the standard and authoritative work in the field of anesthesiology and drugs.

Number three, since both Bob Bell and I were from Manhattan and 100 miles from home, we stayed in Monticello, and had dinner together on trial nights – or rather I should say we had drinks together because Bob had about 12 Dewar's and water, and I had about six shots of some whiskey to keep him company. I figured I was doing my lawyerly duty because the next day he surely would not be sober and I would have the advantage over him. But alas, each and every following morning in court, Bob was sober as a judge.

Number four, prior to trial I reviewed a copy of the ER records, and it was clear to me that the records had been changed, but I could not figure out why they had been changed because the change was in our favor. It was obvious that the number 5 in "7.5 cc" had originally been a 0 and that someone had deliberately written over it to make it into a 5. I kept wondering and wondering why the defendants, or someone from the hospital, would increase 7.0 cc to 7.5 cc, which was clearly against their interest. (We were arguing that they gave too much Lidocaine, and here they were *increasing* the amount in the chart.) I never figured it out. But I should not really say "never" – because I did figure it out at the end of the *second* trial. (Fortunately for Mrs. Ferdon and me, there weren't 11 or 12 women jurors on the first trial, or we never would have gotten a chance at a second trial.)

And so, on to the second trial.

It was a disaster. Bob Bell slaughtered us. One, he introduced into evidence the records of the New York City Medical Examiner's Office for the last fifty years and, contrary to what our pathology expert had said at the first trial, there was not a single report of a Lidocaine-caused death.

Two, he brought in Dr. Mazzia – the leading anesthesiologist our pathology expert had testified was an authority on the subject – and he contradicted our expert.

Three, Bob introduced into evidence the autopsy slides of Mr. Ferdon's heart and its vessels, including the aorta, and the slides were very damaging. It was the first time I had seen them, and what I saw was a picture of a vast desert with a little trickle of water running through it. In medical terms, I guess the vast desert was the arteriosclerosis, which filled Mr. Ferdon's heart and blood vessels, and the trickle of water was the opening in those vessels through which the blood flowed.

In any event, all I could do was keep wondering why they changed the hospital records to increase the Lidocaine. It still made no sense.

The night before the summation I did what I should have done before or at least during the first trial, and what I especially should have done before this second trial: I finally looked at the *original* hospital records instead of my photostat copy. And there it was, as plain as day, I could see not just one change (i.e., making the 0 into a 5), but *two* changes. The amount of Lidocaine as originally written was "10" cc. Someone had made the 1 into a 7 by adding a horizontal line to the top left part of the 1, and then added a decimal point and changed the 0 to a 5. The doctors had originally injected 10 cc of Lidocaine into each of Mr. Ferdon's three ribs, and changed the record to make it appear that they only injected 7.5 cc.

The reason I could now see that the 1 of the number 10 had been changed to look like a 7 was because the top horizontal part added to the 1 was written by a pen with different ink. That the horizontal and vertical parts of the 1 were written in different color inks at different times had not come through on the black and white photostat I had been looking at, but was clear on the original. I am not proud of the fact that I did not discover this change from 10 to 7.5 until the last moment of the second trial, but at least it wasn't too late.

The next morning when we went to court, Bob Bell summed up, and then it was my turn. My summation focused on one thing and one thing only. I told the jury that the hospital record was changed. It was changed for a reason. It was changed by the defendants or someone on their behalf. The reason it was changed was because the defendants knew that 10 cc of Lidocaine was too large a dose and they should never have given him that amount, and that was the reason he wrongfully died. I told the jurors that the original hospital record was in evidence and they had the right to take it into the jury room and examine it, and not to take my word for it but see it for themselves. If they saw the change, which anyone could see with the naked eye, they would know the only verdict they could render would be for the plaintiff.

The verdict was in favor of Mrs. Ferdon for $67,000. It was not a lot of money, but this was 1969 and the trial was in an upstate county notoriously more conservative than the city. Moreover, there was no pain and suffering from the Lidocaine as Mr. Ferdon died immediately after it was administered; and Mr. Ferdon's earnings were at the lowest end of the earnings scale, so the loss of income to his surviving spouse was not very much.

I felt sorry for my friend Bob Bell in that he did not have an opportunity to rebut my summation (the plaintiff goes last), but I doubt that he felt sorry for me when he had Dr. Mazzia destroy my expert witness during the second trial. More importantly, it was Bob's clients' hospital record written (and changed) by them, and he had it in his possession for years. His clients knew there were changes in the record and I'm not saying that Bob knew it, but he should have known it.

POSTSCRIPT: After the trial, I became friends with Dr. Mazzia and about six months later he took me to see the first and only open-heart surgery I ever witnessed. It was such an unusual opportunity that I brought along my brother-in-law Pat George, a university professor then visiting from Wisconsin. It was done at New York University by Dr. Frank Spencer, a distinguished cardio-thoracic surgeon, and Dr. Mazzia was the anesthesiologist.

Not only were Pat and I permitted in the operating room, in gowns and masks, but we stood right at the table. I still remember my shock when I heard someone using a saw and I looked over to see that it was being used to open the female patient's chest. (It's a good thing that 36 years later I did not hear the saw when I was under general anesthesia up at Columbia for my open-heart surgery.) In any event, Dr. Spencer was not yet in the room; it was the chief resident who was doing the sawing.

It was as a result of my seeing what an important role in surgery the chief resident plays that I later sought out and met with the chief resident who assisted in the brain surgery performed on my client Betty Crabbe. That neurosurgeon, Joseph Mormino, was kind enough to agree to be our malpractice expert in Ms. Crabbe's lawsuit against his former hospital, Flower Fifth Avenue, and it was due to him that we won the first eight-figure verdict in New York history.

CHAPTER 24

THE SCALES OF JUSTICE

Dunkley v. New York Hospital, tried in 1979 before Judge Albert P. Williams and a jury of eight in Supreme Court, New York County, was a case I remember and include in my memoirs because of two unusual incidents. One had to do with the curious make-up of our jury, the other with what I said about defense counsel to that jury. Even though it wasn't as bad as how defense counsel treated me in Tulchin, I still regret it to this day.

The facts as usual were fairly straightforward. Ms. Dunkley, a married Staten Island woman, who worked at a convent assisting the nuns, had an intrauterine device (IUD) inserted to prevent pregnancy. One day she went to the doctor to have it replaced and he could not locate it. A sonogram was performed and it showed that the IUD had moved. Instead of being at the entrance of the uterus, it was oddly above and outside of the uterus.

It was agreed by the defendant surgeon at New York Hospital and Ms. Dunkley that surgery had to be performed to remove the displaced IUD. Ms. Dunkley told the surgeon that since her IUD had traveled around inside of her, which she presumed could be dangerous, instead of replacing it with another IUD she would rather have her tubes tied as long as she was undergoing surgery anyway.

Surgery was performed and to the surprise of all, the object seen on the sonogram was not an IUD. It was a surgical clip from a prior ulcer operation, which had dropped from its original resting place above the uterus.

Ms. Dunkley was under general anesthesia during the attempted removal of the IUD and so, without waiting for her to wake up and ask if she still wanted her tubes tied, the surgeon just went ahead and tied the tubes.

When she awoke, Ms. Dunkley was told about the ulcer clip and that her IUD had probably loosened prior thereto and fallen out of her body and that her tubes were now tied. She was quite upset about what had happened and what she was put through, and that her tubes had been tied without again discussing it with her. It was one thing if the IUD had traveled internally and caused a risk to her health, she wouldn't want that to happen again. It was quite another, as she now learned, that it had simply fallen out, in which case she had little to fear from an IUD and would have rather had it replaced than have her tubes tied.

She brought a malpractice lawsuit against the surgeon and his employer New York Hospital for the improper reading of the sonogram, and the assault and battery of tying her tubes without her consent because her tubes were only to be tied if the foreign object on the sonogram was indeed an IUD, which had moved from its original site.

The Hospital's defense was 1) the IUD and the ulcer clip were very similar in size, shape and appearance, and very difficult to tell apart, and so there was no departure from accepted medical practice in failing to distinguish between the two on the sonogram; and 2) she had given her written consent for the tying of the tubes.

Six experts testified for the defendants; one for the plaintiff. The defendant surgeon was a young doctor for whom a great career was predicted by the New York Hospital people, and he played the part when he testified with abundant confidence. Unfortunately for him, and the Hospital, the six women on the jury voted against him and awarded Ms. Dunkley $100,000 in damages.

The first incident about the trial that was so unusual related to the jury. The six women on the jury were all African-American, and one of the two alternates was also an African-American woman. (The other alternate was a Caucasian man.) Ms. Dunkley was Caucasian.

During the trial, the judge, an African-American man, called defense counsel Peter Kopff and me to the bench and started to ask: "How in the world did you manage to pick a jury and get seven - -," but before he could say his next word, I – as I had a habit of doing – finished his sentence for him (to myself) with the word "Blacks." I was shocked that he would mention this to us. However, I was wrong. He finished his sentence with the word "women." I admit I was pleased that seven of my jurors were Black, and that is what I saw. He, however, did not see seven Blacks, he saw seven women.

The second unusual incident related to Peter Kopff and me, and I am sorry for what I did, especially to such a gentleman and fine lawyer as he. The case was tried at the end of winter and it was still cold in New York. On the day scheduled for our summations, I wore a sweater under my jacket, and the sweater covered most if not all of my tie. The tie was one of my favorites, blue with the scales of justice in gold. For some reason, summations were adjourned to the following day. The jury had not seen my tie, but Peter apparently did. To be noted: had we summed up that day, I would have removed my sweater before I gave my closing argument for all to see my tie.

On the following day, I wore a different tie and was very surprised to notice that Peter was wearing an exact replica of the tie I had worn the day before, same color, same golden scales of justice. He summed up first and although he did not mention the scales of justice, there they were for all the jury to see. They could not miss them.

I then summed up and said to the jury: "Beware of these trial lawyers who want to seem so pure and just and truthful, and wear the scales of justice on their ties. Do they wear such a tie because they are pure, just and truthful? Or do they wear it to subtly, subliminally even, manipulate you into thinking that justice is on their side and their side only?"

Once again I say I am sorry for what I did to Peter, but he did outnumber me six experts to one, and he did copy me by wearing my tie. And the old adage does apply: "All's fair in love and war," and this was war, as were all of my other trials.

Part IV

Luck and the Law

In the 6½-month period from January to mid-July 1987, 23 malpractice cases were tried to verdict before me. In all but two, the jury found in favor of the defendants.

–Judge Ira Gammerman
NY County, Supreme Court
(tenure: 1981 to 2004)

Doctor, imagine you are watching a baseball game – the batter hits the ball – instead of running to first base, he runs to third base. That is a departure.

–Judge Ira Gammerman
Crabbe v. Flower Fifth Avenue Hospital
New York (1982)

I Mel Patrick Lynch make the following free and voluntary statement. About two years ago, I got the idea I would like to kidnap someone. About that time I saw the name of Edgar Bronfman in the newspaper.

–Mel Patrick Lynch, Defendant
State of New York v. Lynch and Byrne
FBI-HQ, New York (1975)

CHAPTER 25

THE CHRISTMAS PHOTOGRAPH

It may be hard to believe that in 1982 the first eight-figure verdict in New York history - $10,000,000 - came about because of a 10-cent photograph taken on a Christmas day. As in most every trial I was involved in, luck played an important part in the outcome - we were lucky to have a great judge - a great jury - a great expert witness. But without the photo I doubt that we would have won, let alone set a record.

On Christmas Eve, December 24, 1975, Betty Crabbe, an African-American woman in her thirties, had a severe headache. She went to the emergency room at Flower Fifth Avenue Hospital, which was near her home in Manhattan where she lived with her three daughters. She complained of a right-sided headache and a droop of her eyelid over the top half of her right eye. She was examined, told it was nothing more than a headache for which she should take some aspirin, and sent home.

She returned to the ER with the same complaint and the same result three more times during the following week, when finally on New Year's Eve she was admitted to the hospital. A diagnosis of right-sided subarachnoid hemorrhage was made upon admission. She was medicated to stabilize her, and surgery was performed two weeks after admission.

A few minutes following the surgery a major artery at the operative site spasmed and she was left severely and permanently brain damaged.

When Ms. Crabbe's daughters first came to our office in 1976, I was on trial in the Bronfman kidnapping case and they were interviewed by my partner Tom Meagher. At that time and at all times thereafter, Ms. Crabbe was unable to communicate either orally or in writing.

Following receipt of her medical records and our consultations with medical experts we were stymied: 1) there was no mention in the four ER records that a ptosis was present (i.e., a droop of the right eyelid); 2) the spasm, which caused the brain damage, was a well-recognized complication of the surgery she underwent, occurring approximately ten percent of the time; and 3) none of the medical doctors who reviewed the case for us believed that malpractice occurred.

However, we went ahead and filed a lawsuit against the hospital because we believed that Ms. Crabbe's complaint was a legitimate one. First, she must have had the life-threatening condition (and ptosis) when she went to the ER on Christmas Eve – but wasn't listened to – because a person does not go to a hospital at such a time unless she is in dire distress. Second, the weeks of delay in diagnosing her condition and operating on her must have increased the likelihood of complications during and after surgery.

We then did what we often had to do: we took depositions of all those involved to try to discover the truth. Ms. Crabbe could not help herself; the doctors could not help her; perhaps we, the lawyers, could.

Unfortunately, seven years passed, it was now 1982 and the case was scheduled for trial and we were still stymied. We had not uncovered anything helpful in all that time and most important of all, we still did not have a medical expert who would testify on behalf of Ms. Crabbe, which is required in medical malpractice lawsuits.

And now, luck came into play and it snowballed.

LUCK (1) – THE RESIDENT

In preparing the case for trial I decided to do what should always be done: I reviewed everything available again, starting over from the beginning. And the beginning was the hospital record.

When I reached the last part of the record, I re-read the operative report. It was written by the neurosurgeon who performed the operation. He was the chief of the neurosurgical department at Flower Fifth and he was listed in the discovery papers as one of the experts the defendant would have testify on its behalf at the trial.

For some reason, while re-reading the report I remembered my trip to the NYU operating room after the Ferdon case, and how odd it was to see and hear a resident sawing open the patient's chest when I had gone to see the great cardiothoracic surgeon Frank Spencer perform the surgery. I heard that Dr. Spencer had performed four such surgeries in a day and I wondered how that could be done. I found out. When Dr. Spencer first entered the OR, we had been watching the chief resident for about an hour. Dr. Spencer came in – took over at the operating table – cut into the heart – did what he had to do – and left after about ten minutes.

It struck me now when reading about Ms. Crabbe's surgery that perhaps the chief resident who assisted the chief of neurosurgery might be a person who could shed light on our case. His name was Joseph

Mormino and he was no longer associated with Flower Fifth. I went to see him at his Staten Island office: he was courteous, helpful, straightforward and most important of all, he was willing to testify on Ms. Crabbe's behalf that the defendant hospital committed malpractice and that its departures caused the brain damage. His words to me at the time of my visit and later on at the trial were:

> Of course it's malpractice.
>
> Of course she had the subarachnoid hemorrhage on Christmas Eve or before.
>
> Of course she had the ptosis or the beginning of it on Christmas Eve.
>
> Of course the week's delay until admission was significant and a cause of the brain damage.
>
> Of course because of that week's delay the surgery had to be put on hold until her vitals were stabilized.
>
> Of course during the delay from December 24th until the surgery three weeks later, the hemorrhage was intermittently bleeding causing the brain to get mushier and mushier, so that when the surgery was finally performed the brain was very difficult to work with and so the operation took 11 hours, instead of the usual five and a half to six hours.
>
> Of course because the surgery took an extra five to six hours the operative insult to the brain made it much more likely that the known post-operative complication of spasm would and did occur, dooming the patient.

LUCK (2) – THE CHRISTMAS PHOTO

After I met with Dr. Mormino, the ptosis issue puzzled me even more than it previously had. How could the daughters be so adamant that her eyelid was drooping, and obvious, on Christmas Eve – and Dr. Mormino confirm that they had to be right – and yet no mention was made of it in the hospital ER records?

I, therefore, had the young Crabbe women to my office again. While thoroughly discussing the events of that fateful Christmas week with them it finally dawned on me: that's it, Christmas week, her first visit to the ER was the day before Christmas, and what do people do that next day, on Christmas itself? They get together with family – they exchange presents – sometimes someone gets a camera as a gift and they take pictures with it – sometimes they keep the pictures even after seven years. Certainly, I thought, if photos were taken, Ms. Crabbe would be in them. Certainly if she was in them, they would show her face, including her eyes.

Sure enough Ms. Crabbe's daughters told me that they remembered that Christmas Day 1975 very well. They had a big family dinner at home, their grandparents and their father (who was separated from their mother) and other relatives were over, and they did take pictures. The girls went home and found the photographs. We had one snapshot blown up and later marked in evidence as an exhibit. It showed a smiling Betty Crabbe with a large afro, sitting on a sofa with the girls' father, who had his arm around her shoulders and was also smiling.

The most outstanding feature in the snapshot was the right eyelid, which was half-way closed over Betty Crabbe's right eye. I must confess, at this late date, that I feel bad that I did not think of the Christmas photos before that time, but I feel lucky that it was not too late and that it turned out all right.

LUCK (3) – THE JURY

I remember four things about our jury.

First, on the jury we had one of the most beautiful women I had ever seen. Initially, during the voir dire, I was not sure that she would be a juror I would be comfortable with on a malpractice case because her father was a dentist and she herself had been a nurse in Nepal for a year or two. But it made no difference what I thought. Our trial judge, Ira Gammerman, who sat in on the first of the six days it took us to pick the jury, apparently was also smitten with her beauty and he called the lawyers up to the bench and told us in no uncertain terms that when he came back to have the jury sworn in, she had better still be there because he wanted to have a beautiful face to look at during this lengthy trial. When Gammerman spoke, you listened.

Second, we had a very smart jury. One of those typical end-of-the-school-year Manhattan juries.

Third, one of the jurors – an alternate who at the end did not sit in on the six-member jury's deliberations – came to my office after the verdict to talk to me about an article she planned to write about the trial.

She too was quite beautiful, and she had been a starlet in Hollywood about 20 years before the trial. While we were talking she told me that she had read about an $11,000,000 verdict the year before in Florida and that it was the highest verdict ever awarded in the country. She said that during our trial she told the other jurors about it and told them that they should go for the record. (At the end of each trial day all jurors are instructed by the judge not to talk about the case with each other or anyone else, but it is well known that this commandment is often disregarded.) I have no idea whether her rooting interest in our case played any part in the final outcome, but perhaps.

Fourth, we had a young man who ended up as one of our six jurors, whom I had a difficult time deciding if I should keep or not because there were things about him and his background that I liked and did not like for our case. My strong preconceived ideas and notions about jurors should be clear by now – but what may not be clear is that in the same prospective juror there can be factors which could make him, or her, fit in *both* my very favorable and very unfavorable categories. The difficulty then is to evaluate which factors are more likely to predominate.

For example, my first wife Jo was once a prospective juror on a civil accident case back in the early 1960s when I was still a defense attorney at Reilly & Reilly. The plaintiff's lawyer, Moe Levine, a well-regarded attorney, questioned her and used a peremptory to strike her because he was sure that on account of her background, and particularly her being married to a personal injury defense lawyer, she would obviously side with the defendants and against him. He was so wrong.

By any standard, most of the telltale signs we look for in a juror on a medical malpractice or accident case would scream out "defense juror" for Jo. For example: she was raised in Idaho (a conservative state); her maiden name was Warner, which could mean either English or German ethnicity (conservative); she was the daughter of a doctor (pro-defendant); she was a college graduate (typically more difficult for a plaintiff's lawyer, with the burden of proof, to persuade); she was married to a former prosecutor now trying civil cases on behalf of defendants (pro-defense through and through).

However, at the same time, there were strong signs that Jo could be a "liberal" plaintiff-oriented juror – which in fact she was. First, she was an accomplished painter, and specifically an abstract expressionist back then in the '60s, with three works in the Museum of Modern Art; in other words, Jo did not confine her art or herself to strictures or boundaries (liberal). Second, she was a "women's libber," she used the title "Ms." from its inception, she signed her paintings with her maiden name, and she spoke for herself not caring which side of an issue her defense-lawyer husband was on (liberal). Third, she knew prejudice from childhood and was against it (again, liberal). (The town where she grew up, Idaho Falls, population 35,000, was three-quarters Mormon, and no Mormon was ever a patient of her father, solely because he was *not* a Mormon.)

Now, back to the juror who gave me so much concern. In my mind, the pros and the cons were as follows:

> THE CONS – There really was only one fact I was worried about in regard to him, but it was a very important one: he was a physicist and a college physics professor. I never took a course in physics; I never knew a physicist; but everything I knew, or thought I knew, about them was that they could or would be very dangerous for a plaintiff in a lawsuit. To prove anything to a physicist – who is trained never to assume a fact to be true – the proof would have to be 100%; it would have to be certain; it would have to be beyond a reasonable doubt (i.e., the standard necessary for a conviction in a criminal case, higher than the standard in a civil case). What's more, a physicist would be smarter than I am, and so I might have difficulty swaying him to think and vote as I would want him to do. Therefore, the last person I would want to have on my jury when I represented the plaintiff was a physicist.
>
> THE PROS – First of all, he was African-American and would be the only African-American on the jury, and given my belief that blood is thicker than water, how could I excuse the only Black person, someone who could identify with Ms. Crabbe and her daughters. Second, he taught at Medgar Evers College, which I had heard was a liberal institution. Third, because it took six days to select the jury I made it a point to observe him in the large jury hall in New York County where all jurors assembled before going their separate ways into individual jury rooms. I noticed that he often talked with a number of these other potential jurors, he seemed like a leader, he seemed friendly and, most important of all, the jurors he met with and spoke with were all Black or Latino.

Believing that he would identify with the Crabbe family, the pros outweighed the con and so I kept him.

Although I did not speak with the jurors after the verdict because they were discharged while Judge Gammerman was ruling on motions, I do know he was not against us because the verdict was unanimous. I am sure the defense did not challenge him during jury selection due to the fact that he was a physicist. I guess the defense did not believe the old Brooklyn adage "blood is thicker than water," or whatever it is that physicists study.

LUCK (4) – THE JUDGE

Judge Ira Gammerman was one of the smartest, most strong-willed and best judges I ever appeared before. This was a very difficult case and he kept it under control. We were lucky we had him.

An example of his manner: while I was cross-examining one of the six defense expert witnesses, I was having a difficult time making much headway in having him answer a question about the word "departure," and having him admit that something was a medical departure. The word "departure" was apparently an anathema to him and not in his dictionary. I was using a baseball analogy to make a point with this expert and he acted as though I was talking in a foreign language.

At that point Judge Gammerman said: "Mr. DeBlasio please let me interrupt. Doctor imagine you are watching a baseball game – the batter hits the ball – instead of running to first base, he runs to third base. That is a departure."

The jury and everyone in the courtroom, except the doctor, laughed. Judge Gammerman then addressed me: "Anything else Mr. DeBlasio?" I smiled, took his cue and said "No thank you, Your Honor," and sat down.

I never copied Judge Gammerman's third base example when questioning a witness because on reflection I thought it could backfire and be harmful to a plaintiff. The reason – the example is so extreme that it never happens, except maybe in a Little League baseball game, and the jury could get the wrong impression that a departure is only when a doctor does something that almost no other doctor would do or has ever done, and obviously that is not the law. I understood Judge Gammerman used that extreme example to make a point and make it he did, but it wasn't to be copied.

THE SUMMATION AND VERDICT

I no longer remember the summation, but others have remembered it for me. It was in mid-June, just after my daughters finished their school year and so they were able to come and watch. My older daughter was about to go off to college, and my younger daughter had just finished the tenth grade, and by this point in their lives they had already been to several of my summations. The Crabbe summation was one of their favorites – they say that they and many of the jurors were in tears. (I have always been appreciative that my girls liked to come watch me on trial. It was never anything I asked them to do, and it certainly was not any sort of an obligation. I was just very lucky as a father. I may not have had as much time to spend with them as I would have liked, but they always made time for me.)

My good friend Tom Moore was also present that day, as he reminded me during a recent phone call. He was on trial in the courthouse and had heard that I would be summing up on a big case, so he headed over as soon as he could and managed to catch the tail end. He told me that in the nearly 40 years that have passed, he has never forgotten hearing me tell the jury: "Make Mrs. Crabbe a queen, give her ten million dollars." He said he had no doubt then that the jurors would do exactly as I asked, and that he had just witnessed a record-setting verdict in the making.

Following the $10,000,000 verdict – the highest malpractice jury award in New York history and the second highest in the country up to that time – Judge Gammerman brought about a settlement between the parties. In 1982, the highest award in a personal injury case that was allowed to stand by the Appellate Division, First Department, whose jurisdiction was Manhattan and the Bronx, was $2,000,000. Judge Gammerman told me that he would try to have the defendant forego an appeal and pay $2,000,000. He told the defendant he would try to have me take less than $2,000,000. He, therefore, had us settle the case for $1,900,000, thus pleasing both sides.

Following the trial, Gammerman made a comment about me to one of his friends, later recounted to me: "One thing about DeBlasio – he never asks a question unless it's absolutely necessary." I am still impressed with those words. I cannot say he was right, but I do know that if I had ten points I wished to discuss with a witness and the witness gave an answer damaging to himself on the first one, I did not ask any more questions.

POSTSCRIPT: For Christmas that year, my office staff framed the case-winning photo of a smiling Betty Crabbe sitting next to her girls' father on Christmas Day 1975, her right eyelid half-way closed. "The Christmas Photograph" hung on my reception room wall until I retired in 2006. Ten million dollars for a ten-cent photo, what are the odds.

CHAPTER 26

"I Love Collecting Garbage"

The case of Larsen v. City of New York, which I tried in 1979 in Supreme Court, Staten Island, before Judge Ezra Greenspan, was an interesting case because the trial format for *accident cases* (as opposed to medical malpractice) had recently changed. They were now to be tried in two parts, first the liability phase and, if the jury found the defendant at fault, the trial would continue on to the second phase for the jury to determine the damages. If the plaintiff lost the first part of what was now to be known as a bifurcated or split trial, the whole case was over.

These new rules were strict - against the plaintiff. They favored defendants 100% and were sought by the defense bar. Under the new scheme, jurors were not to hear about or see evidence of the plaintiff's injuries before deciding who was at fault, because defense attorneys feared it might unduly influence their decision.

Naturally this change - this trial bifurcation - posed a serious problem and a challenge for plaintiff's attorneys. The *problem* was that if the facts of the accident made the case appear to be minor - nothing more than bumps and bruises - the jury could think the lawsuit was a waste of their time and simply dismiss it at the end of the liability phase, *not on the merits* but simply so they wouldn't have to sit through the second part of the trial.

The *challenge*, then, was how to let jurors know during the liability phase that a plaintiff's injuries were indeed serious, even if the accident seemed minor, and that the case deserved their full attention and honest consideration. Such was the problem and challenge for me in Larsen.

In 1975, Paul Larsen took a tumble when his motorcycle skidded over some gravel on a Staten Island road, but by the time of the 1979 trial he looked the picture of health - young, handsome and full of life. Thus, during the initial liability phase, the jurors could easily believe that he was unfairly imposing upon their time over some minor accident, and so not bother to consider if the defendant, the City, really was at fault for the tumble.

But nothing could have been farther from the truth than that Mr. Larsen was wasting their time. One of his legs had been severed just below the knee, and I believed that Mr. Larsen had a right for the jury to know that his was a serious case. Not because we wanted the jurors to decide his case based on sympathy, but because he deserved a fair trial, which meant their full attention when deciding his fate. Thus, the challenge of how to let them know about the missing leg.

THE FACTS

Back in 1975 when the accident occurred, Paul Larsen – one of many Staten Island residents of Norwegian ancestry – worked for the Department of Sanitation. He worked on a sanitation truck and was one of the men who walked alongside, grabbing and dumping the residents' garbage bins. On the day of the accident, having finished his shift at 5:00 p.m., he rode his motorcycle from the Staten Island Sanitation Depot onto Arthur Kill Road. He came to a curve in that road, with a posted 15 mph speed limit, and drove over some gravel that had fallen off trucks that were on their way to a highway construction site. Mr. Larsen's motorcycle skidded, its side struck against the curb, his leg got caught between that curb and the motorcycle's footrest, and he watched as his severed leg rolled down the street along with his bike.

At about 1:00 p.m. that afternoon, four hours before the accident, a man who lived at the location where the accident took place telephoned the Sanitation Department and reported the gravel spill on the road. He reported it because he was annoyed that these spills were a daily occurrence since work on the highway had begun. As of 5:00 p.m., the time of Mr. Larsen's accident, Sanitation had not sent workers to clear the road.

THE LAWSUIT

Our claim basically was: 1) there was a dangerous condition on the roadway (the gravel) that could imperil motorists; 2) the Sanitation Department had timely notice of the dangerous condition (four hours via telephone call); 3) the Sanitation Department had a duty to the public to timely remove that dangerous condition; 4) the Sanitation Department was negligent in failing to perform that duty; and 5) the plaintiff drove his motorcycle in a reasonably careful and prudent manner and was not contributorily negligent.

The City's defense basically was: a) it did not have timely notice of the gravel and thus was not negligent in failing to remove it; and b) the plaintiff was driving his motorcycle at an excessive rate of speed over and above the 15 mph speed limit, and thus was contributorily negligent.[2]

When I had Mr. Larsen in to prepare him for trial, I found him to be extremely likeable. I asked him all about his leg both before and after the accident; if the leg bothered him after the accident; and if so when, why, how often and what he did for it. He said, sure it bothered him, he would develop sores, bruises, inflammation at the stump. Weight gain and weight loss played a part in how the prosthesis fit on the stump, as well as changes in the weather, as well as pressure on the stump after a tiring day at work.

He told me to get relief he would have to soak his leg in warm water and put on ointments, and naturally to do this he would have to remove his prosthesis. He told me the prosthesis would have to remain off for several days, but that he was no longer embarrassed when people sometimes stared at him with his pants leg pinned up around his knee.

I then talked to him about jury trials and how the system had changed. I told him how now the jurors had to first consider if the defendant was at fault and to what degree, and how he would only have the chance to talk about his injury if we won that first part of the trial.

I also told him that timing and luck always play an important part in all of life's events, including in jury trials. "There is good luck and there is bad luck," I told him. It was certainly bad luck he lost his leg. And it was bad luck that his trial had to be split into two parts. It also might seem to be bad luck if, during the first part of the trial, his stump were hurting and he couldn't wear his prosthesis, but this I told him could turn out to be good luck. He said he understood.

As he left my office, I wished him "good luck."

---

[2] When we filed the case, New York was still a *contributory* negligence state. However, on September 1, 1975, New York abandoned this harsh regime and adopted a system of *comparative* negligence. Under this system, cases are no longer dismissed whenever a jury finds a plaintiff contributed to the negligence. Instead, the jury compares the parties' negligence and assigns a degree of fault to each (from 0% to 100%), and then the damages award is reduced by the percentage of the plaintiff's negligence. Thus, if a plaintiff is found 40% at fault in an accident and the jury awards $100,000 in damages, the award is reduced by 40% to $60,000. This new system was in place by the time of our 1979 trial.

When Mr. Larsen arrived in the courtroom for the initial liability phase of the trial, his stump had apparently been bothering him for his pant leg was rolled up to his knee. And, just as he had said, he showed no embarrassment as the jurors stared.

Even though I was not permitted at this stage to ask him about his injury, I had to show that he had not contributed to the accident, so that no (comparative) percentage of fault would be apportioned to him at all. Thus, one of my very first questions when he took the witness stand was:

> QUESTION: On the day of the accident when you drove your motorcycle did you have and use your two legs?
>
> ANSWER: Yes.

And with that we had met and overcome our challenge. There was no way now the jury was going to ignore this serious case. They gave Mr. Larsen his due – their full and rapt attention throughout both parts of the trial.

Mr. Larsen went on to testify to his actions when he came to the curve in the road: basically he slowed down to the proper speed, no other vehicles were in the vicinity, he didn't see the gravel in the road until it was a few feet in front of him because the curvature of the road had blocked his view, he tried to swerve to avoid the gravel but still rode over it, and he crashed.

After Mr. Larsen testified as to the accident, the Defendant City of New York produced an eyewitness who was working in a street that intersected with Arthur Kill Road a short distance before the curve. He testified that he heard the roar of a motorcycle, saw it speed into the curve at about 45 mph, and then heard the crash.

When it was my turn to cross-examine the City's eyewitness, I used simple math to put the lie to his testimony about Mr. Larsen's speed. He testified that the width of the street on which he was working, which was perpendicular to Arthur Kill Road, was 30 feet and that there was 10 feet of clearance on each side of the street. Thus, his view of the motorcycle as it passed by him along Arthur Kill Road was at best limited to the 50-foot total width of the road he was working on.

By simple mathematical formula, a vehicle travels one and one-half feet per second. A car going 30 mph travels about 45 feet in a second; a car going 60 mph travels about 90 feet in a second; a car going 45 mph travels about 67-68 feet a second. Had this eyewitness been forewarned a motorcycle was approaching and had he been watching for it, at most he would have had it in his sights for 50 feet and, at the 45 mph he claimed it was going, he would have seen it for less than a second.

But this eyewitness had not been forewarned and was not "on the look-out." It was impossible for his senses and brain to react to the motorcycle roar, look up, see the motorcycle, process what was happening, all in less than one second *and* accurately determine the motorcycle's speed.

On the liability phase of the trial, the jury easily found in favor of Mr. Larsen, and 100% against the City.

We then tried the damages phase of the case. Mr. Larsen told about his life after the accident, basically without frills or fanfare. The part that stands out in my memory and which most impressed the jury went as follows:

> Q – Did you ever go back to work when you only had one leg?
>
> A – Yes.
>
> Q – When?
>
> A – Six weeks after the accident.
>
> Q – Where?
>
> A – Sanitation.
>
> Q – Doing what?
>
> A – My same job.
>
> Q – Walking alongside the truck, picking up residents' trash cans, unloading the contents into the back of the truck?
>
> A – Yes.
>
> Q – Why? Why that backbreaking job?
>
> A – I love the job. I love collecting garbage.
>
> Q – Why?
>
> A – I'm out in the open air – I'm free.

The jury's award was $675,000. Not too much in my opinion. But it is well known that Staten Island jurors are quite conservative in their awards, especially so when the City of New York is a defendant because they are well aware that their taxes come into play.

POSTSCRIPT: After the trial, even though Paul Larsen now had a relatively substantial sum of money, he continued working at his Sanitation job, because there is nothing better than loving what you do, even when that's collecting garbage.

CHAPTER 27

An Invaluable EBT

I tried another bifurcated case several years after Larsen, also involving a traffic accident, but in this one there was no need to roll up a pant leg. My client, David Braun, was rolled into the courtroom in a wheelchair, a quadriplegic, totally unable to do a thing for himself. The case was Braun v. Shaki, and I tried the damages phase in 1990 before Judge Robert Stolarik and a Rockland County jury of six.

We had easily won the liability phase of the lawsuit on summary judgment in October 1989, the judge deciding in our favor without the need for a trial by jury. The undisputed facts were simple. On December 24, 1987, 39-year-old David Braun, a self-employed egg distribution middle-man, was driving his car with his seat belt buckled around his waist, when Defendant Shaki's car crossed into Mr. Braun's lane and struck his car, causing it to overturn. Mr. Braun, trapped in place by his seat belt, was hanging upside down with his neck broken and his aorta lacerated. His wife Ester, who was sitting in the back of the car per Hasidic custom, and was not wearing a seat belt, was uninjured.

The only issue to be tried now in late April and early May 1990 was the amount of damages to be awarded. In my summation, I asked the jury for $20,000,000. But before I tell what happened, I would like to explain how it came about that I could ask so much when the driver only had insurance coverage up to $100,000 and it was my rule never to take money out of a defendant's pocket. Which means we have to go back to the very beginning of the lawsuit, when it looked like we would never even be able to take the case to trial in the first place.

There is no such thing as a perfect case to me – but to be a good case you need at least four things:

1. Good liability
2. Significant injury
3. Sufficient insurance coverage
4. Good luck

We obviously had numbers 1 and 2, but even after intensive investigation, we were still missing number 3. All we had or knew was:

a) The police report listed Mr. Shaki as the owner and driver of the car.

b) The motor vehicle department listed the registration of the car in Mr. Shaki's name.

c) The defendant's Answer to our Complaint stated that Mr. Shaki was the sole owner of the car.

d) A representative of the company that issued Mr. Shaki his liability insurance policy, telephoned me and said that while he realized this was a tragic case, the limit of insurance on the car was $100,000, which he offered me then and there to settle the matter. I thanked him for the call and told him that I could not accept the offer.

In due course, as we always did in civil cases, we issued notice to the defendant that we would take his deposition at an examination before trial (EBT), which meant that we would ask him questions to try to discover facts about the case known to him but not to us. (His attorney similarly got to take the deposition of our client David Braun.) I decided that if we were going to be able to help Mr. Braun in any meaningful way, I would need good luck at the EBT, so that somehow or someway I might unearth evidence that there was more than $100,000 available.

The evidence I was hoping to find, for example, was that perhaps the defendant was using the car in the course of his employment, which would allow us to bring his employer into the lawsuit as an additional defendant. Or if there was a defect in the car caused by the manufacturer or a body repair shop, which caused the defendant to drive into the wrong lane, this would allow us to bring in the manufacturer or the repair shop. Or if there was a defect in the roadway that caused the defendant to lose control – or some other act or occurrence (like the gravel spilled on the road in Larsen) – this would allow us to bring in the municipality or other third party.

At the EBT I got very lucky, but only after a struggle.

Without going into all the details, I asked Mr. Shaki every question I could think of, but every one of his answers kept coming back to his owning the car by himself, without his employment or a car defect or the road's condition playing any part at all in the accident. So, I decided to go over the whole accident a second time with him, finishing up with ownership: where and how he obtained the car. He said he bought it at a Cadillac dealership, on a date I no longer remember.

I was out of questions, and I don't know what made me ask a final one that hardly seemed to matter anymore, but I went ahead and asked how he paid for the Cadillac. He started to answer my question when he suddenly interrupted himself: "Well," he said, "I didn't really buy it, I leased it."

Those words were music to my ears. I couldn't believe it. Once again what I had learned as a young boy came true: "Things are seldom what they seem – skim milk masquerades as cream." It was now a new ballgame and for the rest of his life, Mr. Braun would be provided for.

I may be naïve, but I don't think the defendant had been lying to me before that, when he kept repeating he owned the car. I can understand how some people can think they own a car when really they just lease it; and furthermore, it was only to his advantage, there was no downside, to admit that he leased it.

Under New York law at that time, both the lessor (in this instance, the leasing company GMAC) and lessee (Mr. Shaki) were deemed to be owners of the leased vehicle and thus both were liable for injuries that resulted from its negligent operation. We thus amended our Complaint to include GMAC as a defendant, and its $10,000,000 policy came into play.

We spent four days picking the jury, from April 23 to 26, 1990, during which time the judge tried to get the parties to settle. On about four separate occasions, Judge Stolarik had us meet with him in chambers. The meetings, all of which his law clerk attended, were not amicable. I was asking $9,000,000 and the lawyers for Defendants Shaki and GMAC were offering $4,000,000.

Judge Stolarik, whom I had never met before that time, turned out to be a dyed-in-the-wool defendant's judge and his bailiwick, Rockland County, was a defendant-oriented county. After I refused on several occasions to settle for the $4,000,000, the judge became furious with me and kept insisting I tell him how much I thought a Rockland County jury would award my Hasidic client. I repeatedly told him that I never dared to predict how a jury would decide a case I was about to try, and only after he *ordered* me to answer him did I say "twenty million."

Judge Stolarik said I was crazy and used other choice words about me and, as a final warning, he told me I'd better not flood his courtroom with "Hasidics." I told him that was the last thing I would do, I did not try my cases that way.

On May 7, 1990, I gave my summation. As soon as the jury left the courtroom to deliberate and the judge returned to chambers, Judge Stolarik's law clerk, a Major in the Army Reserves, walked over to me and said: "I heard your entire summation. Now I know what you meant when you told Judge Stolarik that you thought the jury verdict would be for twenty million. I want you to know, I agree with you and believe twenty million it will be."

The judge's law clerk proved prophetic because two days later, the jury rendered the highest verdict ever in Rockland County up to that time – $20,110,500.

Judge Stolarik reduced the verdict to $12,110,500. I believe that his law clerk – who liked my summation and liked me – must have talked him into that relatively high figure. But for the clerk – another bit of luck in this case – I think the judge would have reduced the verdict to the $4,000,000 the defendants had stuck to during our contentious settlement conferences.

After Judge Stolarik's reduction, the defendants finally agreed to pay $9,000,000. I refused to accept it. I demanded $10,000,000.

I gave the defendants my reasons as follows: the Appellate Division, Second Department, which had jurisdiction over Rockland County, had a short time before our trial permitted $9,000,000 as the highest award it had ever affirmed, and thus $9,000,000 was the new precedent for cases such as ours. I told them to assume that, in the next five years, GMAC lessees were going to be involved in 100 cases in which quadriplegia occurred and that those cases would be capped at $9,000,000.

But if I went ahead and appealed from Judge Stolarik's reduction and the Appellate Division decided to permit $10,000,000 of our $20,110,500 verdict to stand (which was not far-fetched), then $10,000,000 would be the new precedent. GMAC's insurance carrier would then be subject to lose an additional $1,000,000 in each of those 100 hypothetical cases, thus adding up to $100,000,000.

We could avoid that additional $100,000,000 future loss to GMAC, I explained, if now they would just pay $1,000,000 more than they wanted to. I would not appeal, the Appellate Division need not become involved, and $9,000,000 would remain the precedent.

They paid us the $10,000,000.

Good luck, and the value of the EBT, were never more impressed upon me than in this case.

POSTSCRIPT: One month after the trial, I saw David Braun at his daughter Chava's wedding. I attended it with my daughter Alessandra, although she and I enjoyed the reception on different floors per Hasidic custom. Afterward, David continued to stay in contact with me, making it a point to call several times each year to see how I was doing and to tell me of his own life. He never spoke of his condition, never complained, he just talked about his family and their accomplishments.

Under other circumstances, David would have made a very fine juror on one of my trials, no doubt stating in voir dire that his greatest achievement was his children, and his grandchildren.

Me and my client, Dominic Byrne, during the Bronfman trial.

Dominic, the limousine driver, and Mel Patrick Lynch, the NYC fireman. Two very lucky Irishmen. I am on the far right.

CHAPTER 28

THE LUCK O' THE IRISH

Shortly after midnight on August 9, 1975, Samuel Bronfman II, 21 years of age, telephoned his father Edgar – the billionaire CEO of Seagram Distilleries – at his 100-acre estate in Westchester County, New York. "Dad, I've just been kidnapped," he said, to which Edgar made a one-word reply: "Bullshit."

One and a half years later a Westchester County jury, which heard three months of testimony in one of the nation's most unusual celebrity kidnapping trials, in effect repeated Edgar's word back to him when it brought in a not guilty verdict for Dominic Byrne and Mel Patrick Lynch, the two men charged with the kidnapping.

Byrne and Lynch were the two luckiest criminals ever to go to trial. Their judge was a godsend, their jury was a gift from God, and the government could not have made more of a muck-up in preparing and trying their case. Witness after government witness was caught up in some blunder or gaffe so damning that by the end of trial, the jury had long since lost all confidence and even interest in what the prosecutor had to say.

For this inconceivable verdict to come about in the most slam-dunk, open-and-shut criminal case that one could possibly imagine, the stars had to align perfectly for Byrne and Lynch in every possible way and completely against the prosecution, such that there was a total eclipse of the sun by the moon. And perfectly align they did. By the time all was said and done, a greater trial farce was never had and a falser verdict never won.

Who were these lucky Irishmen, how did they become kidnappers, why did they choose Sam Bronfman (the unluckiest of millionaires), and what did they do during the nine days they held Sam captive? But more than anything, how and why did the jury vote as it did?

THE KIDNAPPING

On Friday, August 8, 1975 Sam Bronfman, height about 6'3", weight about 180 lbs., a recent graduate of Williams College where he played on the varsity tennis team and the junior varsity basketball team, had dinner with his father Edgar Bronfman at Edgar's recently acquired estate home in Yorktown Heights. Edgar, age 46, a billionaire, was the CEO of Seagram, then the world's largest liquor conglomerate, which was founded by his father from whom he inherited most of his wealth.

After dinner with his father, Sam drove to his mother's estate in Purchase, also in Westchester County. Sam was living alone there that summer and was about to start work at Sports Illustrated Magazine in the fall. He was the oldest of the five children of Edgar and his first wife Ann Loeb Bronfman, heiress to the Loeb fortune. Sam's parents had only just divorced in 1973, and now his father was about to marry for the third time, to a woman only four years older than Sam. This, shortly after he had his second marriage annulled.

When Sam exited from his car just after midnight on Saturday August 9, Mel Patrick Lynch, age 37, height about 6'0", weight about 190 lbs., an Irish-born New York City fireman, came running at him from the woods along one side of Sam's mother's house. Lynch, wearing a ski mask and gloves, with a revolver in hand, ordered Sam to get to the ground and told him not to look at his face or he would be shot.

Lynch handcuffed Sam's hands behind his back, held his gun at Sam's ribs and shoved and prodded him along, around the back of the house, past the pool and tennis courts, down a hill and over a dam on a lake, through the woods and into an overgrown field, all the way to the very edge of the 50-acre estate, which abutted the Hutchinson River Parkway. Lynch told Sam to sit down and close his eyes, he put a piece of wool on each eyelid, and wrapped an adhesive-tape blindfold around his head. Lynch then removed the ski mask he had been wearing, went over to the shoulder of the Parkway, gave the pre-arranged signal for Byrne to come collect him where he had dropped him off more than an hour earlier, and then he and Sam waited some ten minutes or so. When the car pulled up, there was Dominic Byrne, age 53, height about 5'2", weight about 125 lbs., sitting in the driver's seat. Lynch opened the front passenger door, got partway in, and pulled Sam in after him.

Lynch and Byrne had been friends for seven years. Like Lynch, Byrne was Irish-born, and like Lynch, he lived in Brooklyn. Unlike Lynch, however, Byrne did not know a kidnapping was about to happen and was in fact happening, and when he saw Lynch get into the front seat of the car with a gun in hand, and a man who was blindfolded, he let out a shriek that Sam later told the FBI agents he believed was made by a woman. (In those days, neighbors used the term "effeminate" to describe Dominic Byrne, in part because of his high-pitched voice, his high-heeled shoes and his general demeanor.)

To interrupt the narrative – a few words about Byrne's and Lynch's relationship. They were complete opposites. Lynch lived alone in an apartment; Byrne was married and the father of a 19-year-old girl and a 12-year-old boy who all lived together in a house they owned above a liquor store that they had once owned. Lynch was taciturn, dominant and forceful. Byrne was talkative, docile and feeble. At age 53, Byrne was still childlike, always smiling and giggling and chattering, and so everyone called him Dominic, just as one would call a child by his first name. Dominic was indiscriminately friendly and when walking about his neighborhood with his Irish wolfhound he would invariably greet everyone with a "Top 'o the Morning to Ye." He was extremely devout, he was a regular usher at Sunday mass, and he would do anything for anyone to make them like him. (When I was a boy, there was a well-known Irish actor who often played the part of an Irish priest in films. His name was Barry Fitzgerald. Dominic was the reincarnation of Barry Fitzgerald.) In a word, Dominic was the most unlikely person you would expect to commit a crime, let alone abduct someone and hold them against their will.

Dominic was a limousine operator and he and Lynch originally met when Lynch rented a limousine from him, to supplement his fireman's pay by chauffeuring people around. Soon thereafter, Lynch was a frequent visitor at Dominic's home, eventually endearing himself to Dominic's two children and his wife Liz. It reached a point finally where Dominic was almost a guest in his own home and Lynch the paterfamilias.

Lynch by all accounts had been a hard-working, well-respected fireman for 12 years at a firehouse in Brooklyn. He had one problem though – some called it the "Irish Curse" – he drank a lot. Rum and coke was his favorite.

When he drank, he had dreams of grandeur and those dreams included improving his lot and to do that he needed money – lots of money. And then one day in 1973 an idea came to him. At the firehouse, among all the magazines and tabloid newspapers and comic books and dime-store novels, he came upon a true-crime thriller written by a college co-ed (as they were called back then), Barbara Mackle, who survived being kidnapped and buried in a box in the Georgia woods for 83 hours. Lynch was, in a word, captivated.

At the same time that Lynch was reading about the abduction of this girl whose father was a wealthy Florida land developer – and about the kidnappers (a young man and his girlfriend) who almost made off with half a million dollars in ransom – he was also reading articles in the local tabloids about Edgar Bronfman's divorce from his first wife, with his immense wealth prominently featured. Lynch decided to look up Bronfman in WHO'S WHO IN AMERICA and not only found out the names of his children, but addresses for them in Purchase (Westchester) and on Manhattan's Park Avenue. And so Lynch in his private reveries, fueled by "the drink," hatched a plan to kidnap one of Edgar Bronfman's older children from the Purchase home and hold him or her for ransom.

Lynch foresaw a problem though. He couldn't just build the kind of box with an oxygen supply that the Mackle kidnapper had designed. He would need to keep the Bronfman child at his apartment and so he would need an accomplice to guard the child while he was at work and, eventually, when he was picking up the ransom money. Who better to play the babysitter than the child-like Dominic, who wasn't too bright and who would do whatever he was told?

So was born the saga of what was to monopolize the nation's news and TV media for nine days in August of 1975 – the Sam Bronfman kidnapping.

For almost two years leading up to the kidnapping, from the late summer of 1973, Lynch followed the same routine on at least 20 occasions: Lynch would be at Dominic's home talking and drinking with Liz and the children, usually in the evening, when he would abruptly tell Dominic: "Get my car. We're going for a ride." Dominic, without objection, would do so. Dominic would then drive for about an hour with Lynch seated in the back of his Cadillac limousine drinking. Dominic would let him out along the side of the Hutchinson River Parkway, go to a gas station to wait awhile, and then circle the area getting on and off the exits until he saw Lynch's signal at the drop-off and pick-up site. Lynch, in the meanwhile, would walk through the woods observing the Bronfman grounds (the estate in Purchase), particularly the house. After an hour or two of surveillance, he would return to the Parkway, signal Dominic, get into the car and tell him, "Let's go home." And as Dominic drove, Lynch would resume his drinking.

Dominic didn't fully understand what Lynch was doing on those many evening trips they took up to Purchase. He was such a naïf, a simpleton, that even though Lynch confided to him he was planning a kidnapping, as far as Dominic knew Lynch might have been going there to spend time with an Irish maid employed in a rich person's home. Dominic, after all, had his own secrets. As he confessed to the FBI after his arrest, he liked to "frequent" gay bars, particularly Clancy's and Uncle Charlie's in Manhattan, and he had "contacts" as well with gay men in Asbury Park and Atlantic City. (One bit of luck we had in this case was that I was able to keep this information out of the trial, in great part because it was considered a personal "detail.")

And so the saga continued until the fateful night of August 9, 1975.

After Lynch pulled Sam into the car's front seat (Sam sat by the passenger door), Dominic drove the car into the city and back to Brooklyn. When they got to the Belt Parkway, Lynch directed Dominic to pull the car to the side of the road where there was a bank of public pay telephones. He asked Sam where his father was at that moment and for the telephone number.

Dominic got out of the car as he was told, put coins in the phone, realized it was not enough for the long-distance call to Westchester and that he didn't have any more. So, he made the call collect. When a man's voice answered he handed the receiver, which was on a long cord, through the window and across the front seat to Sam, who then pleaded with his father's butler to go wake his dad. It took several minutes as the butler had to leave his rooms above the garage and walk over to the main house and then up to the second-floor bedroom. When finally Edgar got on the line and Sam, struggling to keep his voice under control, managed to tell him he was kidnapped, Edgar snapped back "bullshit."

A word or two about Edgar Bronfman. At the time of the 1976 trial, Edgar and I were the same age (47), the same height and weight (5'9" and 180 lbs.), and we both wore our black hair and sideburns somewhat long as was the style back then. Those were the only things that we had in common. We lived in different worlds. He, Canadian-born and raised, was the son of a billionaire father. My father worked three jobs. My father's pay as a postal clerk was rather high for those post-Depression days at $40 a week, $2,000 a year. Edgar's father, on the other hand, arrived in Canada from Russia already so wealthy that not only was he able to bring along his extended family but their family rabbi, and he was quickly able to build an international liquor empire.

To give an example of Edgar Bronfman's wealth, in 1940, Edgar's father set up a trust in the amount of $750 million for his four children, two boys, two girls, 30% to each boy, 20% to each girl. Edgar was the eldest of the siblings and his share in 1940, at the age of 11, was $225,000,000. In 1940, the United States had not yet entered World War II. In New York, a ride on the subway and the trolley cost 5 cents, an ice cream cone at Coney Island cost 5 cents, a movie cost 10 cents for children and 15 cents for an adult, a seat in the bleachers at a Yankees or Dodgers game was 50 cents, and the price of a pound of veal cutlets was $1.35.

By the time of the 1976 trial, Edgar owned two penthouses, one on each of Manhattan's two most exclusive avenues, Park and Fifth, and he also owned and lived part-time in his Yorktown Heights (Westchester) mansion. His company owned the landmark Seagram Building in New York, among many other properties worldwide. All of his homes were staffed by numerous servants, and he owned limousines and a helicopter and employed two chauffeurs and two pilots.

Edgar sat in court (in the audience section set apart for the families) almost every day during the three-month trial (from September 8 until December 10, 1976). He also testified for two days as a government witness. I watched him pretty closely during most of that time, basically to size him up - to observe his demeanor - to observe his interactions with the people around him, namely his first wife, his third wife, his public relations man, his Wall Street lawyers, his children and the FBI chiefs - and his reactions to the witnesses, the judge, the jury and the lawyers. One of my reasons for doing this was to get as clear a picture of the man as I could, and to know him as well as I was able, so that I would know how to treat and question him when he took the witness stand and, as importantly, to know how the jury would react to me and him at that time.

My impression of him was that he was not likeable, not pleasant, not simpatico, but dictatorial and commanding in every manner, shape and form. He was the perfect example of what a witness should not be - he was "numero uno."

After Sam's collect phone call, Edgar called the FBI and Dominic drove on to Lynch's apartment building. Dominic stopped a few car lengths from the front entrance and he and Lynch helped the blindfolded Sam out, put sunglasses and a hat on him, and draped a jacket over his shoulders to cover the handcuffs behind his back, in case anyone on the street were to see them. They then went into the building and to Lynch's apartment.

For the next nine days Sam stayed there, continuously blindfolded and with his hands tied loosely together by rope in front of him, either sitting on the living room couch or lying on the bed. He listened to the television and radio, ballgames and tennis matches mostly, and occasionally he heard news of his own kidnapping. When Lynch was there with him – when not at the firehouse or drinking with Dominic's wife – Dominic would stop by with food for them. When Dominic was there alone with Sam, he would feed him, help him to the bathroom, wash his face below the blindfold with a cloth, change the TV and radio stations for him, ask if he was too warm or too cold, get him blankets, prop his head up on pillows, tuck him in, tell him he loved him and kiss him goodnight.

After two failed ransom-delivery attempts worthy of their own story, on the eighth day of captivity Lynch finally met with Edgar in Queens in the early hours of Saturday August 16. Lynch drove back to Brooklyn with $2.3 million stuffed into two black garbage bags (the equivalent of 1 million Irish pounds), oblivious that he had managed to evade dozens of FBI agents who had been surveilling and tailing him.

As Dominic continued to babysit Sam, Lynch drove directly from the ransom pick-up to Dominic's apartment and sat awhile with his wife Liz. He (or they) came up with a plan where to hide the money – at the apartment of a friend of Dominic's who was then in the hospital. And he (or they) concocted a story to tell if they were caught. The story went like this: Lynch and Dominic would tell the police that while they were trying to pick up limousine fares at the Plaza Hotel in Manhattan, two men accosted them, forced them at gunpoint to drive to Westchester to abduct Sam, and then told them to guard Sam at one of their apartments.

Lynch then left Liz's place. He returned to his own apartment, told Dominic about the Plaza Hotel story, got the friend's apartment key from Dominic's keychain, and went to stash the money. When he returned, Dominic went home.

In the meanwhile, before losing sight of Lynch's vehicle altogether, the FBI had managed to have an agent in a position to read his license plate number. As Lynch slept, the agents traced the car's registration to him, and upon discovering that the vehicle had not been declared stolen, they began to stealthily take up positions in a two-block radius around Lynch's apartment building.

But they weren't too stealthy, because by late Saturday afternoon, Dominic noticed an unusual car with men lingering about near his home, which was a block and a half from Lynch's. By Saturday night, Dominic was frightened that these men might be gangsters who had discovered they had stashed a lot of money in his friend's nearby apartment, and after discussing the situation with his wife Liz, they decided to send their 19-year-old daughter to the police with a note.

Shortly after midnight, two skeptical detectives arrived at Dominic's. He pointed out the unusual car from his window and the detectives radioed for assistance. Two officers with guns drawn approached the vehicle and ordered the men in the car to show their hands. After some frantic gesticulating, the two undercover FBI agents managed to get out their credentials. All four men then went upstairs to confront Dominic. And Dominic confessed that he and Lynch had been caring for Sam on account of two men at the Plaza Hotel who forced them to kidnap him.

Calls were made to FBI headquarters; Dominic was brought in for questioning; he convinced the agents in charge that he really did know where Sam was even though they told him they didn't believe his Plaza Hotel story. A contingent of FBI men escorted Dominic back home, where they directed him to call Lynch to say he was coming by right then, at 3:30 in the morning. Some among the FBI thought this was nuts, warning Lynch; others thought it was the only way to avoid a shoot-out as they went in to rescue Sam.

They left Dominic's, the agents and police officers on foot, while the chief of the FBI's New York Regional Division with other top officials drove the one-and-a-half blocks in a government limousine together with Dominic. In the alcove by Lynch's first-floor apartment door, about 30 agents and police officers crowded together, some spilling back into the lobby. Then, just as in the Marx Brothers movie A NIGHT AT THE OPERA, when Dominic opened the door with his key, they all tumbled in headlong. Lynch was restrained – Sam was unbound – two guns were seized – fingerprints were lifted – and Dominic was transported in an FBI vehicle smiling and chattering wee-wee-wee all the way back to headquarters sure that he would be hailed a hero.

Two hours into their separate 14-hour confessions, Lynch asked to meet with Dominic. In the presence of two agents, Lynch told Dominic to abandon the Plaza Hotel story and tell the truth. Dominic began to cry, wondering out loud what would happen to his children. Lynch told him not to worry, reminding him that it was just the two of them who were responsible; in other words, his wife Liz would be free to care for the children. Each returned to his own interrogation room with his own set of agents and proceeded to confess to their crimes.

A CHANGE OF VENUE

The first great piece of luck we had was getting the trial *out of* federal court. Lucky because defense lawyers have far more control over their cases in state court – they're allowed to actively participate in the jury voir dire for one thing – and because state prosecutors' offices don't have nearly the breadth of talent and experience that the federal U.S. Attorney's Offices are known for. And our *keeping* it out of federal court came about in a rather incredible way.

This had been a federal case from the get-go, from the first moment that Edgar refused to deal with the Yorktown Heights and Purchase police, insisting instead on the Federal Bureau of Investigation. Kidnappings and extortion were the FBI's bailiwick. Extortion, by use of the federal mail and/or federal communications lines, was inherently an interstate crime; and kidnapping, when the victim was transported across state lines, was as well.

When Dominic went to the NYPD, the feds immediately took over. And during the 14 hours that Lynch and Dominic were confessing to the FBI (not the NYPD), federal prosecutors were literally alongside, drafting the criminal Complaint to present the following morning, Monday, August 18, 1975 in federal court in Manhattan.

So how did the federal government's firm grip on the case get derailed? It came about as follows.

On the Sunday of the arrests, I called the FBI office at 2:10 p.m. to try to speak with Dominic and to advise the prosecutors to stop all questioning now that he had a lawyer. But I got the run-around for half an hour – by one of the directors of the FBI no less – before I was able to speak with the Assistant U.S. Attorneys handling the case, Gerald Alan Feffer and his partner Laurence Barry Pedowitz. "No," they informed me, I couldn't speak with Dominic then, but they would arrange for me to have a few moments with him the next day, Monday, before court. I should meet them in the morning at their office. (If I weren't on vacation in New Hampshire with my family, a seven-hour drive away, I would have gone straight to the FBI office on Sunday and demanded access.)

At 8:00 Monday morning I was making more calls, and at 9:00 a.m. I was at the U.S. Attorney's Office, where I again got the run-around. Dominic, they said, was still over at the jail – it turns out that he wasn't, he was in a next-door room – but they handed me his confession to read before court and said they'd like to talk with me for a few moments once I was done. As I was reading, seven federal prosecutors assembled themselves in a nearby room: the lead case attorneys Feffer and Pedowitz, two other Assistants from the Manhattan office, and three Department of Justice attorneys who'd come up from Washington DC, among them a young Rudy Giuliani (the future U.S. Attorney in Manhattan and later

Mayor of New York). When I'd had time to finish reading, they came to get me, and then tried to ambush me.

They told me that the criminal Complaint they were going to present in federal court that day only included an extortion charge, not kidnapping. This was so because Dominic had so far insisted that the entire affair occurred only in New York State. They needed to add the kidnapping charge to the federal indictment if they were to be able to keep the case in federal court – which they wanted more than anything – but they could only do so if Dominic admitted that while circling from exit to exit on the Hutchinson River Parkway as he waited for Lynch, he sometimes went an extra exit north, crossing back and forth over the Connecticut line. Or better yet, they wondered aloud, perhaps in the heat of the moment, once he had Lynch and Sam in the car heading south, Dominic became confused and drove the wrong way.

"You were an Assistant U.S. Attorney," they praised me, "you understand how much better and more efficient the trial would be in federal court, and" – they tried to reason with me – "with Mr. Byrne's conviction a foregone conclusion you have to think about the sentencing consequences. In state court, he will get a mandatory life sentence, and spend it in a state-run prison, whereas in federal court it isn't automatic that he'll get life, and whatever sentence he does get, he'll spend at a federal facility, which is easier time." All faces looked expectantly, if haughtily, toward me.

I thanked the men for their concern and advice, but told them that subornation of perjury was not a part of our modus operandi when I was an Assistant U.S. Attorney 20 years earlier, and it would never be, no matter what the consequences.

More disgusted than disappointed, they reluctantly allowed me to finally see Dominic, but only because they knew the judge would ask Dominic in open court if he'd had the opportunity to speak with me about the charge. If Dominic were to say no and the judge reprimanded the government, they'd have hell to pay, because Feffer and Pedowitz's boss was going to be the one handling the hearing on account of the expected media frenzy and a courtroom ripe with reporters.

After I met with Dominic for just a few minutes, we appeared in front of U.S. Magistrate Judge Martin D. Jacobs. He set a bail hearing for ten days out, but to the very great chagrin of Assistants Feffer and Pedowitz and, I imagine, Rudy Giuliani as well – whose days in the spotlight would have to wait two more decades – we never did make it to that hearing. While the federal prosecutors were plotting to have me and Dominic commit perjury, the Westchester County District Attorney Carl A. Vergari and the Kings County (Brooklyn) District Attorney Eugene Gold were scheming to steal the case out from under the feds – and no doubt fighting between themselves as to who would ultimately get the case, Westchester, the site of the abduction, or Brooklyn, the site of the captivity.

Immediately after our Monday arraignment in federal court on the extortion charge, D.A. Vergari announced that his office would be seeking an indictment for extortion *and* kidnapping. The reason he gave to the public for the change of venue? The federal extortion charge had a maximum penalty of 20 years' imprisonment, but the New York State kidnapping charge's maximum was life.

Even though we wouldn't be on my home turf in Brooklyn – no doubt the State powers-that-be decided Brooklyn had to be avoided at all costs because its jurors were considered more "liberal" than those in Westchester and they couldn't risk a hung jury on the Bronfman trial – at least we wouldn't be in federal court and so we'd have a fighting chance.

I never could have imagined in my wildest dreams what a godsend our Westchester judge and jury would prove to be for me and Dominic. The luck o' the Irish.

LOSING THE TRIAL

How could a Westchester prosecutor have lost this case?

In all of my trials, I was never known to become friendly with the other lawyer or lawyers on the case, although I always tried to be polite. We were both out to achieve one result – to win – to defeat the other fellow. And it is difficult being buddies and two-faced as you try to destroy someone. So I never got to really know the prosecutor, the Westchester Assistant District Attorney Geoffrey Orlando, except to say good morning and good afternoon.

What I had heard was that he was very personable and supposed to be the leading trial lawyer in his office. But he tried this case by the book, like he might have been taught in law school, or instructed to do by a more senior but uninspired prosecutor when he was still a junior Assistant. Or maybe it was Edgar Bronfman's personal lawyers from the Wall Street firm Simpson Thacher, who were present daily at the trial, who directed him to try it as he did. As the reporter M.A. Farber wrote in THE NEW YORK TIMES on November 15, 1976, more than halfway through the trial:

> The 32-year-old prosecutor, a tall, erect man who speaks in a monotone without a trace of emotion, has actually said very little in court. He just calls the prosecution witnesses – usually FBI agents – and asks them to "tell us what happened." He rarely interrupts and almost never asks questions following cross-examination.
>
> "Let it all hang out – even the contradictions," has been his policy and the policy of his superiors in this case.

Whatever the reason, Orlando's two biggest errors, which lost him the jury and cost him the trial, were: 1) the order he put on his witnesses and evidence; and 2) his playing for the jury a cassette tape, which Lynch had Sam record after the first two ransom-drop attempts had failed, a tape that was laced with foul language.

The first, and more egregious, of the two errors was that Orlando approached his case like an automaton, calling to the stand 53 witnesses, chronologically: first, the Yorktown Police detective who on day one of the kidnapping interviewed Edgar's butler; second, the postman who on day two of the kidnapping delivered a letter to Edgar's Park Avenue apartment; third, the Park Avenue doorman who paid the 10 cents overdue postage; fourth, the elevator operator who brought the letter upstairs to the penthouse apartment Edgar had vacated a year before; fifth, the building's residential manager who on day three called the Seagram offices to say there was a letter that might be of some importance; sixth, the FBI agent who went to the building to pick up the letter; seventh, an FBI agent who put a notice in THE NEW YORK TIMES advising the kidnappers that the letter was received; eighth, a different FBI agent who put the same notice in the DAILY NEWS; ninth, yet another FBI agent who put the same notice in the NEW YORK POST; tenth, the agent who oversaw the ransom preparations; and so on. If it's mind-numbing to read, you still can't imagine how boring it was to listen to in court. It was the worst beginning to a trial I had ever been a part of – but what great luck for Lynch and Dominic.

By the time we finally got to the FBI agents who played a significant role in the investigation, they proved ill-prepared and I was able to pick them off, one, two, three. After the first of these agents testified, the jury was dazed and dumbstruck. By the second, the jury was disbelieving and dismayed. By the third, the jury was doubled over in laughter, as was some of the court staff. The agents' ineptitude was, as my 12-year-old grandson might say, "legendary."

Had Orlando done nothing more than introduce *on the very first day of trial* Sam's putrid blindfold for the jury to touch, see and smell, the verdict would have been his without having to put on a single witness. The jurors would have been as horrified and disgusted as I was the first time I saw it, just before our opening statements.

The blindfold smelled to high heaven and told the whole, true story of the kidnapping. One look at it, with ripped-off pieces of Sam's flesh and his facial hair growing into the adhesive tape, and the jury would have known beyond all doubt that the kidnapping was no hoax as Lynch's lawyer declared it was during his opening statement. What hoax? Nobody faking their own kidnapping would wear a blindfold, and it was clear from this putrid mess that Sam had indeed been wearing it for nine stench-filled days. (Lynch's lawyer told the jury in his opening remarks that Sam was the mastermind of this fake abduction but real extortion scheme, and had forced Mel Lynch, his supposed homosexual lover, to go along with it or he would ruin his career by revealing to the Fire Department that he was homosexual.)

Then, for good measure, Orlando should have immediately had the jury listen to Lynch's confession, the true contemporaneous story of the kidnapping, and not the gay-lovers fairytale Lynch invented over the course of a year as he waited for trial. Read the confession on day two and the trial would have been over. We defense attorneys never could have gained the jury's attention, let alone its trust, after that.

But Orlando, oblivious to the quality of the evidence in his arsenal, did not bring out the blindfold until his 34th witness took the stand (and he did not read the confession aloud until his 38th witness). By then, the jurors had laughed too hard at too many of the government witnesses' gaffes to bother about looking at, let alone smelling, some ratty old blindfold.

The second egregious mistake Orlando made was playing audio tapes for the jury. The tape in which Sam asked his father to pay the ransom and secure his release was, for me, perhaps the greatest gift the prosecution gave us. In my mind, after Orlando offered it into evidence and it was played and heard on a loudspeaker in open court, there was surely no way that a certain strong segment of the jury would ever vote against us.

My two favorite jurors in this regard were two middle-aged Irish mothers who sat side by side in the jury box. I had never been in the presence of nuns while I was growing up, but these two women both looked just like the stern-faced no-nonsense ones I had seen in movies, and I don't mean Ingrid Bergman, my favorite actress. In their background, those Irish women had to have family members and close friends who reminded them of Lynch and Dominic, and there was no way they knew or socialized with anyone in the wealthy Bronfman circle.

It was a no-brainer that these two would be turned off during the trial when they heard of the exploits of a man who divorced his wife after 25 years of marriage, after she had brought five children into the world for him, and then took two more wives. But the coup de grâce of the disgust they would feel toward the Bronfmans, père and fils – as well as toward the prosecutor himself – was, I knew, going to be when they heard the audiotape of Sam to his father.

The playing of that tape for me was, and I knew it would be for them as well, a bombshell. When I first heard it played in chambers with the judge and the lawyers I was taken aback; even though I had been brought up playing in the streets of Brooklyn and had served my time in the Navy, I had never heard such filthy language in my entire life, let alone when addressed to one's father.

All during my childhood I never heard any of the four of us in my family curse or use any of those bad words you heard in the streets. My family went every other Sunday and most holidays to my grandmother's house (a railroad-flat apartment with the toilet in the common hallway) for dinner. There was never any cursing there by any of my aunts, uncles or cousins. In fact, I do not remember any cursing in any house I went into when I was a boy, and certainly not directed at a mother or father. I felt sure that the same prohibition against cursing prevailed in the homes of these two Irish jurors, my two "nuns," from the time they were children and through the present.

How did it come about then that the audiotape was played and the two jurors were left shell-shocked for the remainder of the trial? At the end of each trial day it was Judge Beisheim's custom to have the lawyers announce in open court, with the jurors present, who the next day's witnesses would be. One reason was so that the jurors could request that seats be reserved for any family members they would want to have attend.

When Orlando said that he intended the next day to call an FBI agent who would identify the tape so that it could be marked into evidence for all to hear, one of the two Irish women jurors said she would like to have a seat reserved for her 12-year-old son, even though he would have to miss a day at his parochial school to come to court.

I knew then and there that the juror who was going to have her sweet, innocent son in court to listen to the tape was going to rue her decision so much that she would probably go to church that night to plead for forgiveness. When the tape was aired my eyes were fixed on her.

As soon as the first "F" word was uttered, she turned to look at her son, not taking her eyes away from him until the tape was over. During the 10 or 15 minutes of playing time, she appeared to me to be a victim who was undergoing an exorcism. Her friend, the Irish woman juror seated next to her, seemed to be in a similar state of shock, biting her lip and near tears. I was surprised that the first one did not get up from her seat, step down from the jury box, walk over to her son and escort him out of the courtroom, followed closely behind by the second one.

The tape went as follows:

> Dad you've got to get off your 'f---ing' ass and get me the 'f---' out of here. This is no 'f---ing' bullshit. It's 'f---ing' real.
>
> Don't be your usual 'f---ing' selfish self and think of me for 'f---ing' once.
>
> You've already 'f---ed' up the ransom two times. I don't know how 'f---ing' long I and they can hold on.

And so it continued, on and on. Sam must have used the "F" word in anger 30 times.

From that point forward, neither of the two Irish women ever again looked at Sam or Edgar Bronfman, even when they were on the witness stand. They could no longer be fair and impartial; their upbringing had come into play, as it always does in times like these, and they became biased and prejudiced against all that the prosecution tried to prove thereafter.

Why Orlando had the jury listen to that tape is beyond me. It served no purpose for the prosecution in proving its case. My best guess is that he was so programmed in the way he planned his trial that he just introduced something in evidence because it happened to occur during those nine days in August 1975. Or maybe it was his superiors, or Edgar's Wall Street lawyers, who simply insisted.

If I were to add a third major error in the prosecution's trying of this case, it would have to be Orlando's mistake in putting Sam's father Edgar on the witness stand. He was the last government witness to testify and if by then not every single juror had already been turned off, they were by the time he stepped down.

Most of the time while Edgar was on the stand, half of the jurors would not and did not look at him. (To be noted, a juror is required to look at a witness because one of the ways jurors are to fulfill their fact-finding duty of determining credibility is by observing the witness's demeanor, by which I mean his appearance and manner of speaking.) Orlando did not request that the judge direct the jurors to look at Edgar, and Judge Beisheim did not take it on his own to so direct them. I remember wishing that the jury would look at Edgar, but that wish was counterbalanced because it was obvious the jury turned away because they disliked him, if not really hated him.

Nor did Edgar look at them. On the witness stand he looked straight ahead, never to his left where the jury was seated. He never made eye contact with any of the jurors. Every lawyer worth his or her salt always instructs witnesses that when answering a question, they should turn to and look at the jury, and in as sincere a manner as possible. Of course, there is an art to this. It often takes a good deal of time and preparation with a witness to accomplish it, but it also takes a witness who is willing to learn and follow directions. I, therefore, do not fault Orlando because it was obvious that Edgar would not welcome advice and would not follow orders. The CEO of Seagram was not one whom you direct or order what to do and how to act. He gives the orders because that is what a "numero uno" does.

Apart from his demeanor, why would and did the jurors hate this "victim," which surely Edgar had to be as the father of an abducted child? The answer was simple. His way of life – his humanity or lack of it – was at the opposite end of the poles from theirs.

First, there was the disclosure that Edgar divorced the mother of his five children after 25 years of marriage. If that was not bad enough in and of itself, he divorced her so that he could gain a title by marrying into British royalty, marrying a "Lady" who was the daughter of a "Marquess." To add to that disgust, he sued to have this second marriage annulled within days of the wedding on the fiction that the marriage was not consummated. (To be noted, there was no claim of lack of consummation *before* the wedding.) His then marrying a third wife, half his age and only just shortly after the annulment was granted, was too much even for the most liberal and progressive members of the jury.

Second, there was his admission that the first and only word he said to his son Sam – upon hearing that he had been kidnapped – was

"Bullshit." I am sure that no loving parent I knew, nor any parent on the jury, would ever have said such a thing. I'm sure the jurors would have expected something more along the lines of: "Oh my God, please help us, please let this be a bad dream I'm having, a nightmare. Don't be afraid my child, I'll do everything to get you home, safe and sound, as soon as possible, no matter what it costs. I'll move heaven and earth, please have faith in me and trust me. I love you." That is what a decent human being of a father would have said. (Too bad Edgar's public relations man, who was in court with him every day, was not available during that phone call to feed the right words to him.) Instead, Edgar's saying "Bullshit" meant: "You're a liar – an idiot – a nut – getting me out of bed with this nonsense – you ought to be ashamed of yourself." The jury probably felt, as I did, like saying: "No, Edgar, you're the one who ought to be ashamed."

Third, there was the proliferation of filthy language on the part of Sam. To me, it was inconceivable for someone to use such language, especially a son to a father. What kind of upbringing was this? What kind of household was it to permit and tolerate such conduct? I have always believed you learn to speak and act like Sam and Edgar did in one of two ways: either at home or in the streets. The "streets" have to be eliminated from the equation because the trial testimony was that Edgar and Sam both grew up in gated estates and did not play in the streets. Ergo, Sam had to have heard that language at home, from his father. Thus, it is often true that "you reap what you sow."

Orlando never should have let Edgar testify, as I did not have Dominic Byrne testify, even though in my opening statement to the jury three months earlier I had left the door open. Sitting with Dominic throughout the trial as he smiled and waved at each FBI agent who approached the witness stand, telling me they were his friends, convinced me that he was a little strange, somewhat weird, and grossly out of touch with reality. I am sure that had Dominic testified, he would have been in all his glory, and he would have willingly and happily said anything Orlando wanted him to say, true or not, for one reason and one reason alone, he would have wanted Orlando to like him. So I say, one does not necessarily have a person testify just because he was a witness to some event, no matter how necessary it may seem. If he is going to turn off the jury, or lose the case for you, you should not have him testify.

Edgar's testimony served no purpose for the prosecution in proving its case. The government did not need him to testify to the phone call (they had other witnesses), the money (they had agents and photos), the three trips to deliver the ransom (they had the FBI agents from the surveillance), or the audiotape (they had Sam). Instead of adding anything to the prosecution's case, putting Edgar on the stand allowed me to bring out on summation everything that turned off the jury: his wives, his wealth (homes, estates, limousines, helicopters, chauffeurs, pilots, etc.), his greed (marrying for an English title), and his foul mouth.

This case couldn't be won by us on the facts, and it was never about the truth. What I needed for my summation was a villain even more contemptible than a kidnapper. And in Edgar, the jury and I found our man.

****

For those who are interested, I include here Lynch's confession, the one he made to the FBI immediately upon his capture, before he had the chance to fabricate the most magnificent tale of lies ever told at a trial. The confession was hand-written by one of the agents, and read over by Lynch, who dictated minor corrections to the text, and initialed them when made. I do not include the crossed-out words, but simply Lynch's corrections. The confession exists to this day, in the archives of the Westchester County Courthouse, in both handwritten form and as transcribed during the trial when the prosecutor read the confession aloud for the jury. (As for Lynch's trial testimony recanting this confession, I save that fairytale for another book.)

New York, NY
August 17, 1975

> I Mel Patrick Lynch make the following free and voluntary statement to Special Agent J. Kevin O'Brien and Special Agent Richard F. McCarthy of the Federal Bureau of Investigation. I have been advised that I have a right to remain silent, that anything I say can be used against me in court, that I have a right to talk to a lawyer before any questions are asked to me and to have a lawyer present during questioning, that if I cannot afford a lawyer one shall be appointed for me before questioning by a court and that if I decide to answer any questions or make any statement now without a lawyer present I have the right to stop answering questions or making a statement at any time. I

understand these rights and I freely and voluntarily waive them. No threats or promises have been made to me.

About two years ago, I got the idea I would like to kidnap someone. About that time I saw the name of Edgar Bronfman in the newspaper. From then on I considered that kidnapping someone would be an easy way to get some money. I assumed that Bronfman would have some family, and thought of kidnapping one of his family members, assuming that he would have children.

To obtain knowledge of him I went to the library and looked him up in "Who's Who in America." I recall Mr. Bronfman children's names were in the book but I do not recall it gave their age. It gave his address as 60 Lincoln Ave, Port Chester, New York.

Sometime later I went to the address, looked at it. I did this several times but just looked at the entrance of the home. I place this period of time as sometime in the summer of 1973, as an article concerning Mr. Bronfman and the Seagram Co. appeared in The New York Times.

About this time I spoke to Dominic Byrne about my proposed plan. I don't recall where this discussion took place, but it was either in his car or mine. I do not think he was interested in the beginning. At this time Dominic Byrne had been a friend of mine for about seven years. During this time I would bring up the subject of the proposed kidnapping on some occasions when I would see him. After a period of time when at times we would discuss this subject I convinced him that it could be done easily and no one would get hurt. At this time he agreed to assist in this plan.

Sometime later I had Dominic drive me up to the house and drop me off near the house so I could observe at a closer range. I think we probably drove up in my car. This first trip was at night and was probably in September 1973. I remember that the house was not fenced in and I observed that there was a way to get in and out of the grounds easily. From this time until the end of 1973 Dominic and I made three or four trips for the same purpose usually from eight to nine o'clock at night at which time I would spend about one hour observing the activities of the Bronfman home. During these trips I recall that there was [a] little activity at the Bronfman house and I did not get too close so that I would not be seen.

Just prior to this time I had been out for a ride by myself, and found two guns. I think that it was the finding of these guns that gave me the idea to kidnap someone.

I found these guns one an automatic and one a small revolver with ammunition in a Chase Manhattan bank bag made of cloth in a wooded area adjacent to a parking stop on the Palisade's Parkway.

I wish to state that the trips I made with Dominic were probably all made before the end of September 1973. I recall this because on the last trip in September the house was closed. I think because of the fact the house appeared vacant that I decided that I would put off the kidnapping till the following summer.

I do not think that we made any further trips to the Bronfman home until the early summer of 1974. In early summer we, Dominic and I started our observation trips to the Bronfman home on weekend evenings, after dark. We made about eight or ten of these trips, Dominic and I during the summer of 1974. On these trips I got closer to the Bronfman house but I did not get to know who any members of the family were.

Sometime after the idea of the kidnapping became a reality with me and after seeing the article in The New York Times concerning Mr. Bronfman, I saw another article in the Daily News about Mr. Bronfman and his divorce proceedings, this article only served to keep my plan in mind. I do not think I ever discussed this article with Dominic Byrne.

About the end of June or the beginning of July 1975 Dominic Byrne and I started to take observation trips to the Bronfman home. I would like to state that I had no other source of information concerning the Bronfman family and as far as I know Dominic Byrne had no source of information about the Bronfman family other than our observations.

My plan concerning the kidnapping of any member of the family, was that I would kidnap one of the children in the vicinity of the house who was alone. I did not ever intend to go near the house. I did on one occasion see Samuel Bronfman in the company of another individual but I never did plan to kidnap two persons. In the summer of 1975 Dominic Byrne and I made about half a dozen trips to the Bronfman home altogether. On each occasion I had the necessary equipment in my possession to effect the kidnapping and might have, if the opportunity presented itself, done it sooner.

On the evening of August 9, 1975 Dominic Byrne and I went to the vicinity of the Bronfman home at about 10 PM. We drove to the Bronfman home in my 1973 black Cadillac. Dominic dropped me off on the Hutchinson River Parkway and [I] proceeded in the general vicinity of the house approaching from the east the Bronfman residence to an area wooded about 200 yards from the Bronfman home. I observed the house, to see if anyone was moving about, and didn't see anyone. I then went closer, at about 11:30 PM I saw a car drive in. This car a B.M.W. I think black in color drove into the garage. I saw the person who had been driving this car get out but I did not know for sure it was Samuel Bronfman. When he got out of his car, which was in the garage, I ran toward the garage as he was coming out of the garage. I said, I think, "This is a stick-up." I had the automatic weapon in my hand. I had the mask on, and gloves. I told him to lie down, and I put handcuffs on him behind his back. These handcuffs I had obtained from a mail order house in the south. I told Sam to get up and we walked out toward the road through the woods. Just before we, Sam and I got to the highway I told him to lie down at which time I put a blindfold on him. I made the blindfold by putting wool on his eyes and adhesive tape over it. Dominic Byrne came in a few minutes. I signaled him with a flashlight. I put him in the front seat. Sam was next to the door. I put him on the outside to prevent him from interfering with the driver.

Dominic then drove south on the Hutchinson River Parkway to the Whitestone bridge. Then the Van Wyck Expressway to the Belt Parkway west and someplace near Canarsie we left the highway to make a telephone call. At this phone booth Dominic dialed the number of Bronfman's home. I do not remember if I told him what to say but I told him he would have to speak to his father. I do not think we ever told him he was kidnapped. He knew himself. We then drove to my apartment at 601 E. 19th Brooklyn. I brought Sam into this residence through the basement. I think it was 2:30 or 3:00 in the morning by the time we arrived at my apartment 1C, 601 E. 19th St. Brooklyn.

When we arrived at the apartment I put a set of handcuffs on each hand. I also put a piece of chain between each set of cuffs behind his back. This way he had enough room to move his hands, feel his face, or anything he wanted to do. I am sure the handcuffs were in front of him rather than behind him.

On the same morning Dominic Byrne and I kidnapped Samuel Bronfman Dominic Byrne mailed a Special Delivery letter to Samuel Bronfman father Edgar Bronfman to 740 Park Ave. This letter was prepared in June 1975 by me at my apartment on my Remington electric portable. This typewriter is blue and white or blue and yellow. I would like to state that in this letter I used some of the phraseology I had obtained from a book on the Mackle kidnapping. I do not remember where Dominic Byrne mailed the letter. Just Sam and I stayed in the apartment the rest of that evening, Dominic returned at least a few times with food.

I would say that on Sunday Dominic Byrne came around 5 PM as I had to go to work and he stayed with Samuel Bronfman until I returned from work a little after nine a.m. on Monday.

I recall that by this time the kidnapping was on the news both Radio and TV and in the papers. Dominic left sometime Monday.

On Monday afternoon I told Sam to write a note. Sam was sitting on the bed and I told him what to say, but not everything as he knew what to say. This note was to let the Bronfman family know that Sam was alright and alive. I think I mailed that letter in the evening probably in Queens. As best I can recall I stayed with Sam alone that evening. Tuesday was much the same as other days when I was not working, Dominic brought food and was at the apartment. My original plan was that if the original letter was received early sometime on Saturday the payment of the money could be made by Monday night and this whole thing could be over. That is why I had Dominic mail it special delivery. However I learned from the press that it was not received early. Therefore I suggested the tape recording to which Sam agreed. I told Dominic Byrne to bring the tape recorder I knew he had to my apartment and also to buy new tapes.

The first I told Sam what to say, but not everything. I think this tape was made on Tuesday. This tape was made in the bedroom. Just Samuel Bronfman and I were in my apartment. Dominic Byrne mailed this tape but I do not know where it was mailed.

On Wednesday Dominic was at the apartment a few times with food. During this period of time I did not answer any telephone calls except from Dominic. On Wednesday it was the first night I went to pick up the money. On this night I told Mr. Bronfman by phone to go to [the] KLM counter maybe I only said KLM. I made the call from Queens. I also tried to make [a] call to page Mr. Bronfman but I could not get him. At this time I called his home and told him I lost contact. Maybe I said Sam was alright. I don't remember the rest. I imagine it was made Wednesday night, that is, the next tape with Sam and myself alone in the apartment.

This tape was mailed the same night by Dominic Byrne, but I don't know where it was mailed I think I told him to take it to Queens or Manhattan.

Thursday I went to work and Dominic took care of Sam. Thursday night I made a phone call from Queens. I do not know exactly where. It was a call to Kennedy [Airport] and I told Mr. Bronfman tomorrow. Thursday was also the day that I suggested that he write another letter. Sam thought about it and he said he would write to his mother. I suggested that he might desire to send something in it. He decided to send the picture. This letter was mailed I believe by Dominic Byrne but I do not know where.

On Friday morning I went to work and Dominic Byrne came to take care of Samuel Bronfman. That night with my own car 1971 Toronado NY-692-KLQ, I drove to Queens Blvd. and made successions of calls, one to the number given him, one to TWA, one to [the] phone that he supplied at my instruction, one to [the] Mobil Station on the Southern State Parkway and one to the Burger-Shake, all giving him instructions relating to the passage of the ransom money. I selected the exchange spot just before he got the last call.

I met Mr. Bronfman, got in the car with him and told him to drive around. The exchange spot was just past a trestle [a support pillar for an elevated train track] on 69th St. near Queens Blvd. On my instruction after driving a short distance he left the car, at which time I drove Mr. Bronfman station wagon to my own car, which was parked a block or so away. I transferred the money, drove to Northern Blvd to Queensboro Bridge to Manhattan to FDR Drive southbound to Brooklyn Bridge then to Brooklyn Queens Expressway to Prospect Expressway to my residence arriving approximately 3:15 AM.

After a discussion with Dominic Byrne he gave me [the] key to the apartment of a friend of Dominic Byrne at the corner of east 17th and Foster Ave. I have drawn a diagram of this location. The apartment number is twelve. I went to this apartment and took the ransom money, a gun and a mask and put them under one of the beds.

I did not release Samuel Bronfman that night because it was too late. I did not think I could release him safely and kept him in the apartment until I was sure it would be clear outside. I probably would have released him early Saturday morning but I thought I was under surveillance.

I had made no plans for the use of the money. The money received was in no way connected with any political movement.

I would like to say that at no time would I harm Samuel Bronfman as I have since told him if he offered any resistance I would have run away. I would like to state that after two days I took the handcuffs off Samuel Bronfman and tied his hands loosely with rope. I would also like to state that I did not physically harm Samuel Bronfman in any way.

I Mel P. Lynch have read the above statement consisting of sixteen pages, and made corrections.

He stated that he does not desire anything to be added to this statement, or anything deleted from it, or anything further corrected in it. He does not feel that it is in any way inaccurate but, because of the seriousness of the case, he does not wish to sign it until a lawyer representing him has read it.

Witnesses:
J. Kevin O'Brien, Special Agent, FBI, New York, NY, 8/17/75
Richard F. McCarthy, Special Agent FBI, New York, NY 8/17/75

Part V

Examinations

I very much appreciate your kindness to me yesterday and also your special qualities as a person and a professional. Even if it might have appeared that we were on opposite sides, in the more important sphere, you and I are in unison.

–A. Bernard Ackerman, M.D.
New York (1995)

How many people do you think would let me do my work and operate on them, if I scared them with all the risks?

–Bellucci, M.D.
New York (ca. 1969)

I did not want to spoil her Mother's Day.

–Sonoda, M.D.
New York (1993)

Q – In your mind, in *your* mind, did you ever have the opinion, after review of these records, that this patient's demise – just think to yourself – may very well have been preventable?
A – Yes.
Q – With good proper medical treatment?
A – Yes.

–Mastrota, M.D.
New York (1984)

I am cross-examining Samuel Bronfman on the 25th day of trial, Friday, November 19, 1976. Sam was the 52nd witness to testify, the second-to-last of the government's witnesses. His father Edgar was the last. Seated to my left are the defendants and to my right are the jurors.

CHAPTER 29

THE ART OF THE EXAM

At all trials there are two main types of witness examination. There is the direct examination of one's own witness, and there is the cross-examination of the opponent's witness.

On direct examination, lawyers are a little constrained in their questioning as they are not permitted to lead their own witness toward a specific answer. Take, for example, the question: "When you entered the intersection was the traffic light green?" On direct examination the lawyer would have to ask: "What color was the traffic light?" Simple really. Instead of leading – prompting – the witness to the color "green," the lawyer asks what are known as open-ended questions to allow the witness to choose the answer. The witness informs us, we don't inform them. (There are always caveats and exceptions; for example, when an expert or someone with specialized knowledge is testifying, the lawyer may be permitted to ask some leading questions to focus the responses.)

The opposite is true on cross-examination. On cross, typically you don't want to give witnesses the opportunity to go off in any direction they want, you want to target them to specific details, and this is done by asking yes-no questions: "When you entered the intersection, the light was red, wasn't it?" (The question is best asked simply by intonation without the need for suffixes like "wasn't it?," "correct?," "yes or no?" But sometimes these phrases can be used for effect, or to vary the questioning; and demanding "yes or no" can be useful to cut witnesses short when they insist upon injecting explanations or excuses.)

There is not much to say about direct examinations. Either you know the facts of your case, or you don't. Either you know how to ask questions, or you don't. These things can't be taught. If a lawyer isn't born with this innate ability, then he or she must work hard to master the facts of each case, so at the time of trial their mind is free to listen to and hear what the witnesses have to say. Only in that way will the examining lawyer be able to seize upon what is helpful and cast doubt upon what is damaging.

I have never been particularly fond of direct examination, though I did love examining Dr. Yukio Fukuyama in the Tanabe case, which I include in this section, because he was such an extraordinarily gifted and talented individual. I say this because the direct examination usually lacks drama, which is as it should be since you don't want to have your own witness or client take you by surprise at trial when on the stand. (There is little worse on direct examination than not knowing what your witnesses will say – or not knowing that they will contradict one another as happened to my opponent in Tulchin when he called the two Bloomingdale's porters.)

Even if not fond of it, the direct examination must be done well, and to do it well, you must prepare your witnesses. A well-prepared witness occasionally can single-handedly win the lawsuit for you (as happened for my good friend Peter Kopff in Rivera, which I include in this section), but more often it's the case that an ill-prepared witness will doom your trial. This is what happened to the government in Bronfman, where witness after ill-prepared witness took the stand – some without even reviewing criminal case reports they'd written – allowing me to embarrass them on cross-examination and make a mockery of the prosecution. A journalist who covered every day of the trial captured the resulting chaos:

> [T]he FBI agents and several city detectives, many of whom have testified about the same events, have repeatedly contradicted one another under cross-examination. Some jurors have found it impossible to control their laughter, not only at these contradictions but also at admissions by law enforcement officers that they did not 'nail down' some seemingly elementary aspects of their investigation last year.

M.A. Farber, THE NEW YORK TIMES, "BRONFMAN ABDUCTION STILL RAISES QUERIES," November 1, 1976.

Which brings me to cross-examination of which I am particularly fond. Why particularly fond? Because cross-examination has the potential for high drama, which is the trial lawyer's bread and butter. It's why we try cases, why we put ourselves out there day after day, and later feel as if we are dying each and every night, as the incomparable Arturo Toscanini captured it so perfectly. And make no mistake, we trial lawyers are performers, the courtroom our theater, the jury our audience, the applause our raison d'être. Dramatic? You bet.

The cross-examination is usually where you win or lose your case, as in the Aldycki trial, when I asked the defendant hospital's expert doctor one final question: if when he first reviewed the hospital record he didn't think to himself that this patient's death was preventable and, somberly and truthfully, he admitted that he did. It had been his sole mission on trial to defend the hospital and deny its liability at all costs, but by the end of the cross-examination I had made him my witness.

All things otherwise being equal, in a close case, the jury will find in favor of the best cross-examination, aspects of which should be reprised on summation (as in Aldycki). When all things are not equal, when the case is a "dog," you can achieve the improbable, and even the impossible, with a great cross-examination. And sometimes you can simply win when your opponent misses his own great cross-examination opportunity, as in Kaye, where left was right and right was left, but my opponent's mind was not free to catch what was there to be caught.

There is also what's known as redirect examination, following opposing counsel's cross-examination. Redirect should be used sparingly and with surgical precision to rehabilitate one's own witness if the cross-examination was particularly damaging on a subject. In the Bronfman case, I had to conduct a redirect examination of one of the co-defendant's witnesses when the prosecutor tore a hole in his story (and potentially our entire defense) on cross-examination. That witness was one of only a few defense witnesses in our three-month trial, which had seen over 50 government witnesses testify, so I couldn't just sit by and let it happen.

Finally, or really I should say first, there is a type of witness examination that takes place long before the trial begins or the jury is empaneled. It is the Examination Before Trial, known too as an EBT or deposition. When done well, an examination of a party or expert medical witness before trial can cause the opponent to realize a settlement is his best option, thereby avoiding the tremendous time and expense of a trial and possible appeal. It can also, in unusual circumstances, lead a plaintiff's attorney to dismiss an action against a defendant, as was the case in Rivera when, after deposing the most brilliant doctor I ever knew, Dr. A. Bernard Ackerman, I discontinued our case against him.

In this section I have included a few of my favorite examinations, including many excerpts from cross-examinations on the Bronfman trial. The examinations within are verbatim from trial transcripts that I have. (When cases went up on appeal, we obtained the transcripts and I kept many of them.) In the Bellucci story, for which I do not have a transcript, I recreated the examination from indelible memory.

CHAPTER 30

In Memory of Dr. A. Bernard Ackerman Who Brought Imagination and Creativity and Iconoclasm to a Pretty Sterile Field

Examinations Before Trial (EBTs), or depositions, are a vital discovery tool in *civil* cases. I was basically brought up doing them at Mr. Reilly's defense firm. All that we did at Reilly's were EBTs and trials. Usually when we finished an EBT of the plaintiff, he and his case were destroyed and the trial was just the finishing touch.

EBTs are almost always held in an attorney's office. Judges and juries have nothing to do with the EBT. Present are the parties' lawyers, the person who will be testifying under oath - either a defendant or plaintiff or expert or eyewitness - and a court reporter to transcribe the testimony. The attorneys usually manage to conduct themselves in a civilized manner, despite the absence of a judge, and if any disagreements should arise, such as one attorney's objections to questions asked by the other attorney, they are preserved for the judge's ruling at the time of trial.

The purpose of the EBT is at least twofold. One is to discover facts about the case in advance of trial, in part to facilitate settlement negotiations. A second purpose is to memorialize testimony, in part to "box in" a party or witness, the EBT transcript to be used against them should they have a change of heart when testifying at trial.

Probably the two most important EBTs that I conducted in my career were in the Braun case and the Rivera case. In Braun, the EBT helped me to discover the existence of the car leasing company GMAC, which ultimately made it possible for my quadriplegic accident-victim client to recover $10,000,000 of the $20,000,000 jury verdict, instead of just the defendant driver's $100,000 policy. In Rivera, the EBT led me to discover the existence of the malpractice itself, which up until that moment had seemed improbable and unprovable.

The facts of the Rivera case were simple. In 1992 Ramiro Rivera, a young man in his 20s, noticed a growth under his arm and went to see a dermatologist, Dr. Manrique (subsequently, a defendant in our lawsuit). Dr. Manrique biopsied the growth and, as per his custom, he forwarded the biopsy specimen to the Medical Center at New York University (NYU) in order to have the Chief of Dermatological Pathology, the great and brilliant Dr. A. Bernard Ackerman, diagnose the growth and report to him his findings and recommendations.

Dr. Ackerman (the second defendant in our lawsuit) diagnosed the specimen as a Spitz nevus, a benign condition, and recommended that Dr. Manrique excise (i.e., remove) the complete growth. Dr. Manrique did not follow Dr. Ackerman's recommendation.

A year and a half later, the growth had metastasized and it was discovered that it was not then and never had been a Spitz nevus. Instead, it was a life-threatening melanoma. Mr. Rivera had surgery to remove the growth, and subsequently was referred to our office to look into filing a medical malpractice lawsuit.

We had some of the leading dermatopathologists in the country review the original biopsy slides, and to a man all agreed that they did not find melanoma. (A dermatopathologist is a medical doctor who interprets sections of biopsied skin specimens by conventional microscopy.) Not only did all agree with Dr. Ackerman's original Spitz nevus diagnosis, but all agreed that it was not custom to remove benign growths such as Spitz nevi and that what Dr. Manrique did, which was absolutely nothing at all, was the accepted practice. Each and every one emphasized, however, that Dr. Ackerman was the leading dermatopathologist in the country – "a half-step above the rest of us" – and that his flouting custom by recommending removal of this particular growth, a recommendation none of them would have made, was an example of Ackerman's brilliance. Even if he could not see melanoma on the biopsy slides, he knew something was not right with the specimen. He was, in a word, a genius.

Thus, what I knew going into the EBTs was that Dr. Ackerman had not committed malpractice and, even though Ackerman had directed that excision be done in this particular instance, Dr. Manrique apparently had not committed malpractice either. I also knew that unless I learned something during Dr. Ackerman's upcoming EBT, something which I and everyone else had missed, there was no case and the lawsuit would have to be dismissed.

Learn I did – namely that Dr. Ackerman was indeed brilliant and that he was honest and believed in righting a wrong. Unfortunately for Dr. Manrique, Dr. Ackerman placed the final wrong squarely on his shoulders for failing to remove the entire tumor as Dr. Ackerman said he was mandated to do.

Our EBT on April 27, 1995 lasted several hours and although Dr. Ackerman and I started out as adversaries, midway through we began to form our own private mutual admiration society. Ackerman admired and helped me, so much so that I got exactly what I wanted – he became then and there my expert witness against Dr. Manrique. (At one point during the EBT in answer to a question of mine Ackerman said: "I must tell you that . . . I like very much your approach to precision and exactness, I mean, I try to do the same thing in my professional life.")

In equal measure, I admired and helped Ackerman, so much so that he got exactly what he wanted – I discontinued the lawsuit against him and proceeded solely against Dr. Manrique. (Among the many things I liked very much about Ackerman – who was a founder of the field of dermatopathology – was his total devotion to his craft and his tirelessness in pushing its limits. In the ten or so years since he had become Director of Dermatopathology at NYU, he achieved a 100-fold increase in the number of specimens the dermatopathology lab was able to examine in a year, from approximately 2,000 in the mid-1980s to 200,000 by 1994.)

As helpful as I believe it would be for one to read here Ackerman's beautiful command of language and knowledge of the subject matter, time I am afraid will not permit it and so I will try to summarize the crux of his testimony during my examination of him.

Ackerman explained how two days before the EBT he re-examined the original 1992 biopsy specimen. Upon re-examination he now saw that the lesion was a melanoma not a Spitz nevus. Thus, he admitted: 1) "I missed a diagnosis"; and 2) "I made a mistake." I like things repeated, so that there can be no mistake, no retraction later, and therefore I asked him: "If the melanoma were like a star in the sky, was it possible that there was a cloud of Spitz nevi blocking the melanoma from your view?" He answered: "Absolutely not. The melanoma was not blocked, it was there to be seen."

When I then asked him why he looked at the specimen again before our EBT and didn't just rely on his 1992 reading, his response made clear why he was a half-step above the rest: "Well, for several reasons. One was whenever I miss a diagnosis, I always study the case, and not just once, I want to make sure to the best of my ability it's not going to happen again; and secondly, I want to find out why it happened; and thirdly, I want my students to learn from my mistake."

With those honest admissions, I knew that he had made our case for us, and for the remainder of the EBT he became our expert witness, albeit not against himself but against Dr. Manrique.

Depending upon who is describing it, the most complex subject can be made to sound simple and the simplest made to sound exceedingly complex. Ackerman's explanation of how the missed diagnosis came about was simple.

Back in March 1992 when he originally reviewed the patient's (Rivera's) specimen, as was his custom Ackerman looked at it with a 21-headed microscope, so that he and 20 of his students could examine the slide together. (In addition to his role as Director of Dermatopathology at NYU, he was also a full professor of dermatology and of pathology, and these 20 students were dermatologists, pathologists and dermatopathologists who were then taking an advanced course in dermatopathology with him.) Although now in 1995 he no longer recalled this particular specimen review, he knew from re-reading the report and his general custom that his diagnosis was Spitz nevus and that the other 20 doctors present agreed with the diagnosis.

There was a caveat, however. In his report, he included a note to the clinician, Dr. Manrique, that "because the changes were unusual, the lesion should be completely removed." Although Ackerman no longer recalled the "changes" that led him to issue this unusual directive in this particular instance – he did *not* write such notes in 99.8% of his Spitz nevi reports – he believed there was something subliminal that interfered with his Spitz nevus diagnosis here.

Now in April 1995 when he re-reviewed the patient's specimen in preparation for the EBT, Ackerman again looked at it with a 21-headed microscope with 20 of his students. (Ackerman was now Director of the Institute for Dermatopathology at Jefferson Medical College in Philadelphia, and again the 20 students were medical doctors studying for advanced degrees.) Ackerman did not inform them that this patient was subsequently diagnosed with melanoma – he just asked them based on their review of the slides what the diagnosis was. Everyone said Spitz nevus. He was hoping, he said at our EBT, that one or two of them would "chirp up" melanoma, but to no avail. He added that back in 1992, if one of his students had said "melanoma," which they were free to do, "the brakes would have been applied" and a more intensive search might have turned up the melanoma.[3]

In regard to why in 1995, when looking at the 1992 specimen for the second time, he now realized that he was looking at a melanoma and not a Spitz nevus, his answer was simple: "This time I was told in advance that I was going to see melanoma and obviously that colors one's judgment. One doesn't look with a tabula rasa."

Ackerman knew that since Mr. Rivera's melanoma was metastatic when found in 1993, it was the melanoma and not a Spitz nevus that was in the 1992 specimen, for the simple reason that Spitz nevi do not metastasize and melanomas can. Dr. Ackerman explained how now in 1995 he could be so sure:

> The crucial features that enabled the diagnosis to be made by me [two days ago], who wasn't looking with a completely objective view, but nonetheless, these were things that were there, were in the dermis, aggregations of neoplastic cells, which became confluent in many foci, forming a somewhat reticulated pattern, and that pattern, especially the confluence of the aggregations, is not a feature of Spitz nevus, but can be a feature of melanoma. That was the major factor. That was enough for me to make the diagnosis of melanoma.

After explaining how and why he missed the diagnosis in 1992, Ackerman went on to state how and why Dr. Manrique committed malpractice. Dr. Manrique, he testified, had three options upon receipt of the report stating that the lesion *should be* completely removed: 1) speak with Ackerman and Ackerman would then explain in detail why the lesion had to be removed; 2) obtain a second opinion from a different dermatopathologist; or 3) remove the lesion. "Manrique had to do something," Ackerman testified at the EBT. "You just can't do nothing."

Why did I proceed against Dr. Manrique but let Ackerman out of the lawsuit? Was it because I was naïve like Dominic Byrne, and wanted this great and brilliant man to like me? Not at all. I let Ackerman out because he did not depart from the accepted and proper practice of medicine in reaching the wrong diagnosis:

---

[3] A "metastatic melanoma," Dr. Ackerman explained, is a malignant neoplasm of melanocytes, which he then translated as a proliferation (or tumor) of cells that make melanin, which has the capability to kill a person. He explained that a "Spitz nevus," named after Dr. Sophie Spitz, is a benign proliferation of melanocytes characterized by some cells with round or nevus (spindle-like) shapes.

Q (Mr. DeBlasio) – If I ask you questions about accepted and proper medical and dermatological practice, would you understand what I'm talking about?

A (Dr. Ackerman) – Surely.

. . .

Q – In your opinion, with a reasonable degree of medical certainty, were you in conformity with accepted and proper medical practice and standards when you noted "the changes are unusual"?

A – Yes.

Q – Were you in conformity with accepted and proper medical standards when you said "the lesion should be completely removed"?

A – Yes.

Q – So now I just go to the other way. Had you not said there are changes that are unusual and had you not said the lesion should be completely removed, would that have been a departure from good practice?

A – No.

Q – Why not?

A – Because I suggest that if those [specimen] sections were seen by the outstanding dermatopathologists in the world, a hundred of them, 90 would have called it a Spitz nevus. If that's the case, then the standard is that it's possible to misinterpret this particular neoplasm as a Spitz nevus, and if that's the case, the vast majority of them would not have added the note at all.

Q – Beautifully answered. Beautifully answered. What you did was above and beyond the call of duty?

A – I think so in some ways. I mean, I still missed it, but I think that --

Q – You missed the diagnosis, but you covered it?

A - Yes.

Q - Whether you missed it or not, you call it by any other name, if you say take it all out, what does it matter?

A - Same.

MR. DeBLASIO: I have no further questions.

The day after our EBT - our mutual admiration society meeting - I received the following handwritten note:

Dear Mr. DeBlasio,

I very much appreciate your kindness to me yesterday and also your special qualities as a person and a professional.

Even if it might have appeared that we were on opposite sides, in the more important sphere, you and I are in unison.

Thank you once again from

Bernie Ackerman

I must commend as well the brilliant lawyer who represented Ackerman at the time of the EBT, my good friend Peter Kopff. It was no doubt on account of Peter's great counsel that Ackerman was so well-prepared and adaptable throughout the EBT, which led me to immediately drop him from the lawsuit and adopt him as my expert. What's more, once I discontinued the case against Ackerman and advised Dr. Manrique's counsel who my medical expert witness would be, we settled before trial for $700,000, which was paid by Dr. Manrique's insurance carrier.

POSTSCRIPT: When Ackerman returned from Philadelphia to New York in 1999 to found his own institute, the internationally acclaimed Ackerman Academy of Dermatopathology, we became close social friends. The last dinner we had together was at the elegant restaurant Jean-Georges on Central Park West in about 2006, and my daughter Alessandra joined us. Sadly, my friend Bernie Ackerman died not long afterward, and far too soon.

I may have had a subliminal feeling that he would pass on before me, because toward the end of that long-ago EBT I asked him, in effect, to give his own eulogy:

> Q – If a person had made a complete study of your entire career and you were up for the Hall of Fame of Dermatopathology and that person was your spokesperson, what are the highlights, what would that person say why you should be admitted? And you know, this is not you, this is that person, so there is no question of modesty or immodesty, I achieved this, I've done this, I've received this honor, this award, etc., etc.
>
> A – Well, what I hope they would say is he took it seriously, he went beyond the outer limits of his possibilities, he played no political games, he was honest and he brought imagination and creativity and iconoclasm to a field that heretofore was pretty sterile.

He was an elegant, eloquent man, who knew how to turn a phrase and pen a pun.

CHAPTER 31

"How Many People Would Let Me Operate If I Scared Them?"

One of the quickest and most effective cross-examinations I ever conducted in my life occurred in a malpractice case involving informed consent back in the 1960s, when the concept of "informed consent" was in its infancy. Back even before I tried Komoroff.

In this case the plaintiff, who had been a bomber pilot in World War II, years later sustained a perforated ear drum in his left ear when he was a passenger on an airplane flight from California to New York. Upon landing, he telephoned his cousin who was a surgeon in California and the cousin arranged for him to see the best ear man (otolaryngologist) in New York, Dr. Bellucci.

The plaintiff (whose name I unfortunately no longer remember) saw Dr. Bellucci and explained why he was there. Dr. Bellucci examined him and told him yes, he had a perforated left ear drum, and it would be no problem for him to treat and repair. But what he was really interested in, Dr. Bellucci told his patient, was what he saw (or really didn't see) in the right ear, namely that his ear drum was missing.

"Yes," the plaintiff said, "I perforated my right ear drum twenty years ago in the War and that's the result." Dr. Bellucci asked how he was getting along without the right ear drum, and the plaintiff said he still had partial hearing in the ear, adding: "I just have to plug up my ear every time I shower, but that's usually no trouble."

"Look," Dr. Bellucci then told him, "your left ear will be fine, but about your right ear, we're doing wonderful things these days with people who have no ear drum. We operate and we give them a new ear drum that is as good as, or even better than, the one they had. The operation is called a tympanoplasty."

The plaintiff said: "It's good to hear there are these new operations, but really I'm only interested now in my left ear and I'm glad to hear it will be okay. I've lived with my right ear this way for twenty years and I'd rather leave it as it is."

Dr. Bellucci persisted. He assured his patient that he was an expert on tympanoplasties and had so far only had wonderful results. After additional persuasion to get his right ear operated on, the plaintiff agreed to the procedure in order to bring his hearing back in full.

Dr. Bellucci operated, and the plaintiff went completely deaf in the right ear.

The plaintiff came to see me and, after we discussed the case, I told him I would order all of his medical records. If after reviewing the records I thought the case had merit, I would send them on to one or two doctors in the field of otolaryngology to try to determine if they, too, believed that Dr. Bellucci committed malpractice during the surgery.

I obtained the records, I read them, and I found a doctor willing to review them. The expert's opinion? No malpractice. The patient's resulting deafness was a known risk, hazard and/or complication of tympanoplasties, which could and did occur through no negligence of Dr. Bellucci.

I had another expert doctor review the records, and again no malpractice in the performance of the operation.

I had been turned down before by experts in many cases that sounded like they could be malpractice, and I had accepted that, but this case sounded different. I thought back on what a very bright and very honest cardiothoracic surgeon friend of mine from Texas once told me jokingly, though I knew that many a true thing is said in jest. His standard for deciding whether a doctor committed malpractice was: if the case made him want to spit, it was malpractice – if it didn't, it wasn't.

The Bellucci case made me want to spit.

It didn't sound right to me: a man goes to a doctor for his left ear and ends up with his right ear being operated on – because the doctor basically insists that's the way to go – and the man becomes deaf in that ear and then is told "that's life, that's the way the cookie crumbles."

I had the plaintiff in again and questioned him more thoroughly. I knew that there was something new in town, a new legal doctrine that permitted lawyers to sue a doctor even when a surgery was properly done. If a patient suffered an injury that was a recognized risk or hazard of that particular surgery, but was not warned ahead of time about the possible negative outcomes, the patient could sue on the theory that the doctor had failed to obtain his *informed* consent. If Dr. Bellucci had operated on the plaintiff without informing him that even if performed perfectly the tympanoplasty might result in complete hearing loss, then he might be liable for the injury suffered.

These "lack of informed consent" cases were still in their infancy in the 1960s, and no lawyer I knew thought much of them. What's more, they were worth very little in damages. But we had nothing to lose.

I now asked the plaintiff in more detail about his conversations with Dr. Bellucci, with particular emphasis on what he was told about the tympanoplasty. He repeated that Dr. Bellucci told him he was an expert in tympanoplasties with wonderful results. I asked if Dr. Bellucci ever told him about what could go wrong as a result of the operation, and he was firm in his answer that he was never told about anything going wrong, or about risks or complications. I decided we had a legitimate case against Dr. Bellucci for failing to obtain informed consent, and we sued him.

At trial in New York County, I called Dr. Bellucci as my initial witness. First, a few words about defendant-witnesses. Unlike in criminal cases, in a civil case the plaintiff has the right to call the defendant to testify. (There is no Fifth Amendment right to refuse to answer questions on the grounds of self-*incrimination*, since the defendant is not here charged with a crime, just with negligence.) Furthermore, even when called as a plaintiff's witness, the defendant is considered "hostile" and so the plaintiff's lawyer is allowed to cross-examine him. In other words, I could ask leading questions, forcing him to answer me "yes" or "no," instead of the usual way with one's own witness, asking open-ended questions that would allow him (and not me) more control in how he answered.

In response to my initial open-ended questions, Dr. Bellucci gave his reasons why the plaintiff went deaf in his right ear following surgery. It was either because during the surgery some microscopic bones in the ear were inadvertently moved and caused the deafness, or because the plaintiff was ultra-sensitive to the high decibel sounds of one of the operative instruments, both of which were not departures from accepted and proper medical standards and practices and thus not malpractice. He said these occurrences were well-known risks of this type of surgery, but had never before happened in his cases.

I then asked if there were other risks to the surgery. He said of course. I asked if it was standard medical practice for the surgeon in a case such as this to tell his patient about the risks before operating. He agreed it was, and I asked if the failure to disclose these risks would be a departure from accepted medical practice. He agreed it would be.

I asked if he told the plaintiff of the risks, and he said he definitely did so. I then asked him to tell us what these risks were, listing them in order of seriousness to the plaintiff's well-being. Naturally, being such a nationally renowned surgeon, he was happy to enlighten us with his knowledge. The risks, he testified, were as follows:

1. Death
2. Paralysis
3. Brain damage
4. Stroke
5. Deafness

and on and on until he listed about 20 horrible scenarios. (It was like the commercials for medicines we see and hear on television these days, with a seemingly endless list of possible horrible-sounding side effects. These warnings are in fact a direct and important consequence of decades of our medical malpractice and products liability lawsuits.)

When Dr. Bellucci finally finished telling us of the risks, I then asked him in true cross-examination style, one by one:

> You told him as a result of surgery you can die – yes or no? *Yes.*
>
> You can become paralyzed – yes or no? *Yes.*
>
> You can get brain damage – yes or no? *Yes.*
>
> You can get a stroke – yes or no? *Yes.*
>
> You can go deaf – yes or no? *Yes.*

After he yessed all my questions about the twenty or so risks, I asked:

> After you told the plaintiff all of these risks and complications, and asked him if he still wanted to undergo the surgery on his right ear – the ear which he didn't come to see you about and which had not really caused him any problems in twenty years – his answer was, "Sure, go ahead, what do I have to lose?"

Dr. Bellucci's answer? "Well not in those words, but he did agree."

I then said the famous "no more questions," and with that the case was over. Before Dr. Bellucci's lawyer could get up to ask his own questions, the judge excused the jury, called me and his lawyer to the bench, advised him to call his insurance carrier to settle the case, and a few moments later the case was settled.

One of the jurors approached me afterward in the hallway and said: "Boy, you sure showed what a liar he was." The juror was right. On our way out of the courthouse Dr. Bellucci and I bumped into each other and spoke. As I remember it, he said:

> DeBlasio, what's the matter with you? Do you know what you're doing? You're preventing me from doing good work. How many people do you think would let me operate on them, if I scared them with all the risks? I know what I'm doing. I mean well. I almost never fail. This was just an unfortunate case and I may even have been able to fix him up if given the chance.

I guess it's all in the eyes, or maybe the ears, of the beholder. Even though I didn't feel sorry for him, I liked Dr. Bellucci and thought he was an excellent doctor – so good in fact that a few years later I sent my sister-in-law to him when she went temporarily deaf in an ear.

POSTSCRIPT: In 2016, I read a very compelling book by Henry Marsh, a British neurosurgeon born in 1950, who sounded like a lovely, compassionate person and brilliant doctor. In his chapter on Haemangioblastoma, he wrote at length about informed consent and expressed the doctor's dilemma not very differently than did Dr. Bellucci more than 50 years earlier:

> I told [my 40-year-old patient] that there was a one or two per cent risk of his dying or having a stroke if the operation went badly. In truth, I did not know the exact figure as I have only operated on a few tumours like his – ones as large as his are very rare – but I dislike terrorizing patients when I know that they have to have an operation. What was certain was that the risk of the operation was many times smaller than the risk of not operating. . . .
>
> Would he have chosen not to have the operation if I had said that the risk was five per cent, or fifteen per cent, or fifty per cent? Would he have chosen to find another surgeon who quoted lower risks? Would he have chosen differently if I had not made any jokes, or had not smiled?
>
> I asked him if he had any questions but he shook his head. Taking the pen I offered him he signed the long and complicated [consent to operate] form, printed on yellow paper and several pages in length, with a special section on the legal disposal of body parts. He did not read it – I have yet to find anybody who does.

Henry Marsh, DO NO HARM: STORIES OF LIFE, DEATH, AND BRAIN SURGERY, St. Martin's Press, U.S. Edition May 2015.

CHAPTER 32

THE BOW TO THE WAIST

On June 18, 1993 a Japanese woman walked down an aisle carrying her crying son, who was grossly contorted. At that moment, another Japanese woman rose from her seat, bowed down to her waist while looking at the mother and boy, and started to scream and wail, continuing until the boy was well past.

One might have thought that this scene took place in Tokyo at a religious shrine. Not so. It happened in White Plains, New York, at the Supreme Court where Judge Samuel Fredman was presiding at the trial of Tanabe v. Sonoda and Lawrence Hospital. The woman carrying her son was Mrs. Tanabe; the woman bowing toward them out of respect and for forgiveness was Dr. Sonoda, the obstetrician who delivered the boy, Ken Tanabe, ten years earlier on Mother's Day 1983 at Lawrence Hospital in Scarsdale.

In 1983, the two women were patient and doctor. Now in 1993, they were plaintiff and defendant.

Doctor Sonoda's screaming and wailing and bowing were done in front of both the presiding judge and the jury of ten (six regular jurors and four alternates), which had been selected to render a verdict in this malpractice lawsuit. It had taken two weeks to pick the jury, from June 1 to June 15, and the trial started on June 16, 1993.

Doctor Sonoda's outburst occurred on our third day of trial testimony. The trial ended almost a month later, on July 12 when a verdict was rendered. In a case filled with drama, her outburst stands out as the moment I will always remember, and I knew then that the trial was over, that no juror could erase that event from his or her mind.

The Tanabe case was a simple one. It could be summed up in one word: Demerol.

Demerol is a drug, an opiate. A 50-milligram dose was given by injection into the buttocks of Mrs. Tanabe when she was in labor at Lawrence Hospital. It was given to lessen the pain. Dr. Sonoda ordered it from home when talking by telephone to the nurse who was monitoring Mrs. Tanabe.

We sued Dr. Sonoda, claiming that she should never have ordered the Demerol. We also sued the hospital and an anesthesiologist, claiming that once the Demerol was given, the nurses did not timely recognize the damage it caused to Ken, and the anesthesiologist was not able to intubate him. Our damages claim was that Ken's life was destroyed at birth.

When the jury saw Ken, he was ten years old.

He could not talk.

He could not walk.

He could not stand.

He could not control his bowels.

He could not understand anything.

He could not follow commands.

He could not care for himself in any way.

Basically, all that he could do was crawl like a baby (but not like a normal baby, because his arms and legs were misshapen); suck on objects; be spoon- or hand-fed with soft food; and laugh inappropriately when stimulated. At ten years old he had the brain and abilities equivalent to those of an infant of six to nine months, or possibly one year of age.

All of the above injuries and conditions are permanent, and will never improve, and will continue on for the next 60 or so years of his life expectancy. A more tragic life and human being cannot be imagined.

Since the age of two, Ken has lived in Tokyo with his parents and older brother, and he has been under constant medical care. When she was on the witness stand that day in June 1993, while holding Ken, Mrs. Tanabe said that she would never institutionalize Ken but would care for him until the day she dies.

Why is Ken this way? Because he stopped breathing for several minutes within his first 20 minutes of life and his brain suffered irreversible damage due to lack of oxygen.

Why was that? Because his mother was given Demerol, which passed through the placenta into the blood stream of the fetus (when Ken was in utero), one hour before he was born, and it depressed his respiratory system to the point where he could no longer breathe.

Why include this case? Because of the direct examination of one of the world's greatest physicians. But before I get to his testimony, some background on the birth, the Demerol given, and the malpractice of two doctors and several nurses.

THE BIRTH

In 1983, Mr. and Mrs. Tanabe, she 29 and he in his early 30s, were a happily married couple who had a healthy four-year-old son. They had come to the United States two years earlier, when Mr. Tanabe who worked for the National Bank of Japan was sent to manage one of its branches in the New York area.

Mrs. Tanabe became pregnant and selected Dr. Sonoda, a Japanese-speaking obstetrician in her 50s, as her physician. Mrs. Tanabe did not drink, did not smoke, did not take drugs, and had a normal, uneventful pregnancy.

In the early hours of Sunday May 8, 1983, which was Mother's Day and also the fifth wedding anniversary of the Tanabes, Mrs. Tanabe's labor started. At about 3:00 a.m., Mrs. Tanabe telephoned Lawrence Hospital, spoke to a nurse in the obstetrical department, and told her about the labor. The nurse called Dr. Sonoda at home, waking her. The nurse called Mrs. Tanabe back and said to stay at home and call when her water broke or the contractions increased in frequency. At about 4:30 a.m. the membrane ruptured and water broke, and Mrs. Tanabe called the hospital. She was told to come in and that Dr. Sonoda would meet her at the hospital. The Tanabes arrived there at about 7:00 a.m.

Shortly after 7:00 a.m. a nurse telephoned Dr. Sonoda at home, waking her again, to say that the Tanabes were at the hospital. Dr. Sonoda said she would be right over. (Dr. Sonoda's home was 10 minutes from the hospital by car.) Unfortunately, Dr. Sonoda fell back to sleep.

In the meantime, an obstetrical nurse was tending to and monitoring Mrs. Tanabe. Upon first examination, Mrs. Tanabe's cervix was apparently dilated about two centimeters. (When a cervix is dilated ten centimeters, the baby is about to be born.)

About one hour later, around 8:00 a.m., when Dr. Sonoda still had not arrived, the nurse called and woke her up again. The nurse told Dr. Sonoda that Mrs. Tanabe was complaining of pain and was asking for medication. (Mrs. Tanabe denied this when she testified.)

Dr. Sonoda testified that she asked how many centimeters Mrs. Tanabe was dilated, and that she was told *three to four* centimeters. Dr. Sonoda told the nurse to give 50 mg of Demerol and that she would be at the hospital shortly. This call was at 8:20 a.m.; the Demerol was given at 8:25 a.m.

At 8:30, after giving the Demerol, the nurse checked the dilation of the cervix. The nurse testified that it was *four to five* centimeters dilated, and she said that is what she wrote in the hospital record. The hospital record, however, proved that she was not being truthful. It was clear that the numbers as originally written in the record were "*7 to 8*" centimeters dilated and that "4 to 5" had been written over that. (While the nurse was on the stand, I asked Judge Fredman for permission to show the record to the jury at that time, rather than during deliberation, and he allowed it.)

Dr. Sonoda arrived at Mrs. Tanabe's bedside at 8:45 a.m., 20 minutes after her talk with the nurse. Dr. Sonoda examined the cervix right then, and she testified on trial that she was "amazed" that the cervix was fully effaced at ten centimeters. She immediately began preparations for the birth.

The baby was delivered at 9:23 a.m., 58 minutes after the Demerol was given. Upon birth, the baby was slow to cry and it was a weak cry. The hands and feet were cyanotic (i.e., a dusky color), signs of possible respiratory distress, which could be a result of the Demerol.

The APGAR at one minute was eight (out of ten), two points taken off on account of somewhat poor respiration. At five minutes, the APGAR was ten (the highest and best level).

The baby was kept in the delivery room for about seven minutes, tended to by a nurse who was swaddling him in two blankets while Dr. Sonoda was removing the placenta and suturing the episiotomy. When Dr. Sonoda declared the baby stable at about 9:30 a.m., the nurse put a cap on his head - so that the only visible part of his body was a portion of the face - and carried him to the nursery and placed him in an isolette.

There were two nurses in this nursery. At the moment the newborn Ken arrived, each of them was busy washing a baby, so they just glanced his way and did not immediately assess him as was required. About five minutes later, at 9:35 a.m., one of the nurses finally examined him.

When she removed the blankets swaddling him, what she saw was what looked like a limp, discolored ragdoll barely breathing and with an abnormally slow heartrate for a newborn (just 65 beats per minute), and no reflexes. She called for help. She knew the baby was in respiratory failure, and she tried to give mouth-to-mouth resuscitation. (She testified that when the delivery-floor nurse originally brought the baby into the nursery, she did not tell her the mother had been given Demerol and that the Demerol had been given only one hour before delivery.)

Dr. Kerrigan, the anesthesiologist then on duty, responded to the call at 9:45 a.m. He spent 15 minutes trying to intubate the baby, but was unsuccessful. Another physician was called to come assist.

It was not until 10:00 a.m. – 25 minutes after the original call for help – that a neonatologist (Dr. Basca) arrived at the nursery and, within seconds, was able to intubate Ken. Ken then "pinked up," but the brain damage he had already suffered was irreparable.

(Ken was transferred to New York Hospital that day at about noon, and he stayed there for one week. Pediatric neurologists continued to care for him thereafter and, when he was two years old, his family moved back to Tokyo where he came under the care of one of the world's most revered neurologists, Dr. Yukio Fukuyama.)

DEMEROL

In order to understand what happened to Ken Tanabe, it's necessary to understand how Demerol works and the risks it poses to a fetus.

In 1983, Demerol was universally given to women in labor for one reason: to lessen the pain of the mother in labor. When given, it crosses the placental barrier to the fetus within a minute or two. Demerol has a four-hour lifespan, which means that it is gone from the mother's body, and the fetus's body, in four hours.

The amount of Demerol to be given depends on the weight of the mother. The standard is one milligram for one kilogram (about 2.2 pounds). Mrs. Tanabe weighed about 135 pounds when she was given the Demerol. Thus, the 50 mg dose she received was appropriate. Not so for Ken, in utero, who was receiving a comparable level across the placental barrier, but weighed only about seven-and-a-half pounds.

Ken received about 15 times the appropriate dose for his weight, which would prove catastrophic as, upon birth, he was left to metabolize the Demerol on his own, his mother's body no longer doing the work for him.

Demerol can and does depress respiration. The larger the dosage, the greater the depression. Our expert testified that the peak of respiratory depression, which lasts about one hour, begins 20 to 30 minutes after it is given. The Demerol was given to Mrs. Tanabe at 8:25 a.m., it began to peak at approximately 9:00 a.m. and the birth was at 9:23 a.m.

Thus, as Ken's body emerged from the womb and his mother was no longer breathing for him, the respiratory depression was at its peak and continued at that level through the first half-hour or so of Ken's life. And the extent of the respiratory depression he experienced was out of all proportion to his weight.

The respiratory depression was not immediately noticeable, though, at Ken's birth, and indeed his APGAR score was quite good. However, as our medical expert explained at trial, this was simply because the traumatic birthing process, with the sudden change from the warm dark womb to the outside world, energizes and activates the newborn. After only a very few moments, when Ken was swaddled in blankets and lying down in the warm nursery environment, the respiratory depression caused by the Demerol overwhelmed him, sending him into a state of extreme respiratory distress. The lack of oxygen left many of his brain cells unnourished and caused them to die.

THE MALPRACTICE TRIAL

The main claim of malpractice against Dr. Sonoda was that she should not have ordered the Demerol. The secondary claim was that once she realized the birth was imminent, she failed to have in place all that was necessary to counteract the harm the Demerol would cause the baby.

Dr. Sonoda admitted at trial that at the time of the 8:20 a.m. telephone call when she said to give the Demerol, there was no reason to have done so because she would be at the bedside in 20 minutes, when she could determine for herself the stage of labor and then decide if Demerol was appropriate. She also testified that had she known the cervix was seven to eight centimeters dilated, she never would have ordered the Demerol - it would have been a departure from good and accepted practice - because the birth was imminent. (Given that the record before alteration indicated the cervix was *7-8 centimeters* dilated at 8:30 a.m., just five minutes after the Demerol was given, it was unlikely that Dr. Sonoda asked and was told - as she testified - that the cervix was only *3-4 centimeters* dilated at 8:20, five minutes before she ordered the Demerol.)

When she arrived at the hospital at 8:45 a.m., and found Mrs. Tanabe fully dilated, she knew she faced a serious problem on account of the Demerol. She testified she was hoping the baby would be born immediately so that it would be before the peak hour of the Demerol's effect. Unfortunately, that was not to be as the delivery took almost 40 minutes.

It was as Dr. Sonoda prepared to deliver the baby that she committed another, graver error, one that sealed Ken's fate. Knowing the birth was imminent, knowing Demerol had been given only 20 minutes earlier, knowing the Demerol could cause severe respiratory problems, it was mandatory that she have adequate oxygenation provided from the moment of his birth, by intubation if necessary. Most obstetricians are trained in and know how to intubate a baby. Unfortunately, Dr. Sonoda was not so trained. She had never intubated anyone and she did not know how to do it.

Given those circumstances, it was mandatory that *before the birth* Dr. Sonoda have a doctor experienced in intubation present in the delivery room with her. A pediatrician, Dr. Edis, was on call for such a purpose, and Dr. Sonoda knew this.

When I asked Dr. Sonoda at trial why she did not have Dr. Edis come to the delivery room, she responded: "I did not want to spoil her Mother's Day." (Instead, she spoiled Mrs. Tanabe's Mother's Day, that day and forever thereafter.)

It was also mandatory, one of our experts testified, to have Narcan (an antagonist of opiates such as Demerol) in the delivery room. They should have used it, and while it was taking effect, Dr. Sonoda should have started artificial respiration, at a minimum mouth-to-mouth or a mask and bag. Failing to take any of these steps, she should not have sent the baby off to the nursery where there were no doctors present.

As for Dr. Kerrigan, we sued him for his negligence in failing to achieve the only thing he was called in to do at 9:45 a.m., intubate a baby. His negligence wasted 15 of the 25 most critical minutes of Ken's life – from 9:35 a.m. when he was discovered to be limp as a ragdoll until 10:00 a.m. when Dr. Basca arrived to save Ken's life.

With regard to Lawrence Hospital's gross negligence, we claimed that it was liable on account of: 1) the nurse who changed the records from 7-8 to 4-5 centimeters to cover up Dr. Sonoda's Demerol error; 2) the delivery-room nurse who failed to inform the nursery-room nurses that Demerol had been given; and 3) the nursery-room nurses who failed to timely and properly examine and treat Ken upon admission to the nursery.

One might wonder at this point was there a defense and, if so, what was it?

There was a defense, and it was the old "so-what defense": *We didn't do anything wrong, but if we did, so what? It didn't matter, because this condition was caused by a genetic deficiency*. Quite literally, that was their defense.

To counteract this defense, I had to bring in three medical experts who were as marvelous a group of doctors as I ever assembled in any one case. First, Dr. Albert Bartoletti, a neonatologist from Albany, testified about Dr. Sonoda's and the hospital staff's departures from accepted medical practice, and he explained the life cycle of Demerol and its effect on the respiratory process and the brain. Second, Dr. Kristjan Tomas Ragnarsson, Chief of Physical Medicine and Rehabilitation at Mt. Sinai Hospital in New York, testified both about Ken Tanabe's needs for the rest of his life and that he would have a normal life expectancy. Third, Dr. Yukio Fukuyama, a pediatrician and pediatric neurologist, a full professor and the Chairman of Pediatrics at Tokyo Women's Medical University in Japan.

Of the three, I only discuss and include portions of Dr. Fukuyama's testimony, because he was brilliant on direct examination and put the death knell on the defendants' claim that Ken's affliction resulted from genetic causes.

THE DIRECT EXAMINATION OF DR. FUKUYAMA

Dr. Fukuyama's professional credentials were as great as, if not greater than, the most celebrated medical witnesses I ever examined. First, he was one of the very few living doctors who had a disease named after him: "Fukuyama Congenital Muscular Dystrophy." In 1960, when he was in his 30s, he identified and described one particular condition, a disease entity, which had never been described in any medical textbook before, and so it now bears his name.

Second, one year before our trial, while president of the International Child Neurology Association, he received the Frank Ford Award. This global award is bestowed only once every four years, and only upon a single doctor selected from among the world's greatest living pediatric neurologists. (Dr. Ford was the eminent pioneering pediatric neurologist who served as the chief of pediatric neurology at Johns Hopkins University.)

Third, Dr. Fukuyama had more than 1,000 articles published, including ten books on child neurology written in English; and in the ten years preceding our trial, at least once each year he would give a series of lectures on pediatric neurology in a different part of the world, including in the United States at Columbia and Harvard Universities. (Immediately after our trial he was to present a lecture in Pisa, Italy, to pediatric neurologists from around the globe specializing in the rare condition "cortical dysplasia.")

At our trial, Dr. Fukuyama testified in English without the assistance of an interpreter, as excerpted here on direct examination.

QUESTION (DeBlasio) – Doctor, have you flown to the United States at my request; have I asked you to fly here? Did I ask you to come?

ANSWER (Dr. Fukuyama) – I have been responsible for taking care, taking medical care for Ken for the last eight years. I was always responsible for the medical aspect, medical problem that Ken have had. So, I knew Ken quite, let's say, well, and I'm very afraid about his future, so I would be happy to present my knowledge about Ken, the conditions.

Q – Thank you. I'm just going to ask you a limited number of questions. A limited number. Have – you already told us but I would just like to put it specifically, from 1985, May 9th, when Ken was two years and one day, until the present – have you been his treating doctor at the Tokyo Women's Medical College?

A – That's right.

Q – And please tell us, Doctor, the last time that you saw Ken was about when? The last time?

A – It was March, this year.

Q – All right. As a result of your treatment of Ken over that eight-year period, do you have a diagnosis of what his condition is at present; do you have a diagnosis?

A – Yes.

Q – Would you please, slowly . . . tell us what his diagnosis is?

A – My diagnosis is chronic brain dysfunction . . . due to neonatal anoxic encephalopathy.

Q – Continue, please. What other diagnosis is there?

A – Brain damage can be expressed by breaking down into the four categories. That is, number one is mental retardation, number two is cerebral palsy, spastic quadriplegia, and number three is epilepsy, having various seizure types, and number four is microcephaly. That's all.

Q – All right. Now, these conditions, the mental retardation, the cerebral palsy, the epilepsy, the microcephaly, please tell us how they affect Ken. What does he do, what does he not do, what can he do, what can he not do? Do you understand my question?

. . .

A – I understand. Ken is now able to move his extremities but not in skillful way. . . . He cannot feed any food by himself. Every feeding should be given to him by some other people, person. He never able to speak any single meaningful word. He will react to stimuli from the environment. He can feel pain by the noxious stimuli, but usually he will respond to such noxious stimuli with, let's say, uncontrollable laughing or smiling, so that I feel there is a big contradiction between the stimuli, which should be noxious to the normal baby, but the reaction Ken show is quite unreasonable. His vision and auditory function, hearing, is well preserved, but in a very elementary way. He recognize a person but he will not be able to distinguish between the people who are quite friendly to him and people who are not familiar.

Q – He will not be able to distinguish?

. . .

A – Cannot, cannot distinguish the people. And he cannot control sphincter. Sphincter means urination or defecation will occur quite automatically and he never able to take care of it, let's say, defecation and urination by himself. And he cannot move around, he cannot stand up with his own foot. He requires the wheelchair all the time. So, my evaluation of Ken's life is totally dependent upon the parents' care. Otherwise Ken cannot survive. So, the very basic fundamental function to live was not acquired by Ken.

Q – What do you mean by that, Dr. Fukuyama?

A – I meant that feeding, defecation, and let's say, to feel the environment is not acquired, clothing or toileting is not acquired, everyday activity is dependent upon the parents' care.

Q – Age-wise, we know Ken is now ten years and a little more than one month old, can you tell us with a reasonable degree of medical certainty, can you tell us what age person is Ken like?

A – I would say that he's level, development level is almost equivalent with as the level of a six to twelve months old baby. . . . Both mental and physical ability is nearly equivalent with the level of six to twelve months old baby.

Q – All right. Now, Dr. Fukuyama, what has happened to Ken's body, any part of his body, or his brain, as you mentioned; what has happened that has brought all this about? Why is he limited to being six to twelve months of age and limited to not being able to do the things that you've told us? What inside him is stopping that, or has stopped it?

A – Well, I saw Ken at his age of two and afterwards I always watching the baby, the child, for the last eight years, at least during that period of time there was no serious problem happen so --

Q – No serious problem?

A – Problems, causal event never occurred during that period, so that the cause of the brain damage should be existing before my first consultation, and the neurological. The handicaps already present, already developed when I saw the patient, so I looked at the period before my consultation, from his birth to my consultation. That is the period of two years. And I found that by history taking, by detailed history taking some problem happened to occur during his neonatal period.

Q – All right. I just want to stop you there . . . these conditions that you've described of Ken, without me repeating them, do you have an opinion, with a reasonable degree of medical certainty, whether or not those conditions will be permanent or not? Do you have an opinion?

A – I believe that the condition I am seeing now is certainly permanent.

. . .

Q – His inability to talk; do you believe he will ever be able to talk?

A – I believe that he will never be able to acquire the speaking ability. . . .

Q – Do you have an opinion, well, it's all within a degree of medical certainty, in ambulation, movement, will Ken ever be able to do anything more than crawl?

. . .

A – Never able to stand up, nor walk; perhaps the maximum motor ability acquirable will be just crawling. It's still a very clumsy way, not a normal crawling, not normal crawling.

. . .

Q – All right. Now, Dr. Fukuyama, we're talking about Ken, he's now ten. When he becomes twenty years old, a man, twenty-five, is he still going to be crawling on the floor?

A – Yes. Yes I think so.

. . .

Q – When Ken gets to be twenty, twenty-five, in your opinion is he going to be able to feed himself?

A – No, I can't believe that.

Q – Is he going to be able to control his bowels?

A – No. He will never acquire.

Q – Is he going to be able to put on his clothes or take off his clothes?

A – No.

Q – Is he going to be able to do anything except crawl and hold objects; is he going to be able to do anything else? He crawls, he holds objects; is he going to be able to do anything else, purposeful?

A – Well, I can't remember his purposeful movement ever. When I saw Ken always he looks like a kind of toy with very smiling face and automatically moving the extremities in irregular way, and I don't think such movement of his own intention. That is very involuntary movement.

. . .

Q – Doctor, you mentioned before in one of your answers that he can feel pain.

A – Yes.

Q – How do you know?

A – Well, when we tried to get blood by injecting the needle then Ken will try to draw his arm to try to avoid such a painful stimuli. But he will not get so angry by the sticking of the needle in his arm, in comparison to the normal baby.

Q – He will not get as angry as the normal baby?

A – No.

Q – Okay. You mentioned before noxious . . . stimuli . . . often bring about a smile or a laugh. . . . What does that mean?

A – For example, I tried to examine Ken by holding his arms to test the muscle tone and . . . let's say, pick up the skin . . . will cause pain in a normal baby, but the patient, Ken, will show the more smiling face to my try of examination. So, his reaction seems to be quite unexpected to me.

Q – This condition you said of his being at six months to twelve months development, do you have an opinion, with a reasonable degree of medical certainty, when he's an adult, twenty, thirty, forty, fifty, do you have an opinion, will he still have the mental and motor ability of a six month old to a twelve month old?

A – Yes, I think so. Yes.

Q – Do you have an opinion, with a reasonable degree of medical certainty, from the time you first saw him at two years until the day he dies, will he need 24 hours attention and care like a baby of six months to twelve months of age?

A – That true. That is my opinion, yes.

. . .

Q – From what you know about Ken, and from all your examinations and all your testing, is Ken's condition hereditary?

. . .

A – It is not, not hereditary.

. . .

Q – All right. You may have already told us, but please now tell us why you, with your training, your experience, your background, why you never imagined a genetic problem with Ken? Why?

A – Because of the physical finding shows, let's say, clinical course, which was reviewed by detailed history taking, as well as the detailed physical examination and long term follow-up for the last eight years by myself, always showed, all those things showed the clinical course was rather stable or, let's say, yes, stable and stationary, so this kind of clinical course don't suggest the possibility of genetic disease.

. . .

Q – Doctor, do you have an opinion, with a reasonable degree of medical certainty, of the competent producing cause of Ken's brain damage, retardation, and other conditions you described? Based on what I say, assuming it to be true, assuming it to be true, in your opinion, what caused his brain damage?

A – The event which occurred almost immediately after birth, during which the baby couldn't breathe sufficiently for about half an hour. . . . My opinion is neonatal anoxic encephalopathy occurred during the neonatal period.

Q – And when you say during the neonatal period, is that what you just told us, that half hour right after birth?

A – That's right.

Q – And what is encephalopathy?

A – That means, that special word is used for, let's say, a unspecific term for the brain dysfunction in any sense.

. . .

Q – What's anoxic, the anoxic before encephalopathy; what does that mean?

A – It means encephalopathy was caused by cerebral anoxia.

. . .

Q – All right. Doctor, cerebral, is that the brain?

A – Yes, brain.

Q – Anoxia, is that lack of oxygen?

A – Lack of oxygen, yes.

Q – Okay. Just a few more things. What, in your opinion, what happened to the brain cells or to the brain as a result of this approximate half hour of anoxia, what happened actually to the brain cells, or brain?

A – Well, the brain, to function normally for the brain the oxygen is very essential substance, because brain can utilize only oxygen and glucose as an energy source of the cell function. If the oxygen supply is stopped then brain cannot make any function, and so just like the asphyxiation of the human being, then the brain and the brain cell is quite sensitive to the lack of oxygen, so even the lack of oxygen during the short period of time, brain may suffer from the lack of oxygen in various degree.

Q – And what happens to those brain cells when they suffer?

A – The most cells will die and never regenerate afterwards.

. . .

Q – All right. Once dead, as soon as brain cells are dead, is there any way, by operation, or anything else, that can make them come back?

A – No. No.

Q – Those dead brain cells, are they what's causing the problems to Ken?

A – Yes.

Q – In what part or parts of the brain are these dead cells?

A – I think that the damage occurred rather broadly, extensively, but there are still some selectivity of the damage.

Q – Selectivity of the damage?

A – Selectivity of the damage, within the huge number of brain cells. Not all 100 percent brain cells will die at once, so that some brain damage will get very serious hazard and die, in such a way there is some selectivity of damage and, in my opinion, the cerebral cortex was damaged more seriously in comparison to other parts, especially to the brain stem.

Q – Cerebral cortex, c-o-r-t-e-x?

A – C-o-r-t-e-x.

Q – And what does that control?

A – The cerebral cortex have a different function covering motor, sensory, visual, auditory, and especially the consciousness and perception and, let's say intelligence in general.

Q – All right. Any other part of the brain, like the cerebral cortex, any other part especially damaged?

A – The other parts which were affected more seriously in the case of Ken would be basal ganglia. . . . Ganglia is a place where the cell will control or regulate the motor, tone, let's say, motor, muscle tone. Ken have hypertonicity of the muscle, that is called spastic, that is dependent upon the injury of the basal ganglia specifically.

Q – And, in your opinion, with a reasonable degree of medical certainty, was it that period of about a half hour after birth with the anoxia which was the competent producing cause and a substantial factor in bringing about this damage?

A – That's right.

MR. DE BLASIO: Thank you very much, Dr. Fukuyama.

When Dr. Fukuyama finished, there was very little the defense lawyers could or did do in their cross-examinations to negate this powerful testimony. They could not and did not have him retract, withdraw, or change one word in his testimony.

Dr. Fukuyama's fee for his trip from Japan for the trial was $25,000. It was well worth it. In summation, I asked the jury to consider awarding Ken's parents $5,000,000 and Ken himself $20,000,000; the jury rendered the highest verdict ever in a personal injury action up to that time in Westchester County, $25,000,000.

POSTSCRIPT: A note on the lawyer's cut, the "contingency fee," and how it works. By law, by state statute, personal injury attorneys may not charge the client up front, may not charge a consultation fee, may not charge an hourly rate, but should cover all costs and expenses of the lawsuit through the final appeal. The cost today to bring a case to trial can easily run a lawyer over $100,000. In medical malpractice cases, as in Tanabe, a single expert can cost upwards of $25,000 to review records and appear as a witness, and there are many cases which involve several experts (18 in Baumgarten).

Moreover, in personal injury cases generally, it's not just *medical* experts we need at trial to explain the plaintiff's injuries, but economists and actuarial experts to explain loss of earnings and expected lifespan, and then depending on the nature of the case, we might also need for example an accident-reconstruction expert - all of whom we must compensate for their time spent on record review, at deposition, and in trial. Even above and beyond these expert fees are the steep costs of deposing witnesses (hiring stenographers and paying for the voluminous transcripts), copying medical and business records, and any and all other imaginable expenses, just to get a case to trial. All this comes out of the lawyer's pocket, from the first attorney-client meeting through trial and final appeal, a process that can easily take four to fourteen years after the injury.

If we lose the lawsuit, we earn nothing and we absorb all the costs and expenses; the client pays nothing. We earn only on the contingency that we win the case. To offset the losses and keep our businesses afloat, when we do win the firm's percentage of the jury award or settlement offer is significant.

Upon winning, the costs and expenses are first deducted from the verdict to reimburse the lawyer; the amount remaining is then divided between the client and the lawyer according to the percentage set by statute. In accident cases in New York, the client receives two-thirds and the lawyer one-third. In medical malpractice cases, however, the split is different. Back in the 1960s when I began as a plaintiff's attorney, the contingency split was the same for all personal injury cases, two-thirds one-third, medical malpractice cases included. Since that time, though, tremendous lobbying by the American Medical Association, and insurance companies generally, led the New York legislature (as well as other states' legislatures) to reduce and structure the attorney's fee, so the higher the medical malpractice verdict the lower the percentage the lawyer receives.

In Tanabe, the defendants' insurance companies paid just $3,100,000, despite the $25,000,000 verdict. After expenses were deducted to reimburse the firm, the Tanabe family received close to $2,500,000, and we earned less than $500,000 in fees.

CHAPTER 33

"No Man Is an Island"

On March 1, 1979, Louise Aldycki, 45 years of age, gave birth to her sixth child, a son, by Caesarean section at Staten Island University Hospital. Two days later, she was diagnosed with pneumonia. Two days following the diagnosis, she collapsed and was brain dead by the time a Cardiac Code Team reached her.

On March 8, one week following the delivery, she died. This is the sad story of Ms. Aldycki's last week on earth as was brought out in Supreme Court, Richmond County, in 1984 before Judge Royal Radin and a Staten Island jury.

It is also the story of how friendship, honesty and bravery came together on the eve of trial to reveal the truth about Ms. Aldycki's death. And how a cross-examination capitalized on that truth to compel the defendant hospital's expert to concede liability on the witness stand.

THE FACTS

Ms. Aldycki was four weeks shy of her due date when she was admitted to Staten Island University Hospital on February 28, 1979 for possible pneumonia. Cultures were taken that day, but before the results were ready, her obstetrician decided to go ahead on March 1 and deliver the baby by C-section. Two days later, on March 3, the cultures came back positive for pneumonia and Ms. Aldycki was assigned to an isolation room on the maternity floor. The next day, Ms. Aldycki began to have difficulty breathing and became very emotionally upset; at around midnight going into March 5, she told one of the nurses who happened to be a long-time family friend (Joan Espisito) that she needed her husband to be with her right then, even though he had been at the hospital just two hours earlier.

Permission was given for Mr. Aldycki to be with his wife at that late hour, and he arrived at her room a few minutes after midnight. From that time on, he was with her while she was wringing her hands, was very distraught and was muttering that she was afraid to close her eyes out of fear that she would never wake up.

At about 1:40 a.m., the floor nurse (Ms. Kim) gave Ms. Aldycki a 5 mg Valium tablet. Ten minutes later, Ms. Aldycki turned very pale and complained of more difficulty breathing, so much so that she removed her false teeth, which was the first time she had ever let Mr. Aldycki see her without them.

Ms. Aldycki then started to turn blue. Mr. Aldycki left her room to find Nurse Kim and told her to please call a doctor because his wife was having great difficulty breathing. As they rushed back to Ms. Aldycki, Nurse Kim told him that she had called the resident on duty four times that night, and when she spoke to him at 1:30 a.m., he ordered the Valium for her anxiety and had said that she would be alright in a few minutes.

As soon as Mr. Aldycki and Nurse Kim returned to Ms. Aldycki's room, Mr. Aldycki saw his wife gasping for air and then, within moments, at about 1:50 a.m., she collapsed into unconsciousness. By the time the Code Team arrived, her pulse was absent, her eyes fixed and dilated, her brain dead.

THE LAWSUIT

We sued the obstetrician who delivered the baby, for his failure to delay the elective C-section until after the pneumonia culture results, because if the culture was positive (which it was), it was better practice to treat the infection before operating. This was particularly so when the due date was still four weeks out. We claimed as well that the obstetrician failed to timely transfer Ms. Aldycki to the ICU on March 3, immediately upon learning of the positive culture and pneumonia.

We sued the anesthesiologist at the delivery for improperly giving Ms. Aldycki the highest grade for anesthesia, which typically is reserved for healthy non-smokers, which Ms. Aldycki was not; and for her failure to advise the obstetrician that Ms. Aldycki was not a proper candidate for surgery at the time on account of respiratory difficulties.

We sued Staten Island University Hospital for its failure to timely and properly recognize that Ms. Aldycki was deteriorating rapidly due to lung obstructions, which resulted in inadequate blood flow and oxygenation to her heart and brain, leading to her death. We also claimed that the hospital failed to timely transfer her to the ICU, and to timely and properly resuscitate her.

During jury selection, the obstetrician and anesthesiologist settled for $300,000. I did not consider this a lot of money for a death such as Ms. Aldycki's, but the reason I settled was because I believed the case against them was a weak one: even if they erred in going ahead with the C-Section (possibly on account of an error in calculating the due date), and in giving too high a grade for anesthesia, the errors did not necessarily play a *substantial* role in Ms. Aldycki's death.

I made the same relatively low $300,000 demand of the hospital for a similar reason, because our medical experts who reviewed the hospital record were not impressed that we had a strong case. A secondary reason for the low demand was because in those days the law mandated that before going to trial, an impartial malpractice review panel had to consider the record and give its opinion. In this instance, the review panel concluded there was no malpractice on the part of the hospital, and that finding I knew would be introduced into evidence on the trial to assist the jury in its final determination.[4]

Unlike the doctors, the hospital did not agree to settle the case and so we were to come back to court the next day to select a *new jury* and

---

[4] In 1975, a law came into effect requiring that before any medical malpractice case could go to trial in New York State, it first had to be reviewed by a screening panel composed of one judge, one lawyer, and one doctor for each medical specialty implicated in the lawsuit. This meant that for each and every case, a panel had to be convened to read the medical records and legal briefs, and then hold informal hearings for the parties' lawyers to present argument. (The individuals involved – the complaining patient and accused medical personnel – did not appear.) If a panel's decision was unanimous, either that malpractice occurred or did not, then at the forthcoming trial the jury would be informed of the decision and could accept or reject it, based on the evidence produced at trial. If the panel was unable to reach a unanimous decision on a case, the jury would never even know that a panel had been convened.

In theory, these new panels were to weed out false claims of malpractice and to facilitate settlements, thereby reducing court backlogs. In practice, however, the panels had the opposite effect: settlements became scarcer as plaintiffs made higher demands and defendants made lower offers, depending on who prevailed at the panel stage; and court backlogs surged on account of delays in finding doctors and lawyers willing to participate on the panels. In 1982 Judge Gammerman, who had been named to oversee these panels for New York County, declared that they were "ill-conceived" and "should be repealed as soon as possible." The law was not repealed in time for our trial in Aldycki, and the defendants having won the panel decision had little incentive to offer much money in settlement. Thus, I only demanded $300,000.

start trial. (The decision to disband the jury we had just selected was discretionary, but both parties wanted it. The hospital's attorney wanted a new jury because the original jurors knew two defendants had dropped out and likely settled, and so they might infer that the hospital was also liable; we wanted it for the opposite reason, because the jury might believe the hospital was *not* liable because if it was, it too would have settled and dropped out.)

It seemed an inauspicious start, settling against two defendants and going ahead against another when everyone seemed to think we did not have a strong case. And yet we won.

THE TRIAL

There were a number of reasons why we won the trial:

1. Because of the inestimable aid given to me by the obstetrician's lawyer at the last minute.

2. Because Mr. Aldycki was at the hospital in Ms. Aldycki's room with her continuously from just after midnight on March 5 until she became unconscious at about 1:50 a.m. and thereafter.

3. Because Nurse Espisito, who had known Ms. Aldycki and her children when they lived in the same neighborhood 15 years before, and who was assigned to the maternity floor at that time, agreed to testify about the events leading up to the collapse even though she was still employed by the hospital and was fearful that she would be fired after she testified.

4. Because the hospital called as its expert witness an obstetrician who had failed to read the hospital record as carefully as he should have and made a fatal error from which he could not extricate himself.

1. FRIENDSHIP: LAST-MINUTE PROOF

Right after I settled the case against the doctors, luck, honor and friendship changed everything. The lawyer for the settling obstetrician – against whom I had tried many cases and whom I respected for his skill and integrity – knew something important regarding the hospital which he knew I didn't know. As he left the courthouse that day, he told me to look at the hospital record again and check the time of the Code.

That evening I did so. I quickly found the time the Code was *called* (2:00 a.m.) in the "Progress Notes" of the hospital record. This notation of 2:00 a.m. was what I, my firm and our medical experts all had known about and relied upon. What none of us had noticed, though, was that on a separate page at the end of the hospital record, mixed in with the "Order" sheets, there was an "Arrest" page that listed the time the Code Team *arrived* as 2:27 a.m. - 27 minutes after the Code was called.

Every hospital has an Emergency Code System and a Code Team meant to respond immediately - within one to two minutes - after a Code is broadcast over a loudspeaker, signaling that a patient in a certain room needs to be resuscitated. The short response time is critical because it is estimated that a patient will become brain dead if the brain is deprived of oxygen for between four and eight minutes.

After I finished reviewing the hospital record, I had found only those two entries about the Code: the 2:00 a.m. call time that Nurse Kim, the maternity floor nurse, wrote in the Nurses Notes; and the 2:27 a.m. arrival time that Nurse Tighe, the nursing supervisor, wrote on the Arrest page.

If both times were accurate, malpractice was assured because it was mandatory in all hospitals that a Code Team respond to a call within one to two minutes, and the 27-minute response time was incomprehensible and inexcusable. If one or both times were *not* accurate, if for example the Code was not called until 2:25 or 2:26 a.m., malpractice was assured because it was mandatory that the Code be called when Ms. Aldycki collapsed, which was between 1:50 a.m. and 2:00 a.m., and the 30- to 35-minute delay was incomprehensible and inexcusable.

Here then was the key to the case. Either the Code Team was inexcusably delayed in arriving; or the maternity nurses inexcusably delayed calling the Code until 2:25 a.m., which Nurse Kim tried to cover up by writing that they made the call at 2:00 a.m. Under either scenario, the hospital was grossly at fault.

When we returned to court the following day to select the new jury, I told the hospital's trial lawyer Anna Waldherr that I would not renege on my $300,000 settlement demand if the hospital met it at that time, but that once we started on trial, the demand would be withdrawn and we would have to take a verdict. She understood and still refused to settle the case. And so we went to trial and to verdict, and the jury awarded us 20 times the $300,000 figure we asked.

2. HONESTY: A WITNESS WHO GAVE VOICE TO THE VOICELESS

Mr. Aldycki was the perfect witness for a Staten Island jury, the reason being he had been a fireman – until forced to retire because of a spinal injury that even with surgery left him permanently disabled – and Staten Islanders are known to revere firefighters more than anyone else.

Mr. Aldycki's story was simple and clear, and he told it honestly and without the slightest embellishment. He told the jury that he and Ms. Aldycki (née Scaramuzzo) lived together for five years raising her five children and, even though they were not formally married, they held themselves out to be husband and wife. He told them how he had always wanted a child of his own and, even though Ms. Aldycki was 45 years old, she agreed to have another child.

Mr. Aldycki then told the jurors about his wife's terror as he was at her bedside in the isolation room shortly before she slipped into unconsciousness. He told the jury about the muttering, the hand-wringing, the gasping, her removing the false teeth, her fear of closing her eyes and then her turning blue. He also told them that the Code was not called at the time his wife collapsed.

He told the jury how when his wife turned blue, Nurse Kim left the room and came back with Nurse Espisito. Nurse Espisito then said that they needed to get additional help immediately, and they left together and returned with two nursery room nurses. The four nurses tried to revive Ms. Aldycki, but without success and, according to Mr. Aldycki, it was not until about one-half hour after Ms. Aldycki collapsed that one of the nurses called the hospital operator asking that a Code be called. When the Code Team arrived, Ms. Aldycki was unconscious. The Team tried to resuscitate her and then took her to the ICU.

Mr. Aldycki did what not many witnesses can, which was to give voice to the deceased in the moments leading up to their death. His presence in his wife's room, continuously from midnight until she became unconscious at about 1:50 a.m., meant that he was able to relay to the jury what she in death could not: the fear, the pain, the suffering and the knowledge that she was about to die. And from Mr. Aldycki's demeanor, the jurors knew that what he said was the unfortunate truth.

3. BRAVERY: A SELFLESS NURSE

Nurse Espisito was a 35-year-old Licensed Practical Nurse on the 11:00 p.m. to 7:00 a.m. shift (March 4-5), assisting Nurse Kim. They were the only two nurses caring for 25 women then on the maternity floor. Ms. Espisito was the family friend who telephoned Mr. Aldycki at about midnight, after she had stopped in to say hello and Ms. Aldycki asked to have her husband return to the hospital to be with her because she was afraid she was about to die.

When I spoke to Nurse Espisito just prior to trial, she told me that she had nightmares about the events of March 4 to 5 because of how everything had gone wrong in the treatment of Ms. Aldycki. She also told me, however, that she could not testify as a witness for the family because she still worked at Staten Island University Hospital and she was the sole supporter for her three children and she knew she would be fired immediately if she took the witness stand.

When I told her that I would subpoena her to testify and that the subpoena should protect her, especially since all we would ask her to do was tell the truth, she begged me not to do so because she could not afford to lose her livelihood. I tried every way I possibly could to persuade her to do what she had to know was her duty to do, namely to be a neighbor in the truest sense of the word for another mother's children and try to see that justice was done for them.

She continued to tearfully beg me not to compel her to do what she knew would end up harming her own children. I asked her to seriously think about it overnight and if, the next day, she still refused I would understand and not call her as a witness.

The next day, the first witness I called to the stand was not Nurse Espisito but Nurse Kim. One reason being that she was the only one who had written anything in the hospital record about Ms. Aldycki between midnight and 2:30 a.m. on March 5. Her testimony was basically that she attended to Ms. Aldycki and 24 other mothers who had recently given birth, and that she and Nurse Espisito were the only two nurses on the maternity floor.

She told the jury that there was only one doctor on duty for her to call if one of her patients on the Maternity Ward had to be seen and examined by a doctor, and that he was a first-year resident who was *also* the only doctor in charge of the Delivery Room, as well as the Obstetrics Department's ER that night. She said she had tried to reach him via beeper and through the telephone operator on four occasions in regard to Ms. Aldycki, and the only time she spoke to him by phone was at 1:30 a.m., when he ordered the Valium for Ms. Aldycki, which Nurse Kim administered at 1:40 a.m. The last time that he had been to the Maternity floor was shortly before midnight.

Nurse Kim also testified that she wrote in the Nurses Notes that she called the Code at 2:00 a.m., when Ms. Aldycki had taken a turn for the worse, and that the Code Team had arrived within one or two minutes.

When Nurse Kim had finished testifying, a tearful Nurse Espisito appeared in court. She agreed to testify, and her testimony was devastating for the hospital.

Nurse Espisito, extremely emotional on the stand, put the lie to all of Nurse Kim's testimony. She testified that at about 2:00 a.m., Nurse Kim came to her in a state of semi-shock and said she needed help with Ms. Aldycki, who had just become unconscious with a barely palpable pulse and blood pressure that had dropped to shock level. Nurse Kim told Nurse Espisito that she did not know what to do. Nurse Espisito told her to call the Code. Nurse Kim responded: "I don't know how to, I've never been in a Code." Nurse Espisito said to call Nurse Tighe, the nursing supervisor for the Maternity Ward. When Nurse Kim called her, Nurse Tighe said: "Don't call a Code until I get there and I evaluate the patient."

Nurse Espisito told the jurors that as Nurse Kim was speaking with Supervisor Tighe, she went to the Nursery to get two more nurses and together they went to Ms. Aldycki's room, checked her vital signs and performed CPR while waiting for Supervisor Tighe to arrive. One of the Nursery nurses telephoned Supervisor Tighe when she still had not arrived on the floor, and told her that this was an emergency and that they needed the Code to be called.

When Nurse Tighe told her not to do so until she saw the patient, the Nursery nurses disobeyed her orders and called the Code. Nurse Espisito testified that although she did not know exactly how many minutes had transpired, "it seemed like a long time" from when Nurse Kim asked for help – saying she didn't know how to call a Code – until they finally called the Code and the Code Team arrived.

4. CROSS-EXAMINATION: COMPELLING THE TRUTH FROM AN EXPERT

As Shakespeare might have phrased it, the cross-examination testimony of the Defendant Hospital's medical expert witness, Dr. Vincent Mastrota, was *the quietus* (death knell) to the hospital's attempt to deny liability for the omissions and commissions of its resident doctor and nurses in their non-treatment and treatment of Ms. Aldycki.

On direct examination by the Defendant Hospital's attorney Ms. Waldherr, Dr. Mastrota, an obstetrician, testified that there was no malpractice on the part of the hospital regarding the calling of and response to the Code. He told the jury that a Code is not to be called until there is cardiac or respiratory arrest and that when the Code Team arrived at 2:27 a.m. Ms. Aldycki still had a pulse and a measurable blood pressure and so was not in cardiac arrest and, therefore, there was no malpractice. However, as it came out during my cross-examination, Dr. Mastrota did not know the facts as well as he should have, because the hospital record was clear that when the Code Team arrived Ms. Aldycki did *not* have a pulse or measurable pressure.

If this error wasn't bad enough, he made truly fatal mistakes in the following exchange with Ms. Waldherr during his direct testimony:

> Q (Waldherr) – Can you tell us whether in your opinion . . . the telephone order [on March 5 at 1:30 a.m.] for 5 milligrams of Valium by mouth was appropriate?
>
> A (Dr. Mastrota) – Yes, it was, particularly since the patient was in I.C.U. . . . Because I.C.U. nurses are very good at reporting the patient's condition.

Dr. Mastrota's first mistake? He "volunteered" after he gave the answer "yes" that she was in the I.C.U. My first rule with all of my clients and witnesses is never volunteer information. The reason being that when you volunteer, your answer is not responsive to the question and, if it is helpful to your case, it will be stricken from the record, but if it is harmful to your case, it will be used against you on cross-examination.

Dr. Mastrota's second mistake? He did not know the hospital record as he should have. Ms. Aldycki was *not* in the ICU on March 5 – where we claimed she should have been – and it became obvious from Dr. Mastrota's answer that he too believed that's where she should have been, and that the hospital was at fault.

With all these mistakes during direct examination, Dr. Mastrota was ripe for cross-examination, and cross-examine him I did. From then on, it was all downhill for Dr. Mastrota and the hospital, so much so that Dr. Mastrota was forced to admit that the hospital staff departed from accepted and proper medical practice. His testimony was the death knell for the hospital, especially since Dr. Mastrota was the last witness of the trial and there was no time or opportunity to pull him from the game and bring in a relief pitcher.

The following are excerpts of Dr. Mastrota's testimony during my cross-examination, which belie his direct testimony. (One thing to note in my examination is when I ask him to "assume" certain facts. When lawyers question experts – whether on direct or cross – we are seeking their opinions. To allow them to reach these opinions, we are entitled to and indeed must state the facts upon which the opinions will be based.

But because the jurors have yet to "find" these facts, we ask the experts to *assume* them to be true, not wanting to invade the province of the jury.)

Q (DeBlasio) – Now, you mentioned yesterday – do you remember about the telephone call, you were asked about the valium?

A (Dr. Mastrota) – Yes.

Q – And do you remember saying, "Oh, that telephone call, that was okay, particularly since the patient was in ICU"?

A – Right.

Q – Which is short for intensive care unit?

A – Right.

Q – And intensive care unit nurses are very good?

A – Right.

Q – Number one, that's true. Intensive care unit nurses are very good. Right?

A – Yes.

Q – And when you said they're very good, I take it, I take it, and no criticism of anyone else, but that was to distinguish them from regular floor nurses; right?

A – In the sense that they are more accustomed to critically ill patients.

Q – More aware?

A – Yeah.

Q – More knowledgeable?

A – Not necessarily but they're –

Q – Accustomed, accustomed means more experienced?

A – True.

Q – If you got more experience, if you got brains, the more experience you get, the better informed you are in how to react and when to react; right?

A – Hopefully.

Q – Now, you said the phone call is okay, particularly since she was in ICU. When you said that, when you said that, is it a fact you believed she was in ICU?

A – Yes.

Q – And is it accurate for me to say the reason you believed it was because that's where she would have been if you were the doctor?

A – That's reasonable.

Q – Right. And that's good practice?

A – Yes.

Q – That's why she would have been there?

A – Right.

Q – And to be in ICU you have to be a certain kind of a patient?

A – Right.

Q – A patient who needs constant, constant monitoring and care?

A – Correct.

Q – A patient who is in critical condition or certainly on the road to being there?

A – Yes.

Q – And that's good and accepted and proper medical practice, to put a patient such as this in the ICU?

A – Yes.

Q – Good. When would you have put her there?

A – Well, probably sometime on the 3rd of March.

Q – You know for a fact now, don't you, she didn't go there until after she had her arrest and no pulses and was brain dead, you know that?

A – Yes.

Q – That was a bad departure, wasn't it, not to put her –

WALDHERR: Objection.

Q – That was a bad departure, wasn't it, not to put her in the ICU before that?

WALDHERR: I withdraw the objection.

A – I feel that it was less effective treatment than it should have been.

Q – All right. Just try to answer my questions. I'll leave out the bad. That was a departure not to put her in the ICU?

A – I would agree.

. . .

Q – Assume that on March the 4th, March 5th, the night of the 4th and the early hours of the 5th; assume that this patient, Miss Aldycki, was not in ICU. . . . Assume she had blood-tinged sputum.

Assume that after the husband got there, shortly after midnight, he observed his wife looking physically terrible, telling him she felt terrible, telling him she was having difficulty breathing.

Assume that a nurse's assistant . . . said that the patient appeared very anxious, in great distress, was continuously wringing her hands, and told her she felt "I am dying," she was afraid, afraid to close her eyes. . . .

Assume that this patient had a pulse of 134, 136, assume that this patient was short of breath. . . .

Assume that her blood pressure, which had been 130/70 in the afternoon of the day before. It was now 104/60, something like that. A drop of significance.

Assume that the nurses called the resident on call on three or four occasions informing him of all these events. Assume all that.

Assume that from a little after midnight to about 1:30 in the morning. Assume the resident did not come, assume no medical doctor came. And assume no treatment whatsoever was given to the patient. . . .

The circumstances I gave you right now, confine them to my circumstances.

That's good and accepted practice, don't do anything for her for the two hours, no doctor come and see her. That's good?

A – It's not good.

Q – That's not good?

A – No.

. . .

Q – Doctor, take into consideration under your review of this file that patient should have been in intensive care at that point. Okay? That's what you told us?

A – Yes.

Q – You told us that the failure to have her in intensive care was a departure from accepted practice. That is what you told us?

A – I didn't tell you it was a departure from accepted practice.

Q – Didn't you say that a few minutes ago when I was –

A – If I did, I didn't understand your question.

Q – You didn't?

A – You asked me would I have put her –

Q – Don't tell me what I asked you. You will confuse me. I will ask you again.

A – Okay.

Q – This patient, who according to you, had pneumonia from February 28th that was not diagnosed until March 3rd and was delayed four days to be given antibiotics and when they were given, wasn't given timely and wasn't given vigorously and wasn't given sufficiently. Did you not say – did you not say that those were departures?

A – Yes.

Q – Did you not say that the patient should have been in ICU from March 3rd?

A – I said I would have preferred her in ICU.

Q – Because that is what good practice called for; right?

A – It doesn't say she couldn't have gotten good practice elsewhere.

Q – All right. So you are telling us now, Doctor, you are telling us now, you didn't say on this record that good practice and accepted practice mandated her being in ICU?

A – I said that was my preference.

> THE COURT: I don't want to encourage or permit argument between counsel and the witness.
>
> Ladies and gentlemen, you will remember what the doctor said, and it will be your recollection that will count.

Q – In your opinion, you would have put this woman in intensive care unit because she was in a critical state or in a state that would lead to a critical state; right?

A – She was very ill, yes.

. . .

Q – Now, you got the code record in front of you?

A – Yes.

Q – What were the pulse – what was the pulse? Was it present or absent when that code team got there?

A – Absent.

Q – How long had it been absent before the code team got there?

A – I couldn't say that from this record.

Q – All right. You don't know?

A – I don't know.

Q – A pulse absent means what?

A – A pulse absent means there is no or little cardiac output. Not enough to provide a peripheral pulse.

Q – It could mean no cardiac output?

A – Yes.

Q – Which means what, no heart beat?

A – Right.

. . .

Q – Doctor, a very serious condition?

A – Absolutely.

Q – Okay. "Pulse absent." How long were they absent? Do you have any idea?

A – No. I told you I don't.

Q – They were absent when a team got there. You don't know how long they were absent before; right?

A – I don't.

Q – Okay. "Pupils fixed and dilated."

A – Correct.

Q – When the team got there; right?

A – Right.

Q – Do you know how long the pupils were fixed and dilated before the team got there?

A – No, I don't have any idea.

Q – All right. Pupils fixed, what does that mean?

A – It means that they fail to react.

. . .

Q – Does that have something to do with brain damage?

A – It is strongly suggestive of a significant neurological injury.

Q – Brain damage?

A – Brain damage, yes.

Q – All right. Pupils dilated; what does that mean?

A – Well, that goes along with fixed.

Q – Whether it goes along with it or not, what does it mean; widened?

A – Widened, widely open.

Q – Widely. So you look at a person who is dead or dying, and you are going to see wide pupils and fixed?

A – Well, it depends on the cause of death.

Q – If there is brain damage?

A – Yes.

Q – That's what she had when the code got there; right?

A – Yes.

Q – Doctor, how long, how long does it take before the brain is starved of oxygen for the pupils to get fixed and dilated?

A – There's not an absolute answer to that question, but generally, it's – usually, we would regard it between four and eight minutes as a critical period.

. . .

Q – Do you know what time the nurse says she called the code?

A – I don't remember. It's in the notes, the Nurses Notes.

Q – It says two o'clock?

A – Okay.

Q – Right? Do you know if that is true or not?

A – I don't know for sure.

Q – Certainly if she called the code at two and they didn't get there until 2:27, that is certainly way too long; right?

A – It is not a good response time.

Q – No. Certainly if she should have called the code at two, and didn't call it until to two-twenty-five, or two-twenty-six, that is not good either; right, if the code should be called at two and you delay a half hour or 25 minutes. That is not right either?

A – Not good.

Q – That is a departure from accepted practice?

A – Definitely.

. . .

Q – Now, in any event, going back to my question, assume that with all these conditions going on, at 1:50 a.m., according to the verified Nurses Note, the husband called the nurse.

Assume the husband has testified that just before he called the nurse his wife said, "I feel terrible. I can't breathe." She lifted up her oxygen. She took out her false teeth, which she never did before in her life, in his presence. They were only together four or five years. Took out the false teeth. Gave them to him. "I can't breathe" and collapsed, head rolled back, unconscious.

Assume that is 1:50 a.m.

A – Okay.

Q – He went out in the hall and yelled for the nurse, "Please come in. Help my wife."

Assume the nurse and nurse's aide came in, checked the patient's condition. Immediately called for a doctor at 1:50 o'clock.

Was that accepted and good practice for the nurse to call for the doctor immediately?

A – Yes.

Q – Assume the doctor – the doctor – the doctor never came, never called until he came with the code team at two 2:27, 37 minutes later.

Was that good practice for the doctor not to come?

A – The patient was unconscious during this time?

Q – Yes.

A – No.

Q – That was bad practice?

A – It was not appropriate.

Q – That was a departure from good practice; right?

A – Yes.

Q – Not only was the patient unconscious during this time, the nurse couldn't obtain a pulse. The nurse had difficulty in obtaining a blood pressure. It could only get 60 for systolic.

The nurse didn't know what to do with the doctor not coming, so the nurse then went to other nurses on the floor, who were ICU nurses for infants, and asked for help. Okay.

Assume they came in, they got thready pulse but no significant pulse, no significant blood pressure.

The doctor still didn't come during all this time, from ten minutes to two until 2:27. No doctor came. That's a departure from accepted and proper medical practice in this community at this time?

A – During this time the patient was pulseless, with –

Q – Thready pulse, no obtainable blood pressure.

A – Not responsive?

Q – Absolutely not responsive. That's departure from accepted and proper medical practice, isn't it?

A – Yes.

Q – On the part of the nursing or medical staff of the hospital; right?

A – Whoever was responsible.

. . .

Q – Doctor, had the doctor responded at that time, what would good and proper medical practice have been to do?

A – Well, obviously immediate supportive measures, CPR, intubation perhaps, oxygen, et cetera. Stimulants, perhaps.

Q – And those measures are measures which are designed to prevent the patient from dying; right?

A – Yes.

Q – Designed to prevent the patient from becoming brain dead so that if she was going to live, she is not going to be a vegetable; right?

A – Yes.

Q – Designed to get the oxygen flowing in the heart, working as it should.

A – Designed to return the patient to normal physiologic function.

Q – Right. And had they given prompt and proper treatment at that time, is it reasonable to say that, based on the facts given to you, prompt and reasonable treatment could have prevented the irreversible brain damage?

A – I don't think anybody can say that one way or the other.

Q – Could have prevented the death?

A – Once again, I don't think anybody can say that one way or the other.

Q – Just think to yourself, think to yourself. In your mind, in *your* mind, did you ever have the opinion, after review of these records, that this patient's demise – just think to yourself – may very well have been preventable?

A – Yes.

Q – With good proper medical treatment?

A – Yes.

MR. DeBLASIO: Thank you.

THE OUTCOME: JUSTICE DONE AND PARTIALLY UNDONE

In my summation I quoted John Donne, the great English clergyman and poet, from his essay well known for its line "For Whom the Bell Tolls" written 350 years before our trial. I thought it appropriate because in it he writes that no man is an island entire of itself but part of the mainland, and that any man's death diminishes me because I am part of mankind.

I adapted his words to the island where we in the courtroom were sitting. Staten Island, though an island, was still part of the mainland and still part of the greatest city in the country, and we deserved not to be treated like an impoverished Third World country when we were as prisoners in a hospital. We too were entitled to the best medical care that New York was known for, as opposed to providing two nurses for 25 patients, and just one resident doctor for the Delivery Room, Emergency Room and the entire Maternity floor.

For that one doctor not to see Ms. Aldycki for two hours after being told that she was worsening and possibly dying, and for the nurse in charge of the maternity floor to never have been in a Code and to never have been trained in Code procedure, were gross departures from proper medical and hospital practice anywhere in the world let alone in New York City.

I asked the jury to toll the bells that John Donne had written about, not only to announce the death of one of our neighbors but to be a wakening call. I asked the jury to be the conscience of the community in preventing what happened to Ms. Aldycki and her family from happening in the future to their neighbors. I then said what I believed would be fair and just was $5,000,000: $4,000,000 for her children for her wrongful death, and $1,000,000 for her pain and suffering. The jury gave a million more than I asked.

The jury awarded a total of $6,000,000: $4,500,000 for wrongful death, and $1,500,000 for Ms. Aldycki's pain and suffering. The jurors found that the hospital was 80% liable and the obstetrician with whom we had settled was 20% liable. The hospital was therefore responsible for $4,800,000. (Had the obstetrician not settled for $300,000, his portion of the verdict would have been $1,200,000.) The verdict of $6,000,000 was the highest award ever recorded in Staten Island up to that time in a personal injury or wrongful death case.

After the verdict, Ms. Waldherr told me that John Donne was her favorite poet. However, I guess her principals at Staten Island University Hospital did not feel the same way because they appealed the verdict on two grounds: 1) my summation was inflammatory and the John Donne quotation improper; and 2) the award was excessive.

The Defendant Hospital had a legitimate reason to argue on appeal that the award was excessive because it was more than I had said in my summation would be fair and just. I think the reason the jurors added that extra $1,000,000 to the award I asked for was because they felt that punitive damages were proper in this case.

The Appellate Division did not agree with the jurors. The judges reduced the award to $1,000,000: $750,000 for wrongful death, and $250,000 for pain and suffering. The $250,000 I can understand; the $750,000 I cannot.

Only $750,000 for Mrs. Aldycki's four surviving children under the age of 21, to compensate them for an unimaginable loss. The birth of the new baby was to be a time of joy and instead it grossly altered the course of her children's lives. The three children in high school at the time of her death all quit school immediately or shortly thereafter, completely grief-stricken and unable to ever return to get their degrees. And her infant, delivered prematurely, was not only left to grow up without his mother's love, attention and embrace, but to know that it was the circumstances of his birth that led to her death.

In regard to my summation, the Appellate Division found no error. However, when I later met with Justice Sybil Kooper, one of the appellate panelists on our case, she said: "Peter, next time you quote John Donne's 'For Whom the Bell Tolls' in a summation, quote it accurately." I accepted her scolding as appellate permission for me to continue with my "For Whom the Bell Tolls" summations, which I did. And from that time on, no trial judge or appellate court ever criticized me for doing so.

POSTSCRIPT: In so many of my cases I wanted to give money to lay witnesses who had been helpful to us at trial, particularly those like Joan Espisito who risked their careers to do what was right and what was just. But to pay a witness even after trial, as a sign of gratitude and not at all to influence their testimony, would violate ethical rules we had to follow. So, I never did get to thank Nurse Espisito in a way I think she deserved.

As to what did ever happen, if the hospital fired her as she feared it might, I cannot be certain, but I think I would have heard from Mr. Aldycki if it did.

As for Staten Island Hospital, it did not have the insurance coverage nor its own funds anywhere near sufficient to cover the record-setting $6,000,000 judgment. Who knows what it would have done if the amount were not so drastically reduced to $1,000,000. Fortunately, in the 21st century, Staten Island Hospital has been well run and well staffed and is now the leading hospital in Staten Island, providing good medical care to its patients - me among them.

CHAPTER 34

"A *LITTLE* CRIMINAL EXPERIENCE"?

I once conducted a direct examination of myself. It was under such unusual circumstances that I doubt many, if any, other lawyers before or since have ever done such a thing. And so I include the story here.

It came about during the Bronfman trial, or actually just before it, and the underlying facts were complicated.

During the year that we waited for the trial to take place – in large part due to Lynch's two prison escape attempts and serious resulting injuries when he jumped out a window – I made a motion to keep Dominic's signed confession out of the trial. On September 8, 1976, the day we were finally scheduled to begin trial proceedings, Judge Beisheim held a hearing on my motion. Higgins had also filed a motion to keep Lynch's confession out and, as he was the lead defendant, his hearing occurred first. The two hearings took 12 court days.

The thrust of my argument was that while the agents and prosecutors were interrogating Dominic following his arrest on Sunday, August 17, 1975 (beginning at 3:30 a.m.) – but before he signed his confession (at 5:15 p.m.) – I had telephoned the FBI offices (at 2:10 p.m.) and asked to speak with my client. When my request was denied, I directed the prosecutors to stop questioning Dominic. When the prosecutors, Assistant U.S. Attorneys Gerald Feffer and Laurence Pedowitz, ignored my direction they violated Dominic's constitutional right to counsel, particularly as I was advising that he remain silent.

Thus, the confession Dominic signed for the FBI agents after my call, as well as the two statements he signed for the prosecutors (one on Sunday late-afternoon, one on Monday morning), had to be suppressed. The jury should never hear what Dominic admitted.

In his written opposition to my motion to exclude the confession, Orlando included sworn statements from Assistants Feffer and Pedowitz that I had *not* asked them to cease all questioning.

I am arguing the motion to suppress Dominic's confession, after examining myself and cross-examining two federal prosecutors and several FBI agents, regarding my 2:10 p.m. phone call to FBI headquarters to stop all questioning of Dominic on the day of his arrest. Judge Beisheim credited my testimony above that of the others, and suppressed Dominic's written confession as it was signed only after my call. In Solomon-like fashion, however, he allowed the two FBI agents who questioned Dominic to testify at trial about everything he confessed to them up to the time of my call.

Geoffrey K. Orlando, the Assistant District Attorney prosecuting the case, is in the foreground. Dominic is seated in the background.

Judge Beisheim had to determine the facts – who was truthful – me or the two Assistant U.S. Attorneys. Did I or did I not say the questioning was to cease?

To do so, Judge Beisheim held a suppression hearing. Orlando called ten witnesses, including Assistants Feffer and Pedowitz and the two FBI agents who questioned Dominic. I cross-examined them and then called the two agents I spoke with at 2:10 p.m. (Mertens and Ingram) when trying to hunt down the Assistants – and I called myself as a witness.

When I appeared before Judge Beisheim for that hearing, I was not sanguine about success. Over the previous year, I had made several motions for bail, always assigned to different judges, and then when each motion was denied, I had appealed it. Thus, by the time of the suppression hearing, I had appeared before just about every Westchester County judge, including Judge Beisheim, and had felt every judge's disdain, though I was never quite sure if it was because I was representing someone they likely found reprehensible, or because they thought I was not competent to do so. By the end of the suppression hearing, however, I was shockingly surprised and grateful by what seemed to be Judge Beisheim's radical change of attitude toward me.

At the hearing, just about every FBI agent I cross-examined left the witness stand with their testimony riddled by inconsistencies and their reliability in question. The testimony that proved most galling, though, was that of James Ingram, the FBI Special Agent in Charge of Internal Security, whom I had called as a witness. It came about as follows.

When I first phoned the FBI office at 2:10 p.m. on the day of Dominic's arrest, I spoke with Ingram and he gave me a real run-around, saying he didn't know where Dominic was, or if he'd even been arrested. He advised that I call the U.S. Attorney's Office to find out. I did, only to be told that the attorneys assigned to the case, Feffer and Pedowitz, were over at the FBI office and I should call there to speak with them. It wasn't until 2:40 that I finally got through, and only later did I find out that the whole time I was making these phone calls, Dominic was being interrogated in Ingram's 10th floor corner office.

When I asked Ingram about this on the witness stand at the suppression hearing, his response was: "I was unaware of all the intricacies of the case and who was where." I don't think that Judge Beisheim believed or appreciated it when the New York FBI's #3 man stated under oath he did not know that one of two suspects in the biggest kidnapping case in NY-FBI history was being questioned in his very own private office.

Then I cross-examined Assistants Feffer and Pedowitz about my call requesting that they advise Dominic that he had a lawyer, and that they stop interrogating him. They readily admitted they didn't advise Dominic he had a lawyer, but they denied I ever spoke with them about stopping the interrogation:

> Q (DeBlasio) – When you returned to the room with Dominic Byrne after my call to you, did you then tell him that a lawyer who had been retained by his family had spoken to you?
>
> A (Feffer) – No, not at that time.
>
> Q – Did you at any time tell him that I had called you?
>
> A – Yes.
>
> Q – When did you tell him that?
>
> A – After the interview was completed.
>
> . . .
>
> Q – And did I not ask to speak to Dominic Byrne?
>
> A – No.
>
> Q – No conversation of that at all?
>
> A – Absolutely not.
>
> Q – In no way during that conversation did you make the assumption or get the impression that I was calling asking to speak to Dominic Byrne and if that were not possible that Dominic Byrne was not to be questioned from that time on?
>
> A – Quite to the contrary, my sole assumption from that conversation was that you were in New Hampshire and you were concerned as to when you had to physically be present in court.

Orlando, for some reason, decided to get up on redirect to ask Feffer a single question, which then allowed me to really blast Feffer on recross:

> Q (Orlando) – Do you recall the substance of the conversation that took place with Mr. DeBlasio?

A – Yes, I do. . . . He asked me several questions about the procedure that was going to be followed in our courthouse. He indicated that he had little of any criminal experience and that his field was negligence law.

MR. ORLANDO: Thank you very much. I have no further questions.

RECROSS EXAMINATION

BY MR. DeBLASIO:

Q – I indicated a "*little*" criminal experience?

A – I think you told me that you had --

Q – Four years Assistant United States Attorney prosecuting only criminal cases, perhaps 50 to a conclusion.

A – I think --

Q – Wait, wait. Is that what I told you?

A – If I can answer it. I don't know if you are making a statement or you want me to answer the question.

Q – You say I told you I had "little" criminal experience?

A – You said --

Q – No, no. Can you answer that yes or no?

A – I would like to answer the question.

Q – Don't explain it yet. Can you answer that yes or no?

A – I cannot answer --

Q – Now, I believe, Mr. Feffer, you just stated that I indicated to you I had little criminal experience; is that a fair statement of what you said?

A – I believe that is exactly what I said. . . . You had no idea, for example, as to when the time period was for us to indict. . . . You told me that you had been in the United States Attorney's office in the '60's, but since that time you had been involved principally with negligence. You told me about a million-dollar verdict which

> you had recently secured in the negligence area. And I repeated your comments to many other people in the office at that time. And that answered my question as to why the previous day you had not instructed the FBI or myself not to speak to your client.

Judge Beisheim barely hid his disgust during Feffer's testimony. What I imagine most affected Judge Beisheim was Feffer's arrogance and brazen unethical behavior: in one breath mocking my legal skills, while in another casually agreeing that he ignored his duty to advise a defendant that he was now represented by counsel.

I called myself as the final witness.

> THE COURT: If you will, please.
>
> THE WITNESS (DeBlasio): Yes.

> Q (by DeBlasio) – What is your occupation?
>
> A (by DeBlasio) – I am a lawyer.
>
> Q – On August 17, 1975, did you make a telephone call to the F.B.I. offices in New York City?
>
> A – Yes, I did.
>
> Q – What time was that call?
>
> A – 2:10 p.m.
>
> Q – Did you speak to anyone?
>
> A – Yes.
>
> Q – To whom did you speak first?
>
> A – I spoke to a lady at the number of 535-7700, area code 212, and I asked her name. She said her name was Mary L. Mertens. I asked her to spell the Mertens. It was: M-e-r-t-e-n-s.
>
> I told her my name was Peter DeBlasio, that I was an attorney and that I was making a call, having spoken to the Dominic Byrne family, and I was calling the FBI offices to speak to someone in charge about Dominic Byrne.
>
> She asked me to hold on.

> Before that, I asked her to please make a note of the time. I remember at that time I said the time I had was 2:12.
>
> She asked me to hold on, and then I spoke to a man. I asked his name. He said it was Ingram. I asked if he were an FBI agent. He said he was. I told him my name, told him that I was a lawyer, that I had been an Assistant United States Attorney. . . . I told him that I had been retained . . . to represent Dominic Byrne. . . .
>
> I, therefore, asked Mr. Ingram for permission to speak to Dominic Byrne. He told me he did not know where he was. I asked if he was arrested. He said, "I don't know that." I asked him when he was going to be arraigned. He said, "I don't know." . . . I said, is there somebody there who can give me this information and who could let me speak to Dominic Byrne, and he said, "I suggest you speak to the United States Attorney." I asked him, the Southern District or the Eastern District? He said he didn't know.
>
> . . . . I asked him if . . . he would try to find out some of the answers to the questions I was asking . . . . He said he would try.
>
> We hung up. At 2:40 I called the same number again. I asked to speak to Mr. Ingram. A man [Feffer] got on the phone and I asked if it was Mr. Ingram. He said, "No." I said . . . I had spoken with Mr. Ingram [and] [h]e said he was going to try to get some information. [Feffer] said, "Yes, I know all about that. . . . In answer to your questions, Dominic Byrne has been arrested [and] he is going to be arraigned tomorrow on Monday. . . ." I asked if I could speak with Dominic Byrne. He said he didn't know where he was.
>
> I said, "Is there anybody who does know where he is?"
>
> He said, "No."
>
> I told him that . . . I wanted it noted that I was representing Dominic Byrne, been retained by him and I wanted no questions and no answers of or by him without me being present.

Orlando then cross-examined me, and we were done.

What the basic legal issue boiled down to at the hearing was credibility. Judge Beisheim had to determine who was truthful – the Assistant U.S. Attorneys or me. To do so, he had to consider and weigh the demeanor and background of the antagonists, again the Assistant U.S. Attorneys and me.

His finding? I was the truthful one.

The day before we began picking the jury, Judge Beisheim issued a written decision and in it he blasted the Assistants, effectively calling them liars but with carefully chosen and polite words:

> There was some difference in the recollection of Mr. Feffer and Mr. DeBlasio as to what was said in their conversation. The court finds, however, that Mr. Feffer was vague and indecisive and had a hazy recollection and accepts Mr. DeBlasio's testimony as to what was stated in this conversation, the important parts of which were that Mr. DeBlasio told Mr. Feffer that he represented the Defendant Dominic Byrne and that he wanted no further questioning of Byrne or for Byrne to sign any statements except in his (DeBlasio's) presence.
>
> Mr. Feffer was unable to state what statements contained in the so-called pre-arraignment statement of Byrne were taken before the telephone conversation with Mr. DeBlasio and what part of the statement was taken after the telephone conversation. Mr. Feffer also admitted that he did not tell Byrne that his attorney had called until the pre-arraignment interview was completed at about 2:50 P.M. and Byrne had signed the statements. Mr. Feffer and Mr. Pedowitz took a second pre-arraignment statement in the early morning of August 18, 1975, before Mr. DeBlasio arrived for the arraignment.

Judge Beisheim, I repeat, was a great judge. While the *federal* prosecutors more than earned his admonishment, Judge Beisheim recognized that the *state* prosecutor's office did not deserve to have Dominic's confession to the FBI completely excluded from their trial in state court. And so he continued in Solomon-like manner.

He suppressed the *written* document that Dominic signed and gave to the FBI, because Dominic signed it after my initial 2:10 p.m. phone call, but he was *not* suppressing the *oral* statements that Dominic made up to 2:10 p.m. – he was going to allow the FBI agents to testify at trial as to everything Dominic confessed to them *before* the 2:10 p.m. call. (On account of Ingram's interference, he didn't go by the 2:40 p.m. call when I actually spoke with Feffer and Pedowitz.)

As for Dominic's *oral* statements to the FBI *after* 2:10 p.m., which Judge Beisheim was suppressing, the judge found that they were "of minor significance." He believed the FBI agents when they testified that everything important they learned from Dominic they learned before my call. According to them, after my call Dominic just spoke about matters of personal social history – that he smoked marijuana and frequented gay bars – nothing substantive about the kidnapping offense itself.

As for the federal prosecutors Feffer and Pedowitz, Judge Beisheim excluded them and everything they had to say utterly and completely from the trial: he would not permit the two written statements that they had Dominic sign in blatant disregard of my phone call, nor would he allow them to testify as to Dominic's oral statements to them.

Obviously, Judge Beisheim granted me a Pyrrhic victory – the jurors would not read Dominic's confession, but they would hear all about it from the FBI agents. But I was pleased. Although I lost that pre-trial battle, the judge's mindset toward me had changed, he had found that I had integrity (at least more than the federal prosecutors). And this may have been why he allowed me so much leeway when we began jury selection the next day, which is what of course clinched the trial. This bizarre and incredibly unusual direct examination of myself, in a way then, ended up playing an important role in our ultimate victory.

POSTSCRIPT: Lynch did not have an attorney at the time of his arrest and confession; the court appointed one for him the following day, at the initial appearance on Monday, August 18, 1975. Thus, unlike Dominic, nobody called in on his behalf to stop his interrogation, and so he didn't have much of an argument to make to suppress his statements.

Even though Lynch had not signed his confession – ever savvier than Dominic – it didn't matter, he had initialed that he understood his rights and was making his statement voluntarily. As a result, Higgins was not successful in keeping it out of the trial. The jurors not only saw the handwritten confession, but they heard it read aloud. After the verdict, Higgins appealed Judge Beisheim's ruling admitting the confession into evidence, and he attached a copy of the initialed statement, which is why in addition to the trial transcript, a copy of the handwritten statement has also been preserved.

A courtroom artist's sketch of me during the Bronfman trial.

CHAPTER 35

THE BEST AND THE BRIGHTEST

Before the Bronfman trial, I would have told anyone, if asked, that I had never met a better class of men than the Special Agents of the FBI. I had worked closely with many FBI agents in the 1950s – and in those days the agents were all men – when I was an Assistant U.S. Attorney. They were our investigators, companions, friends and witnesses, and they were of immeasurable aid to me and all of my federal prosecutor colleagues when we tried cases against individuals charged with committing federal crimes, such as bank robbery, transporting stolen goods in interstate commerce, transporting kidnap victims across state lines, and the like.

Up until the start of the Bronfman trial, I respected them for their professionalism, honesty and devotion to duty. However, as I began to cross-examine them at trial, I very quickly became more circumspect in my praise. They were ill-prepared, their recollection was often faulty, they became easily confused, they misspoke, and on occasion they skirted the truth. By the end of trial, I do not think that anyone in the courtroom was more disheartened than I at the FBI's reputation in near shambles.

Almost without exception, I exposed a blunder or gaffe so unbelievable that the jurors, and eventually the court staff, were caused to laugh uncontrollably and it was like being back in Brooklyn at the Loew's Oriental movie theater watching one of the Marx Brothers' zaniest films. These once mighty men left the witness stand fearful for their career advancement, not knowing what had just hit them.

I had to do it. The facts were 100% against us. The only way to win this trial would be on cross-examination, by distraction, confusion, sleight-of-hand, smoke and mirrors, magnifying glass, whatever it took to get the jurors to turn their backs on the privileged Bronfman family and the pretentious FBI agents. I needed the jurors first to lose confidence in the government, and then to lose interest in their case altogether.

To accomplish these goals, I thought I'd inject some humor into the proceedings. I started on day one.

POSTAGE DUE

On Thursday October 14, 1976, our first day of trial, Orlando called a number of civilian witnesses to the stand. His third witness was Frank Vida, a doorman at Edgar's posh Park Avenue apartment building. He had been the one to receive the initial ransom letter, by special delivery from a postman. I knew immediately from the direct examination that I could get a laugh out of the jurors, and not at Vida's expense.

Orlando asked Vida just a few questions, among them what he did when the postman handed him the letter. He said he gave him ten cents for the excess postage, and that he wrote on the back of the envelope: "Doorman Frank Vida paid postman ten cents for postage due." Orlando left off at that. Higgins, as counsel for the lead defendant, went next and spent about four times as long on cross-examination as Orlando had on direct, and didn't ask much. My turn came and I started right in:

Q – Mr. Vida, did you get the dime back?

A – No, sir.

Q – Didn't? Part of the hazards of the job?

A – Yes, sir, yes.

The jurors loved it. I had hand-picked them for a reason. They were regular citizens, everyday blue-collar workers just like the first few witnesses: the postman, Bronfman's doorman Frank Vida, Bronfman's elevator operator, and the superintendent at Bronfman's building. These were people I'd known all my life, they were like my father and mother, my father a postal employee himself, and my mother a garment factory worker.

From the very beginning of the trial, I had the jurors identifying with the little man at the expense of the ultra-wealthy Bronfmans. At the time of the kidnapping, a dime was nothing to Edgar Bronfman, who inherited $225,000,000 at the age of 11. But to a doorman – and to many of my jurors – ten cents was a calculable percentage of their hourly wage. "Hazards of the job?" It was a joke, but it was no joke. I knew it and the jurors knew it.

WHAT'S IN A NAME? (OR IN INITIALS, AS THE CASE MAY BE)

Our styles as lawyers were very different. It's difficult to describe oneself, and not always kind to describe another, so I leave it to THE NEW YORK TIMES reporter M.A. Farber, because I think it's worth knowing, to get a sense of the mood of the trial on a day-to-day basis. In a long article he wrote toward the end of the trial, Farber compared and contrasted us and, as in most things, he was in my opinion just right: Orlando spoke in a monotone, without emotion, and said very little in court, rarely interrupting anyone; Higgins was tenacious, but painstakingly slow, "tending to stare out the window for as much as a minute between questions," sometimes even apologizing to the jury for his delays; and I was "rapid-fire" and "far more assured in manner." Farber continued, quite perceptively, that Higgins and I "mirrored the demeanor" of our clients: Lynch sitting somberly, while Dominic seldom stopped smiling, at the jurors, the judge, the reporters, his family, and everyone else in the courtroom. M.A. Farber, THE NEW YORK TIMES, "Reporter's Notebook: Enter Samuel Bronfman 2d, the 48th Witness," Nov. 15, 1976.

I think that's right. I felt it was my courtroom, I could smile, laugh, joke, whereas Orlando and Higgins never felt comfortable doing so.

When Orlando began calling his FBI agent witnesses, I picked them off rapid-fire one, two, three. The first up was Special Agent John T. Kunst, a six-year veteran of the FBI. Following Orlando's strict chronological order, Kunst took the stand immediately after the building super, from whom he picked up the ransom letter on Monday, August 11, which was two days after the kidnapping and 24 hours since the letter had been sitting outside the door of Edgar Bronfman's vacated Park Avenue duplex penthouse apartment.

Kunst was the last witness of the first trial day, and during the dry direct examination he was shown the ransom letter and asked if it was the very same one he picked up from the building super more than a year earlier. At Orlando's request, Agent Kunst dutifully looked at the back of the letter and testified that he knew this was the very same one because of the initials. Orlando then offered it into evidence. (One of the techniques agents use for purposes of identification is to write their names or initials as well as the date on the evidence, or sealed evidence bag, when they discover or recover it at a scene, and then at the trial they are able to establish the authenticity of the item by identifying the signature or initials as their own. In this instance, as more than one agent had handled the letter and envelope during the investigation, there was more than one set of initials and in different color ink on the back of both of them.)

It was now our turn to question Kunst. Whenever a lawyer *offers* into evidence a letter, or photo, or other item, before the judge *admits* it, opposing counsel is permitted to "voir dire" the witness through whom the item is being offered. As it sounds, the purpose is to get at the truth. In the case of the ransom letter, in the middle of Orlando's direct examination of Agent Kunst, at the moment he offered the letter and its envelope, Higgins and I objected to their admission and were permitted to cross-examine, or voir dire, Kunst. We asked questions to determine whether the letter and envelope were the same true *originals* he had handled the year before, to make sure they were not altered, not copies, not fakes, not forgeries. (In the case of a *copied* document or a photo offered into evidence, the voir dire would be similar: we would ask questions to make sure the item offered was a true and accurate representation of the original or, if a photo, that it was a true and accurate depiction of how the scene appeared at the time the photo was taken.)

What then unfolded was straight out of the Joe Pesce and Marisa Tomei movie "My Cousin Vinnie" – or maybe the movie copied from us. Higgins went first, and while he was asking a few questions, in his very slow, deliberate manner, I had a chance to look at the letter and envelope, which I had not seen before. I pulled out of my briefcase the magnifying glass that I was in the habit of bringing to court since my days as an Assistant U.S. Attorney, and took a closer look. When Higgins finished, I nearly rocketed out of my seat. I handed the letter to the deputy to give to the witness, and I got straight to the point with my first question:

> Q – Are your initials, Mr. Kunst, in the black pen or the blue pen?

There was a long pause as Kunst studied the back of the letter, confusion registering on his face, then disbelief. He looked up, gazed toward Orlando, then lowered his eyes, resigned to the battery of questions he had to know would now be coming his way.

> A – As I look at it closer, I am not sure if these are my initials or not.

> Q – Well, you have testified they are your initials.

> A – I thought they were at first.

Q – You didn't say, "I thought they were," you said they were.

A – I had believed they were at first. Now I look at them closer --

Q – I am not arguing with you. I want to get certain things straight. You did say, "They're my initials."

A – Yes, I did.

Q – You did say, "I put those initials there on Monday, August 11th."

A – Right.

Q – Then you were shown the letter and certainly the date is obviously August 17th, correct?

A – Correct.

Q – Then you said, "Well, in the excitement I must have put the wrong date down."

A – That is right.

Q – Now, I show it to you again and there are two sets of initials and ask which are yours? And now I think you say you are not sure if they are your initials.

A – That is correct.

> MR. DeBLASIO (with magnifying glass in hand): If I may, may I give the witness, if it will aid him –
>
> THE WITNESS: I don't think it will.
>
> MR. DeBLASIO: Just try, don't guess, just try; look and then tell us (handing him a magnifying glass). All right.

BY MR. DeBLASIO:

Q – Does that in any way aid you in determining whether those are your initials?

A – They don't look like my initials now as I look closer.

Q – That is not the question. Does it aid you?

A – Yes.

Q – It aids you, and now what: they are not your initials or you don't believe they are your initials?

A – I don't believe they're my initials.

> THE COURT: Excuse me. I think the record should show that everybody, by the use of the word "it," is referring to a magnifying glass.
>
> MR. DeBLASIO: Thank you, Your Honor, yes.

BY MR. DeBLASIO:

Q – What is there that you now have seen with this magnifying glass that makes you say, "I don't believe they're my initials"?

A – It looks like different initials; that's all I can tell you.

Q – What does it look like, what initials?

A – E. J. something.

Q – What are your initials?

A – J. T. K.

Q – One of them looks like E. J. something. What does the other one look like?

A – I didn't look at the other one because that is the one which we are talking about. The one in the blue ink?

Q – Yes. Or do you know that obviously is not yours?

A – It obviously is not mine.

Q – Then you don't have to look at it. Now, let me ask this, Officer Kunst, or Special Agent Kunst: as an FBI Officer, when you receive a document such as the one you have before you, the letter, and the envelope, is it not your FBI practice and training that you are supposed to initial the document when received?

A – That is correct.

Q – Did you place your initials on the documents, on the envelope and the letter which you opened on Monday, August 11, 1975?

A – Well, I would like to see the envelope before I answer that anyway. (Envelope handed to the witness.)

A – No.

Q – Is there any date of August 11, 1975 on the envelope or the letter?

A – No, not that I see, no.

Q – Those two pages of the letter, are they the identical, are they the exact two pages that you saw on August 11, 1975?

A – I believe they are.

Q – How do you know that?

A – What I read of it reads the same.

Q – How do you know it's not a copy?

A – The letter, I don't. I don't.

Q – You don't know? Your Honor, then I object to its admission into evidence.

> THE COURT: May I see it, please. I haven't seen it since it was marked. (Exhibit 2-A, the letter, and Exhibit 2, the envelope, shown to the Court.)
>
> Well, I am going to sustain the objection for the moment . . . I will defer a ruling until there is further proof, if there is some. . . . I think this is probably going to take, if I know attorneys, a few minutes. I think I might as well let you go home early, ladies and gentlemen.

And that's how the first day ended. A total catastrophe for the government. It looked to the jury as if the government was too incompetent to get into evidence the ransom letter – one of the most important documents in the case – and the jurors watched in amazement as the very first FBI agent fell apart on the stand. We were off to a good start.

As the judge summed it up privately to us the next morning: "Ordinarily I would have let the letter in, but what I was troubled with – I don't think this witness covered himself with glory as far as recollection – I don't think he was intentionally lying about anything but when a man misstates two other initials with a different date for something of his own, it sort of leaves you with a feeling of dissatisfaction. I think what happened was the man came in cold and he just wasn't, just wasn't prepared, and he was doing what he thought ordinarily he would have done."

After he had his say, in Solomon-like fashion as was his wont, Judge Beisheim said he would admit the envelope and letter into evidence. He explained that had it been a gun, or drugs, which can look alike, the agent's initials would certainly have been necessary to make sure there had been no substitution; but here, as it was a document with contents that the agent testified appeared to be the same as in the letter he read a year earlier, the rule was different and it was admissible. And so we started up trial day number two.

There was no question all along that the ransom letter (and its envelope) had to be allowed in evidence, but it was the theatricality that I had been after. And I got it.

WHAT'S IN A DATE? (OR IN A POSTMARK, AS THE CASE MAY BE)

When it came time to offer into evidence the second letter from the kidnappers, this one received on Wednesday, August 13, addressed to Edgar's Westchester estate, Orlando put a fresh set of agents on as witnesses. He called them in order: 1) the agent who retrieved the letter from the Yorktown Heights post office and brought it to agents encamped at Edgar Bronfman's Yorktown Heights estate home since August 9; and 2) the agent who received it at the home, opened it and arranged for it to be brought down to FBI headquarters in Manhattan. This letter, which contained Sam's blindfolded scribblings and included the family's nickname for his father, "Tree," had been mailed late Monday to let the Bronfman family know that Sam was alive.

We were at the end of day two when Orlando called Special Agent Drew H. Carr. Orlando's direct examination was quick and to the point. He asked Agent Carr where he picked up the letter (at the Yorktown Heights post office), if he opened the envelope (no), if he looked at it (yes), and what he did with it (he brought it to Edgar Bronfman's estate house where he handed it off to another agent).

While Orlando was questioning Agent Carr, I asked Judge Beisheim for permission to see the letter and envelope, neither of which I had seen before. At the direction of the judge, Orlando handed both of them to me and, as he asked his last few questions, I picked up my magnifying glass to have a look.

I immediately noticed something on the envelope that struck me as odd, too good to be true, that I had to double check it. Then I pointed it out to Higgins. It was an anomaly so extraordinary that in an instant I knew the trap I would set on cross-examination.

Higgins got up to cross-examine first, and I immediately regretted having shown him what was on the envelope because he almost foiled my plan, nearly alerting the agent to the anomaly. Luckily, he didn't hand the envelope up to the agent, and he didn't know how to snare him:

> Q (By Higgins) - Is there anything about this envelope in particular - the date, for example, do you remember what the postmark date on this is?
>
> A (Agent Carr) - No. No. The stamps I remember primarily.
>
> Q - How many stamps are there?
>
> A - I believe there are seven stamps on the front and I believe three on the back.
>
> Q - All right.
>
> . . .
>
> Q - What is the postmark date again?
>
> A - I never said. I am not familiar with the postmark.
>
> Q - You don't know what the date is?
>
> A - I do not.
>
> HIGGINS: No more questions.

We really were like a one-two punch vaudeville team, as some journalists referred to us. Or for those who prefer sports analogies, Higgins would load the bases and then I'd step up to the plate to hit the next pitch out of the ballpark. (I, and my daughter Caralee after me, were both homerun hitters.) And so, I rose to cross-examine my unwitting prey.

"How long do you anticipate your cross-examination will be of this witness?" Judge Beisheim asked me. "A minute or less," I assured him.

I asked the courtroom deputy to hand up the envelope to Agent Carr, and went straight at him (figuratively):

> Q – This envelope has a postmark of 1974 on it, doesn't it?

He couldn't answer. There was literal silence in the courtroom. We had all heard it a hundred times by now, the kidnapping happened in 1975. How, then, could the envelope have a 1974 postmark? He couldn't believe it and stared down at the envelope an inordinately long time.

At this point for Agent Carr, there was really nothing to be done, no dissembling, no dissimulating, no blame-shifting, nothing to be said but what he finally managed to mumble just loud enough for the court reporter sitting next to him to hear:

> A – Yes, it does.

As it had already been admitted into evidence, I asked Judge Beisheim if I might have the envelope passed right then to the jurors so that they could see the date for themselves. Judge Beisheim had his clerk first pass the envelope to him, so that he could take a look, and then the clerk handed it over to the jury.

Each juror looked at the envelope, amazement in their eyes. None of them needed to use my magnifying glass.

The misdated postmark – a clue as clear as the nose on their faces – had escaped the notice of this expert investigator and the entire FBI for more than a year. And here I, a lawyer with a magnifying glass, in the heat of trial, spotted it in under a minute.

I suppose I could have sat down right then – destroyed with one question – but the theater of it was just too great to pass up:

> Q – Did you know on August 13th, Wednesday, 1975, that that letter that you picked up from Mr. Nolte at the Yorktown Heights post office had a postmark of 1974?

A – No.

Q – No? You know it now today?

A – I know it now after you brought it to my attention, right.

Q – If you look at it you can see it?

A – Correct.

Q – Now, when you picked it up, didn't you look at it?

A – No, sir.

Q – You just, although you were an FBI agent, I take it there are different gradations, right, it's a hierarchy?

A – Correct.

Q – You didn't even open it. You had to bring it to another man who had the authority and power to open it?

A – Correct.

Q – You just went and got it and brought it to someone else, is that it?

A – That's correct.

Q – And you just counted the stamps.

> THE COURT: Any redirect? Any further cross?
>
> MR. ORLANDO: No, Your Honor.
>
> THE COURT: You are excused. Thank you, Mr. Carr. Madam Forelady, ladies and gentlemen, we will recess now until Monday at 10:00 o'clock, that is Monday, October 18th.
>
> As usual, I must tell you not to talk about the case to anyone or let anybody talk about it to you.

The end of day two, another perfect day.

On that Monday morning, October 18, as day three was about to begin, a short article by John Randazzo and George James ran in the Daily News:

> ... As the trial opened, Higgins and Peter DeBlasio, attorney for co-defendant, Dominic Byrne, acted as a kind of one-two punch vaudeville team with Higgins setting up FBI agents on the witness stand for DeBlasio's humor.
>
> DeBlasio, who has characterized the 53-year-old Byrne as a victim of FBI harassment, made light of the testimony of prosecution witness Drew H. Carr, a six-year FBI veteran. He said that Carr had noticed the number of stamps on the envelope of what was thought to be a second ransom note, but not the fact that the postmark was 1974, one year before Bronfman was kidnapped.

Orlando, true to form, started off day three by putting on the agent to whom Carr had handed the envelope at the Bronfman house, Agent John O. Long. Even though the witnesses were not allowed to know about the testimony of previous witnesses, someone obviously told Long to take a close look at the date of the postmark before he took the stand, because when I asked him about it, he said he had noticed it a year earlier, when he first saw the envelope. But he didn't stop there. He went so far as to say that everybody else, including Agent Carr, had noticed the wrong postmark date too. It was one lie too many, and I had him. My cross-examination of Agent Long was relentless:

> Q – In regard to that letter, did you study and examine the letter and the envelope?
>
> A – I read it, yes.
>
> Q – Did you make any special note of the envelope?
>
> A – I did not, no.
>
> Q – Did anyone in your presence?
>
> A – To my knowledge, no.

Q – Did you, on that day that it was received, know that on that envelope the postmark was 1974?

A – I recall that, yes.

Q – You knew it that day?

A – Yes.

Q – How did that come to your attention?

A – It was unusual, number one. And I just – everybody there was aware of it. It was just something that struck your eye.

Q – Being unusual is not how it came to your attention. How did it come to your attention?

A – I saw the envelope.

Q – You saw it?

A – Yes.

Q – You were examining that envelope rather carefully, right?

A – Yes.

Q – You saw "1974"?

A – Yes.

Q – Did you see any other date on that envelope? We are talking about People's Exhibit 38. Did you see any other year on that, other than 1974?

A – I don't recall.

Q – And you realized this before you sent it to FBI headquarters?

A – I think the letter had left the [Bronfman] house before any discussion took place about it.

Q – What about the envelope? Did you send the envelope?

A – It all went down in one package.

Q – You saw it before you sent it, obviously?

A – That's true, yes.

Q – Right?

A – Yes.

Q – You said you saw it before it was sent to FBI headquarters, "1974," and you knew it was 1975?

A – Yes.

Q – And you said everyone else saw it, correct?

A – Those who examined the letter.

Q – Who examined the letter?

A – Richard Staedler, Special Agent; John Downey, Special Agent; myself and I believe Drew Carr, Special Agent.

Q – So you four examined the envelope and did someone say out loud, "By the way, look, it's '1974'"?

A – I don't recall really how it ever – it came up. It came up in conversation. I do recall that.

Q – It came up before it was sent to FBI headquarters in Manhattan or not?

A – To my knowledge, the letter had already left the Bronfman home.

Q – Let me go back now. You looked at this envelope and examined it. You saw "1974." You didn't say anything to anyone. No one else who examined it said anything to anyone, and it was sent to FBI headquarters and then sometime later someone mentioned, "By the way, it had '1974' on it"?

A – To my knowledge, yes.

Q – Did the FBI headquarters in New York tell you that it had "1974" on it?

A – No, they did not.

Q – You fellows knew that before you sent it?

A – I saw it.

Q – I know you saw it. Did you write it down any place?

A – No, I did not.

Q – Now, when you saw "1974" written on this envelope, what did you do to check whether or not that was a correct date or a mistake or something else?

A – I didn't.

Q – Didn't do anything?

A – No.

Q – Did you inquire maybe this letter had been – stayed like in the post office for a year?

A – I did not personally inquire, no.

Q – Did you have someone, one of those FBI agents who you sent over there, did you have someone go over and check, see their stamp machines, see what they are stamping with?

A – I did not, no.

Q – Did anyone to your knowledge in the FBI check out how this alleged ransom note received in August 1975 had a 1974 stamp on it, anyone in the FBI check out with the post office people at all?

A – To my knowledge, I don't know.

Q – You certainly didn't tell anyone to do it?

A – No, I did not.

Q – Did you tell the people at headquarters in New York that it had a "1974" postmark on it?

A – I don't recall telling them that. I know they were informed of it.

Q – How do you know that?

A – At some time --

Q – How do you know that?

A – How could I know that?

Q – Yes.

A – I am sure someone at the [Bronfman] house called them.

Q – When you say you are sure, that is what I want to know. Are you sure because that is what good FBI practice would be, or are you sure because you overheard it, or what? How are you sure someone at the FBI called New York and told them this has a 1974 date on it?

A – I would just say that they had to know at some period during the investigation.

Q – Why? Because it's as clear as the nose on your face, or because the FBI does things very thoroughly. Why did they have to know?

A – If I didn't tell them, I know somebody else had to see it.

Q – Yes.

A – So I would say I am sure that they became aware of it.

Q – Maybe the other person at the house who saw it figured you saw it and you told them, maybe he is assuming you told them, and you are assuming he told them, and no one told them.

A – All I can tell you is I saw it and I didn't tell anybody. It was discussed later at the house.

Q – All right. Discussed with you agents who were there?

A – Yes.

Q – What was the discussion?

A – It came up in conversation.

Q – Tell us, please, what was the discussion?

A – Someone mentioned, I don't recall who, that the date was 1974.

Q – And did someone say, "Gee, we better go and check it, maybe this letter was written or mailed a year ago"?

A – No.

Q – No one said anything like that?

A – Not to me they didn't.

Q – No one checked it out and that is the end of it?

A – To my knowledge, I don't know.

MR. DeBLASIO: Thank you.

THE COURT: Any redirect?

MR. ORLANDO: No, Your Honor.

It couldn't have been clearer to the jury that Agent Long was lying through his teeth, trying to cover up a truly humiliating FBI gaffe. These agents, and indeed all the agents on the search and rescue detail, were the best and brightest in the world's greatest investigation bureau, and yet they all missed the misdated postmark. Sure, they scoured the *letter* for clues, for any hint, in any shape or form whatsoever – hairs, fingerprints, syntax – to help them locate the kidnapped heir to one of America's great fortunes. But the envelope? What could *that* have told them? Too many people had touched it to be able to lift the kidnappers' fingerprints. And they noticed all the stamps, but that was meaningless. The rest of the envelope? Equally useless, they thought. It couldn't possibly offer up a clue as to Sam's whereabouts. And so nobody thought to look at – or even just by sheer dumb luck happened to notice – the date and place the kidnapper mailed his letter.

The import of this clue was not lost on anyone in the courtroom. Had the agents noticed the date on that Wednesday, August 13, 1975, five days into the kidnapping, they could have located the specific post office with a machine incorrectly set to 1974, and then zeroed in on the neighborhood where the kidnappers most likely were hiding out. And they could have staked out that post office branch to see if the kidnappers returned to mail another letter to Edgar Bronfman – which they did – and then possibly have been able to apprehend them.

I'm not sure that the prosecution ever truly recovered from the damage done by these witnesses, and this was just the third day of trial.

WHAT'S IN A PHOTO?

Orlando next called a group of agents to testify about the ransom money. They fared no better than their compatriots who enlightened us (or really didn't) about the letters and their envelopes.

Special Agent Joseph E. Mayer was in charge of preparing the ransom payment, initially set at $4,600,000, but reduced by Lynch to $2,300,000 when he realized he'd be on his own at the pick-up and literally couldn't pick up the weight of $4,600,000 in bills. (The $2,300,000 ended up being delivered in two suitcases weighing 80 pounds each.)

I may make light of the agents and their colossal ineptitude, and even the buffoonery of the kidnappers themselves – *during the abduction making a traceable collect call to their victim's father* – but this was a very serious kidnapping. And when Edgar Bronfman and the FBI received the original ransom letter, the situation became more ominous than even they had originally imagined. Preparing the ransom just right was literally a matter of life and death, as is evident from the ransom letter that I include below, which was read aloud at trial.

A few words of background on the ransom letter. First, Lynch confessed that he typed the ransom letter a couple of months before the kidnapping, and before he knew which of the Bronfman boys he would have the chance to abduct. Thus, in the letter, he never names Sam, but rather refers to the person kidnapped as "a member" of the family, "that person," "your son" and "your boy." And Lynch leaves vague the day of the week the ransom letter will arrive, because he had no idea when he would have the opportunity to carry out the kidnapping, and then mail the letter.

Second, much of the letter was copied verbatim from the ransom note included in the book 83 HOURS TILL DAWN, by the kidnap victim Barbara Mackle, which Lynch confessed he read, which explains the weird reference to holding the person in a remote place with a limited air supply, and the list of tests he says he'll run on the bills. Third, the seemingly odd amount of the ransom, $4,600,000, is simply that it was the equivalent of an even 2,000,000 Irish pounds, something the FBI never pieced together. Fourth, as to the address and telephone number Lynch had for Edgar, he confessed he found them in WHO'S WHO IN AMERICA, but he had looked in an out-of-date edition, which is why the letter went to the vacated Park Avenue penthouse instead of Edgar's recently acquired Fifth Avenue apartment.

The ransom letter:

> Sir: We are holding a member of your family for ransom. That person is quite safe though somewhat uncomfortable. He is being held in a remote place with enough food, water and air to last a limited period of time after which the air supply will be cut off automatically. There is no chance of him being able to escape and there is less of a chance that he might be found. We had to take these precautions to insure the success of our mission. As you know, what we have embarked upon is considered a very serious matter with serious consequences so we do not intend to make mistakes. We are veterans of the Viet Nam war who are addicted to drugs as a result of that stupid, senseless war. Now we find ourselves outcasts in our own country with no hope for a decent life or anything to look forward to.
>
> Contemplate if you will the position this puts you in. If you pay the ransom within the time we have allotted you will be informed of your son's whereabouts before his air supply runs out. Should you not follow our instructions carefully, you will be condemning your son to die. We have done our research and planning very carefully and we expect a happy ending for you and us. Remember it is all up to you from now on. If you do not want a tragedy in your family you will do exactly as we say. By the way, we know quite a bit about you and your family.
>
> The police are not to be contacted on any level as to do so would only tend to scare us off. Besides when police are involved in a matter of this nature, it could lead to a tragic end for the victim that is being held. You are probably aware of what happened recently in Florida. Since we are not fools we must anticipate police involvement in this case but be assured that your communication with them or their actual involvement will be detected and we will break off all communication with you. We have tied into several of the possible means of communication with the police and are keeping them monitored. By this we mean all police agencies.

The ransom will be as follows: $4,600,000 (four million six hundred thousand dollars) in recently issued bills. The breakdown as follows:

$500,000	in	$20.	bills	(one suitcase)
$1,500,000	in	$50.	bills	(one suitcase)
$2,500,000	in	$100.	bills	(one suitcase)
$600,000	in 20,000 tens 3,000 hundreds 2,000 fifty's (one suitcase)			

Here are the requirements you must meet in this matter: the notes must not be older than 1950 series. They must have a great variety of serial numbers and not be merely shuffled. They must be Federal Reserve notes of standard configuration. No more than 50% (fifty percent) may be uncirculated. No forms of markings will be accepted on the bills.

The bills will undergo intense examination and counting for several hours before we let you know where your son can be found. We will run tests on a large representative sample of the bills. We plan about 40 tests. These include every chemical and physical test. No shaving, cutting, spotting, omission, counterfeiting, irradiating or additional numbers will go undetected.

You will need four suitcases of approximate size 32 by 19 by 6 inches. Purchase these suitcases and lock the bills inside. Then tie the keys to the respective suitcase handles, two keys to each case. You will keep the different breakdowns as described above in separate cases.

It is of the utmost importance that you keep exactly to these instructions and use the greatest speed as the life supporting devices that sustain your son are only designed to last a specific length of time. If you do not comply exactly as per these instructions time will run out and your son will die. He has been concealed in such an ingenuously [sic] devised place that we feel he would not be found for a thousand years if you were not told where to look for him.

From the time you receive these instructions you will have until closing time of the banks on the next business day to get the money ready. For instance, if you hear on Saturday you must have the money ready by 3 p.m. on Monday. If you hear on Tuesday, you will have until 3 p.m. Wednesday. We will not tolerate any deviation from these instructions.

Strict secrecy is to be maintained at all times to avoid the possibility of impostors getting the money. The police, and we mean all police at any level, are not to be involved in any manner. The FBI would like to make up for their blunders in California, but be assured that they would only be endangering the life of your son and yourself. Have no doubt in your mind we will do as we say.

As we said before, we have done our research well and we are very well equipped with the latest technology to carry out our mission. For instance, we will be using voice altering devices during any telephone calls. Also we have a good supply of bullets with lethal doses of cyanide poison. There will not be any fingerprints or any other evidence on this or any subsequent notes you receive.

The money is not to be photographed or the serial numbers recorded on tape or any other way or to be recorded in the National Crime Information Center in Washington or any other agency. The money must be clean as we instruct. You will include with the money a signed statement that you or any member of your family will never testify against anyone accused of this kidnapping. Even this typewriter cannot be traced.

This note or any others you receive is to be returned with the money and it is not to be copied. There are not to be any bugging devices in the suitcases or in the money or car that delivers the cash. You are not to use any form of communication, once the delivery has started follow our instructions. You are not to be followed by anyone either in a car or by light plane or helicopter. We have a very good system to check out your moves.

If any of us are caught, we will instantly commit suicide as we have nothing to lose. Then your boy will surely die. Only one of us knows the place where your son is being kept. The rest have been taken there under tight security blindfolded. Also if any of us are caught the others will come out of hiding on suicide missions to kill you and all who are near and dear to you. Bear in mind that we are desperate people who are committed to doing exactly as we say. Your brother and sister's families will become as much of a target as you yourself.

The choice is yours. Do as we say and all will be well. We need the money more than you will miss it. It will give us the chance in life that we have been denied. What we are asking for is what we want and need. Get in touch with your banker friends and have them get the money ready in the time allotted. You can tell them any story you like as to why you need the money but make sure they do not go to the police.

If you try to double-cross us you will become a marked man. We will cut you down when you least expect. If we do not get the money we would be better off dead. If we are going to die then we will take you and any members of your family we can with us. Remember no Secret Service, FBI or any other law enforcement agency is to be notified now or in the future. Let us give you our word that if you cooperate we will let you have your son returned unharmed. Pay the ransom, forget about police and the publicity which you do not need as someone else might try the same in the future.

We will use the code word <u>RAVEN</u> to prevent an imposter getting the cash. On the day you are to have the money ready for delivery you will place the following ad in all editions of New York City newspapers <u>Jack please come home, your mother is very anxious. We will be happier in the future. Sign the ad Fred Dollard</u>.

Edgar M. you are to be the one who delivers the money, you cannot use a stand-in or look-alike. We know you well so do not try to fool us. The cash is to be delivered from 740 Park Avenue, so make sure it is there at exactly 3 p.m. We will call [###-####]. The telephone is to be answered on the first ring. The

> conversation will be brief so make sure you get the instructions correct the first time. We will not repeat ourselves so do not try to stall for time. We must see the ad in the paper before we call you. You are not to use a spectrograph machine on the phone. At the delivery site you will be covered by a high powered rifle and scope loaded with poison bullets.
>
> The Raven

Immediately after the FBI received this ransom letter on Monday, August 11 – and made copies at Manhattan-HQ so the original could go right to Washington DC for lab analysis – a team began to work with Edgar Bronfman and his bankers, assembling the money in a vault at the Manufacturers Hanover Trust Company at 40 Wall Street. Quite rightly, the FBI ignored Lynch's instructions about not photographing or recording the serial numbers.

The Seagram people counted the money and Special Agent Mayer supervised as agents stacked the bills, recorded the serial number of the top bill of each stack, wrapped the stacks in brown manila paper and placed them in bundles of like-denominations in four green plastic garbage bags, one with $100 bills, one with $50 bills, one with $20 bills, and one with a combination of $100 and $50 and $10 bills, exactly as described in the ransom note. Then they placed one garbage bag in each of four brown leather suitcases. The agents photographed the entire process, which was time-consuming and required many agents because they were under incredible time pressure to get it done by 3 p.m.

On Tuesday August 12, at 2:30 in the afternoon – barely within the timeframe the kidnappers allotted – the original ransom letter made it back to Manhattan from Washington DC to be enclosed together with the $4,600,000, per the kidnappers' instructions. The suitcases were then transferred uptown to the Armory on 67th Street and Park Avenue, a few blocks from FBI headquarters, and placed in the trunk of a Seagram Company car parked there in the garage. Another team of FBI agents then waited with Edgar at his Fifth Avenue apartment for the kidnappers to telephone with instructions for delivery. (The telephone number was the same one he'd used when living at the Park Avenue penthouse.) Nobody called.

On Wednesday morning, a special delivery envelope with a cassette tape arrived at Edgar's office with instructions on where to deliver the ransom money that evening, and which vehicle he was to use. He was to drive the Vista Cruiser station wagon that belonged to his ex-wife (Sam's mother), to JFK Airport, where he would await further instructions.

The tape also quite unexpectedly told Edgar to cut the ransom in half. So, the agents took the money out of the Seagram Company car, brought it upstairs to a classroom in the Armory, removed the $4,600,000 and repeated the whole packaging process, this time with only $2,300,000 and in just two suitcases. They again photographed the entire procedure. And then they loaded the two suitcases into the back of the Vista Cruiser station wagon, which by now was parked at the Armory.

Later that evening, Wednesday, August 13, Edgar drove to the airport for his first attempt at handing off the ransom. It would not be until his third attempt, two nights later, that he would be successful.

A year later at trial, Agent Mayer testified about the ransom-preparation process and how very important and laborious it had been. Counting out $4,600,000 was time-consuming, as was bundling the money, recording it, packaging it, photographing it, and repeating the process when they were told to break it down into $2,300,000.

On the stand, however, Agent Mayer came off as a bit arrogant, and more so with each of the 18 photographs passed up to him to identify (which Orlando had to do to move them into evidence). The photos, Agent Mayer told the jury, were of himself in a room with the 12 agents he was supervising, as they worked for hours without respite.

During cross-examination by Higgins, Mayer explained how the agents carefully wiped the suitcases with alcohol to clean them of all their own fingerprints, so they would be able to lift the kidnappers' fingerprints after the fact, if the bags were ever recovered. The garbage bags, however, were not handled in a similar manner. No care at all was taken to wipe them clean of agent fingerprints. The reasons Mayer gave were somewhat odd and incompatible: 1) they ran out of alcohol; and 2) unlike the suitcases, the garbage bags had no handles and, at about 80 pounds, they were large and unwieldy and two or more agents were needed at a time to pick them up and corral them into the suitcases, and so there were too many fingerprints to wipe away. According to Mayer, apparently nobody bothered to wear gloves.

Agent Mayer's explanation was confusing and I capitalized on that in my cross-examination, the purpose of which at this point was just to make him, and the agents generally, appear bumbling and befuddled, not to challenge the facts.

As Higgins took his time questioning Agent Mayer, I looked at the 18 money-sorting photographs, which I had not seen before, thinking of what hook to use on cross-examination. I picked up my magnifying glass, which by this stage of the trial I simply kept on the table, and looked to see what was there to be seen. It was like the postmark episode all over again. I immediately noticed an anomaly, could not believe my eyes, did a double take and then smiled. As the saying goes, it was déjà vu all over again.

When it was my turn to cross-examine Agent Mayer, I started with the running-out-of-alcohol issue, which was absurd, before setting him up for what I really wanted to get him with:

> Q – Mr. Mayer, the alcohol was used on the original four suitcases in which the $4.6 million was?
>
> A – That's correct.
>
> Q – And the alcohol was used where, at the Manufacturers Hanover?
>
> A – No, it was not.
>
> Q – Where was it used?
>
> A – I believe it was at the Armory.
>
> Q – Where did the alcohol come from? Was it in a – what kind of a container?
>
> A – I believe it was one we brought from the office.
>
> Q – Brought from the FBI office?
>
> A – That's correct.
>
> Q – In some container, obviously?
>
> A – Yes.
>
> Q – Now you say the reason that you didn't use alcohol on the garbage bags which were at the Armory was because you had no alcohol?

A – At that time, correct.

Q – It was either evaporated, was all used or was taken back to the office?

A – Taken back to the office.

Q – Which is two blocks and something away, right?

A – Correct.

Q – Five minutes away?

A – Correct.

Q – So the reason you didn't use it was because you had no alcohol and no one went the five minutes to get it back, or say, ten minutes to go back and forth, right?

A – Correct.

Q – No other reason?

A – Time element, that's all.

Q – You mean the five or ten minutes?

A – No, we were rushing to get the packages complete so they could be put into the car.

. . .

Q – Now, wasn't anybody – you say the FBI agents, they were touching these bags with their fingers?

A – Not everyone, just the ones who picked them up.

Q – Some of them, at least?

A – Yes.

Q – Weren't they using gloves?

A – No.

Q – No one used gloves?

A – Not to my knowledge.

Q – Not at all during this procedure?

A – No.

I then asked for and received Judge Beisheim's permission to approach Agent Mayer, because I wanted to point out something in one of the money-sorting photographs now in evidence. When I handed him the particular photo, I pointed to an agent in the back upper-right-hand quadrant, and asked if he could see that individual clearly.

Q – Look at Exhibit 35 in evidence and see if it refreshes your recollection (handing to witness).

THE COURT: That's in evidence so you can tell us what you see.

Agent Mayer hesitated at the strange question, and looked down at the photo he had seen so many times in preparation for his appearance in court, and saw it as if for the first time. His rather haughty mien dissolved in an instant.

A – The man has gloves on.

As he said this, a few of the jurors just started laughing out loud. I continued:

Q – What is he doing with the gloves?

A – I can't tell.

Q – Not combing his hair, is he?

A – No, he is not.

Q – He is standing right by the package, isn't he?

A – He is behind it, yes.

Q – A few inches behind?

I then asked Judge Beisheim if I might pass the photograph to the jurors so that they could see the gloved hands for themselves.

MR. DeBLASIO: May I just show this one to the jury?

THE COURT: Yes.

Judge Beisheim had his clerk first pass the photograph to him so he could take a look, and then the clerk, with a smirk, handed it over to the jury. Those who were not already laughing now joined in.

BY MR. DeBLASIO:

Q – So we note, in looking at this Exhibit 35 that is a brown wrapping paper around something which contains $1,150,000?

A – That's correct.

Q – Which was then put into the green garbage bag?

A – Yes, sir.

Q – And this picture you were – were you present when it was taken?

A – Yes, I was.

Q – I show it to you again. Was it taken at the Armory?

A – Yes, sir.

Q – By an FBI photographer?

A – Yes.

Q – And that's an FBI agent who has gloves on?

A – I believe so.

Q – And that big heavy load right next to it, does that relate to the 80 pounds or something that that thing weighs?

A – I don't know.

Q – It was a heavy load though?

A – Yes, it was.

MR. DeBLASIO: Thank you.

THE COURT: Any redirect?

MR. ORLANDO: No, Your Honor.

It was like the Marx Brothers and Keystone Cops together in one great movie, like the movies I used to love as a boy, the way these agents testified about running one way and the photos showed them running in the complete opposite direction. I had them chasing their tails. And by the rise I constantly got out of the jury, I knew already at this early stage of the trial - Agent Mayer was just the tenth prosecution witness - that I could not lose.

THE NYPD WAS NOWHERE TO BE SEEN

One of the later FBI witnesses Orlando called to the stand (his 34th witness overall) was Special Agent Leo P. McGillicuddy, who was in charge of the FBI's rescue operations team. He was called toward the end because his testimony concerned the late stage of the investigation, the moments when the FBI and NYPD entered Lynch's apartment to rescue Sam after Dominic unlocked the door for them.

One of the first things that Agent McGillicuddy did when he took the stand was to take full credit for the rescue - as if the NYPD was nowhere to be seen - and contradict the testimony of NYPD Detective James E. Schry, which the jury had heard just a few days earlier. The jurors had all listened very attentively to Detective Schry as he testified to heroic acts in finding and freeing "a dazed and dirty" Mr. Bronfman. And the jurors had watched as Schry broke down on the witness stand, wiping tears from his eyes, describing how he and his partner NYPD Detective Thomas J. Cerbone were the first to break into Lynch's apartment, and how Sam hugged them and prayed together with them at the rescue scene. Detective Schry even told the jury, proudly, about the Police Department commendation he and Cerbone had received for their valor.

Then here comes Agent McGillicuddy to the stand: "I pushed [Lynch's] door in, followed by FBI directors LaPrade and Beane."

So I began my cross-examination with the contradiction, making McGillicuddy dig himself in deeper, highlighting the pettiness between the FBI and NYPD, and undermining all of his credibility:

> Q - Mr. McGillicuddy, I want to start off by just getting one phase of the questioning out of the way, if I may, and then I won't go into it.
>
> There's an exhibit in evidence, Defendants' Exhibit D. I am going to read just a little part of it to you and ask if it's the fact. It's by the Police Department and it's in regard to Department

> Recognition for Detectives Schry and Cerbone. Reading from page 3, paragraph 9:
>
> "Byrne was instructed to insert the key in the lock and open the door by Detectives Cerbone and Schry."
>
> Is that a fact?
>
> A – No, sir.
>
> Q – "As Byrne opened the door, the two detectives led the entry into the apartment followed by the FBI agents."
>
> Is that a fact?
>
> A – No, sir.
>
> Q – "Lynch was quickly overpowered by the two detectives before he could react."
>
> Is that a fact?
>
> A – No, sir.

One rescue, two irreconcilable stories. The "jurors seem astonished," the ever-perceptive reporter M.A. Farber wrote on the day after McGillicuddy's testimony in THE NEW YORK TIMES. Unfortunately for Orlando, he had waited until McGillicuddy's testimony to introduce into evidence the blindfold that had been around Sam's head for nine stinking days. It was the first opportunity the jurors had to see – and smell – it. But by this time, the jurors had had enough, and they simply turned their backs on McGillicuddy and didn't bother with his offer of the blindfold.

A FOOL'S CONFESSION – TURNING THE TABLES

I really lit into and was relentless with the two agents who had taken Dominic's confession, and who were allowed to testify about it, even if the signed confession itself was not permitted into evidence by Judge Beisheim. I needed to distract the jury, keep them from focusing too closely on the substance of the confession, and I did this by highlighting the sloppiness of the agents' interview with Dominic, grilling them on all the questions they foolishly didn't think to ask. The sloppier the agents seemed, the less reliable the confession they obtained, and the less the jurors cared.

The two agents left the witness stand very demoralized from my pointing out their shortcomings, but I'll leave it to Mr. Farber to give an idea of how those cross-examinations went:

> A number of jurors looked astonished when the first of the two agents who questioned Mr. Byrne after his arrest, Robert McGonigel, said under cross-examination that he could not recall having asked Mr. Byrne why he wanted to kidnap Mr. Bronfman, what his share of the ransom was to be, what Mr. Bronfman said to him during the nine days of his alleged captivity in Mr. Lynch's apartment, what Mr. Bronfman's condition was, whether anyone else came to Mr. Lynch's apartment that week and a dozen other questions.
>
> Mr. McGonigel looked puzzled while testifying – his eyes darted about the courtroom and his mouth hung open between answers – and he often sought to "refresh" his recollection with documents he had last seen the previous week. He heaved a deep sigh as he stepped down from the stand.
>
> Mr. McGonigel was followed by Myron Fuller, the other agent who had questioned Mr. Byrne. Mr. Fuller said that a number of the questions that Mr. McGonigel forgot had, in fact, been asked of Mr. Byrne but that Mr. Byrne had not been responsive to most of them.

M.A. Farber, THE NEW YORK TIMES, "BRONFMAN ABDUCTION STILL RAISES QUERIES: After 12 Days of Often Contradictory Testimony, Most Major Issues in Trial Haven't Been Detailed," Nov. 1, 1976.

It would take another book to cover all of the agents and highlight all of the contradictions and moments of uproarious laughter during my cross-examinations of them. Maybe one day my daughters will write that book. But for now, I'd like to end on a high note, commending a few stellar and special FBI agents.

THE FBI'S BEST AND BRIGHTEST – ITS WOMEN

Special Agents Sheila Wakefield Horan, Marylou Mertens and Suzanne Monserrate were among the six women and more than 100 total agents on surveillance in the early morning hours of Saturday, August 16 at the time of the ransom hand-off. These women provided the sole shining light in what was otherwise a spectacle of ineptitude.

Their roles were simple. Agent Monserrate was assigned to act as a backseat passenger in a taxi, accompanied in the backseat by another FBI agent (her real-life husband), driven by a third FBI agent. The taxi was to be part of a surveillance convoy, keeping an eye on Edgar while watching to see who tried to make contact with him. Agents Horan and Mertens were backseat passengers in another surveillance taxi, also driven by an FBI agent, assigned to follow the kidnapper's car after the ransom hand-off.

It was obvious to me – having by now only seen or heard men agents on the witness stand and in photos – that the senior FBI men running the entire operation used the women on this tactical surveillance mission not because of their particular skill sets – anybody could sit in a taxi – but solely on account of their gender. They were there to make a few of the many surveillance vehicles in the area look less conspicuous, just a husband and wife or two girlfriends returning home late after a Friday night on the town.

Boy was the FBI lucky it chose these talented women, even if for the wrong reason. They were the ones who saved the day and possibly even Sam Bronfman's life.

But first, I'll set the scene.

The assignment for these three women, and indeed all of the agents on the ransom delivery detail, began a little more than two days earlier on Wednesday evening, August 13, when they converged on Kennedy International Airport (JFK), in Queens. Lynch had told Edgar to get to the airport on Wednesday by 8:00 p.m., park his car, go into the International Arrivals building and then wait by two adjacent public phone booths, for which he gave Edgar the numbers.

Edgar drove his ex-wife's Vista Cruiser station wagon from the Armory in Manhattan to JFK, covered "at every angle" by "a caravan" of FBI operatives, their vehicles in front and behind and off to his side, he testified a year later. He arrived, parked, went into the building, found the phone booths and then made himself visible as he was told to do. He was also told to make sure that nobody else used those two phones, they were to be kept free, which was difficult, because each time a plane arrived the phone booths became very crowded.

After about an hour, one of the two phones rang, he picked it up and a voice told him to go to the KLM counter. He saw a small counter directly opposite him, on the other side of the corridor. He went, he waited, and he wandered. As nothing seemed to be happening, he began to look constantly over at the airport's message board, and then wandered some more, until eventually a well-disguised FBI agent brushed passed him and said to expect a page on the loud speaker system. They would be addressing him by his family nickname "Tree." A few minutes later, there was a page, he made his way to the Information Desk, and received a message that he was to go back home to await further instructions.

He wasn't sure which home, he told the jury a year later, whether he was to go to wait by the phone at his Fifth Avenue apartment or to wait for another letter addressed to his Yorktown Heights house. He finally just left the airport at about 1:30 in the morning and drove to the Armory, where he left the car with the money in back. Supervisory Special Agent Mayer's team would keep round-the-clock watch over it.

On Thursday evening, even though nobody had heard from the kidnappers, the FBI suggested that Edgar return to JFK. By 8:00 p.m., he and the 100-plus member surveillance team were again in position, and Edgar did the same as the evening before, he made himself visible. At about 9:30 p.m., a call came to the same phone as the previous night, and the kidnapper told him the exchange would take place the next evening. Edgar went back to the city and prepared to follow the same routine on Friday.

On Friday afternoon Edgar received the infamous tape from Sam, laced with profanity, alternately scared and angry at his father for botching the ransom delivery. Edgar reacted by becoming more frightened for his son's life. The previous two evenings had been a frenzied circus, but not this time, he told the FBI agents in charge, he was no "little boy," he didn't need or want "the cavalcade" again. It was too risky.

Furthermore, he told them, this time he wasn't going to wear nearly as much electronic gear as the nights before, like the recording device they'd given him to slip over telephone handsets to record conversations. He was afraid that if the kidnappers were watching him from a distance and saw him slip the device over a phone, his son's life would be in danger. He felt in his "bones" that this was going to be it, this time, this night, and he didn't want any "slip-ups."

Up to this point, neither Edgar nor anybody at the FBI knew if the kidnappers had Edgar under surveillance the last two evenings, and had gotten spooked by the very many suspicious people around him, despite the agents' disguises. What they hadn't realized, but should have, was that the first evening's colossal failure was not due to their being spotted, but because of an incalculable blunder on their part. There was not just one, but two KLM counters and while Edgar and the entire FBI contingent was at one counter, the kidnapper was calling a set of phones at the other counter, incessantly dialing and re-dialing, increasingly infuriated. As for the aborted attempt the following night, what they couldn't have known was that Lynch had been drinking, and when he got to Queens that Thursday evening to make the initial call from a public phone, he was simply too drunk and decided to put off the ransom exchange until the next day. The kidnappers hadn't gotten spooked, they were simply incompetent.

The FBI chiefs did know they were dealing with amateurs. They knew it from the moment they read the initial ransom letter. These were copycats. William F. Beane, the agent in charge of the Bronfman operation, had been the lead FBI agent on the Mackle case six and a half years earlier and he instantly recognized that at least half of The Raven ransom letter was taken verbatim from the Mackle ransom note. But even hapless amateurs might be reckless enough to kill the boy if they were to discover the FBI on scene at the ransom delivery. So when Edgar demanded he be allowed to proceed with the delivery the way he wanted to do it, the agents in charge conversed and decided to let him do as he wished.

On Friday evening, Edgar left the Armory with the FBI detail following at a more discreet distance. He knew by now how to drive himself to the airport on his own, how to get to the parking lot, how to make his way to the telephone booths. He arrived at about 8:00 p.m. and waited around the phones until a call came in between 9:30 and 10:00 p.m., telling him to go to the TWA terminal.

Then it got complicated. The TWA terminal was large and noisy and Edgar wasn't sure what he was supposed to do there. He wandered around until he thought he heard someone paging "Mr. Tree," and he searched in frustration until he saw the Information Desk and spotted a red phone, which he picked up. A woman's voice came on and told him he was too late, the man who called to speak with him had hung up. Edgar became so aggravated and angry that after he slammed the phone down, he picked it back up to give the woman a piece of his mind, and instead there on the phone he heard the kidnapper's voice. The conversation was brief. Lynch directed Edgar to put the receiver on the counter, go over to the first pay telephone that he could see, get the number, come back and give it to him. Edgar did as he was told and gave him the number.

After he hung up the red phone, Edgar checked the minimal electronic equipment he had on him to make sure he was still in contact with the FBI, and then he went to stand by the pay phone. Lynch called and told him to give him the number of the phone next to the one he was on, he did so, and then Lynch called him at that one. This time, they spoke for a few minutes. Lynch assured Edgar that Sam was fine; Edgar assured Lynch that he was alone; and Lynch then gave him instructions where to go next to get further instructions.

Perhaps no longer a cavalcade, but certainly a charade. Edgar was to take the Belt Parkway to the Southern State and right after the toll, he'd see a gas station on the island dividing the roadway, and he was to park there and go to the bank of telephones. He'd been given a number so he'd know precisely which phone to stand beside. Edgar complained to the kidnapper that he didn't know the area at all and was afraid he might get lost. They agreed he would have 50 minutes to get there.

When Edgar made it to the gas station, the phone was already ringing. And while he picked up the receiver in time, it was nearly impossible to hear – it was drizzling and the cars racing along the wet roads on either side of him created too much noise. After a lot of back and forth, with Lynch believing he was stalling for time, Edgar finally got the instructions clearly enough to understand his next move: he was to retrace his steps back toward Kennedy Airport, take the Belt Parkway to Queens Boulevard, to about 59th Street where he'd see a food joint called Burger Shake. He was to wait outside the restaurant at a bank of pay phones for another call.

Predictably, since Edgar was nervous and didn't know the area, and signs were difficult to read in the rain and the darkness, he missed a turn-off and things went awry. He veered sharply to the right as he tried to get his bearings around Kennedy airport, and very nearly crashed into a small red car. He had come so close to causing an accident in fact that the little red car began menacing him, driving right up behind him, on his bumper, and continued "dogging" him as he switched lanes to try to get away. And it got worse still. He noticed a Port Authority police car coming up fast from behind chasing both of them.

The police forced the two vehicles to stop, and Edgar began to panic because he didn't have his driver's license and the inordinate delay this would cause might make him miss the Burger Shake rendezvous. Luckily for him, he hadn't refused all electronic devices that the FBI had suggested he wear, so he was able to tell them what was going on. A few minutes later, while Edgar was in discussion with a very disbelieving police officer, the FBI got word to Port Authority, which radioed the officer to stand down. If this weren't a kidnapping, it would have been comedic.

It was about midnight when Edgar made it to his destination, without additional incident, pulled into the driveway of the Burger Shake and stopped his car in the parking lot. But then things got dicey again. The telephone rang, he picked up, the kidnapper asked what he had in the car (the two suitcases), how the back seat of the station wagon was positioned (down), where the suitcases were (in the rear). The kidnapper then told him to open all the doors of the car, and leave them open, and pretend like he was cleaning it out.

Edgar did as he was told, but he got jittery, he figured the kidnappers were going to drive by to have a look into the car, to be sure nobody else was with him, and that made him wonder what would happen if one of the kidnappers were to get in the car with him. Even just a cursory search would reveal the electronic equipment on him, the earpiece, earphone and transmitter. So he decided to ditch them all, but just before he did, using the codenames the FBI had assigned for the mission, he said aloud for the agents to hear: "Iris, this is Rooster, I am getting rid of all the electronic equipment I have on me. The only contact we now have is what you can hear through the car transmitter, but I won't be able to hear you." He then walked over to some bushes by his car and tossed the equipment, surreptitiously observed by agents in nearby vehicles and restaurant dumpsters, who had been keeping a close watch over him all along.

The kidnapper had told him to wait for another call, and so Edgar stood by the phones, but as it was taking so long he went back to his car. As more and more time passed, he was sure he had misunderstood the kidnapper's instructions, so he just kept going back and forth between the bank of telephones where he'd wait a while, and his car where he'd wait a while, then to the telephones, then to the car, for about two hours. On one of his return trips to the telephones, a man dressed in a chef-like uniform came out of the Burger Shake and said he was wanted on the telephone, pointing to the bank of phones Edgar had been heading toward.

The phone was ringing and he picked up to a screaming voice, alternately irate and disappointed, and then accusing him of disobeying and trying to set a trap. After Edgar managed to calm the kidnapper's rage, barely able to keep his own rage in check, he told the kidnapper that the FBI was not going to let him go out a fourth night like this on his own, and that anyway his nerves were raw. Lynch said his nerves were raw as well and that the result would be bloodshed. They both got ahold of themselves and continued on, Lynch giving Edgar his next set of instructions.

It was clear to Edgar that the kidnapper had checked out his car because he knew which way it was facing when he gave him the directions to their rendezvous. Edgar was to go along the Queens Boulevard service road, turn right onto to 69th Street heading south, pass under the elevated tracks, cross 47th Avenue and then stop on the right-hand side of 69th Street, by a row of trees.

The 100 or so FBI agents in the area of the Burger Shake and cruising Queens Boulevard – deployed on foot, bicycle and motorcycle, and in cars, vans, a Ryder truck and at least two taxis – started to reposition as soon as Edgar stated the meet-up point over his car's transmitter. Some agents drove ahead to 69th Street, and others followed behind at a distance, radioing in the Rooster's every move.

And now to our heroines.

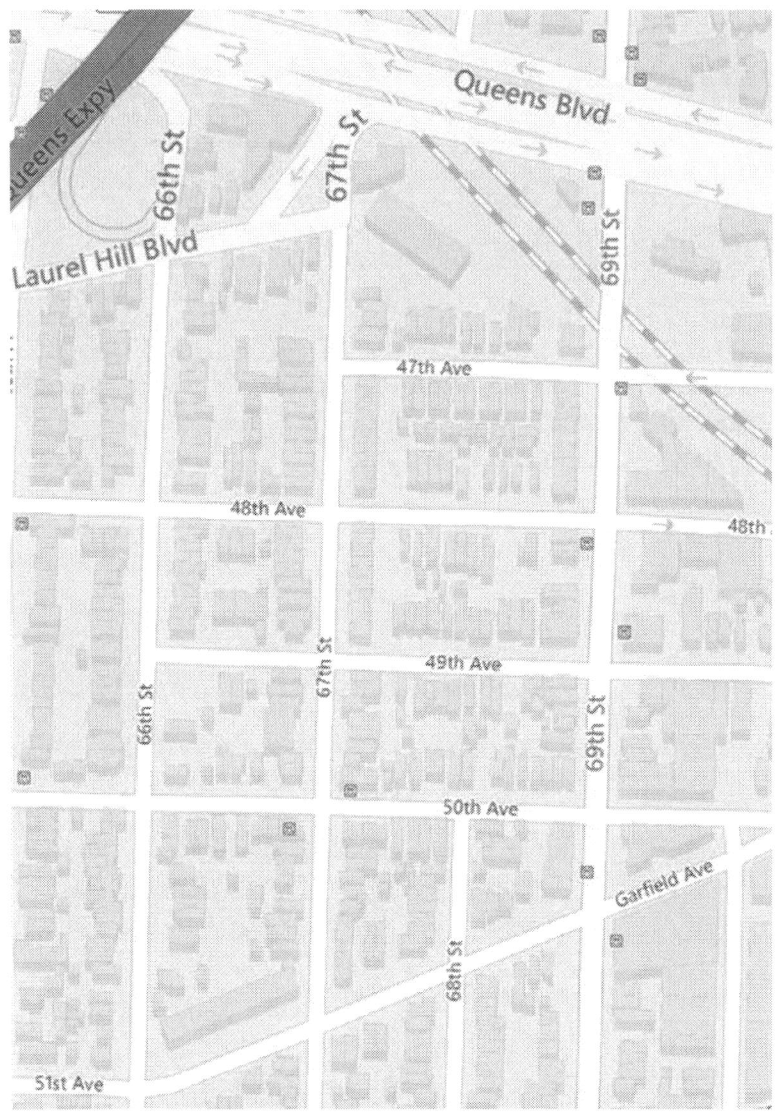

The site of the Bronfman ransom delivery, Queens, NY, August 16, 1975. Lynch got into Edgar Bronfman's car on 69th Street between 47th and 48th Avenues, facing south. He directed Edgar to take a series of right and left turns, and after a circuitous route they ended up just about where they started, coming to a stop on 48th Avenue near the corner with 69th Street, facing west toward 67th Street. Lynch ordered Edgar to get out.
Lynch then drove Edgar's car west on 48th Avenue to his own car parked on 67th Street between 48th and 49th Avenues, facing south. He moved the $2.3 million ransom money from Edgar's car to his own, and drove south on 67th Street, west on 49th Avenue, north on 66th Street, east on Laurel Hill Boulevard and onto Queens Boulevard heading east.

Agent Suzanne Monserrate was in a taxi with her husband Agent Frank Monserrate and Agent Charles Domroe who was their driver. Their assignment was to watch to see who made contact with Edgar in his station wagon. After leaving the Burger Shake, knowing the meet was to take place on 69th Street, they went on ahead, and drove up and down the street on the look-out for Edgar's car to appear. On one of their passes, going north, Agent Suzanne Monserrate spotted a man in a burgundy and white checkered shirt at the northwest corner of 69th Street and 47th Avenue, peering down 69th Street. She took notice because he was the only person out on the otherwise deserted street, he was near the rendezvous point, and he was clearly looking for someone or something. When the man walked west on 47th Avenue, they turned and drove past him, trying to get a look, but he turned his face completely away. They radioed it in at 2:25 a.m. They drove on, made a series of left turns, and came back north on 69th Street.

It was 2:30 a.m. when Edgar reached the designated spot on 69th Street between 47th and 48th Avenues, facing south. Not long after he came to a stop, a man in a burgundy and white checkered shirt wearing a ski mask, with something hidden in his right hand, leaned into the passenger-side of the car, peered through the window, opened the door and got in. He told Edgar not to look at his face.

As the Monserrate taxi was again driving north on 69th Street and crossing 48th Avenue, Suzanne now spotted Edgar's car facing in their direction, about halfway between 48th and 47th on her left-hand side, with a figure on the sidewalk getting into the front passenger seat, the same man in the checkered shirt she had seen a few moments before. They radioed it in, continued straight ahead one block, and made a U-turn. As they were coming back, they saw Edgar's car pull out, and they followed from a distance of two to three car-lengths, stopping when he stopped for about half a minute in front of a place called Sammy's Topless between 48th and 49th; and when he started up again, they continued on with him another two blocks until he went through a red light and turned right onto 51st Avenue. They didn't want to be seen, so they radioed it in for others to pick up the tail.

Edgar told the jury how as soon as the kidnapper – whom at trial he identified as Lynch – got into his car, he directed him to start driving. He ordered him to go straight and then told him to make a series of seemingly random right and left turns. He noticed that every time Lynch saw a car's lights in front or behind them, he "wiggled" in his seat like he was "overly apprehensive." When their circuitous route led them back to 69th Street (heading north), just about a block from where they had started, Lynch told him to turn left onto 48th Avenue, immediately pull over to the right, and back up to the corner.

As Edgar was moving right, and about to back up, a two-door blue Torino with four men inside came at them slowly from the opposite direction going east on 48th Avenue, the driver's window down in the heat of the night, with the radio blaring. The blue Torino drove just beyond Edgar's car, turned off its lights, and glided to a stop by the curb. As the four men inside slid down in their seats, the driver rolled up his window, hoping that Edgar and the kidnapper had not heard the incoming radio transmissions about the ransom exchange in progress and requests for updates on their whereabouts. As quietly as possible, one of the four agents radioed in their location, and advised that they now had eyes on the Rooster.

Oblivious to the radio broadcasts emanating from the blue Torino just across the street, Lynch told Edgar he was commandeering his car and ordered him out. He instructed Edgar to wait in place for at least ten minutes before going to look for his car, which he would find one block ahead and to the left on 67th Street. Edgar made to get out, but as he started to open the driver-side door, he was nearly struck by a guy on a motorcycle careening around the corner too wide.

It was Agent Martin C. Coyne, who from a distance of about 100 yards had been tailing Edgar's car as it drove north on 69th Street. He followed the car's route exactly and made the left onto 48th Avenue, purposely taking the turn wide so his headlight would not shine directly into Edgar's car up ahead of him, which might have alerted the kidnapper to the tail. But as he went into the turn, he saw Edgar's car unexpectedly parked right near the corner and he had to veer quickly and violently left to avoid hitting it. He missed the car (and Edgar), he testified, by no more than one foot. Regaining control, he continued down the block and turned *right* onto 67th Street – there was no 68th Street along 48th Avenue – passing a row of parked cars, one with several agents inside. He backed his motorcycle into the curb behind the agents' car, nodded in acknowledgment, and then he sat and waited.

Lynch had moved into the driver's seat once Edgar managed to get out, and he began to drive straight ahead, unwittingly reversing roles with Agent Coyne whose route he now followed. But at 67th Street he turned *left* instead of right. The agents ducking down in the blue Torino, across the street from where Edgar was standing, couldn't see where the car with the money had gone. But Agent Coyne, straddling his motorcycle, saw it make the turn onto 67th Street, and he kept close watch.

It was very dark and the streetlight didn't quite reveal the whole area, but Coyne saw Edgar's car stop on the right-hand side of 67th, halfway between 48th and 49th Avenues, which was only about 150 feet from his position and on the same side of the street. He watched the kidnapper get out of Edgar's car, go to the back, take out what looked like a large garbage bag, bring it to a car parked in front of him, return to Edgar's car for a second large bag, bring it forward as well, and then open what must have been the car's trunk. A light came on allowing Coyne to see the man put the bags inside, and then it went out and he could see the figure walk into the street and get in on the driver's side. As the car started to move forward, south on 67th Street, he started his bike. He called over the radio situated in his helmet that the suspect was in what looked like an Oldsmobile "Toronado" and that he was in pursuit.

Coyne followed in the direction of the kidnapper's car, trying to get close enough to read the license plate, and almost made out the number when the Toronado sped up and made an abrupt right turn onto 49th Avenue heading west. He stood down, fearing he might have been made. The agents who had been parked in the car next to Coyne had also started in pursuit, following Coyne's motorcycle following the kidnapper's car, and radioed in that it was a gold bottom, black top Toronado. But they too gave up the chase when the kidnapper made the quick, sharp right.

As they likely were contemplating the wrath of their superiors for failing in their sole mission – to stay with the kidnapper's vehicle while keeping out of sight – all noticed a yellow Checker taxicab appear on the scene. It was traveling west on 49th Avenue and was closing in on the Toronado. They prayed that it was one of their own, the decoy Checker with the two female agents.

Agents Sheila Wakefield Horan and Marylou Mertens were indeed in the Checker cab. A male agent, Steven Carbone, was posing as their taxi driver. They had just heard the radio transmission describing the kidnapper's car when Horan and Mertens spotted what they thought might just be a two-tone Toronado turn onto 49th Avenue a block ahead of them. They told Carbone to pick up the pace and, when they were near enough to confirm it was indeed the suspect's vehicle, Carbone slowed down to tail it from a discreet distance.

They were under the strictest orders not to stop and arrest the kidnapper, because the FBI brass thought they'd lose all chance of finding Sam. They were to follow the kidnapper to his destination, undetected –

they had to avoid spooking him at all costs. He had proved himself erratic and unreliable so far, and they couldn't risk him pulling over to the side of the road to call his accomplices, if he thought he was about to be caught, and direct them to kill Sam. So Carbone kept his cab about four car lengths back at all times.

The Checker cab followed when the Toronado turned right from 49th Avenue onto 66th Street, then another right onto Laurel Hill Boulevard, and a quick right onto the Queens Boulevard access road heading east. But Queens Boulevard presented the agents with a problem. As the access road's two lanes changed into three, the kidnapper could easily pull ahead, and if they were to try to match his speed and every random maneuver, their big yellow Checker was sure to be noticed.

With no other FBI vehicles in the vicinity to substitute in for them, Horan and Mertens made a tactical call. They knew the Checker could not follow the kidnapper all the way to his destination undetected, no matter what their bosses back at headquarters might believe. Instead, they would pull up close enough to read the license plate and then break off. It was a gutsy decision, totally contrary to orders, but to them the kidnapper had appeared amateurish and so perhaps his plates, if not his car, would lead them to his door. As Agent Horan testified a year later, "it was integral" that they see that plate. Sam's life depended on it.

It took Carbone about a half mile on Queens Boulevard to get them close enough to the kidnapper's car, without raising suspicion, for Agents Horan and Mertens to be able to read the license plate. And as it turned out, no sooner had they radioed it in – 692 KLQ, an orange New York plate with navy blue print – than Lynch took a sharp right off Queens Boulevard onto 51st Avenue.

Lynch went on alone to Brooklyn, oblivious that he had just evaded 100 special agents. He went straight to Dominic's, to share a celebratory rum and Coke with Dominic's wife Liz, while her husband was out babysitting Sam.

Edgar, in the meantime, had gotten out of his car with "a mixture of a certain amount of relief coupled with a great deal of tension," he told the jury. He felt he had done everything he could, he had accomplished what he had set out to do that evening. Now there was a chance he'd get to see Sam again. But the drama wasn't quite over.

He was alone, at nearly 3:00 in the morning, on a deserted side street in Queens, biding his time as the kidnapper had instructed, when he noticed an odd man approaching him. He was "terribly frightened," he later admitted to the jurors, when "a very tall Black gentleman" came up alongside him and, addressing him as "Mr. Bronfman," told him to stay where he was. If he were an FBI agent, he surely would have called him by his code name. This man had used his real name, like the kidnapper did. Maybe this was one of his associates, as the FBI had warned him. So Edgar ignored the nearly 7-foot-tall man, and nervously took off in search of his car. But the tall Black man followed him.

If Edgar didn't yet know what was happening, the Black man did. He was used to people such as Edgar taking fright and/or ignoring him, so he spoke again, quietly and unhurriedly, this time addressing him as "Rooster." James A. McIntosh, a seasoned FBI agent, had been assigned to keep watch over Edgar – the FBI couldn't be sure the kidnapper didn't have an accomplice waiting somewhere nearby – and when all was safe and clear he made his imposing presence known. Reassured and relieved, Edgar walked with Agent McIntosh to where Agent Coyne had seen his car abandoned.

When they turned onto 67th Street and spotted the car across the road, Edgar left McIntosh at the curb. He walked over alone, found the keys on the seat, and drove himself to the Armory in Manhattan. There he dropped off his ex-wife's Vista Cruiser station wagon, never wanting to see it again in his life, and got a lift home to 960 Fifth Avenue.

POSTSCRIPT: Agents Sheila Horan, Marylou Mertens and Suzanne Monserrate were true trailblazers. When they were sworn in as FBI Special Agents, between 1973 and 1975 respectively, they were among the first women in the Bureau's history. (The very first two women FBI agents had only taken their oaths in July 1972, just months after Director J. Edgar Hoover's death – because literally it was only over his dead body that he would ever allow a woman to become an FBI agent.)

Agent Horan rose to be acting head of the FBI's National Security Division, and eventually Deputy Assistant Director for Counterintelligence in Washington. She became one of the FBI's highest-ranking women ever. Among her many accomplishments, in 1998 she was in charge of the on-site investigations into the U.S. Embassy bombings in Nairobi, Kenya and Dar es Salaam, Tanzania.

I always imagined that when Agents Horan and Mertens returned to Manhattan headquarters after their successful surveillance operation, they faced quite a ribbing from the men when a trace of the license plate the *ladies* called in revealed the Toronado's owner to be Mel P. Lynch, a

New York City firefighter, obviously not the man they were looking for, indeed the very last person who would carry out a kidnapping. And I imagine the FBI men mocking Horan and Mertens, trying to bring them down a notch and deny them a hero's credit for the greatest success of the entire search and rescue operation: "That car was obviously stolen. No kidnapper uses his own car. You'll see, Lynch will have called it in a few days ago as missing." I like to believe that the FBI women stood their ground – and were ultimately acknowledged as heroes – when it was discovered that Lynch indeed had not reported his 1971 two-door two-tone Oldsmobile Toronado sedan stolen.

Agents Horan and Mertens, despite working around the clock for at least three days straight, had remained focused and had managed to outperform their male counterparts. Their heat-of-the-moment decision to abandon the tail in favor of getting the license plate number not only likely saved Sam's life, but went a long way toward repairing the FBI's damaged reputation, which was at a low point in mid-August 1975. Indeed, the day after Sam's August 17 rescue, alongside pages of stories about the triumphant work of the FBI on the Bronfman case, both THE NEW YORK TIMES and the DAILY NEWS ran articles about the FBI's ongoing failures in the Jimmy Hoffa and Patty Hearst cases. The FBI had made no headway in finding Hoffa – the former president of the Teamsters Union and one of America's most powerful men – who had gone missing, apparently kidnapped, on July 30. Nor had the FBI yet managed to locate and arrest Hearst – the kidnapped heiress turned bank robber – who had been a fugitive for more than a year. (In September 1975, the FBI finally did succeed in capturing Hearst; Hoffa's disappearance remains a mystery to this day.)

As for Lynch's monumental ineptitude in using his own vehicle to pick up the ransom money, NEWSWEEK journalist Pete Axthelm captured it brilliantly in his December 6, 1976 article "Who Snatched Sam?":

> In terms of logistics, whoever plotted this caper set some new standards for bungling. The snatch occurred on a weekend, when banks were closed and ransom money inaccessible. When the group stopped at a roadside phone, no one had the right change and they had to call Edgar Bronfman collect. Later they dispatched a ransom note to the wrong address. Lynch hoped to convince the jury that Sam ordered that mistake to insure that nobody would suspect a hoax; the prosecutor countered that Lynch made the error by looking up the outdated address in an old newspaper.

Perhaps such blunders can be explained by the vast quantities of rum-and-Coke that Lynch said were consumed throughout the caper. As kidnap or hoax, the whole case seems to offer at least one warning to future rookie criminals: get all the addresses and phone numbers straight before indulging in any mid-crime cocktails. As for Lynch's final mistake – driving his own car to the ransom drop spot so his license plate could be traced – this could be easily explained without waiting for the jury to face its decision. "For a good Irishmen," said one veteran Irish reporter, "either a real kidnapping or an elaborate hoax may seem like a great adventure for a hero. But stealing a car to carry it out – why, that would be a mortal sin."

Defendant Mel Patrick Lynch, the greatest witness ever to take the stand. Two of his sisters, who attended the trial every day, are in the background.

CHAPTER 36

A Tale to End All Tales

I can look back now after a 50-year, 600-trial career and say that among the thousands of witnesses I observed, nobody approached the magnificence of Mel Patrick Lynch. His performance during the Bronfman trial was nothing short of masterful. He was the Arturo Toscanini and Enrico Caruso of witnesses. He turned a horror story into a tragedy of operatic dimension. The jurors were mesmerized. If they could have, they would have exploded in applause and cried for an encore when, spent but heroic, he stepped down from the witness stand, his podium, his stage.

After 51 government witnesses, two of whom Orlando recalled for a second turn on the stand – so really after a total of 53 – with Edgar up last, it was finally our time to put on a case and Higgins as always went first. After three months of boastful agents, nearly all falling on their faces, the jurors were ready for someone who spoke without flourish, without doubletalk, and in plain everyday language. They got what they wanted in Lynch.

In the (figurative) spotlight, he looked wan, and he looked tired. He had on the same blank face he'd worn all trial, which stared ahead as though concentrating on something in the distance. He spoke with his soft Irish brogue. He was simple. He was convincing to anyone who was eager to be convinced. And, if this took place not in a court of law where the ideal is that the "truth" be told, but in a theater, on the stage, by a great actor, then one might and could say he told the "truth" – and one might and could forgive his audience, spellbound, swooning even, as they listened intently to the man's gentle voice, resonating faintly through the courtroom and faintly resonating, spinning a tale to end all tales.

It was so, so simple. And so brilliant. What could he say about the kidnapping when he was caught red-handed? When the proof was so overwhelming that 100 out of 100 judges I know would have pronounced him guilty without a moment's hesitation?

He said the only thing he could say that might possibly let him escape a life sentence. Strike at the heart of the prosecution's case and say that there was no kidnapping. "*It was a hoax*," Lynch told the jury. "It was a scheme that Sam – my homosexual lover – devised and forced me into aiding, to get money from his father, which money was going to be rightfully Sam's in a few years down the road, but he wanted it now. I was forced into it because homosexuality in the Fire Department is a curse, you're an outcast, you're not wanted, you're not 'one of the boys.' Sam blackmailed me by threatening to expose me."

During his testimony, Lynch even went so far as to tell the jurors that when the news of Sam's kidnapping broke on Sunday August 10, he was watching television at the firehouse and immediately called Sam and told him to go home, to please just go home. But Sam, he said, told him not to worry.

Lynch made up the gay-lovers extortion-kidnapping story because he couldn't bear the thought of life in prison and he knew it was the only way he could possibly distract and disgust the jury enough to be acquitted. As it was, he had already tried escaping from jail, twice. Within a month of his arrest he made his first attempt, but was unsuccessful and was moved to a higher-security facility. Six months later, and days before our trial was originally set to begin, he complained of chest pains, got himself transferred to a hospital and there jumped out a window. He broke several bones, which delayed the trial by five months and left him with a permanent limp. Lynch was ready to do anything to avoid a life sentence, so a few months of ostracism and humiliation – which was often the result in the 1970s when someone publicly announced their homosexuality – was a small price to pay for his freedom.

When it came my turn to cross-examine Lynch, I did not get out of my chair.

Up until that point I was not sure if, to save Dominic, I would have to sacrifice Lynch, make him out to be a monster who preyed upon his feeble-minded friend Dominic, forcing him under duress to aid in the most terrible of crimes imaginable, the abduction and threatened murder of a young person. The first and perhaps the only subject I would have brought up on cross-examination, to show that Sam was indeed kidnapped, that it was not a hoax, was why Dominic was in this case at all. I would have asked Lynch, if this were a hoax, a plan with his lover, for what reason did he need Dominic? We'd heard the FBI witnesses testify about Dominic's confession, how he was often at the apartment guarding Sam, and we'd heard Sam's testimony about the "little guy" caring for him. Sam wouldn't have needed guarding if he was in on it, and certainly not if he was the mastermind. Guarding from what?

What's more, if it were just a hoax, the worst thing to do would be to bring in a third person. How could he and Sam trust that person not to go to the police? And of all the people to choose, Dominic would have to be the last as it was in his nature to do what he finally did, turn himself in. Lynch and Sam didn't choose Dominic for a hoax; Lynch chose Dominic for a real kidnapping, because he needed a driver and a grocery shopper and a babysitter.

But after witnessing the maestro on the stand, I knew our case was won and kept my seat.

Orlando did get up, but he couldn't touch Lynch on cross. As Pete Axthelm wrote in "Who Snatched Sam?" in NEWSWEEK a few days afterward: "Orlando attacked Lynch eagerly, scornfully and at length . . . at times smitten with a kind of Perry Mason fantasy, perhaps hoping that under enough browbeating Lynch would suddenly cry out a confession to a triumphant Orlando."

But Orlando's efforts were futile. Lynch simply turned the cross-examination into a second opportunity to lay all the blame on Sam.

When the spotlight went out and the curtain came down after four days on the witness stand, no one on the jury could be confused about the issue they had to decide: Did they want to believe Mel or Sam?

Poor Sam, Mel played his role to perfection.

CHAPTER 37

To See or Not to See

Higgins should not have called any more witnesses, but he had promised the jurors in his opening statement that he would bring three people to prove that Sam concocted the entire scheme, that he forced his lover Mel Lynch to be his accomplice in extorting his father – under threat of exposure to the Fire Department – the death knell for Lynch's career.

The first witness Higgins promised to call was a young man who was supposed to testify that Sam had previously approached *him* to aid and abet in extorting money from Edgar Bronfman. That witness did not show up, nor was any excuse or reason given to the jury for his failing to testify. The second witness he promised to call was another young man who was supposed to testify that Sam and *he* had been homosexual lovers. That witness did not show up either, nor again was any excuse or reason given to the jury for his failing to testify. The third witness Higgins promised to call was Andrew Cokley, the doorman from Lynch's apartment building, who was supposed to corroborate that Lynch and Sam knew each other, and testify that he had seen them enter the building together, one time, in about June or July 1975. He did show up. Would that he hadn't.

When I arrived at the courtroom the morning that Cokley was to testify and took my seat at the defense table, Higgins looked like he had just been knocked over by a truck. I asked him what was wrong and he told me that he could not put Cokley on the stand because a few minutes before, when he was preparing him, Cokley reneged on the statement he had given back in September 1975, that he had seen Lynch and Sam Bronfman together.

Higgins told me he was going to tell the judge that he would be resting his case without calling any more witnesses. I was stunned. I said, essentially: "How can you not call him? You told the jury he was a star witness. You told them yesterday he would be here today. He is here. He is your only possible tie-in to Sam. He did sign an affidavit a year ago that he saw Lynch and Sam together. You can't just ignore it. How could you explain to the jury you're not calling him?" Higgins finally agreed that he had no choice but to have him testify.

On direct examination, Higgins did the best he could. He showed Cokley a newspaper photograph of Sam taken in August 1975 and asked him if he had not told him (Higgins), when they met shortly after the kidnapping, that the man in the photo (Sam) resembled the man Lynch entered the apartment building with earlier that summer. Cokley agreed.

On cross-examination, however, Orlando asked Cokley if he saw that man in the courtroom, and when he answered "No," Orlando had Sam Bronfman stand up and asked if he was the man who accompanied Lynch. Cokley then dropped a bombshell when he said: "I can't say because I didn't see his face."

When Orlando sat down, the judge asked Higgins if he had any redirect examination, and he said no. The judge then asked me if I had any questions for the witness and I said yes.

I didn't like to interfere with another attorney's witness, but this situation was now critical. All of the good that had been accomplished by the defense on cross-examination throughout the trial could be lost. More importantly, I had now pegged Dominic's fate to Lynch's and so the damage that just occurred affected Dominic too, and I had to try to make some repairs on my own client's behalf.

When I got up to cross-examine Cokley (which the judge insisted was really direct examination and so did not permit me to lead the witness), I tried to put him at ease as much as possible. I began my questions getting him to repeat his earlier testimony that the man he saw with Lynch was a certain height and weight, which matched Sam's build.

I asked him whether his memory about the man he saw with Lynch was better or clearer more than a year ago – when Higgins showed him a photo of Sam and he said it looked like the man – or better today. He said it was better a year ago.

Then I asked him to describe in detail the exact layout of the building entrance, where he positioned himself, and what precisely he did when Lynch entered with this other man. (I had seen photographs of the entranceway of the apartment building, and I was very familiar with it because I grew up in a similar Brooklyn apartment house, although we did not have a doorman.)

He explained that the building had two sets of doors, and that people entering from the sidewalk would push open the first set of doors on their own and walk into the lobby area. Then, about 12 feet from the first set of doors there was the second set of doors, with glass, which the doormen would open as the people approached. (Lynch's building had two doormen who worked separate eight-hour shifts, one started at 8:00 a.m., and Cokley started at 4:00 p.m.; there was no doorman on duty after midnight.)

I then got to the point. I had to rehabilitate him as our witness, show how even though he told Orlando he hadn't seen the man's face, of course he must have done so when the man was entering and coming toward him.

I asked him to watch me closely. I stepped back about 12 feet from the witness stand. The jury sat to my right and Cokley was in front of me. I told him I was going to make believe that I was Lynch walking from the sidewalk through the first set of doors, and then the 12 feet over to the second set of doors, and for him to make believe the other man was walking beside me. I started walking slowly forward:

> Q – Mr. Cokley, when you opened the door for Mr. Lynch and the gentleman, what were they doing?
>
> A – Just coming in.
>
> Q – All right. When you say "coming in," were they coming toward you?
>
> A – They come towards me. Everybody come in, they got to come towards me.
>
> Q – When they were coming towards you were they walking? Was the front of them coming towards you?
>
> A – The front, yes.

I then did an about-face, went to my starting point, and walked the 12 feet towards him, but this time backwards, so that all he could see was my back. (I had learned a thing or two about courtroom theatrics from my friend Peter Johnson.)

Then I stopped. I turned around to face him and asked:

> Q – Was the back of them coming towards you?
>
> A – No, the front.

He was laughing hard. So, too, were all the jurors and much of the courtroom.

I returned to my starting point and, as I slowly walked the 12 feet, this time facing forward, I asked:

> Q – What was coming towards you, what part of their body was coming towards you?
>
> A – The front.
>
> Q – The front. When you say "the front," does that include the head?
>
> A – Everything come toward me.
>
> Q – Right. And about how close, or how near, or how far were they from you when you saw them, the front of them, coming toward you?
>
> A – When I opened the door?
>
> Q – Yes.
>
> A – Just about that far --

He was indicating about eight feet away. I continued my slow walk forward as he finished his answer:

> A – I opened the door and they come on in.
>
> Q – Tell me when to stop. I am coming towards – make out I am them, coming towards you like this. . . . You got the door there.
>
> A – I got the door.
>
> Q – All right. Tell me when to stop.
>
> A – Right there.

(I was about five feet from the witness box)

> Q – Like this?
>
> A – Yes. They would be closer to me.
>
> Q – May I come here?

(I was just about up at the witness box)

> A – They come right close.

Q – Like this?

A – Yeah. I opened the door for them.

Q – About three or four feet?

A – And they come around and . . . the other man was closer to me.

. . .

Q – May I ask how tall you are, Mr. Cokley?

A – I am 5'5".

Q – And this man, this man was taller than Mr. Lynch?

A – About an inch taller than Mr. Lynch.

I then gestured with my arm sweeping up and down in front of my body and asked:

Q – What did you see?

A – I seen the head and he turned his back and his head.

I thanked Mr. Cokley and sat down. Orlando, per his custom, did not recross the witness.

* * * * *

The purpose of an examination, whether direct, cross, redirect or recross, is to elicit background facts that move the trial along, but more importantly to bring to light critical facts that make (and hopefully don't break) your case. But once accomplished, what does a trial lawyer do with all these brilliant facts, with his bag of dazzling trial gems?

As much as I might like to play Hamlet and stop the trial with a soliloquy immediately after – or even during – a witness's testimony, to enlighten the jurors about the significance of the new critical fact just revealed, the law does not allow it. So, what to do? We cannot just hope that by the time of jury deliberation the jurors on their own will remember all our great points, especially those from the earliest witnesses in long trials.

What we do is what writers and composers have known since time immemorial, and here I think particularly of opera and musical theater – I still remember my brother in the fifth grade starring in his school play "The Pirates of Penzance" – we recap the trial in one long, glorious finale, reprising our greatest moments.

This finale – our "summation" – is the trial lawyer's biggest challenge and, when done well and right, it is the pinnacle of the trial. A great summation only comes together after a lot of focus and concentration throughout the trial, collecting and assembling in one's mind the main points from the more significant witnesses. In the Bronfman trial, Mr. Cokley was one of those witnesses. It was, if not critical, at least important that I rehabilitate him after the bombshell blast, explaining away his comment that he didn't see Sam's face, which wiped out the only objective evidence we had linking Sam and Lynch.

So during my summation I spoke at some length about Mr. Cokley – who had testified that he was born in 1901 and had left school before learning to read or write – about why he was credible and how the jury should interpret his testimony about not seeing, but really seeing, the face. I started by acknowledging that Mr. Cokley did not remember some things, but I reminded the jurors that he was not trained as an FBI agent. When he was opening the door for Lynch and the other man back before the alleged abduction, back in June or July of 1975, he obviously was not thinking that he had to memorize the man's face so that a year later he could describe him to a jury at trial.

I reminded the jurors that Mr. Cokley said the man he saw was a little taller and a little thinner than Lynch, just like Sam was. And I addressed head-on his statement, "I didn't see the face." "What did he mean by that?" I asked the jury.

We all had seen that Mr. Cokley was Black, we all had heard his southern accent, and we all could do the math, that he was only a single generation removed from slavery and from the Civil War. When he grew up, his life had to have been unimaginably difficult, in a way none of us could fathom. And in addition to the constant indignities he must have suffered, he did not get the benefit of any sort of an education, but spent his lifetime illiterate.

On summation, I explained to the jury that he expressed himself differently than many of us might, he wasn't adamant about what he saw, but that didn't matter:

> I don't know Mr. Cokley, but I do know things about human

beings. Especially when he is not learned, education-wise, he might be the smartest man in the courtroom, but you know we all use words differently.

Do you think he meant he didn't see the man's face when he comes in here to court and identifies a picture of the man? When the only way you can identify it is the face? When the man went right by him? He might have meant a hundred things.

To him, not seeing the face might mean, "I didn't memorize it, I didn't study the eyes, I didn't do an artist's conception." It's the way he talks. There is no question, I am sure, if he didn't see the face, what is he here for?

Is he here to lie? Is he here to commit perjury? Is he here in a kidnapping case of such importance to just come in and make a fool of himself? . . .

Now, we go to the next step. How do you know, now, positively, he is telling the truth? Because, remember, I said there were 40 FBI agents brought in this case. Well, on Mr. Orlando's cross-examination of Mr. Cokley, he told you about two more [who] questioned him. . . .

I say it's reasonable to infer Mr. Cokley told those two agents exactly who it was he saw with Mel Lynch much better than he told us here now, much better. . . . That's why Mr. Cokley is telling the truth, not just because he is 75, not just because he knows Mel Lynch, not because he worked hard, obviously, and he is a decent man. He is telling the truth because the prosecution had the means to show he wasn't telling the truth and they didn't. . . .

They could have brought in the agents who interviewed Mr. Cokley. They didn't do it, and I tell you why. Because they know whatever they said, would have gone against their case.

* * * * *

But again, I am getting ahead of myself.

To return to the trial, it was now *my* opportunity to call witnesses. I didn't need to put on anyone, but after three months it would have looked a little strange if I made absolutely no effort at all. So, with a bit of tongue in cheek, I called the most clichéd witnesses imaginable: Dominic's 14-year-old son who was an altar boy (literally); and Dominic's parish priest, Father Raymond Neufeld.

The person I didn't call was Dominic. If Mel was the greatest witness I'd ever seen, Dominic hands down would have been the worst. There would have been no reining him in. As badly as I knew he wanted to take center stage himself, to receive the prosecutor's and agents' and the Bronfman family's adulation and adoration, I kept him firmly strapped in the kiddie chair beside me. And I rested my case.

Part VI

My Clients

This man had a skill level that no one could touch. His actions and words were simply brilliant. So brilliant that at times I forgot the case was about me. . . . How is it possible for someone to be sitting and listening to a case and forget it's about them? I know how it's possible. When what you're seeing in front of you is so amazing and so phenomenal, you do forget. . . . My only deep hope and desire is that he knows what an honor it was to have him be my voice.

–Deepa Avula (2003)

Watching you in Court was an experience I will never forget. You were absolutely brilliant and each day was more fascinating and overwhelming than the day before. I learned so much watching you. Your personality, humor and of course your brilliance captivated not only myself but the jurors and everyone else in the courtroom. Even Judge O'Brien and all the court clerks also thoroughly appreciated and were in awe of your amazing deliberations. You were a genius at work and certainly gained everyone's respect and admiration. You put your heart and soul into this case and it showed and we are so indebted to you.

–Jean Wall (1996)

CHAPTER 38

"She Won't Be Selling Pencils on a Street Corner"

I remember many, and indeed most, among the hundreds of clients whose cases I tried. Over the many years it took to get their cases from the initiating Complaint to trial, I got to know them well. Some of my clients went on to live long lives and I have been happy and fortunate to hear from them from time to time. Others died too young too soon.

In this section, I include a few stories about clients who, while they themselves did not have anything particular in common with one another, there was something about them that makes them stand out in my mind, something either unusual about their circumstances or unusual in the way I responded to those circumstances.

* * * * *

I tried Deepa Avula's case in 2003 in Supreme Court, Staten Island. As already noted, Staten Island was not a plaintiff's paradise during my 60 years of trials. The population of about 500,000 citizens boasts about 40% Italian-Americans, including me, since I moved here when I remarried in 1986. Most of its working people are blue-collar, police and firefighters. They do not like to part with money, especially when the expectant recipient does not fit into their mold.

Deepa – the daughter of Indian-born doctors – did not fit their mold. And had I not settled with one of the defendants, her ophthalmologist, just before summations, she would have received far less in damages than she deserved. I know because of a comment one of the jurors made to me after the case, which I have never forgotten because it so disgusted me.

I remember Deepa very fondly because she was quite an amazing young girl. She was 13 years old in 1995 when she and her parents came to my office for the first time, and in a very mature way Deepa told me of her congenital eye problems and a pediatric ophthalmologist's poor treatment that caused her significant and permanent loss of vision. For the next eight years I met many times with Deepa and her parents in preparation for trial, and at the age of 21 she was still amazing for her grit and determination, and her ability to face all challenges and basically overcome them.

From birth, Deepa had very little vision in her right eye, and over her lifetime had undergone several operations to keep both eyes functioning. Her mother, a pediatrician, was primarily responsible for obtaining medical specialists throughout the years to treat her, including ophthalmologists, neuro-ophthalmologists, neurosurgeons and the like.

In 1995, at age 13, Deepa suddenly developed excruciating headaches upon waking in the morning, which interfered with all facets of her life including school studies at which she excelled. Once again her mother sought treatment from specialists, but malpractice ensued.

The prime wrongdoer was her ophthalmologist against whom we settled the case. The prime wrong was that he misread the visual field studies, which he took as normal when they were abnormal. In addition, although he found swelling of the optic disc when he examined the fundus (back part) of the eye, he did not consider it worthy of follow-up. In fact, it was a dangerous condition called "papilledema" (a swelling of the optic disc), which could and did lead to damage to Deepa's good eye (the left).

When a neuro-ophthalmologist finally examined and treated Deepa, he placed a shunt into her skull, but the delay in his treatment brought about by the ophthalmologist's lack of follow-up led to permanent loss of some visual acuity and peripheral scotomas (gaps in sight), which amongst other restrictions prevents her from ever being able to drive a car.

Before I come to the juror's comment that so upset me, there are a few things of note about the trial. First, our trial judge Joseph Maltese, before whom I tried a number of cases, was totally impartial, analytic, and one of the brightest judges I have ever known.

Second, this was the only case I tried where a defendant doctor, to minimize his own fault, placed all of the blame on the plaintiff-patient's mother. The defendant doctor testified to the jury that it was Deepa's mother, the pediatrician, who was the one and only person to commit malpractice on the girl. In my opinion, this was totally wrong and unfair. In no way did Dr. Avula treat her daughter for any of her visual problems – she was not familiar with or capable of handling them – instead she, like all mothers, tried to get the best care for her daughter.

Third, I remember the defendant himself as someone particularly inept both as a doctor – he had to admit at trial that he failed his Board Certification tests three times – and as a witness on his own behalf, his answers argumentative, inconsistent and contradictory. He was also stubborn to a fault. For the eight years that it took to get the case to trial, he refused all efforts by his insurance company's lawyers to reach a settlement, adamant that a jury decide the case.

When the case was fully tried and all the evidence in, however, the defendant doctor's insurance company was finally able to convince him to settle before I got to my summation. The company agreed to our demand of $900,000, just short of the full policy coverage. By settling, the insurance company avoided what it believed was sure to be a verdict above and beyond the policy, and we were able to avoid their appeal.

I generally didn't like to settle once a trial started, just as I told Ms. Waldherr the defense lawyer in the Aldycki case. For one thing, if my opponents thought that I was the type to settle mid-trial, they would have little incentive ever to settle beforehand, figuring they might as well roll the dice knowing that they could bail at any point if the trial looked to be going against them. As it turned out in this case, it was a very good thing I went against my general rule.

When I left the courthouse right after the verdict – there was another defendant still in the case so we did go on to summations and a verdict regarding him – I saw one of our jurors. He was a middle-aged Italian-American man and I went over to speak with him.

I asked how he liked the case. He liked it. How he liked Ms. Avula. He liked her. How he would have voted. For the plaintiff. How much he would have awarded against the ophthalmologist. $300,000. I was taken aback. I told him we settled for $900,000. Why would he vote so little a sum as $300,000? I must say his answer to that question disgusted me: "We know she won't be selling pencils on a street corner."

To those of you not of my generation, shortly after World War II, some blind or near-blind veterans of the War, who were impoverished, used to stand on street corners and sell pencils for a penny each. I still sadly remember them, and I still sadly remember this cruel-hearted juror. I always felt that he must have thought Deepa was lucky to have two parents who were both doctors, and that she had to be rich and therefore would never have to worry about money in the future. Fortunately, that is not the law. We are to treat all people alike and not distinguish between the rich and poor.

Now that I continue to think about the possible reason, I consider the faint possibility – I hope – that he might have felt because Deepa did so well in school she was sure to earn a good living and do well on her own. But I doubt it. I think he was mean-hearted.

After the trial, Deepa wrote me a letter, which my office staff had framed. It hung in the office for the three years until I retired. I brought it home, one of the most treasured keepsakes from my career.

June 2003

Hi, Mr. DeBlasio:

My original intention in writing this is to thank you for all you have done for me but I'm going to interrupt myself to tell you a little story. I know that seems a little rude and I should be focusing on the purpose of writing this but I do have a story I want to tell and you're already reading, so why not just continue?

I met this man – his name escapes me at the moment – a few years back; I believe it was 1999. I went to him because I was wronged by some doctors a few years prior which had caused me the loss of most of my vision. I had gone to this man because I needed help with this situation. I remember talking to a colleague of his and then going in to see him. From the very first second I met him, I knew he had interest in me. I could tell just by looking at his face. I felt his interest in me. I didn't even have to be able to see a thing and I would have felt that desire he had to help me. I just knew he would be able to help me, Mr. DeBlasio.

Some years passed by and I had to return to his office for what these law folk call a "deposition." This time I only saw him for a few seconds. And I distinctly remember him asking me how I was doing and how I was getting along with my vision. But there was something strange about the way he asked, Mr. DeBlasio; he asked like he cared. Now I know that seems a little odd that I would say that's strange, but you know what I mean. Sometimes people just ask for politeness' sake or even just for the sake of asking. But his asking me was very different. As time went on, I always remembered the way he asked me. Some more time passed and I returned to his office just a few weeks ago.

It's strange. I keep making references to time "passing" or "years going by" and for me that's exactly what they did. But for him, the time just didn't "go by." The days and the weeks and the months were spent learning about me, learning about my case, learning about my eyes, my sight. When I went back to see him about two years later, I could tell that's how his time was being spent. I knew, again, from the second I went into his office that his last few months and years didn't just pass. I left there again that day with the same feeling I had on our first meeting. I knew this man would help me. I just knew it. But how much he would help me – no one, not me, not him, could have ever imagined.

Believe it or not, Mr. DeBlasio, the story has not really begun yet. It really begins about two weeks after my visit to his office. I was a little nervous upon my entrance into the courtroom for fairly obvious reasons I suppose. But again something strange happened. He came in the room and greeted me and my family and all of a sudden I wasn't nervous anymore. It was so odd, Mr. DeBlasio, he didn't say or do anything any normal person would not have done. But there was something different about him. We were in his arena now and I knew there was nothing to worry about.

The trial started and I knew my feeling was right. There was nothing at all to worry about. Certain people have this ability to shine in their profession like no one else can shine. Do you know what I mean, Mr. DeBlasio? I have seen it all my life. I've seen great lawyers, great doctors, great teachers, great professors. I've seen people who are at the top and I've seen how great they can be. But what I saw before me, for two and a half weeks after my entrance into that courtroom, I've never seen before. This man was incredible, Mr. DeBlasio. I wish you could have seen him. It was better than the best. Better than all that greatness I had seen throughout my life. I watched in absolute awe as he did his job. His mind was sharper than anything I had ever seen, his words were more passionate than anything I had ever heard. Even his opponents knew. Even they knew they paled in comparison. You could tell just by looking at them. They knew. I knew. Everyone knew. This man had a skill level that no one could touch. His actions and words were simply brilliant. So brilliant that at times

I forgot the case was about me. How is that possible, Mr. DeBlasio? How is it possible for someone to be sitting and listening to a case and forget it's about them? I know how it's possible. When what you're seeing in front of you is so amazing and so phenomenal, you do forget. I watched just to see where his mind would go next, where his expertise would lead him. Remember all those months I had talked about? I said I had known he spent time on me and my case. I could never ever have guessed how much. Mr. DeBlasio, this man crushed and destroyed leading specialists in the medical profession. Can you imagine the work he had to do in order to do that? He's a lawyer – he's not supposed to be able to surpass doctors on medical knowledge. But remarkably enough, he did on more than countable occasions.

He was doing something else, too, and I don't think he realized it at all. He was giving me back focus and interest. I had been interested in his profession for a little while and then for whatever reason just lost focus. Reading was too difficult, too tiresome. Who'd want to put in so much time and energy? I can just do something easier. But watching him made me remember why I had interest in the first place, made me see all the things the mind is capable of doing in this profession. I knew I'd never be as good as him. No one ever could be. But if I could even reach one-tenth of his level of intelligence and skill, that would be more than sufficient. Just watching him gave me back what I had lost. And he had no idea he ever did that. That was actually part of the beauty of his skill. He had to have known he was brilliant. Everyone else knew. But he never took himself for granted. Never once stopped questioning himself. He even once asked me if I were scared watching a direct examination of a witness. During the whole trial, I was never ever for a millisecond scared with him by my side. He had no idea how great he truly was.

As the days went on, his mind only got sharper, his case only got stronger. No matter what levels his opponents stooped to – and they went pretty low – he never even for a second considered meeting them down there. He was only concerned with truth and honesty and wouldn't give that up for anything in the world. That was another thing about his skill that was just so impressive. He knew he could play games just like the rest but that wasn't what he was about. He was about doing things the right way, the honorable way. No other way would be acceptable.

The last day of the trial arrived and I was sure there was nothing more he could do to impress me any further. Nothing more, he had done it all. But, I was proven wrong. His summation was the most beautiful, touching thing I had ever heard. It was so passionate and so heartfelt and no one could have put it better than he did. It was the strangest thing, Mr. DeBlasio. He knew what it was like to be me. I have never in 8 years felt as though someone "got it." I will never forget that on June 17, 2003, someone actually did. Someone understood and articulated it better than even I myself could have. He understood. How did he understand? How did he know about the metro? How did he know about the winter? I never told him. I know I didn't. I don't think I ever told anyone. But, he knew, Mr. DeBlasio. He really knew. It was amazing. He had shown me so much more than the level of his skill; he had shown me the level of his compassion and kindness. . . .

In 1995, I was sick and four people didn't believe me. But on November 1, I met someone who did. I haven't thought much about the four people, just the one person who helped me. That is what has gotten me through. Hindsight is the road that leads to foresight he said. . . .

In his summation, he brilliantly made reference to the Titanic. He has made sure that there is a difference between me and the Titanic. Because of all he has done and the heart and caring he has shown me, I know I will never sink.

I don't wish anything was done differently. My only deep hope and desire is that he knows what an honor it was to have him be my voice. I hope that he realizes that he has made sure that next time when one of these people sees a young girl or boy, this won't happen again. I hope he understands how much he has helped me and just how incredible he truly is. Do you think he does, Mr. DeBlasio? For some reason, I don't think he gets it. I mean, really, truly gets it. I wish more than ever that he did. I don't know how to make that happen. I wish he knew he was great. Maybe one day I should tell him?

Anyway I'm sorry for going on with this story. I hope that I didn't bore you. This man just made such an impression that I wanted to share it. Thank you for listening and for everything else. You have been truly wonderful.

With sincere love and appreciation,

Deepa

* * * * *

Staten Island, 2020

Dear Deepa,

All that I can say is thank you for the kindest words and sentiments anyone has ever expressed about me. I will lovingly carry them with me to my grave and because of them I will rest in peace.

Your friend Peter

CHAPTER 39

THE FARMER SAID: "IT IS COLD – LET'S GO IN FOR A CUP OF TEA"

In November 1985, Pamela Winston,[5] single and 29 years of age, employed by TWA as a flight attendant, was repeatedly raped while at the Lexington Hotel in Manhattan, in the room she was assigned following her flight from St. Louis landing at JFK.

In March and April 1993, her civil suit against the hotel's owner, Lextaj Corporation, for money damages for injuries (post-traumatic stress disorder) sustained at the time of her rape, was tried before Judge Carol Arber and a jury of six in New York County.

Civil suits of rape are rare. The basic reason being that the perpetrator of the crime, the rapist, is almost never sued because he does not have money to satisfy a judgment against him. To make a civil suit regarding a rape financially worthwhile there has to be a third party who is, in some manner of causality, also responsible for the rape.

In the Winston case that third party was the hotel.

From the plaintiff's point of view, the case against the hotel was open and shut in that the hotel provided services to the public, for a fee, and as such was duty-bound to offer and see to it that its guests were reasonably and safely cared for while on its premises. Adequate and safe security was a must.

From the defendant hotel's point of view, the case against it was without merit because it had nothing to do with the crime and, to the contrary, it complied with and exceeded all modern-day security and safety measures for the care of its guests.

The defendant fought this case tooth and nail for five weeks, led by attorney John Lyddane, a very tenacious and worthy adversary.

---

[5] I have changed the name for purposes of this story.

THE FACTS

At about 7:00 p.m. two days before Thanksgiving 1985, Ms. Winston and her TWA co-workers arrived at and were assigned their individual rooms at the Lexington Hotel. The hotel, at Lexington Avenue and 48th Street in the heart of Manhattan, was a 27-story building with 740 rooms for guests. There were six separate entrances from the street, one of which was open 24 hours a day, and five of which were open from 8:00 a.m. to midnight.

Ms. Winston and her co-workers were assigned to rooms on the ninth floor. Ms. Winston's room number was 916. Shortly after 7:00 p.m., one of the flight attendants while walking to an ice machine on the ninth floor saw and was spoken to by a large unkempt man with a beard and a foul body odor, who asked if she was one of the "stews" (i.e., stewardesses) who had just arrived with TWA. She was upset by this encounter and reported the incident to a telephone operator when she returned to her room shortly after.

About an hour later, Ms. Winston and four of her flight attendant friends (not including the one who saw the man roaming the hall) went to dinner in Manhattan, and then to another restaurant for a drink, returning to the hotel at about 1:00 a.m. Ms. Winston and another attendant talked for a few minutes while in the hallway outside of Room 916 and then Ms. Winston unlocked her door, entered her room, and went to the bathroom to get ready for bed. When she was done and stepping out of the bathroom, she was suddenly confronted by a large unkempt bearded man who lunged out from behind the window curtains, with a knife in hand, and rushed toward her. He warned her not to make a sound, tied her hands and feet with rope, blindfolded her, and forced her to lie on the bed.

Ms. Winston, who had been trained in dealing with terrorist and hijacking attacks on airplanes, tried to humanize herself and her attacker to keep him from killing her, which she thought was probably what was going to happen. For the next three hours, he repeatedly raped and sodomized her. He also went through her pocketbook and baggage asking her about and taking her jewelry, credit cards and the like.

At about 4:00 a.m., he finally told her he was going and that he would leave her room key outside the door, presumably so that whoever saw it could rescue her later that morning. When the door closed, she waited until she was sure he was gone, then unbound herself and, realizing that her attacker had cut the telephone wire, she went into the hallway and called out for help and was taken to a hospital. She shortly thereafter returned to her hotel room and was interviewed by the police.

Ms. Winston flew back to St. Louis that evening and when she entered her apartment together with one of the crew members, her phone was ringing. She answered and was panic stricken – the rapist was calling her with one of the telephone charge cards he had taken from her. From that day on, she was continually gripped by fear and the effects of post-traumatic stress disorder (PTSD) because of what he had done to her, and was still doing. This fear and PTSD lasted up until our trial, even though she had testified in his criminal case in 1989 and knew he was convicted and sentenced to be imprisoned for 25 years to life.

THE CIVIL TRIAL

Looking back on the trial, I think there were five crucial factors that played prominent roles in the outcome of the lawsuit:

1. One question for the first time in my life I asked a jury panel, on the fourth day of jury selection.
2. Salvatore Schillizzi, our expert locksmith.
3. Lawrence Stanton and Anthony Richardson – two Pinkerton security analysts.
4. Isaac Yeffet – the head of security for El Al Israel Airlines.
5. Pamela Winston herself.

Number 1. On the fourth day of intensive questioning in jury selection, I decided to bring up a subject for the first time in order to keep the jury's attention. I don't believe I had a subliminal feeling about it, but rather just asked the question to vary the proceedings and keep them interesting. I frankly could not conceive of anyone being critical of a rape victim but, in any event, I told them about her terrorism and hijacking training and I said that as a result, she did not fight the rapist and did not resist. I then asked if that factor would in any way affect anyone about their feelings for Ms. Winston.

I was shocked when one of the prospective jurors said it would affect him. He was a middle-aged Black man who had been one of my favorites on the jury. He said that he was a Jehovah's Witness and its teachings instilled in him the absolute belief that when one is assaulted, as in the case of rape, that person had to resist to the death even if it came to that. No matter what I said to him after that, he remained adamant.

Immediately following that, a Black woman juror whom I also liked said that she too was a Jehovah's Witness, and she also believed that it was wrong for Ms. Winston to acquiesce and not resist, even if it were to cost her life. Both jurors were then excused because they couldn't be fair and impartial to Ms. Winston. This religious belief never would have come to light, though, if I had not asked the question about resistance, because one of the tenets of our legal system is that we are not allowed to ask jurors about religion. (I have always wondered what the outcome of Ms. Winston's case would have been if these two people would have remained as two of the final six jurors who voted on this case, especially since we needed five of the six to vote in our favor in order to win.)

Number 2. We had a great expert. Sal Schillizzi was a locksmith who had been voted Locksmith of the Year by a national locksmith association; who had testified as an expert witness before the United States Senate; and who was a lecturer at John Jay College of Criminal Justice in the art of locksmithing.

In November 1986, one year after the rape, an investigator from my office stayed in Room 916, overnight, as a paying guest. Mr. Schillizzi accompanied him and examined and tested the door leading into the room. He found the door to be grossly defective: it had the widest space he had ever seen between a steel door frame and its door. Because of the excessive widening, the lock's latches and dead bolts were worthless. He proved it by inserting a credit card into the space between the door and its frame and then, simply turning the card one time, he unlocked the door within one second. He repeated this maneuver five times and our investigator photographed him doing so.

At trial, Mr. Schillizzi testified that at the time the door to Room 916 was installed, five years before the rape, the excessively widened space already existed and, if due to wear and tear there had been any change in the space over the five years, it would have narrowed and not widened that gap. His explanation of the worthlessness of the lock on the door to Room 916 was simple and completely convincing. When he finished testifying, our theory that the rapist entered Room 916 by use of a credit card and not because Ms. Winston negligently left the door open, as claimed by the hotel, was clear to all in the courtroom.

Number 3. We, therefore, now only had left to prove the second part of our negligence claim against the hotel, that the security it provided to its guests was totally inadequate. This we did by calling two witnesses who were security analysts at the famed Pinkerton Security Agency, Lawrence Stanton and Anthony Richardson.

In October 1985, one month prior to the rape, the hotel entered into a contract with Pinkerton to take over and provide security for the hotel and its guests. Stanton and Richardson, two former officers in the United States Marines, were assigned by Pinkerton to examine and analyze the security measures then in place. Their report to Pinkerton and the hotel management, back in October, could not have been more damning regarding the total inadequacy of the hotel's so-called security and safety procedures.

The following excerpts from their respective testimony show the manner in which they expressed their views:

> STANTON - I told Mr. Bhadah [the hotel manager] in no uncertain terms that the security he insisted we were to provide was impossible – ridiculous – absurd – crazy – nuts – inadequate – and I made it absolutely clear to him exactly what I thought.
>
> RICHARDSON - I told Mr. Bhadah he needed to have closed-circuit TV monitors installed; he needed additional lighting on the 48th Street doors; he needed 3 security officers 24 hours a day, seven days a week, 2 in the lobby and 1 just for the package room (which needed significant renovation); he needed 2 additional security officers 24 hours a day, seven days a week, to patrol the entire hotel; and he needed 1 supervisor, eight hours a day, five days a week. Total 880 hours. I told him that was the absolute minimum.

The end result: Mr. Bhadah completely ignored Mr. Stanton and Mr. Richardson. He told Pinkerton there would be no contract unless they agreed to *his* terms: one security officer in the lobby, one in the package room, and one on patrol. A total of 260 hours a week. And no TV monitors. Pinkerton, whose aim was to get a foothold in the New York hotel market, agreed to Mr. Bhadah's terms.

Thus, on November 1, 1985, less than a month before the rape, Pinkerton took on the security contract. The jury was correctly charged by Judge Arber that the hotel, not the Pinkerton Security Agency, was liable for any negligence on Pinkerton's part, and Stanton and Richardson's testimony proved to be devastating against the hotel.

Number 4. If any more was needed for us to prove our case, it was provided by the hotel when its attorney, Mr. Lyddane, called as a witness Isaac Yeffet, the head of security for El Al Israel Airlines.

In jury selection and in his opening, Mr. Lyddane made much of the fact that the Lexington Hotel's security system was so much respected that El Al, the world's most security-conscious airline, had its flight crew stay at only one hotel in New York, namely the Lexington Hotel.

That farce was put to rest before Mr. Yeffet left the stand. His testimony went as I summarize here:

> El Al's flight crews stayed at the Lexington Hotel when they flew to, and had stay overs in, New York. At all times and without exception the security provided to them at the Lexington Hotel was solely provided by and under the direction and supervision of Israeli security officers. Israeli security was limited and confined to its Israeli crews and no one else in the hotel.
>
> Typically, there were 150 El Al crew members at the hotel at any one time. They occupied five floors in a row where they were the only people on those floors. For safety reasons, they never occupied the hotel's lower floors or its top floor. They averaged 30 crew members on each of the five floors, one person to a room.
>
> There were 30 armed Israeli security officers guarding the 150 crew members at all times, stationed as follows: 1) each floor had two passenger elevators and one freight elevator, and posted at each of the three elevators, on each of the five floors, was one armed guard, 24 hours a day; 2) each floor had two stairways, and posted at each of them, on each of the five floors, was one armed guard, 24 hours a day; and 3) on each of the five floors one additional armed guard patrolled the corridors, 24 hours a day. Thus, at least six armed Israeli security guards were on duty, 24 hours a day, on each of the five floors.

In other words, those five floors of the hotel, but only those five floors, were in fact an Israeli armed camp. No one, but no one, could enter those floors without the permission of the Israelis. Compare those five floors with the rest of the floors and the lobby of the hotel, where only three security personnel were provided in total, and the hotel's claim that its security was top-grade was nothing but pathetic.

Number 5. The final critical piece to our victory was Pamela Winston herself. She was an excellent witness and related her ordeal to the jury in a clear, concise and no-frills manner.

When it came time for my summation, I felt for the first time in my life that I was not equipped to explain to a jury what happened to my client and how it affected that client's life. I was brought up in a different age when rape was not publicized, and so was unheard of. I told the jury that I could not speak for Ms. Winston, but would let her speak for herself:

> When I was thinking to myself all of last night what to say to you today, I thought to myself Pamela Winston should be making the summation. But it is not allowed. She should be making it because who knows more than she.
>
> No one knows more than Pamela Winston, and she made her summation when she made that one bit of testimony that I will never forget – and I will be presumptuous, you will never forget it either – when she told you about her suicide attempt.
>
> She told that story, how she went when she was a young girl to a farm, 30 miles outside where she grew up, and how happy she was there, and how after the rape she went back for that last look.
>
> She had a loaded gun.
>
> But for the grace of whatever you believe in, she was about to fire that bullet and end her life because of what this hotel permitted to happen to her, when a farmer came along.
>
> The farmer said: "It is cold – let's go in for a cup of tea."
>
> How can I sum up better than that? What more summation do you need? What a horrible way to live.
>
> I ask of you, Let Justice Be Done. Thank you.

The jury found the hotel liable and awarded $2,000,000 in damages. The hotel appealed. The Appellate Division affirmed the jury's verdict in all respects, and the $2,000,000 was paid.

POSTSCRIPT: Shortly after the rape, Ms. Winston retired from TWA because of her overwhelming fear of staying in hotel rooms and being attacked again. She moved from St. Louis to Washington State and there she met and married a veterinarian who attended to large animals, including horses, which she had loved so much as a child. She flew in to New York for the trial, and immediately thereafter returned to Washington, where I believe she still lives today and where I hope she has found a degree of peace and tranquility.

CHAPTER 40

The Killer Pillar

Emotion, like many things, has its time and place; the courtroom, however, is not one of those places. Emotion should never come into play there at any time, as I so often tried to explain to my juries. Unfortunately, in a case I tried in 1983 I was so affected by emotion that I did not follow my own advice, and although I achieved what was recognized as a great verdict at the time, unfortunately for my clients it ended up being a pyrrhic one.

Why did I become so emotional that it affected my judgment and veered me off course? Answer - because I felt sorry for the mother of a 20-year-old young man who died in the accident that gave rise to the lawsuit. Why did I feel sorry for her? Answer - because she sat in court every day for a month with two of her sisters who were Catholic nuns, tearfully listening to her boy being pilloried for causing the death of another young man and serious injuries to three 19-year-old women.

Why was he being so unfairly maligned? Because the lawyer representing him was inept and did not put a stop to it. Why was I so concerned? Because I felt an injustice was being committed.

What did I do then to try to correct the way the proceedings were going? I, in the middle of the trial, decided to right the wrong and protect the underdog by becoming an advocate for the mother and son.

Why was that improper? Because not only were he and she not my clients, but we were antagonists as I was representing two of the young women passengers suing his estate. Weird? Yes. Why then do what I did? Because I thought justice called for it. Was I right? Yes, and no. You be the judge.

* * * * *

On April 9, 1978 at about 3:30 a.m. at the intersection of 86th Street and New Utrecht Avenue in Brooklyn, a car driven by James Cassidy struck one of the pillars that supported the elevated subway tracks. Cassidy and his front-seat passenger John Gaffney died at the scene. The three back seat passengers, Debra Cordero (my client), Maria Cacicio (my client) and Patricia Ann Spinelli, sustained injury.

Cassidy and his four passengers had been at a party that Saturday night-Sunday morning at a home on 65th Street near New Utrecht Avenue, about 21 blocks and slightly over one mile from the crash site. Cassidy had volunteered to drive the three young women to their homes, even though they lived in the opposite direction from his home and he was unfamiliar with that area of Brooklyn.

To get to the crash site, he drove on New Utrecht Avenue from 65th Street to 86th Street where the roadway curved from a southerly direction to the east. During those 21 blocks, there were about 84 pillars supporting the elevated subway tracks (i.e., four pillars per block), set about 50 feet apart along the roadway, and about two feet from the right side of his vehicle. The same pattern was true on the other side, for the northbound vehicles on New Utrecht Avenue.

When Cassidy reached the curve at 86th Street and while making a left turn to follow the roadway, he came upon and struck the first pillar placed at the end of the curve. The only safety devices on that pillar were diamond-shaped hazard markers.

Upon autopsy, young Cassidy's blood alcohol content was recorded as .21%, about three times higher than the legal limit allowed when driving a motor vehicle, and a violation of New York's Vehicle and Traffic Law No. 1192 (i.e., operating a motor vehicle while under the influence of alcohol or drugs).

Representing Cordero and Cacicio, we sued Cassidy's estate and the City of New York.

In regard to Cassidy's estate, we claimed he was negligent in the operation of his motor vehicle. In regard to the City, we claimed that the placement of the subject pillar constituted an extreme hazard to traffic, and the unlighted warning and safety device employed there – the diamond-shaped hazard markers – were totally insufficient to warn motorists of the pillar's presence. We also claimed that the City had due notice of this hazard because a local Brooklyn newspaper had published an article about the number of motor vehicle accidents occurring at this specific pillar, and that it was in fact so notorious it was known in the neighborhood as the "Killer Pillar."

The City's defense was that it, as a municipality, was exempt from liability for injuries that occurred at a place such as this where a duly-executed highway plan was in effect. In addition, since 1972, the Borough Engineer had conducted three surveys of the area and in 1977, he considered and rejected a proposal to install a system of blinking hazard lights.

At trial we produced an expert in highway design who testified about the extreme hazard and total insufficiency of the hazard markers in place, especially because they were unlighted; at a minimum, blinking hazard lights should be added. The City produced the Borough Engineer who had done the surveys and he testified that the devices in place were adequate and reasonable, and that the additional safety measure suggested by the plaintiff's expert would actually have increased the existing hazard.

Six lawyers took part in the trial: 1) one for the City defendant; 2) one for Cassidy's estate (the insurance company) as a *defendant*; 3) one for Cassidy's estate (his mother) as a *plaintiff* against the City; 4) one for passenger Spinelli as a plaintiff against the two defendants, Cassidy and the City; 5) one lawyer (me) for passengers Cordero and Cacicio as plaintiffs against the two defendants; and 6) one for the front-seat passenger's estate (John Gaffney's mother) as a plaintiff against the two defendants.

On trial, the three women passengers testified about how gracious Cassidy had been in offering to drive them home and although all of them had been drinking at this party, none of them was drunk and Cassidy showed no evidence of being drunk. They all testified that he drove carefully and within the speed limit for the 21 blocks until the crash occurred at the "Killer Pillar."

The problem in the case for the plaintiffs was that Cassidy had the minimum policy, which was known as a "10 and 20," which meant that his insurance company would pay no more than $10,000 for an individual, and no more than $20,000 for the entire accident. Thus, here, if they received equal shares, the four plaintiffs (the three surviving female passengers and the deceased male passenger) would get no more than $5,000 each. The City, on the other hand, had what was referred to in legal circles as "Big Pockets," meaning there was no limit on the amount it could pay.

Since Cassidy's liability was seen as obvious, the thrust of the case was against the City, proving not just that it was liable, but that it was wholly responsible. My view was that certainly Cassidy with a .21% blood alcohol content was negligent, but his lawyers had a legitimate way out, namely that his drunk driving was not a "proximate" cause of the accident and the injuries (that is, it was neither the main cause nor a substantial factor in the accident). He could have been as sober as a judge and still crashed into the pillar, because the pillar was on a curve, unlighted, and not visible to a car turning left. At nighttime, you had to know the neighborhood to know the pillar was there, and Cassidy didn't. Otherwise, it would only be at the last second that the car's headlights would shine on the pillar to bring it into view.

The City's negligence was also obvious. There should have been blinking lights on that pillar – period. And more importantly, the lack of blinking lights was a proximate cause, if not the *sole* cause, of the accident because with a blinking light Cassidy would have had sufficient time to see the pillar and avoid it.

But midway through trial, it had become obvious to me that Cassidy's lawyer had missed these points and his ineffectiveness was causing an injustice to occur. I felt I had to try to salvage Cassidy's case on account of his mother and his aunts (the two nuns), for two reasons.

First, I could not bear to have a mother live the rest of her life with a jury verdict saying that her beloved son was responsible for the death of another mother's son. It would unfairly multiply the grief and sorrow she was suffering for her own loss.

Second, I always felt sorry for nuns. I could never understand how nuns could give up all of the earthly pleasures of life – including raising children. (I did, however, in a way admire their sacrifice.) And here, I felt doubly sorry for the nuns because young Cassidy was their kin too, their nephew, and I knew that despite all of their prayers for him, the case was doomed.

In summation, I argued as if Cassidy were my client, a very simple, logical argument with words to the effect that:

> If he was so drunk and that's the reason he drove into that Killer Pillar, then let the City or anyone else explain how and why he was able to drive for more than a mile with these pillars two feet from the right side of his car, every 50 feet, and never veer off and crash into one of them. Who in his right mind can think it is pure coincidence that he chose the Killer Pillar to end his life?

But before I get to the verdict, I want to tell about a most unusual happenstance when Judge Frank Vaccaro sent the jury to deliberate, which gives a sense of why I was so sure Cassidy's case would have been doomed if I had not intervened.

One of our six main jurors – a Black woman who was a favorite of mine – told the judge that she wanted to be excused and did not want to take part in deliberating. This was the first time that I had ever seen or heard of such a thing happening, and if I wasn't crushed, I was very chagrined. The judge excused her and replaced her with an alternate.

Lo and behold, when we lawyers went to the hallway outside the courtroom to await the verdict, there she was and she started to talk with the other five lawyers. I made it a point to be alone while a jury deliberated, and so I was sitting on a radiator cover about 20 feet away from the group smoking a cigar, but I could hear some of the talk.

It went something like this:

> The lawyers asked her why she excused herself from deliberations. She told them that she couldn't stand being "cooped up with that dark-skinned Juror No. 4 for another minute." (Juror No. 4 was also a woman and the only other African-American on the jury.) "The way she was smiling and flirting with all of you was making me sick."
>
> The City lawyer asked her how she would have voted and she said, "90% against the City and 10% against Cassidy." He told her he was surprised that she voted against him because every time he saw her in the elevator, she smiled at him and he thought she liked him and was on his side. "Honey, I can smile at you and at the same time put a knife into you" was her response.
>
> She then went down the list of the lawyers and lambasted them one at a time. When she got to the fifth lawyer, who represented Ms. Spinelli, she said: "You, you get up after DeBlasio and do nothing but try to copy him – and you were way short."

I knew my turn to be blasted was next, but I thought it might be cowardly for me to leave, and so I stayed and heard her say: "What can you say about DeBlasio? There's only one DeBlasio and that is DeBlasio." (This was before our city's present mayor Bill de Blasio was elected and became famous, so I guess she was fairly accurate in her assessment.)

As for the verdict, she was wrong about the percentage of fault. The jurors voted 100% liability against the City and none against Cassidy, and so all plaintiffs, including Cassidy, were awarded damages. The two highest awards were to my clients, $1,250,000 to Cordero for a fractured femur (thigh bone), and $500,000 to Cacicio for internal injuries.

The City appealed. The Appellate Division reversed the judgement and sent the case back for a new trial, stating: "The Court refused to instruct the jury that a violation of the statute (Vehicle and Traffic Law No. 1192) would constitute negligence. . . . The unexcused violation of a statutory standard of care is negligence and can create liability if found to be a proximate cause of the accident."

I believe that the Appellate Division's decision to reverse was very wrong because Cassidy's negligence in driving with such a blood alcohol level was obvious to the jury, but the jurors nevertheless and correctly found that his drunkenness was not a proximate cause of the accident. Findings on proximate cause are fact questions not for the Appellate Court, but for the jury – the factfinders – and there was a legitimate basis here for the jury to have decided that Cassidy's driving under the influence was not a proximate cause of the accident and injuries, and that the sole cause of fault was that of the City.

Naturally, the Appellate Division judges were not present at the trial and did not see Mrs. Cassidy and the two nuns, and that is the way it is supposed to be, and I guess that is one of the reasons why the Statue of Justice holding the scales of justice is blindfolded – so that she does not let emotion cloud her impartiality. If I were still trying cases, I guess I should allow myself to be blindfolded, so long as they don't also tape my mouth.

The following year, one of my partners re-tried the case. This time my firm represented all three back seat passengers, because Ms. Spinelli had asked us to replace her lawyer, which we did.

I am terribly sorry that the second trial tried by my then-partner turned out to be a catastrophe. The jury did a complete turn-around, and then some. In regard to liability, it found Cassidy 99% at fault and the City only 1% responsible. And in regard to damages, it awarded Ms. Cordero only $75,000 (as opposed to the $1,250,000 in the first trial), Ms. Cacicio $25,000 (as opposed to the $500,000 in the first trial), and Ms. Spinelli $25,000.

And then to add insult to injury, the jury cut their awards in half – down to $37,500, $12,500 and $12,500 respectively – because it found that the three passengers were *contributorily negligent* in accepting the ride home.

When he returned to our office, I asked one question of my partner: "Why?" His answer: "The jury didn't like drunk drivers." I couldn't resist answering him: "What do you think – that they loved drunk drivers when I tried the case last year?" Harsh but true, and I dissolved our partnership a few years later.

POSTSCRIPT: One year after I tried the case, one of my daughters during a college semester abroad in Bogota, Colombia, was at a party with a classmate, when three young men graciously offered to drive my daughter and her American friend to their respective host-families' homes. Neither of the girls realized that the boys, who had only just arrived at the party, were under the influence of anything. They accepted the kind offer and all five went out to the car. The driver drove carefully through the downtown city streets and then onto a fairly quiet divided four-lane road heading south toward the outer reaches of the sprawling city. He went along fine for about five minutes, the roadway straight as an arrow, when all of a sudden he drove headlong into a lamp post in the center divider, and his tin-can of a Peugeot flipped and landed on its roof.

My 20-year-old daughter, in the front seat between two of the boys, was unscathed and, as neither she nor any of the others was wearing a seat belt, she ended up upright, sitting on what in normal circumstances was the interior roof of the car. (I dare not imagine what would have happened if she, like David Braun, had been strapped in by a belt.) The car had simply flipped 180 degrees around the five children.

All five of them clambered out, afraid that the car might explode. It didn't, and my daughter came home to us months later, but told us nothing about the incident for years.

Even though the Cordero-Cassidy trial took place before my daughter's accident, I believe that in a way her accident – at the time only a potentiality – was one of the reasons I was so emotional about the case. The death of any child, if under only slightly altered circumstances, could be the death of any one of our own.

I have always believed as John Donne so eloquently wrote that we are each of us inextricably bound to all humankind, that we cannot but grieve for the loss of others as we would grieve for our own, that we cannot but make every effort to lessen the burden on the survivors as they, were circumstances different, would do for us. And my way, the only way I know, is by trying their cases.

CHAPTER 41

HEART AND SOUL

In 1996 I tried a case with a terrific client-witness, Lynne Baumgarten, and we ended up winning the highest award for "loss of consortium" in New York history. "Loss of consortium" is a separate cause of action brought within a personal injury lawsuit specifically on behalf of the spouse of the injured plaintiff. Its purpose is to compensate the spouse for the loss of the plaintiff's "services" – which run the gamut from errands done around the home to physical intimacy – during the time the plaintiff is injured. In the Baumgarten case, the loss of consortium claim arose as part of the medical malpractice lawsuit we brought on behalf of Mr. Baumgarten against a neuro-ophthalmologist for injuries suffered when receiving treatment for a brain tumor.

Although the loss of consortium verdict was quite significant, the unbelievable factor concerning this case was that if Mrs. Baumgarten had tried to bring a loss of consortium lawsuit just a few decades earlier, it would not have been permitted in New York (and most of the other states in our country). Not because there was no such cause of action – loss of consortium as a claim has been around for centuries – it simply was not recognized as a ground for *wives* to be compensated.

The reason was simple. In Old England, when a tortfeasor or wrongdoer (the defendant) injured a man's cow or pig, under the law the tortfeasor was liable in damages to the owner for that injury. He had to compensate the owner for *the loss of the services* which that animal – the man's chattel – would have provided but for the injury. In Old England, and New York until 1969, wives were similarly considered a man's chattel and in some instances treated little differently under the law than his cows and pigs.

So, if someone injured a man's wife, he could recover money for the loss of her (his chattel's) services for him. The wife had no reciprocal right to compensation if someone injured her husband, because he was decidedly *not* her chattel. He was not considered to be in the relationship to serve her, and so she had no right when he was injured to claim that she had lost services to which she was entitled.

In 1969, in an action brought by Pauline Millington, New York's highest court finally decided that an action for loss of consortium by a wife could stand. What had always been good for the gander was now considered good as well for the goose. The Millington Court reasoned as follows:

> The concept of consortium includes not only loss of support or services, it also embraces such elements as love, companionship, affection, society, sexual relations, solace and more. . . . It is the interest which may have turned a happily married woman into a life-long nurse and deprived her of the opportunity of rearing children. . . . The loss of companionship, emotional support, love, felicity and sexual relations are real injuries. The trauma of having to care for a permanent invalid is known to have caused mental illness. There may not be a deterioration in the marital relationship, but it will certainly alter it in a tragic way.
>
> . . .
>
> If the husband's potency is lost or impaired, it is both the man and woman who are affected.
>
> . . .
>
> Money . . . is the only known means to compensate [a wife] for the loss suffered and to symbolize society's recognition that a culpable wrong – even if unintentional – has been done.

The vote in Millington was a narrow one, four judges in the majority and three judges in dissent.

But back to the Baumgartens' case.

THE FACTS

In regard to the facts, they followed a pattern familiar in malpractice cases. The defendant's acts of negligence were clear and obvious, whereas the proximate cause (i.e., the causality connecting the negligence to the injuries) created problems in the plaintiff's proof.

In 1982, 33-year-old Gregory Baumgarten went to see his ophthalmologist after about a month of double vision, severe headaches and a sixth-nerve palsy that prevented his right eye from moving to the right. Upon examination, the ophthalmologist believed Mr. Baumgarten presented with classic signs of a brain tumor: the double vision and headaches together with the sixth-nerve palsy. He sent Mr. Baumgarten to a neuro-ophthalmologist, Defendant Dr. Slavin, so that he could either confirm that a tumor existed and then refer Mr. Baumgarten to a neurosurgeon for treatment, or rule a tumor out of the equation.

Dr. Slavin treated Mr. Baumgarten for four months in 1982 and even though a CAT scan taken during that time confirmed abnormalities at the site of the cavernous sinus of the brain (a space filled with blood vessels), Dr. Slavin decided that Mr. Baumgarten had an infection and not a brain tumor. When he discharged him from his care in May 1982, he told Mr. Baumgarten that he did not have a tumor; his problems could have been caused by infection; there was nothing more he could do for him; and there was a psychological overlay to what he was suffering.

Believing in and trusting Dr. Slavin, the Baumgartens were relieved that there was no tumor and did not seek further work-up or care until eighteen months later when Mr. Baumgarten developed a ptosis of his right eye (a droop of his upper eyelid caused by a third-nerve deficit). He then had another CAT scan, which showed an increase of the abnormalities of the cavernous sinus.

A different neuro-ophthalmologist now determined that Mr. Baumgarten did have a brain tumor at that site, and that it had been growing during the previous eighteen months. He sent Mr. Baumgarten to New York Hospital where the Chief of Neurosurgery, Dr. Russell Patterson, performed surgery on the tumor.

Dr. Patterson could not remove the tumor completely because of numerous blood vessels in and around the cavernous sinus. The pathology report at the time of surgery indicated that the tumor was a chordoma (a malignant cancer that is deadly if permitted to continue to grow unchecked). He removed as much of the tumor as he possibly could, then referred Mr. Baumgarten to Harvard's Massachusetts General Hospital for proton beam radiation. (In 1983, Massachusetts General was the only facility in the country using proton beam therapy for this type of tumor, and Dr. John Munzenrider was the pioneer in the field.) Dr. Munzenrider treated Mr. Baumgarten with proton beam radiation in late 1983 and early 1984.

By the end of 1984, however, harmful side effects from the proton beam radiation came to the fore, and Mr. Baumgarten sustained massive permanent injuries, including total blindness in his right eye; half blindness in his left eye; epileptic seizures; total deafness of his right ear; excruciating headaches treated by 500 milligrams of morphine daily; pituitary and endocrine damage necessitating life-long medication to survive; loss of balance; loss of memory; and impotence.

THE LAWSUIT

Regarding liability, we claimed that Dr. Slavin departed from accepted practice not only in failing to diagnose the tumor, but in failing to even consider it possibly existed. We also claimed that by wrongly telling him he had no tumor, he deprived Mr. Baumgarten - who relied on him completely and unconditionally - of the opportunity to seek a second opinion and obtain further work-ups so that a correct diagnosis could be made.

Regarding causality, we claimed that the 18-month delay in diagnosis deprived Mr. Baumgarten of the substantial probability that earlier proton beam treatment - in 1982 when the tumor was much smaller - would not have destroyed nearly as much healthy brain tissue as it ultimately did in 1983. The failure to timely alert Mr. Baumgarten that he had a life-threatening brain tumor doomed Mr. Baumgarten's chances for a cure.

Dr. Slavin's defense regarding the liability was that he did not depart from accepted medical practice in failing to diagnose the tumor because, although he wanted to continue treating Mr. Baumgarten, Mr. Baumgarten suddenly stopped going to him. Regarding causality, Dr. Slavin's defense was that even if he had known there was a tumor back in early 1982, it was not removable then and Mr. Baumgarten would have needed radiation anyway; and what's more, it was Dr. Munzenrider's proton beam radiation treatments that caused the injuries because of Dr. Munzenrider's negligence.

In 1996, 14 years after his initial visit to Dr. Slavin, we went to trial. The five-week trial, at which 18 medical experts testified, was presided over by Judge E.T. O'Brien who was totally fair and knowledgeable throughout.

Lynne Baumgarten was an excellent witness - honest, direct, concise, and without pleas for sympathy. The following are excerpts from her testimony on direct examination regarding her loss of consortium claim.

QUESTION (DeBlasio) – Tell us, please, what have you done for your husband from 1982, say the beginning of '82 to the present, before the tumor was discovered and after the tumor? What services, if any? What aid, what help, what anything have you done? Think slowly, think to yourself. I can't put words in your mouth. Think and tell us and this is basically your only chance to tell us.

ANSWER (Lynne Baumgarten) – I do whatever I can do for him. If he doesn't feel well, stay with him. I try to help him, you know, to feel better. I've taken him to the doctor whenever we had to go. And I try to lift his spirits a little to make him feel better and I try to do whatever I can.

Q – Give us some examples, please. For example, bathing or showering, any involvement?

A – When my husband takes a shower if he's not feeling well, usually I stay upstairs with him, you know, like right – either in the bathroom or right outside because he's afraid he's going to fall while he's in the shower.

Q – Well, give us examples like that. You say, I do things for him and I do whatever I can, that's good, but those are generalizations. Try and give us an idea. We don't expect you to tell us 12 years. Just give us a few little ideas, examples.

A – When, if I'm at work and he's not feeling well, he'll call me and I'll, you know, go right home. If he's having like a seizure, you know, I go right in and I stay with him until he feels better. A lot of times anywhere we have to go I have to assist him. He really can't go by himself. And so wherever we go, wherever he goes, I usually take him. I have to help him walk because otherwise his balance is bad. And he doesn't see. He walks into things. He can't cross the street. He really can't see well enough.

Q – Do you go anywhere for fun?

A – No.

Q – Do you go dancing?

A – No, no.

Q – Did you ever dance?

A – A long time ago.

Q – Did you like it?

A – Yes.

Q – Did you dance with your husband?

A – Yes.

Q – Did you do any sports?

A – Not really.

Q – Does he?

A – No.

Q – Do you go out with friends?

A – Very rarely. We – my husband doesn't like anybody to see him sick. So we really don't have people come over and like we don't have neighbors come in because he – you never know when he's not going to feel well and he really doesn't like anyone to see him that way.

Q – Where do you work?

A – I work for Catholic Charities.

Q –Doing what?

A – I work in a residence home for mentally disabled adults.

Q – How often?

A – I work five days a week.

Q – How many hours?

A – 40 hours.

Q – Who takes care of your husband when you're not there?

A – Well, he's by himself if I'm not there, but my job, I can stay home if I don't feel well. I do paperwork and if he's not feeling well, I can, you know, do it at home. Or if he calls me and says, I'm not feeling well, I can be home in like ten minutes. And my parents live close by, so they'd run over if he wasn't well.

Q – This is your mother here?

A – Yes.

Q – Your father?

A – My father passed away.

Q – When?

A – Just recently.

Q – This subject I want to ask you, with the Court's permission, only two or three questions. If there is something that you know of that sexually is wrong with your husband?

A – Yes.

Q – What is it?

A – He's impotent.

Q – How long has he been so?

A – Probably nine or ten years, I'm not sure.

Q – In the last nine or ten years, have you had any sexual relations?

A – No.

Q – Did you used to when you were young and married with your husband before all this?

A – Yes.

Q – The making of love and the relations, did they give you pleasure and joy and happiness?

A – Yes.

Q – Do you miss that?

A – Yes.

Mr. Baumgarten's testimony about his wife's loss of consortium was perhaps even more powerful than was hers. The following are some excerpts from his direct examination in this regard.

> QUESTION (DeBlasio) – Please tell us, we're in 1996, say this year, eleven months or almost eleven complete months, what does your wife do for you, if anything?
>
> ANSWER (Mr. Baumgarten) – She's a godsend to me. She, number one, if I don't feel good, if she's working, she comes home. She either takes the kids and drops them off to her parents or her mom now, or if she can't, she takes maybe two of them to work and leaves two of them there, or the kids will go across the street to a neighbor's house.
>
> Also, she maintains the house very good. She cooks and makes it easy for me whereas the next day I just have to put the food in the microwave or in the oven to heat it up for me and my children and my wife. She mows the lawn. She takes care of the car. She does put oil in. And that's just one of a few things. She makes sure also that I always have my medicine, the right supply, which we both know is very important. And at the moment, that's all I can think of.
>
> Q – Does she do anything with you in regard to nursing, the broad sense of nursing?
>
> A – Yes.
>
> Q – What does she do?
>
> A – If I'm in very bad pain, she stays with me and she tries to help relieve the pain by keeping the children quiet. And it's very hard for them, but they're very good, four girls, very good. They know by now it's a fact of life. I love them and they love me very much. And also when I'm taking a shower, she stays upstairs to make sure that I don't slip or if I need something, she can come right away to me.
>
> Q – When you say when you have severe pain she nurses you, how often is that?

A – Oh, well, before I took morphine, that was almost daily. Now it's about two or three days a week.

Q – When did you start taking morphine?

A – I'm not sure, but it may have been about two to four years ago.

Q – So this nursing, this caring by your wife has been done by her since when approximately?

A – Since, really since a few months after we got married, because I was, after we got married I was hit by a car, she nursed me through that. And then soon after that we went through the brain tumor, tried to find out what it was. And then we went through an operation. Then I went back to work for several months, then I lost my sight, started getting bad seizures and since the beginning of the marriage she's been a wonderful, loving, caring wife. And also a nurse to me.

Q – There's been evidence that from about August 1987, after you got out of Mercy Hospital the second time, for about a year you were not living with your wife. Do you remember that?

A – Yes.

Q – Why was that?

A – The stress on her, my wife Lynne, was too much and I could see to have somebody in pain all the time around you is hard. And at the time we were having fights and everything. It even bothered the children. But I didn't like it at the time, but that one year apart saved out marriage.

Q – Do you remember the two admissions to Mercy Hospital, one in August of '85, one in August of '87, where you stayed there approximately a month each time?

A – Yes.

Q – Do you know why you were admitted?

A – Yes.

Q – Why?

A – Because each time I took an overdose of medicine.

Q – Was that accidental, was that negligent, was it intentional or something else?

A – It was intentional.

Q – Why?

A – Because I saw myself as an additional burden to my wife. She was being so good to me and just – it's hard to explain, but inside me I didn't feel worth it. We have four small girls and she's trying to take care of them, trying to take care of me, trying to have money to run the house, the family, and I saw if I was out of the way maybe things would be better financially and also emotionally in the house.

Q – Do you still feel that way?

A – No, not now.

Q – Are you depressed now?

A – No.

Q – Are you happy with your life?

A – I've accepted my life.

Q – Are you happy with your wife?

A – Very much.

After the Baumgartens, I called Dr. Munzenrider to the witness stand. I questioned him for half an hour on direct examination. The defendant's lawyer, C.A. Bartlett, Jr., a very worthy opponent, then questioned him for most of that day and the next. At the completion of his cross-examination, which finished just about at the end of the court day, I requested permission to conduct a short redirect examination. I believe that those four minutes of my redirect, which I include here in its entirety, clearly explained, drove home and cemented our case:

MR. BARTLETT: Thank you. I have nothing further, your Honor.

MR. DeBLASIO: May I?

THE COURT: Yes. Can we finish up with the doctor today?

MR. DeBLASIO: I'm going to finish up by a quarter to 5, which I'm grateful I was given four minutes. I'll finish up so we don't bring the doctor back for the third day.

REDIRECT EXAMINATION BY MR. DeBLASIO:

Q – Doctor, nice rapid fire like a machine gun. Did the radiation make Mr. Baumgarten go blind, yes or no?

A – Yes.

Q – Did the delay from 1982 to 1983 in diagnosing the tumor make him go blind, yes or no?

A – Yes.

Q – In 1982, had you treated him with the proton beam radiation therapy, would you have been anywhere near the optic chiasm to cause the blindness, yes or no? [The "optic chiasm" is where half of the nerve fibers from each eye's retina cross over to the opposite side of the brain. The half that do not cross over travel to the same side of the brain, and this split allows each half of the brain to receive visual signals from both eyes.]

A – We would have been able to deliver less dose to the chiasm in 1982 than in 1983.

Q – Would he have gone blind with a reasonable degree of medical certainty with your treatment in 1982?

A – The probability of blindness would have been much less.

Q – Would he have gone blind respectfully with a reasonable degree of medical certainty in your opinion?

A – No.

Q – No?

A – No.

Q – In 1983, to save his life, did you have to radiate the area of the optic chiasm?

A – Yes.

Q – Out of a hundred people exactly like him whom you would have had to radiate in that same way, how many would have gone blind?

A – Between 5 and 10 percent.

Q – He was one of the unfortunate, unlucky 5 to 10 percent in 1983 who would have gone blind?

A – Yes.

Q – With a reasonable degree of medical certainty, if he said I don't want radiation, the proton beam therapy, I don't like the odds, I don't like paralysis, I don't like death, I don't like blindness, I'll stay the way I am, I know they can't remove the tumor but I don't want proton beam – are you with me?

A – Yes.

Q – How long would he have lived?

A – I think he would have probably developed many if not all of those symptoms --

Q – Doctor, we've got to get out by a quarter to 5. How long would he have lived?

A – Three to six years.

Q – He chose willingly the radiation therapy with the chance he could die, be paralyzed or go blind as opposed to obvious and eventual death in three to six years without it, right?

A – Yes.

Q – Put all modesty aside. We all know who you are and what you are. . . . [P]utting all modesty aside, is your radiation proton beam therapy treatment of him, the manner and way it was done, the reason he is alive today?

A – Yes.

Defense counsel Bartlett then asked for permission to conduct recross, to ask an additional question. This was a mistake. After his two full days of cross-examination, he really should not have had anything left to ask.

The judge permitted Bartlett to proceed and so he asked Dr. Munzenrider one last question: "What was the percentage of possible blindness in 1982?" Bartlett was expecting it to be a very high percentage, which on summation he could then argue to the jury showed that even if his client was negligent in missing the tumor in 1982 and delaying treatment until 1983, the patient had a high likelihood of going blind anyway – the oft used "so-what defense." Bartlett was stunned when Dr. Munzenrider answered: "Probably zero to 1 percent, something of that order."

I don't subscribe to the common adage that a lawyer should never ask a question he doesn't know the answer to, but here Bartlett should have followed the adage. Munzenrider's answer was the nail in the coffin.

I was so impressed by Mrs. Baumgarten as a person, a mother, a wife, a daughter and as a client, that I would like to include here what I told the jury about her during my summation:

> You've heard and I want to talk about Mrs. Baumgarten because I'll tell you, she suffered as much as anybody can and she still suffers and she's going to suffer and she doesn't have a tumor. But let's talk about Mrs. Baumgarten. She's entitled to damages. Working at 15, married at 23, she's now 40, has never not worked a day in her life. You've heard Mr. and Mrs. Baumgarten have four children, true. You know what? She has five. She is now a mother to him. He is like a child. How?
>
> He can't do a thing without her. He can't leave the house without her. A child can't leave the house without its mother. He can't go to the doctor without her, a child can't go to the doctor without its mother. He can't go take a walk and have the sunshine on his back and the wind in his face and enjoy it without her. He can't take a shower without her because of his instability, because of his gait, because of his seizures, because of his horrible headaches, he could fall and break something and she's up there every day with him when he takes a shower.
>
> He has to take that medicine three times a day, four times a day, five times a day and you heard, not from me, what happens if he

goes on a desert island and he's got no medicine, Dr. McConnell said he'll be dead in two to three days. He can't be without her, not with his brain damage, not with his memory loss, not with his seizures. That's his mother.

You know the difference in the five children? The four lovely little girls are going to grow up and are going to leave the nest. That's life. He's never going to leave the nest. She's going to have a child on her hands until the day he or she dies.

Do you know another difference between him and a child? Children suffer pain, he suffers pain. Children can't go out and play, he can't go out and play. All the joys of life children don't have because of their immaturity. Children don't know any better. Children don't know what the joys are. Children haven't experienced them. Children haven't lived. It's in the future.

He knows. He was an adult, 31 years, knowing all the joys of life, everything [pointing to different members of the jury] *you* do, *you* do, *you* do, *you* do, roller-blade, cheerlead, fly a plane [reciting the activities they mentioned during voir dire]. Whatever you do, he was able to do. It's all been taken away, but the memory hasn't. He knows he can never do it again. That's the cruel part. That's the cruelty. There's no more anticipation. There's no more hope except, and I've noticed it. He looked better to me every day this case goes on. I notice he doesn't look as bad as he did at the beginning. And you know why? Because he has hope. This case has given him hope.

He sees, he can still hear, he can still understand, he sees what this case is. He finally has really learned all the truth and with learning the truth, he's got a hope and great expectations and thankfully it's improving him because you heard Dr. McConnell say he's aging and going to age faster than anybody else. They'll live the same time, but he's aging faster. You'll be surprised what money can do. You'll be surprised.

Let's talk about Mrs. Baumgarten. For the last 13, 14 – 13 years, almost 14 years, you've heard, I don't have to repeat it, I can't put it clearer, she's a mother to this man. Instead of a wife she's a mother. Forget all their relations. She's tending to him like you tend to a child and she's had to work. She's had to work to make

> $23,000 a year to keep this family going. She deserves a rest. She deserves help. She deserves to be able to stop working and how is that going to happen? That's going to happen with money, with substantial money, for the past and for the future right till they die. They're entitled to that. She's entitled to that. We've proved it. But for [Defendant Slavin's] departures, [Mr. Baumgarten] wouldn't be blind, he wouldn't be brain damaged, he wouldn't be all those things. He wouldn't have suffered and she wouldn't have suffered.
>
> What's fair? What's just? What's adequate for her? Hey, that's why we have a jury. That's why we have six people, all backgrounds, all ages, to put in, you know. We don't want a runaway jury. You know, you read oh, a runaway jury. Forget everything you read in the paper. Go by the evidence. Go by this case, their lives. You know, put aside the two suicide attempts, I mean, you think I can bring out everything that went on for the past 12 years? She has suffered enormously. She's a saint and she's not going to change.
>
> What's fair? What's just? What's adequate for her? Hey, what I say, I'm a lawyer, it's as an aid. You do what you do because you believe it. You think I'm wrong, you do what you think is right. You think I'm too high, you make it lower. You think I'm too low, you make it higher. *For the last 13 years* for what she's gone through, I say fair, adequate and just is two million dollars.
>
> *For the rest of their lives* where he's got a life expectancy of 29 years, realizing that they'll already have the two million dollars, I say another two million dollars, fair, adequate, just, legal for her, four million dollars.

THE VERDICT AND A KIND LETTER

The jury's verdict for the Baumgartens was $9,700,000. They awarded $3,600,000 for Mrs. Baumgarten's loss of consortium claim; and $6,100,000 for Mr. Baumgarten, $5,000,000 of which was for his pain and suffering.

Judge O'Brien reduced Mrs. Baumgarten's loss of consortium verdict nearly 75% to $914,441. On appeal by the defendants, the Appellate Division let the $914,441 award stand. However, the Appellate Division reduced the pain and suffering award for Mr. Baumgarten from $5,000,000 to $2,000,000. Thus, the total verdict affirmed on appeal for the Baumgartens was a little over $4,000,000.

The Appellate Division's decision really shows how far we have come since 1969. The nearly $1,000,000 award for Lynne Baumgarten's loss of consortium claim was equal to almost half of the value of her husband's $2,000,000 award for his pain and suffering, for injuries that were truly shocking and rendered a 35-year-old man an invalid for life.

Following the verdict, I received a beautiful letter from Mrs. Baumgarten's mother, Mrs. Wall, a lovely Italian-American woman who was at the trial every day. I do not think that a trial lawyer can ever feel that his life's work has not served a purpose – in its own small way, toward helping heal those whose lives have been upended by others in whom they placed their trust – when such kind words reach him.

February 6, 1997

Dear Mr. DeBlasio,

Words cannot possibly express how grateful I am to you, Rhoda, Mary and all your wonderful staff for all you have done for my daughter Lynne and her family. I know they never would have received such an unbelievable settlement without you.

Watching you in Court was an experience I will never forget. You were absolutely brilliant and each day was more fascinating and overwhelming than the day before. I learned so much watching you. Your personality, humor and of course your brilliance captivated not only myself but the jurors and everyone else in the courtroom. Even Judge O'Brien and all the court clerks also thoroughly appreciated and were in awe of your amazing deliberations. You were a genius at work and certainly gained everyone's respect and admiration. You put your heart and soul into this case and it showed and we are so indebted to you.

My husband was an excellent judge of character and from the first day he met you, he knew Lynne and Greg were in excellent hands. He had full confidence in your ability to win this extraordinary case and make their lives a little more comfortable. I know he was there in the courtroom with us all the time and feel now he can rest comfortably. Unfortunately, he could not have been there to personally congratulate and thank you and tell you how fantastic you were and that you lived up to all his expectations.

Please accept my sincerest apologies for not writing sooner. Christmas was a very difficult time for me and all the emotions I suppressed during the trial surfaced forcing reality to set in and my having to accept my great loss.

My husband was very special, always with a smile on his face and loved by everyone and we all miss him terribly.

Again, many, many thanks for all you have done. Say hello to everyone.

Fondly,

Jean Wall

CHAPTER 42

The Man Who Would Not Sleep in His Bed at Night

In 1984 I tried a case in Supreme Court, Nassau County, that would have shattered my favorite juror Mr. Bacciagalupo's naïve belief that if the doctor had a diploma "how could he make a mistake?" In fact, he would have been doubly surprised because two doctors committed malpractice on the same patient, which malpractice was so egregious, unforgivable and inexcusable that I could not remember having a case that came close to their total disregard of virtually every facet of the standards of accepted and proper medical practice.

One of the doctors was a surgeon – the other a gastroenterologist. The surgeon's malpractice was one of omission: during surgery he failed to do a biopsy. The gastroenterologist's malpractice was one of commission: following the surgery he gave chemotherapy to the patient without knowing the type of cancer he was treating, let alone if the patient had cancer at all.

THE HISTORY

In 1977, 49-year-old Ignatius Lombardo was sent to a surgeon, Dr. Mishrick, for abdominal surgery for suspected cancer. For more than 20 years, Mr. Lombardo had been suffering from Marie-Strumpell disease with ankylosing spondylitis, an auto-immune condition similar to rheumatoid arthritis, which affected the joints of his spine and pelvis and caused him, among other symptoms, severe bowel problems. For 15 years he had endured constant bouts of diarrhea and recurrent cases of amoebiasis and colitis, for which he was hospitalized many times.

When in 1977 he complained to his family physician Dr. Panzarella of significant recent weight loss, fatigue, abdominal crampiness and blood in his stool, he was sent for a gastrografin enema procedure (a series of X-rays taken after the large bowel is filled with an observable fluid). The radiologist detected a mass suspicious of carcinoma, and so Mr. Lombardo was sent to Dr. Mishrick for exploratory surgery.

Dr. Mishrick opened up Mr. Lombardo's abdomen, observed a four-inch mass in the bowel with enlarged lymph nodes, determined that it was an inoperable metastasized Stage 4 cancer, and performed a "transverse ileostomy" bringing a piece of the intestine, at the site where the small and large intestines intersect, through a surgical hole in the belly and attaching it to an external pouch to collect intestinal waste (feces). As Mr. Lombardo was recuperating from the surgery in Nassau Hospital, Dr. Mishrick told him that he would not live long, but at least he would not suffer much pain now that his inflamed intestines had been surgically bypassed. He would die in bed, Dr. Mishrick told him, peacefully, while sleeping.

Dr. Mishrick told Mr. Lombardo's wife that her husband had terminal cancer and she should buy a plot and make plans for his burial because he only had about 45 days to live. Mrs. Lombardo begged Dr. Mishrick to try to save her husband. He told her there was nothing that he or anyone could do to save him. When she persisted, he advised that they could give him chemotherapy to ease his pain. The Lombardos spoke with their family doctor and he arranged for his partner Dr. Lecchi, a gastroenterologist, to be in charge of administering the chemotherapy.

For more than a year, Mr. Lombardo received the prescribed chemotherapy to thwart the pain. And to forestall the imminent but painless death in bed that Dr. Mishrick had described to him - and which he feared above all else - Mr. Lombardo slept in a chair.

Mrs. Lombardo may not have agreed that it was avoiding his bed that was keeping him alive, but she had no doubt a miracle had occurred. Eventually, though, curiosity getting the best of her, she telephoned their family doctor, Panzarella, to ask how it was possible her husband was still alive 18 months after his death sentence. She also thought to ask exactly what kind of cancer it was that her husband had. Dr. Panzarella said he had no idea, but he would call Dr. Mishrick to find out.

Dr. Panzarella then called Dr. Mishrick, let him know the good news about Mr. Lombardo's remarkable survival, and asked what cancer he had found upon biopsy. Dr. Mishrick said he didn't do a biopsy. According to Dr. Panzarella, Dr. Mishrick told him: "I'm the greatest surgeon on Long Island. I've done thousands of these surgeries. I know cancer when I see it." (When asked later on trial if he had made that statement, Dr. Mishrick said he didn't remember but "it sounds good.")

Dr. Panzarella related this information to the Lombardos and, after several months more passed, Mr. Lombardo was finally sent to Memorial Sloan Kettering Cancer Center in Manhattan. In March 1979, almost two full years after Dr. Mishrick operated, Mr. Lombardo came under the care of two world-renowned doctors: Charles Lightdale, a gastroenterologist, and Joseph Fortner, a surgeon.

Following his examination of Mr. Lombardo and review of Dr. Mishrick's operative record, Dr. Lightdale wrote in his notes: "The description and findings sound more like Crohn's disease than cancer." (Crohn's disease is an inflammatory disease of the large and small intestines.) When his suspicions were confirmed following a colonoscopy, Dr. Lightdale sent Mr. Lombardo to Dr. Fortner for surgery. Dr. Fortner removed several nodes and some tissue, and sent the samples to Memorial's pathology department. The findings? Mr. Lombardo did not then have cancer and he never did have cancer; he had Crohn's disease.

THE LAWSUIT

When the Lombardos came to me about a possible lawsuit, I did not have to send his records per our custom to a medical expert for an opinion as to whether Drs. Mishrick and Lecchi had committed malpractice. I merely had to speak with Drs. Lightdale and Fortner.

When I met with Dr. Lightdale to discuss his treatment of Mr. Lombardo, I found him to be one of the most pleasant and accommodating doctors I had ever met. He treated Mr. Lombardo every three months for the five years between their first meeting and our trial, and he planned to continue doing so into the future.

Dr. Lightdale's educational and professional background were impeccable: undergraduate degree from Princeton University; medical degree from Columbia Physicians & Surgeons Medical School; medical residency at Yale New Haven Hospital; training at the National Cancer Institute; and post-graduate training as a Gastroenterologist Fellow at Cornell Medical College (New York Hospital) and at Memorial Sloan Kettering (the premier cancer care hospital in New York if not the country if not the world). By the time I met with him, he was the Director of the Diagnostic Gastroenterology Unit at Memorial, and had written more than 100 articles published in medical texts, many of them on Crohn's disease and cancer and the difficulties in diagnostically differentiating between them.

When I met with Dr. Fortner I was equally impressed. Dr. Fortner was a surgical oncologist who specialized in abdominal cases and his background was also impeccable: he was the Chief of the Gastric and Mixed Tumor Service at Memorial Sloan Kettering, where he had been an attending physician since 1954; he was a full professor of surgery at Cornell Medical School; he had published 250 articles on surgery and cancer; and he was a lecturer on oncological surgery around the world.

Drs. Lightdale and Fortner were of the same mind with regard to the medical treatment Mr. Lombardo received. Neither of them could believe that Dr. Mishrick did not biopsy Mr. Lombardo, or even attempt to do so, during an exploratory surgery performed specifically to rule out or to confirm the presence of cancer. Nor could they believe that in the absence of biopsy confirmation, Dr. Mishrick advised his patient that he was dying of terminal cancer.

Regarding Dr. Lecchi's treatment of Mr. Lombardo, neither of them could believe that he administered chemotherapy without inquiring as to the type of cancer, because he wouldn't know which chemo to give that might help, and he might give a contraindicated chemo that would be harmful. But that Dr. Lecchi administered chemotherapy without even obtaining positive biopsy proof of *any cancer at all* was a level of incompetence they had never known. Chemotherapy given to a patient without cancer could actually cause cancer, leukemia being among one of the most likely.

Given their superlative backgrounds and experience - and medical opinions decidedly in our favor - I believed that Drs. Lightdale and Fortner would be ideal witnesses for us in this case. At the same time, however, I knew that doctors at Memorial Sloan Kettering, as a rule, would not testify in court as experts on any case and certainly not for a plaintiff in a medical malpractice lawsuit. The problem I faced, therefore, was how to convince them that Mr. Lombardo was worth breaking their hospital's rules.

To my great surprise, it took little to no effort on my part. Both readily agreed to testify in court as experts on his behalf. In their view, the medical departures of both Dr. Mishrick and Dr. Lecchi were wholly inconceivable, inexcusable, unacceptable and just shouldn't have happened.

We went ahead and filed the lawsuit.

Our claim against Dr. Mishrick was that he departed from accepted and proper medical and surgical standards and practices:

1. In failing to biopsy;

2. In failing to attempt to biopsy; and

3. In telling Mr. and Mrs. Lombardo that he had cancer and he would die as a result of it in about 45 days.

These departures, we claimed, were a proximate cause of Mr. Lombardo's injuries, which included:

1. Pain and suffering;

2. Fear of imminent death;

3. Loss of enjoyment of life; and

4. Injuries caused by chemotherapy that likely would lead to a future cancer (leukemia or another malignancy) and premature death.

Dr. Mishrick's defense for not doing a biopsy was that the four-inch mass and the enlarged lymph nodes were so mired in, and surrounded by, blood vessels and inflammatory tissue that not only was it too difficult to safely remove tissue for biopsy, it was too dangerous and the patient could bleed to death on the table. He, as the operator, had to make a judgment call at that time, and he decided to end the operation and wait for a couple of weeks until the inflammation lessened, and then let a gastroenterologist take a biopsy during a colonoscopy. Under these safer circumstances, it could be determined if Mr. Lombardo had cancer or not.

Our claim against Dr. Lecchi was that he departed from accepted and proper medical standards and practices:

1. In initiating chemotherapy without reading a pathology report of a biopsy confirming cancer; and

2. In administering chemotherapy without knowing the specific type of cancer he was meant to be treating, and falsely writing in the Nassau Hospital chart that a non-existent biopsy showed "adenocarcinoma of the colon with contiguous spread of disease to the peritoneum and mesentery area."

Just as we claimed against Dr. Mishrick, Dr. Lecchi's departures were a proximate cause of Mr. Lombardo's past and future injuries.

Dr. Lecchi's defense was as feeble as that of Dr. Mishrick, namely that he inferred from talking to Dr. Mishrick both that a biopsy had been done and that colon cancer had been found.

My belief regarding both defendants was that they lied through their teeth. Dr. Mishrick well knew that there was no possible excuse for not biopsying, that it was mandatory, so he claimed he put it off for a couple of weeks because it was too risky to do it at the time of surgery. One flaw in that argument was that if this were really his intention, why didn't he ever see to it that a follow-up colonoscopy was done? Furthermore, if the patient was doomed to die within 45 days as Dr. Mishrick believed he was upon opening him up, as harsh as it might sound, why not do the allegedly risky but mandatory biopsy at that time because what was there to lose?

Regarding Dr. Lecchi, my belief is that Dr. Mishrick had convinced him that Mr. Lombardo was as good as already dead, and so the type of cancer was of no consequence, the chemotherapy he administered was really just as a favor to the Lombardos, a palliative to give them (a false sense of) hope and to keep Mr. Lombardo from feeling abandoned in his final days.

As I write about this case, I wonder why it even went to trial instead of being settled. I do remember Judge John Lockman, our trial judge, attempted to settle it but met with no success. In any event, we went to trial and it was fought tooth and nail for two weeks by two very skilled lawyers for the defendants – Stephen Warner for Dr. Mishrick and Howard Snyder for Dr. Lecchi. But these lawyers simply couldn't get around our expert Dr. Lightdale's pointed and powerful testimony, which put the lie to the defendant doctors' feeble defenses. (And it must be noted that Dr. Lightdale was no "professional" expert, this was his first time testifying at a trial.)

The following are excerpts from Dr. Lightdale's trial testimony, regarding Dr. Mishrick's failure to do a biopsy.

> A biopsy is essential, failure to *do* a biopsy is a major departure and by that I mean I cannot understand it, I see no cause for it or reason for it.
>
> It's not discretionary – it's essential.
>
> I can't understand what the danger was that the surgeon felt.

Failure to *attempt* to do the biopsy was a major departure.

I have never encountered a case of bowel cancer where it couldn't be biopsied. Either it's localized to one spot and you can remove it, or it's so widespread that it's easy to biopsy. It's got to be one or the other. So I can't understand that a man could say this is widespread but it's too dangerous to biopsy. It just doesn't make sense.

It is inconceivable that a surgeon at Memorial would walk out of the operating room if a biopsy is called for on a bowel case and not either resect the disease or take a biopsy. . . . It would be the most egregious and grossest forms of malpractice.

With something [Dr. Mishrick] felt was so widespread, I can't believe he couldn't scrape a little tissue from that mass someplace and control it. It's just inconceivable and I just don't understand it.

It just doesn't happen . . . it just doesn't happen based on [my] experience in thousands and thousands and thousands of cases. I don't understand why it would happen in this one case. . . . I can't understand why this surgeon could not have taken some time and done a careful exposure of a lymph gland, or an area that he thought was thickened and abnormal, because it was infiltrated with cancer . . . to take a little piece of that tissue, to send it to the laboratory for analysis and stand there and wait for the answer to come back. . . . The diagnosis would have been negative, the diagnosis would have been no tumor seen.

The surgeon when he does a laparotomy has everything under control, everything is at his fingertips. The patient is stabilized by the anesthesiologist. He is not rushed. He's got plenty of time to do whatever he has to do. In this case he hasn't very much to do to take a biopsy. There are descriptions of nodules all over the place. There are descriptions of enlarged lymph nodes. It would take literally one or two minutes to excise a lymph node or a nodule that was described, that was seen. That takes just a few minutes.

It's almost as easy as a haircut for the surgeon. It may be even easier for him because he's got all his instruments, he's got

> everything available to him. It's just sitting there waiting for him, literally for him to snip it off . . . it's just a tiny bit is all they need to put under the microscope to make the diagnosis . . . and he puts a suture around it if there is some bleeding and usually . . . the surgeon then sends the tissue for what is called a frozen section analysis, where it goes to the pathology department by rapid transit, it's frozen there and examined quickly.

The following are excerpts from Dr. Lightdale's trial testimony, regarding Dr. Lecchi's administration of chemotherapy without a biopsy showing cancer:

> To institute chemo without a tissue diagnosis, without a biopsy showing cancer, is a serious departure. It's contrary to basic medical practice. . . . There is no discretion involved . . . that is simply unacceptable . . . without a tissue diagnosis of a specific type of cancer, I don't even know how you would start to give chemo because you wouldn't know what to give.

> [W]ithout a tissue diagnosis of cancer one should never give chemo. You cannot do it. Chemo drugs are designed to target in on the cancer cells . . . they are aimed to kill rapidly growing cells . . . cancer cells are growing the fastest . . . when there are no cancer cells to attack . . . the fastest growing cells in the body are the bone marrow cells, certainly and the drugs certainly affect the bone marrow primarily . . . some of the bone marrow cells will die and some of them will continue to live but be damaged . . . the problem is the cells that are damaged but don't die. They will continue perhaps to grow and make daughter cells that will also continue to grow and some of these cells can be damaged in such a way that they tend to grow in a malignant process. . . . [T]here is medical certainty in this.

> [Dr. Lecchi's report in the Nassau Hospital chart that] "the resection biopsy shows adenocarcinoma of the colon with contiguous spread of disease to the peritoneum and mesentery area" . . . that is a definite departure . . . it's a falsehood. You are supposed to write the truth in the chart.

After testifying to the malpractice, I asked Dr. Lightdale about Mr. Lombardo's prognosis, the likelihood that he would contract cancer on account of the chemotherapy he received:

Q (DeBlasio) – Now, Dr. Lightdale, the other day, again, to bring it back into perspective, you told us about your monitoring Mr. Lombardo and your plan to do so every three months for the rest of his life, and you have also testified about the leukemia risk.

Doctor, will you tell us, please, what is the incidence of leukemia in the adult population of the United States at present?

A (Dr. Lightdale) – The incidence of leukemia in the United States is about 6,000 cases per year, that is in the total 200 million population of the United States. That sounds like a lot of cases, but it's a relatively low-risk disease, and perhaps to put it in perspective for you, if you took a very large stadium, say combined Shea Stadium and Yankee Stadium, and you could have 100,000 people sitting together at general risk, a little simple arithmetic would tell you that only three of that hundred thousand people would be at risk for leukemia, which is really not a very high risk. There are much greater risks of disease than that, and it really wouldn't cause you to worry too much that you might develop it as a general risk disease.

Q – And what is leukemia?

A – Leukemia is a cancer of the white blood cells. It's called cancer of the blood. It's a malignant process in which the blood cells multiply in a wild fashion, usually a single type of cell, and overgrow all the other cells, causing usually a very rapid death.

. . .

Q – All right. Now, you mentioned in your testimony that chemotherapy, such as had by Mr. Lombardo, has placed him in a much higher risk and a greater risk of getting leukemia.

A – That's correct.

Q – Now, will you tell us, please, the people who have received the same chemotherapy such as Mr. Lombardo, give us the numbers on the risk that he has.

A – He has a much greater risk, so much so that if you took only a hundred people and fit them in this room, then four out of that hundred people right at this time would be at risk for that terrible

> disease. Obviously, that would be of much greater concern.
>
> Q – All right, you say four out of a hundred people who had received the same --
>
> A – Who had been treated as Mr. Lombardo has been treated.
>
> Q – And what is it about the chemotherapy that has changed the odds or increased the risk from three in 100,000 to four in a hundred at present, what has the chemotherapy done to these people?
>
> A – The chemotherapy that Mr. Lombardo received was nitrosourea drugs. The nitrosourea drugs damaged the basic stem cells in the bone marrow, the cells that make all the other cells, they damaged them in such a way that they continue to grow and they will grow over the years in an abnormal way. Eventually they produce a malignant cell line that can overgrow all the others, and it becomes leukemia.

On cross-examination the defense attorneys tried to attack our experts, Drs. Lightdale and Fortner, in the usual ways, by challenging their credentials and insinuating bias from the fact that they were receiving a fee from the plaintiff to testify on his behalf. Dr. Mishrick's attorney particularly went after Dr. Lightdale's competence to opine about the malpractice of a *surgeon* (Dr. Mishrick) when he (Dr. Lightdale) was only a mere gastroenterologist. Dr. Lightdale's response was blistering:

> My knowledge of surgery comes from a very careful study of the anatomy of the abdomen. I've done that study for a number of different reasons. I have made my life's work the study of diagnosing diseases in that area so I have learned the anatomy very well. I learned it not just in medical school, not just in my residency training, I have studied it all my life. I continue to study it. I do diagnostic procedures where I place tubes, endoscopes into that area, so I have to know the anatomy very well. I diagnose diseases in that area, so I have to understand how they can affect the anatomy. I have put a laparoscope into that area, made a cut into the abdomen, put the tube through into the space and looked inside there so I have to know what I am looking at, both in normal and diseased tissue and I spend a great deal of time and

> effort doing it, and I teach it, and I teach it at a graduate level to fellows and residents both in surgery and in medicine. I have surgical residents who come under my training and I teach them how to do these procedures. So I work with surgeons, I understand how they work, and I understand how they think, I understand good surgery and I understand bad surgery. I have been to the operating room many times to follow up on the results of my diagnostic efforts to see how accurate they are. I go to the operating room, I look in and verify what is found. That is how I base my expertise in surgery.

Dr. Lightdale then showed that he could be funny, winning over the jury completely. When Dr. Mishrick's attorney finished his cross-examination by asking how much he was being paid to testify at trial, Dr. Lightdale replied:

> I didn't know how much to charge so I asked my friend who was a lawyer. I said, "How much should I charge?" He said, "Well, I get $150 an hour." I said "OK, I'll take the same."

It was a shockingly low amount and took the wind right out of the defense attorney's sails, rebuffing any insinuation that Dr. Lightdale was in it for the money and therefore his testimony was unreliable. When it then came time for Dr. Lecchi's attorney to cross-examine Dr. Lightdale, the first thing he did was to rib him: "Hello Dr. Lightdale. You should have consulted with Dr. Fortner about the fee. You would have done much better. He's getting $5,000."

Dr. Lightdale's deadpan response? "Surgeons usually do better." It was one of the few laughable moments in a very sad trial.

As my last witness, after my experts and various other witnesses including Mr. and Mrs. Lombardo had testified, I planned to call a psychiatrist to the stand to talk about the impact that the erroneous cancer diagnosis had on Mr. Lombardo. To me, the damage phase of this case related to one thing – fear – how enormous Mr. Lombardo's fear had to be that he would no longer sleep in his bed because he was told that was where he would die.

We had retained a psychiatrist to educate the jury about how overwhelming and crippling the fear of death can be. He had reviewed the case and provided us with a written report that I thought was well done and made sense. Not only would he fill the bill exactly, but I thought

I would need only a few minutes before he took the witness stand to prepare him.

In person, however, it was a different story. While I was having a sandwich during the lunch break on the day he was to testify, I gave him instructions on the expected behavior on the witness stand and then I questioned him about the opinions he had stated in his report. He started off by telling me about the discussion with his wife the night before and how she had some good insights into the case, namely: there are many factors why a person behaves the way he does; the same stimuli have different effects on different people; forgotten events from our childhood can make us behave in a way that we mistakenly attribute to a recent experience; we think we lost our temper and threw a tantrum at dinner because the meatballs were undercooked when it wasn't the meatballs at all, but rather built-in frustrations finally erupting like Mt. Etna.

I had heard enough. I thanked him for coming, wrote a check for his fee and told him I would have to continue without him. He seemed relieved when he left. A good defense lawyer would have torn him to shreds and thus done damage to all the good done for us by Drs. Fortner and Lightdale.

When I was young, I thought that I might someday want to become a psychiatrist. I liked analyzing people, determining why they thought as they did and acted as they did. Here, now, I was forced into taking on the role. After the lunch break, I told the judge that I rested my case. I decided that in my summation I would be our psychiatrist and explain to the jury how crippling the fear was for Mr. Lombardo. At least the defense attorneys wouldn't be allowed to cross-examine me.

The jury found for the Lombardos against Drs. Mishrick and Lecchi and awarded them a total of $3,100,000 ($3,000,000 for Mr. Lombardo's past and future pain and suffering; $100,000 for Mrs. Lombardo's loss of consortium action). Although both Drs. Lightdale and Fortner believed and testified that the chemotherapy wrongly administered put Mr. Lombardo at increased risk to develop leukemia or another type of malignancy in the future, the jury chose not to award any damages for that separate claim.

A MOTION TO REDUCE THE AWARD

Counsel for Defendants Mishrick and Lecchi challenged the amount of the jury's award in a motion to set aside the verdict. (They did not challenge the malpractice verdict itself.)

The motion to set aside the award - which means to reduce it - is a common defense practice and trial judges do often reduce the award; and if the trial judge doesn't, then the defendants appeal and the appellate court reduces the award. (Sometimes even, *both* courts reduce the jury award, which is what happened in Baumgarten where the *trial judge* reduced the jury's $3,600 000 award for the wife's loss of consortium to $914,441, and then the *appellate court* reduced the $5,000,000 award for the husband's pain and suffering to $2,000,000.)

This practice of jury-award reduction is the norm not just in New York State, but around the country, *and yet the public rarely hears about the reductions*. (Nor do the jurors themselves ever learn that what they determined to be a fair and appropriate award was drastically reduced. I'm sure the Tanabe jurors, for example, would have been shocked to learn that their $25,000,000 verdict was reduced to $3,100,000.) Instead, the public reads in the media only about an incredibly high jury award - a runaway jury - and it thrills some segments of society who view it as akin to winning the lottery.

But what goes up must come down, and these high jury awards enrage other segments of society - doctors' associations and insurance companies - who characterize the awards as "obscene" and believe personal injury law a travesty. These groups, powerful and organized, periodically spearhead statewide and even national campaigns to place caps on jury awards, and to reduce the percentage of the award the plaintiff's lawyer may receive in fee.

In the Lombardo case - unlike in Crabbe a couple of years earlier where Judge Gammerman forged an acceptable settlement after the jury's record-breaking verdict - the defense attorneys and I fought tooth and nail over the motion to reduce the award, submitting written briefs to the trial judge as well as arguing at a hearing before him.

The following is an excerpt from that hearing where I made the case for respecting the role and integrity of our civil juries and their right to determine the appropriateness of damage awards.

> THE COURT: I have read all of your briefs and I am ready to render a decision on the motion to set aside the verdict, solely on the grounds of excessiveness, having denied all the other motions.
>
> I don't believe there is anything you can add to your excellent submissions. Is there anything you want to say?

MR. DeBLASIO: Yes, Your Honor. I would like to say something if I may?

If Your Honor please, I believe that the words of Chancellor Kent [in Coleman v. Southwick, 9 Johns 45, 52 (N.Y. 1812)], which were written almost two hundred years ago, are still our law . . . "the damages, therefore, must be so excessive as to strike mankind, at first blush, as being beyond all measure, unreasonable and outrageous, and such as manifestly show the jury to have been actuated by passion, partiality, prejudice, or corruption."

I think sometimes we get away from what our law really is. That is our law.

First of all, it says "first blush," which makes it *not* after careful considered reasoning. At first blush, it must strike as too excessive.

Then the jury had to be actuated by passion, partiality, prejudice or corruption. Those are the grounds on which damages are to be set aside.

Now, I think it is clear from this trial that we had an extremely intelligent jury. We certainly had a jury who . . . [awarded] zero damages on the subject of leukemia, and that, as Your Honor well knows, was a question where people who were going to be compelled by emotions or passion or prejudice or bias could certainly have awarded substantial money and certainly have awarded some money.

This jury made a very cold and calculating decision that because there was not, obviously, sufficient proof, they were not going to speculate and they did not speculate. They awarded absolutely not one penny for the possibility of leukemia.

So we look at the words that we must be guided by, "the jury actuated by passion, partiality, prejudice or corruption."

Certainly they weren't actuated by passion, by partiality, and certainly they weren't prejudiced and certainly they weren't corrupt. They awarded money which they felt, and they are the voice of the community, which they felt was legitimate and justified.

Now, as Your Honor may be aware, this case has gotten nationwide publicity. I have received copies of newspapers from the State of Washington, from California, from Florida, from Iowa. I have gotten all kinds of calls from lawyers and people involved. It has been on television. It has been on the radio. There has not been one word by anybody talking about excessiveness or [a] shocking . . . amount of money. To the contrary, this doesn't shock the conscience of the country, of the community, of the people.

Their verdict in no way is anywhere near excessive. One million five hundred thousand dollars to a man in constant fear of death, making his will, getting his plot, wasting away, not going to sleep, for a year and a half.

A million dollars for pain and suffering. He suffered constantly throughout this time.

A meager two hundred fifty thousand dollars for the contemplation of death in the future. This jury wasn't actuated by passion or prejudice. Two hundred fifty thousand dollars for the fear of death. This jury gave what they know this man suffered through.

How? How? Under what circumstances? Under what basis? There are very few cases in history that have had similar patterns. That is why this case has gotten such notoriety. There are very few cases in history where a person has to undergo this. Why, Your Honor?

Most respectfully, why a Court or you should or might want to take it on yourself to make this decision; this is a semi-historic decision.

Now, all the cases cited [in the parties' briefs to this court for] . . . the reductions [are] by an Appellate Division. Every case. It is extremely rare for the Trial Court, once the [defendants] have been given their day in court, and you know, Your Honor, as you said, they had their day. They had every opportunity under the sun. They could have settled this case at a very, very, very minimal amount and they totally refused.

Now, I know you are not here to punish and I'm not here to punish, but as has been said and I thought it was well said by the federal court . . . once counsel, clients and insurance carriers "place their faith in the hands of a jury, they should be prepared for the result, whether the award be considered generously high or penuriously low. They cannot expect the court to extricate them where the award is higher or lower than hoped for or anticipated."

Now, Your Honor, there is no requirement on you legally, morally, ethically or otherwise. You sit alone. You have been so close to this case. You, who have taken part in the settlement negotiations. You have heard figures in settlement negotiations, but that has nothing to do now that a jury has spoken.

I think in fairness and in justice, Your Honor, this should be left to five judges in the Appellate Division, who are removed from this case.

I say, very, very respectfully, you gave us a great trial, but you have been too close to the case. You had to be, for the purpose of trying to settle it. But you have been too close and I think it would be an injustice that I know you don't want to do to the plaintiffs and to me, for you to reduce this verdict; for you to take it on yourself.

You know the Appellate Division will not let stand anything more than five judges believe is right. You know you are not forced to reduce. They get these cases every day not reduced. You are not forced to reduce. They are not going to say, "why didn't Judge Lockman reduce?" The reduction will do nothing, Your Honor. It will still be an appeal. They are going to review the case.

. . .

I respectfully ask you, there is no reason in fact or law why you should touch this verdict and I respectfully ask you to give us the chance to let the Appellate Division decide.

Following my argument, defense counsel made no presentation, and Judge Lockman immediately gave his decision from the bench. He reduced the verdict from $3,100,000 to $1,575,000, cutting in half the $3,000,000 for Mr. Lombardo's past and future pain and suffering, and lowering the $100,000 for Mrs. Lombardo's loss of consortium action to $75,000.

POSTSCRIPT: Very sadly, nine years after our trial, at the age of 65, the malpractice caught up with Mr. Lombardo. Drs. Lightdale and Fortner had been right about absolutely everything. Mr. Lombardo did contract and die from leukemia.

PART VII

SUMMATIONS

You must have done it with mirrors.

–Chief Judge Jacob Mishler
United States District Court
Eastern District of New York (1967)

No man is an Iland, intire of it selfe; every man is a peece of the Continent, a part of the maine; if a Clod bee washed away by the Sea, Europe is the lesse, as well as if a Promontorie were, as well as if a Mannor of thy friends or of thine owne were; any mans death diminishes me, because I am involved in Mankinde; And therefore never send to know for whom the bell tolls; It tolls for thee.

–John Donne
Devotions Upon Emergent Occasions
Meditation XVII (1623)

The streets of heaven are too crowded with angels.

–Tom Hanks, Actor (1984)

Let justice be done.

–Robert Donat, Actor (ca. 1940)

Thank you. Goodbye. God bless you all.

–Josephine Cotilletta
Brooklyn, NY (1986)

CHAPTER 43

"You Must Have Done It with Mirrors"

I loved to make summations, but not always. When I was on trial, I liked to relax in my bathtub, an hour or two at a time, and think of my openings (easy), direct examinations (easy, after a lot of strict preparation of my clients to "never volunteer"), cross examinations (easy), and the finale, the summation (not always easy).

For me the summation, the closing argument to the jury after all the evidence is in, is the most challenging and the most gratifying part of any trial. It must be convincing; it must be uncompromising; it must leave no room for doubt; it must be compelling; it must be unanswerable; it must be believable; it must be sincere; it must be concise; it must be plainly said; and it must be so reasonable and rational, logical and simple, that it will strike a chord with each individual juror so that it cannot be gainsaid or gone against, but eagerly and readily accepted. The summation can offer but one answer, one verdict, and that is for my client to win.

To make such a summation requires a Key, something that all jurors can relate to and which will bring them to the heart and soul of the case. The Key could be motherhood, conflict with a father, perpetual infancy; it could even be something culturally significant about the current date, or a memorable scene from a popular movie.

To discover the Key, I would isolate myself and soak in a hot bath for hours the night before my summation. Almost always, lying in the tub, the Key would eventually come to me. But on one trial, and one trial only that I can remember, I could not find that Key which would unlock the mystery of the case and make my story become complete and believable. If I could not find the Key, then I certainly could not convince the jury that what I was endeavoring to say and show all during the trial made sense.

That one case, a criminal one, was United States v. DeVito, tried in federal court in the Eastern District of New York, in Brooklyn before Chief Judge Jacob Mishler. It was in 1967, nine years after I was a prosecutor in that court, and my client, the Defendant Paul DeVito, was a friend of mine.

I first met Paul in the 1950s, at an Italian-American social club where we were both members called the Progressive Era Association (the PEA). The PEA was known for the best Italian food in the city, and so it attracted and had as its members Italian-Americans from across the community, from politicians to judges to doctors to tax commissioners, even the powerful political bosses Carmine DeSapio and Vince Albano. (DeSapio was a liberal Democrat who was the last and very formidable boss of Tammany Hall; among many other strong-arm changes, he was credited with ending the dominance of the Irish and opening up city leadership, naming the first Puerto Rican Manhattan district leader and backing the first African-American Manhattan Borough President. Albano was a liberal Republican who was chairman of the New York County Republican Committee; he became the most senior of all New York State Republican county leaders, his longevity in very large part due to his good working relationship with New York City's Democrats, without doubt on account of the close alliance he forged with DeSapio at the PEA.)

In any event, one day in 1966, Paul got into trouble. He needed a lawyer to defend him in a criminal matter and so he approached the PEA's leading members, DeSapio and Albano, to see if they knew somebody. As it turned out for Paul, neither man was very helpful, but someone else at the PEA suggested he talk to me. We spoke and I agreed to try to help him.

The case was straightforward. A truck making interstate deliveries of Squibb Pharmaceuticals was hijacked and $300,000 worth of the pharmaceuticals were taken. The goods were recovered by the FBI at a storage shed owned by a drugstore in Rocky Point, Long Island. The owner of the drugstore was arrested and agreed to plead guilty to possession of goods stolen in *interstate* commerce, thus giving the federal government jurisdiction. When questioned by the FBI, he said that DeVito was the one who thought up the plan and they were to share the profits of the crime equally. The FBI then arrested DeVito and after he was indicted, bail was set, and thus he was out of jail awaiting trial when he met with me and I agreed to represent him.

At the time of his arrest, Paul lived in Rocky Point with his wife and four daughters. He was 54 years of age and was a salesman of pharmaceutical goods. He was personable in manner and appearance and had no criminal record.

The evidence produced at trial was:

1. DeVito was a customer of the drugstore and friend of its owner.

2. The stolen cartons were located in the storage shed of the drugstore.

3. The FBI had photographs taken by agents on stakeout of DeVito going into the shed.

4. There were no goods in that shed at that time other than the stolen pharmaceuticals.

5. The FBI lifted and identified fingerprints from one of the cartons as being DeVito's.

6. The FBI, having checked the telephone records made from DeVito's phone at his home, identified that one of the calls was made to the home of one of the actual hijackers of the pharmaceuticals.

7. The owner of the drugstore pled guilty and testified that DeVito planned the crime and participated in it with him.

When DeVito testified at trial, he denied having any part in the crime. Following his testimony, we summed up. It was this summation where the Key – my opening up the case and making all of the pieces fit perfectly together and add up to 100 in my favor – had me stymied.

The answers to the first six points of evidence on my list were easy. I could satisfactorily explain them away. But it was No. 7 that was most damning to our case and, no matter how much soaking I did in my tub, I could not come up with a satisfactory answer and without a satisfactory answer to No. 7, we would lose.

In regard to the evidence, we admitted as true points 1 to 6:

1. Being a customer and a friend – TRUE.

2. The stolen cartons were in the shed – TRUE.

3. The photos were of DeVito and he did go in the shed – TRUE.

4. There were no goods in that shed except the Squibb pharmaceuticals – TRUE.

5. DeVito's fingerprints were on one of the cartons – TRUE.

6. A telephone call was made from DeVito's home phone to one of the hijackers – TRUE.

These admissions were based on DeVito's testimony and the simple story he told, which briefly was:

> My friend the druggist, knowing I was a pharmaceutical salesman, asked me if I would do him a favor and look at something he wanted to show me in his shed. I said sure. I went to the shed. Saw there were a number of cartons. Picked up one near the door. Recognized it was Squibb's and realized that the cartons had been stolen. I told him I wanted nothing to do with this and that was that.
>
> Regarding the telephone call from my home – the druggist came over to my house and while there asked if he could use the telephone. I said sure. He went into the bedroom and made a call. I don't know who he called, but I did not call the hijacker.

No. 7 was the heart of the case. If the jury believed the drugstore owner's testimony that DeVito planned and participated in the crime with him, then DeVito had to be found guilty.

What answer would I have to come up with so the jury would not believe the drugstore owner? Who could and would say, and testify under oath – "My good friend Paul, a happily married man, good husband, loving father of four, a working man, 54 years old, is guilty of committing a serious crime, and I know this for a fact because I am guilty of committing the same crime with him" – *unless* it was absolutely true? Answer – no one.

I could understand – yes commit a crime – plead guilty – and testify against your co-defendant *who is also guilty*, because it will possibly help reduce your sentence. But what I could not understand was – yes commit a crime – plead guilty – but testify against *a totally innocent person*, a friend with a loving family to support, knowing the friend will go to prison and have his life ruined. Who would do that?

Lying there in the tub I think to myself, "That's what I have to figure out to explain Paul's innocence to the jury, but what sort of a person would accuse an innocent friend?" Answer – no one I know, and no one any member of the jury knows. To me you'd have to be a monster to do that to an innocent person; you would have to have a very sick mind to do that to an innocent person.

In the courtroom the next day, as I stood up to give my summation, it suddenly hit me. The Key to this case was that there was no Key, and the answer to No. 7 was that there was no rational answer. And so I began:

> Why did the druggist commit the crime in the first place? The testimony was that he had a successful business and a good life. Why commit this crime? Because he had to have a criminal mind to do so.
>
> And people with criminal minds do things that ordinary people cannot conceive, cannot understand. I cannot conceive why he would do such a monstrous thing as to say his innocent friend was guilty, because I do not have a criminal mind. And since you, members of the jury, do not have criminal minds, you do not and cannot know the answer either.
>
> And if we do not know the answer to why he accused Paul DeVito, we cannot believe him. And without him, there is no credible proof that Paul DeVito committed the crime of which he is charged.
>
> Please be true to your oath to let justice be done.

After the verdict of acquittal was announced, Judge Mishler called me aside and said, "You must have done it with mirrors." I do not know if that was meant as a compliment.

I really do not even know what it means – though I think it might relate to a magician's tricks. But I do know that it took me a long time, with or without mirrors, to come up with the answer even when the answer was simply "I don't know the answer."

Do not forget that when one is a defendant in a civil or criminal case, he does not have to prove anything and so "I don't know the answer" isn't always a bad defense.

POSTSCRIPT: After the trial, I continued to see Paul almost every Tuesday night, which was the night I had dinner and played cards until late at the PEA, with Paul, Dr. Tony DaCunto, Augie Corvino, Vinny DiFiore, and a few others. And then, several years later, when I decided to give up riding the subway every day from the Lincoln Towers apartment where we lived on West 66th Street to the Woolworth Building at Park Place, I bought (leased) a Cadillac limousine and hired Paul to be my chauffeur. For years he drove me back and forth to work, and to the various courthouses, quite glad I'm sure to be waiting for me on the outside.

CHAPTER 44

"100A"

Many of the cases I tried were tragic and sad but none more so than the case of Josephine Cotilletta, which I tried in Brooklyn from April to July 1992. Like many of my cases, the facts were fairly simple.

On May 6, 1986 Ms. Cotilletta was admitted to St. Johns Hospital for the birth of her second child; 42 days later she was taken from the hospital to a funeral parlor for her wake. Her death was due to the gross malpractice committed during a Caesarian section by her obstetrician Dr. Tepedino and the anesthesiologist Dr. Shin.

THE FACTS

Ms. Cotilletta, a healthy 28-year-old woman, was scheduled to deliver vaginally. When it was discovered that the fetus was in a breech position, Dr. Tepedino decided that he would perform a C-section. Dr. Shin gave her an epidural so that the delivery could be done under regional anesthesia. A short time later, Dr. Tepedino cut into Ms. Cotilletta's abdomen with a scalpel - Ms. Cotilletta screamed in pain - Dr. Tepedino told Dr. Shin to give her general anesthesia - Dr. Shin advised against it - Dr. Tepedino told him to do as he was told - and Dr. Shin did.

Dr. Tepedino delivered Ms. Cotilletta of a healthy baby boy and one of the residents closed her up. Ms. Cotilletta then went into shock; an Emergency Code was called; the Code Team tried unsuccessfully to revive her; and she went into a coma from which she never recovered.

The facts according to Dr. Tepedino: As he was performing the C-section, he saw that Ms. Cotilletta's blood was turning dark. He knew that darkened blood could be an ominous sign indicating that the patient was not being properly oxygenated. He told the anesthesiologist, Dr. Shin, of his concerns and asked him how the patient's vital signs were. Dr. Shin assured him that she was fine. A few minutes further into the procedure, Dr. Tepedino saw that the blood had become even darker, and again he expressed his concerns to Dr. Shin, and again Dr. Shin replied that the patient was fine. The patient was closed up and then he left the OR.

The facts according to Dr. Shin: After he administered regional anesthesia (the epidural), Dr. Tepedino told him to put the patient under general anesthesia. He advised Dr. Tepedino against it because he knew the general anesthesia could have a deleterious effect on top of the regional. He told Dr. Tepedino that they should allow more time for the epidural to take effect, but Dr. Tepedino refused to wait. During the C-section, Dr. Tepedino never voiced any sign of concern that Ms. Cotilletta's blood was dark and getting darker, and at no time did he ask how Ms. Cotilletta's vital signs were, which in any event were normal throughout.

Thus, we had two doctors telling completely different stories à la "Rashomon." Were it not for Tina Pisano, an operating room nurse willing to tell what really went on in the OR that day – events that still caused her nightmares six years later – we and the jury would never have learned the truth.

THE TRUTH

According to Nurse Pisano – a magnificent nurse and as great a medical witness as I'd ever seen – Ms. Cotilletta's C-section had been scheduled that day for 9:00 a.m. At that time, however, Nurse Pisano and the other OR nurses, the two residents and Dr. Shin were all assisting another obstetrician on a C-section that was running longer than anticipated. Thus, Dr. Tepedino had to wait until 11:00 a.m. for the team and for an available OR to operate on Ms. Cotilletta.

Eager to get on with the surgery, Dr. Tepedino did not wait long enough for the epidural Dr. Shin had just given to take effect, and Nurse Pisano heard a scream emanate from the patient that she was unable to ever forget. Dr. Tepedino, at the other extreme, calmly looked up to the clock on the wall and told Nurse Pisano: "I want to be out of here by 12:00 – I've got patients I have to see at my office at 1:00 p.m." Turning to Dr. Shin, he ordered: "Put her to sleep, now!"

Dr. Shin voiced an objection that it was not safe to give her general anesthesia on top of the regional he'd given, and asked Dr. Tepedino to wait awhile until the epidural had time to take hold. Dr. Tepedino yelled out loud and clear so that all could hear him: "I SAID PUT HER TO SLEEP NOW." Ms. Cotilletta, who until then was conscious and heard everything, said for Nurse Pisano to hear, "Thank you. Good-bye. God bless you all."

Dr. Shin then put her into a sleep from which she never awoke.

Once she was under general anesthesia, Dr. Tepedino turned again to cut into Ms. Cotilletta. During the procedure, on two occasions he told Dr. Shin – whose manner by now had markedly changed – that the blood was turning darker and darker. On each occasion, Dr. Shin responded like an automaton that the patient was fine. Nurse Pisano, who had never before heard of blood turning dark during a C-section, was curious and so she looked at the operative site. The blood was an unusual deep burgundy blue.

When Dr. Tepedino delivered the baby, he handed him to Nurse Pisano, directed the resident to close the uterus and abdomen, and walked out of the OR as the resident got started.

Ms. Cotilletta almost immediately went into shock.

Dr. Shin did nothing but look at the machines as if he were some kind of Zombie – a robot – paralyzed. Nurse Pisano asked Dr. Shin what he wanted her to do. He said nothing. She asked again. "I have a problem," he mumbled barely aloud. She waited for an order, but he said nothing and did nothing, he just looked at the blood pressure machine and the cardiac monitor for what seemed like forever, for three or four minutes at least. She asked what the matter was, and he repeated that he had a problem, the blood pressure was low. She asked, "What do you want me to do?" He didn't respond. She saw the heart rate was in the 40s and asked, "Do you need help?" Finally, he managed a yes. She asked, "What kind of help do you want, who do you want me to call?" He just stood there. So she asked, "Do you want a medical team in here? You want me to call a Code?" "Yes," he said, "call a Code."

Five minutes had passed from the time Ms. Cotilletta went into shock as Nurse Pisano tried to prompt Dr. Shin into action, and so when the Code Team arrived a few minutes after that, it was too late to resuscitate and save Ms. Cotilletta.

THE LAWSUIT

We obtained the medical records as we always did, and forwarded them to a medical expert to review. We were lucky to have Dr. Mark Johnson – Chief of Obstetrical Anesthesia at the renowned Brigham and Women's Hospital in Boston and a full Professor of Anesthesiology at Harvard – accept the case. The malpractice, he informed us, was clear and inexcusable.

We filed the lawsuit, six years passed, and we began the trial. We were seeking damages for the losses suffered by the baby boy, named Joseph after his mother, the older brother Dino, and their father John Cotilletta, as well as for the pain and suffering that Ms. Cotilletta experienced from the time of the C-section on May 6 until her death on June 16.

Before I get to the summation, there was an interesting dilemma I faced during the voir dire, and then something interesting that did and didn't happen when it came time to proving the defendants' liability, both of which are worth mentioning.

First, as to the voir dire. When we were picking the jury, as so often happened, I had to make a tough decision whether or not I should excuse one of the prospective jurors.

In our favor, this particular juror was about 60 years of age with children of her own and she was a lovely appearing Italian-American woman. To me, therefore, she had the hallmark of a juror who could and would identify with the Cotillettas, and with the deceased Josephine Cotilletta's mother and sister, Mrs. and Ms. Giacalone, all of whom were Italian-Americans and would be witnesses at trial.

However, I knew that just because a married woman such as my prospective juror had an Italian surname, it didn't necessarily mean she *was* ethnically Italian, because back then wives almost always took their husband's last names. In fact, as I learned on a case long before Cotilletta, it could be quite the opposite. On that long-ago case I was representing an African-American woman, in Nassau County, when onto the jury came a Mrs. Taliaferro. She was a stern-looking woman who, although she had an Italian last name, didn't appear Italian to me. So I did something which up to that time I had never done before and had never seen done, or ever heard of being done, and that was to ask her what her maiden name was. This is sensitive territory. There are limits to how deep you can go into a juror's background. But I forged ahead anyway.

I was not surprised when Mrs. Taliaferro answered that her maiden name was "Davis." That answer then brought another question to my mind, again one I had never asked before and had never seen or heard done, and that was to ask her where she was born and raised. Mrs. Taliaferro in a not-too-pleasant tone answered "Mississippi." Her tone was even less cordial when I asked her if she ever went to school with any African-American children and she said "no." Her upbringing may not have affected Mrs. Taliaferro's ability to be fair and impartial to my African-American client, but back in those days I couldn't be sure.

Ever since Mrs. Taliaferro, I always asked all prospective jurors where they were born and raised, and I always asked women jurors their maiden names. Sometimes the jurors didn't like it, but no opposing lawyer ever objected to the questions.

Back to my dilemma on the Cotilletta trial. I asked the Italian-appearing prospective juror what her maiden name was, and when I heard it ended in a vowel, I knew she was an ethnic Italian like me and the Cotillettas and the Giacalones.

So what, then, could there have been about this prospective Italian-American juror that might be a problem for me, and a significant one at that?

One of her children, a daughter, was a medical doctor, and that daughter's husband was also a medical doctor, and they lived and practiced in New York. This raised serious concerns in my mind whether she should sit on this malpractice case.

Myriad questions about the prospective juror's thoughts and feelings in a case such as ours arose in my mind. I think one of the reasons I became a lawyer was because my father always wanted me to be one. So I wanted to know whether this juror had encouraged her daughter to become a doctor and, if so, why. I also wanted to know whether her daughter and son-in-law were ever sued for malpractice and, if so, if that affected her in how she felt about malpractice lawsuits.

I wondered too, when this juror got together with her family for dinner and on other occasions, if she ever discussed the subject of malpractice with her daughter and son-in-law. Did she believe that if someone was injured or died through the negligence of another, such a person had the right to and should be allowed to sue the person who negligently caused the injury and have a jury determine the truth? Did it make a difference to her if the alleged wrongdoer was a doctor? And so on. In as polite a way as I could, I asked her some of these questions. She politely answered them to my satisfaction and, as I felt that she would have no problem identifying with the Cotillettas and the Giacalones, I decided to keep her.

The defense lawyers didn't excuse her either. Obviously, they had to want her on the jury for one reason and one reason alone, her daughter and son-in-law were doctors and so she, of course, should and would identify with *their* clients, the defendant doctors.

Second, as to what happened, and didn't happen, when proving the defendants' liability. At the trial, our obstetrical anesthesia expert Dr. Johnson explained the medicine clearly for all to understand:

1. The regional anesthesia that Dr. Shin first administered dilated (i.e., widened) the blood vessels.

2. The general anesthesia, which Dr. Tepedino subsequently ordered, compounded the widening of the blood vessels.

3. With those blood vessels now widened but with the same amount of blood flowing through, the blood was under less pressure and didn't circulate properly.

4. When the poorly circulating blood went through the lungs, it couldn't pick up sufficient oxygen.

5. When the poorly oxygenated blood then went to the brain, it didn't transport enough oxygen for the brain to function properly, which led to coma and death.

The negligence, Dr. Johnson explained, was equally clear:

1. It was a departure and was incomprehensible that the obstetrician ordered the anesthesiologist to give general anesthesia, which is much more dangerous than regional anesthesia.

2. Not only was it a departure for the obstetrician to leave the operating room when he knew that the blood was so much darker than normal, it was incomprehensible that he did so.

3. The proper amounts of fluids were not given by the anesthesiologist.

4. 100% oxygen was not given as it should have been.

5. Ephedrine, which would have narrowed the blood vessels, was not given.

When Dr. Johnson finished testifying, there was no doubt as to the liability of the two defendant doctors in negligently causing Ms. Cotilletta's death. But it became even clearer when I cross-examined Defendant Shin:

Q – Dr. Shin, failing to give 100% oxygen to a patient with dark blood as testified to about Ms. Cotilletta's blood in this case, is that a departure?

A – Yes, that's a departure.

Then something happened, or really *didn't happen*, for the first time in my career: the lawyer for a defendant doctor (Dr. Shin) did *not* call a medical expert to testify that his client had *not* committed malpractice. He just rested his case. He gave up.

Then, seemingly impossibly, the trial got even better, the liability still clearer, when Dr. Tepedino's lawyer took over.

Unlike Dr. Shin, Dr. Tepedino did not concede negligence, maintaining throughout my questioning of him that he absolutely did not leave the operating room before the operation was finished, and he absolutely did not say anything about the time or tell anyone he was in a rush to get out of there. And unlike Dr. Shin's lawyer, Dr. Tepedino's *did* call a medical expert to testify that his client at all times followed accepted and proper obstetric practices, though the lawyer had to go as far as Florida to find such an expert.

Well, that effort went south as soon as I began my cross-examination. I wasn't even able to finish my first question when the second extraordinary thing happened – the expert from Florida, Dr. Shapiro, interrupted me to raise the white flag:

> Q – Dr. Shapiro, are you telling us that it was perfectly proper for a doctor to see that dark blood and leave that room --
>
> A – You've got me cornered. I admit it's a departure.

THE SUMMATION

The summation is the time for the lawyers to summarize the evidence for the jury, recounting the strengths of their case and the weaknesses of their opponents' case. With themes in mind, it is done extemporaneously, because you can't convince a jury of the absolute truth of your case if you have to rely on a script to remember the story.

The first to sum up on a civil trial is the defendant. The final and choice spot is reserved for the plaintiff, which makes perfect sense if you think about it. Plaintiffs have the burden of proof throughout the trial and, given that responsibility, they are entitled to the first and last words. Thus, at the time of opening statements the plaintiff's lawyers go first, and on summation they go last. (The deliberation stage begins right after the summations, with the judge's "charge" – instructions – to the jurors on the applicable laws and their duties as the sole factfinders in the case.)

As in all my summations, in this one I had a Key. Unlike DeVito, though, I didn't have to soak in my tub to think of it – I was never stymied by it – it was there all along to be seen. I just needed free range in my summation to give it full voice, which luckily I had.

The Cotilletta summation wasn't going to be about the wrongs the defendants committed. They were so obvious, and shocking, that I didn't waste much time on them. I quickly asked and answered why the doctors did what they did and not what they should have done:

> Why did Dr. Tepedino not perform the C-section with regional anesthesia – a relatively safe procedure where the patient is conscious and awake and can alert the physician about any possible complaints – but instead resorted to general anesthesia, which is far more dangerous for the patient, who is unconscious with a machine providing her oxygen? Because he was in a HURRY – he was in a RUSH – to return to his office for office hours.
>
> Why did Dr. Tepedino leave the Operating Room before he completed the surgery when his patient's blood was an ominous dark blue? Because he was in a HURRY.
>
> Why didn't Dr. Tepedino just take the extra few steps to go to Dr. Shin's side of the table to see the vital signs for himself and learn the truth about the dark blood and the oxygenation? Because he was in a HURRY.
>
> Why didn't Dr. Shin properly oxygenate and properly administer fluids and Ephedrine? Because he'd turned into a Zombie.
>
> Why did he turn into a Zombie? Because he was chief of anesthesiology and, where he was born and raised, that rank deserved respect, and here he was caught off guard, totally unaccustomed to public shaming by someone his equal, another doctor, addressing him like a dog in front of the nurses and residents he had to work with every day. He lost face and he couldn't think straight.

The heart of the summation was not going to concentrate on the doctors who killed Ms. Cotilletta (the malpractice), but about what it meant for Ms. Cotilletta's two little boys to grow up without her (the damages). I spoke, therefore, about what I knew in regard to mothers.

The Key to my summation? *My* mother.

Judges give lawyers great leeway on summation, and I usually took it. Although my summations were often objected to, and were sometimes grounds for appeal by defendants, no appellate court ever reversed one of my verdicts because of anything I said or did in summation. In this case, I was particularly lucky that the two defense lawyers who had to sum up before me both took extraordinary leeway, telling the jury all about personal matters not in their clients' lives but in their own. One of the defense lawyers spoke about his five-year-old son. The other mentioned some of the things that happened to him when he was growing up, including playing in the streets (which he called "gutters") in Brooklyn. I, therefore, felt at ease in talking and summing up about my childhood, in other words, about my mother.

> May it please the Court, Mr. Giles, Justice Clemente, Mr. Citrin, Mr. Faillace, Mr. Nicholson, ladies and gentlemen of the jury. I would certainly be remiss if I didn't comment, at this time, on the extreme attentiveness and courtesy you've shown to all of us. . . .
>
> Why have we taken three months of our lives to try this case? Who is Mrs. Cotilletta? Regular, everyday person. Are we trying the case for money? Yes, but she doesn't get any money. What good is it? Why try the case? True, her children will get the money. That is deserved. . . . But that is not the only reason.
>
> For justice? For right to be done? True, those are reasons. But that is not why we're taking three months. . . .
>
> Why? Because Dr. Tepedino tells us today he doesn't know why Josephine Cotilletta died. Dr. Shin tells us today . . . he doesn't know why Josephine Cotilletta died. . . .
>
> We're here to advance. We're here to see that, if possible, a death like this through terrible, terrible, terrible neglect, does not happen to others.
>
> . . . .
>
> I've heard about Mr. Nicholson's five-year-old. I've heard about Mr. Citrin's growing up in Brooklyn playing in the gutters. I played in the gutter when you could really play in the gutter. When there were no cars. And once in a while, "Mister, please, will you move your car off first base?" That's when I played. They

can't play in the gutters anymore. Right here, right at Gravesend Bay before there was a Belt Parkway, I used to play football down in the sand. And I don't like to talk about myself too much in court. But since they talked, I'll talk.

What's this case about damage-wise? Who has been damaged? You haven't seen the one who is most damaged, the little boy Joseph. You haven't seen him. There are good reasons for that. You are not to make your judgment in this case on emotion. You see what happened to Shin with emotion? He couldn't function. The emotion of losing face. We want you to function. We want you to be factfinders. When it's said, "Verdict," coming from the Latin, veritas dictum, truly said, that's what we want. Emotion clouds our reasoning. We're all human.

You didn't see that little boy, six years old. It's one thing to hear about him, but the Chinese say a picture – worth a thousand words. I think about that little boy. You're going to have to think about him in your verdict. You're going to have to use all your powers of reasoning, logic, common sense and experience on what he has been deprived of. That's why we had to go a little bit into who Josephine Cotilletta was – her habits, the kind of woman she was.

And I know they don't say bad things about the dead. I know that. I even told you at the beginning I'm sure she had frailties, I'm sure. I didn't hear any of them come out. Maybe one. Maybe one. I saw in the Operative Record it says last meal 7 p.m. macaroni and beans. That's what we Italians call Pasta Fagioli. It's gonna put the weight on you. Maybe that's a little frailty. Which, unfortunately, a lot of us are affected with. We eat a lot of pasta. A lot of beans. Other than that I didn't hear anything.

(Showing a photograph of Ms. Cotilletta) I have a picture here. . . . Her sister was right, a beautiful face. Happy . . . two days before, two days to live, Sunday May 4th. . . . May 6th her brain went dead. June 16th she was dead. . . .

And that little boy. What's a time in life that children are most happy about? And there is no time in life when we're ever as happy, or should be if we're lucky, as when we're children.

In a cruel way George Bernard Shaw once said, "Childhood is such a wonderful thing, too bad it's wasted on children." They don't appreciate it. They don't understand. They don't understand what it is to get older. They don't understand no matter how old we get we still look out on a world with these same eyes. These eyes I'm looking out with I looked with when I was ten years old. It's the same eyes now I was looking out with then. . . .

Two happiest times in the life of children? Not according to Shaw, according to me. Their birthday and Christmas. Why? I'm not a psychiatrist or psychologist. I would imagine it has to do with getting presents. They get presents on their birthday and Christmas. My brother, a month before October 19th we all knew his birthday was coming. It's all we ever heard for a month. His birthday was coming.

When is Joseph's birthday? May 6th. Every day of his life when his birthday comes what's gonna happen to Joseph?

MR. FAILLACE: Your Honor, I object to this.

THE COURT: I'm going to sustain the objection.

MR. DeBLASIO: Every May 6th, Joseph --

MR. FAILLACE: I still object, Your Honor.

THE COURT: No, I don't know what he is going to say.

MR. DeBLASIO: I'm not allowed to mention the day?

Every May 6th when it's his birthday, I believe, I make a reasonable inference, Joseph is going to remember that's the day his mother died. Every May 6th. Brain dead. The day she delivered him. For the rest of his life.

There are so many other things. I wasn't joking when I asked that doctor about breastfeeding. Hey, don't I know that not everyone is breastfed? Einstein maybe wasn't breastfed, Michelangelo maybe wasn't breastfed. Joe DiMaggio wasn't breastfed. She planned to breastfeed. It's known – it's known that hugging, that loving by the mother, how vital it is.

I don't have to talk about this to you. I picked you. I asked each one of you who was your most influential or important person in your life. You didn't shock me with your answers. I'm not shocked when I watch the football games and these big hulking bruisers score a touchdown and they put the camera on them: "Hi, Mom." Big hulking bruisers, 25, 30: "Hi, Mom." They got a commercial out now, but I said it all the time. Do they ever say, "Hi, Dad. Hi, Pop"? It's always, "Hi, Mom."

Am I here to tell you about motherhood? Your combined years add to more than my years. You know more about it than me. I know about my mother but you know more about it and what it means to be deprived. And the last thing on that subject that I want to say, because they brought in their families. I remember when I was a little boy my mother used to ask me: "How much do you love me, Peter?" And I would say: "Momma, I love you all the money in the world." I grew up in the Depression. In the '30s when money was money.

> MR. FAILLACE: Judge, I object to this, also.
>
> THE COURT: Well, this is hyperbole. I'm going to allow it with the understanding that it's really not what Mr. DeBlasio feels. He is trying to make a point in regard to parental care and guidance. I would allow, of course, some latitude with the jury understanding that your emotional childhood background is really irrelevant except you want to make a point about the facts in this case.
>
> MR. DeBLASIO: Yes, Your Honor. Thank you. I appreciate it and I won't trespass too far.

"All the money in the world" to me was everything. You can't love more than that. Every child has the right to feel that way about his mother. Or her mother. It's been taken away from this boy. I'm a long way from my mother. I still remember.

Just one other point. When I used to go to school we had tests every Friday. And when I would go on Fridays, my mother would say, "I wish you a hundred." And that was great until I came back one day and I got a B or a C in something and I said: "You know, Momma, they are changing it. Now they are giving letters too. You have to also wish me an A." From that day on, "a hundred A," that's all I ever heard. "I wish you a hundred A." 100A.

I've got a daughter. And I told her I was summing up today. She came here to the trial to see me. She said, "Daddy, 100A." I brought it down to my children's generation. We didn't have much, but we got that. The boy is never gonna have it.

All right. I wrote the number 4:35 so I would be sure I wouldn't go for an hour. And I'm not. What's this case worth? You heard our economist expert, Professor Dutka. We have the chart there. I don't care if you throw it away. Everything was the minimum. Everything was conservative. "I didn't take New York City wages. I took the whole country." Pocatello, Idaho, where it costs them 20 cents to eat potatoes, Professor Dutka is using those prices. It's the way she wants to do it. Fine. . . .

Professor Dutka says one million four hundred, whatever it is. That's just an estimate. It could be high, it could be low. That's for you. But that is not the gospel.

We didn't bring somebody here to puff up to five, ten, twenty million dollars. But just remember all those figures Professor Dutka gave you were the basic minimum. I say double at least on those figures. Why give the defendants the benefit because Professor Dutka says the Cotillettas got a mother or a mother-in-law to take care of the children, so they don't need as much money for child care?

Conscious pain and suffering. We had some discussion about it picking the jury. I'm a great believer coincidences aren't just coincidences. There's a reason. . . .

On May 10th, the one day the baby is brought to her, it's in the records. The baby is brought – it is testified the baby is brought on that one day. Ms. Cotilletta in the ICU, in a coma, and she opens her eyes spontaneously. The only day in the entire chart from May 6th to June 16th when she died. Don't tell me this is not a higher power. Don't tell me that if there is anything – don't tell me people don't come out of comas, have lightened comas. If there is anything, what do they say – they put the walkie-talkie on or Walkman – if there is anything that was going to affect her, it was that baby.

The tears? I believe the sister when she testified that she saw tears in Ms. Cotilletta's eyes. I believe the sister. It just happened that day that time? She got a four on the coma scale. A four for the spontaneous and a four for the movement and a one for the verbal and nine out of 20 for the coma just that day? Something brought her out of it. And when she cried? I'm not in her mind. I don't know why she is crying. But I got a good idea. She knew what was happening. She knew she would never see him again. She knew she would never attend a graduation, a birthday, have him love her – all those things.

Honestly I'm not going to make this – bring the children. Nothing. I'm not going into the emotion. This is all honest, straight, down to earth. Honest to goodness facts. We claim that that was suffering. And we claim it's compensable. You will have to, based on your evaluation in this case, decide how much in pecuniary loss in love, services, moral teaching, moral training, setting an example – these boys have lost. From May 6 or June 16 to today. Six years. And then for the future. At least till they're 21. That will be your function.

You'll get guidance from the Court. But it's your function. It's your decision. Based on reason, logic, experience and common sense. Also, how much the husband has lost for loss of his wife.

I'm going to state to you what I think under the law and under the facts in this case is fair, just, reasonable and equitable for each one. You may find what I say too high, you may find what I say appropriate, you might find what I say too low. All that I'm doing is trying to aid you. You can either accept it, disregard it or do anything else you wish.

But I believe that for Joseph Cotilletta, the boy who was born that day, for the total amount of money for the loss of Josephine Cotilletta, his mother, five million dollars. For his brother, Dino, who was two years old, four million five hundred thousand. For the husband, John Cotilletta, three million dollars.

In regard to Joseph and Dino, I believe that the first years until puberty are the most important years for a mother and a child. That's till 12 years of age or thereabouts. We've had six years in the past. Little Joseph is six years old. I believe half of the five

> million, two and a half million for the past; two and a half million for the future.
>
> For Dino, same thing, half: two million two hundred fifty thousand for the past; two million two hundred fifty thousand for the future – four million five. For the husband, same thing.
>
> In regard to Josephine Cotilletta's conscious pain and suffering, I think what's fair, just and adequate is five hundred thousand dollars.
>
> Every case I've ever tried from when I was 24 years old and an Assistant U.S. Attorney here in Brooklyn and I was prosecuting people, I never felt it was my function to say find someone guilty. They were human beings. They had rights. If the evidence was that they were guilty, let the jury say it. I never said it. I always ended every case with the same words which I am going to say now. But they are not my final words here. But every case I've ever ended was with the words "let justice be done." I ask for that in this case. This case, however, I wish in memory of Josephine Cotilletta to let *her* words be the final words, the ones she will be remembered by, as Tina Pisano testified to them: "Thank you. Goodbye. God bless you all."
>
> Thank you.

The jury voted for the plaintiffs in the amount of $6,556,700. Following discussion with the lawyers and the insurance carriers, Judge Nicholas Clemente brought about a settlement: $1,200,000 paid by Dr. Tepedino's malpractice insurance carrier, and $1,000,000 paid by Dr. Shin's malpractice insurance carrier, for a total of $2,200,000.

POSTSCRIPT: As for that Italian woman juror whose daughter and son-in-law were both doctors? It turned out I had been right and the defendants' lawyers wrong. She voted for us, the verdict was unanimous. And as the jurors were leaving – of course not knowing the judge was about to greatly reduce the award they'd just given – she and another Italian woman juror who sat next to her came over to me and said: "Peter, we hope you're happy. We gave you your 100A."

CHAPTER 45

The Lady Who Loved to Ski

In 1994 Marilyn and Thomas Santomauro came to see me about a possible lawsuit they were interested in bringing against the City of New York. On January 27 of that year, Mrs. Santomauro slipped on ice and broke her ankle when she was crossing a Staten Island street, while taking her son Thomas to his grade school. It had snowed a great deal in January 1994 right up to January 27. Mrs. Santomauro's fall occurred in the roadway mid-block in front of the school entrance.

At the time of our meeting, Mrs. Santomauro's fractured ankle had been operated on two times by Dr. Joel Bonamo, a renowned Staten Island orthopedic surgeon. Her injury, it appeared, was healing well.

So why did I agree to represent the Santomauros for a relatively minor injury with a good result, particularly when a person's chances of winning a slip and fall case against the City of New York, due to icy conditions on a Staten Island roadway, were about equal to winning the Irish Sweepstakes when I was a boy? Because the Santomauros were my Staten Island neighbors and they were as lovely a couple as any I knew and I admired how well they were raising their son.

Six and a half years later, in July 2000, we went to trial in Supreme Court, Richmond County, before a great judge, John Leone, and a jury of six.

Except to the Santomauros, this was not a very significant case. But in going through some of my files recently, I realized that it was a split trial in which I summed up twice. I re-read those two summations and I found the difference in my tone and approach from one to the other to be very interesting.

In my career I tried very few bifurcated or split trials, those like Larsen where the issue of liability was tried first and then, if the defendant was found negligent, a second trial went ahead before the same judge and jury on the issue of injury and damages. This was because most of my trials from the late-1970s on, when the bifurcated trial came into effect, were medical malpractice cases and they were always tried with evidence of liability and damages presented together in one trial, everyone understanding the issues were inherently too interdependent to split.

Upon re-reading my Santomauro summations, I realized that the one at the end of the liability phase followed the pattern of my usual summations - slashing - attacking - whereas the one at the end of the damages phase was almost soft and delicate. I attribute this difference to the fact that having won on liability, the jury had to be with me and therefore my biggest hurdle, convincing the jury about the merits of our case, had been cleared.

I include excerpts from those two summations here.

LIABILITY SUMMATION

> May it please the Court, Mr. Justice Leone, Mr. Ryan, ladies and gentlemen of the jury.
>
> I love trying cases. I love it because every time I try a case I learn, I meet new people, sometimes and usually often becoming friendly after the case. Basically, I'm a shy person but in the courtroom I feel different. And I love to try cases because I learn and to me learning is everything in life. Without learning or when learning stops, life is over. And I learn from my mistakes and I always learn about my mistakes as soon as the day is over and I go home and I start thinking, and I say what a mistake I made today. What should I have done?
>
> When Mr. Caputo [the defendant's only witness, an official from the Sanitation Department] was on the stand . . . I should have done one thing. I should have asked him one question and one question only and sat down, after what I heard he had to say on direct, which was nothing: "Mr. Caputo, please tell us why did the Sanitation Department permit an unusually dangerous accumulation of snow and ice to remain on Reon Avenue for almost the entire month of January?"
>
> And it's like the movies, that's all they do, one question, one minute and they're always so right. Why did I have to ask him anything else? Let him answer that question:

> "Why did the Sanitation Department permit an unusually dangerous accumulation of snow and ice to remain on Reon Avenue for a month?"

What could he answer? . . . I doubt he's going to answer the truth, which was "we goofed, we ignored it, we were negligent."

It didn't need an answer. I said to myself you should learn from your errors. Why not in summation just ask that question to the jury and then sit down, why do you have to sum up? The case is so obvious. Just let it be like in the movies, Robert Redford, Al Pacino, Paul Newman.

Let it be like what I learned when I was in law school a long time ago. I always wanted to do it – one question and sit down. I've never done it for two reasons: number one it would be insulting to my fellow colleague; and number two I'm just scared that it may backfire and hurt my client.

Be that as it may, in law school they told us the story of what Elihu Root, a great lawyer and statesman, once did at a trial. After the other lawyer went first on summation and spoke for an hour, Elihu Root got up, and they were all waiting to hear his summation because he was a brilliant lawyer, and he said, "Ladies and gentlemen, I'm going to do exactly the same as my learned opponent has done – and say nothing." He then sat down and he won the case.

I'd like to do that but that would be insulting. There is more to the case than just drama or shouting. There has to be an aid to the jury. This summation is given for a reason, it's not to hear us hear ourselves talk. There is a reason. Especially when you have people who never have been jurors before, and this has got to be all strange and all new but you're fact finders, we told you that at the beginning, facts are the same as the truth.

You're truth finders and when you give that "verdict" in a few moments, you're going back to the Roman days, veritas dictum, truly said. You're going to say what the truth is and what the facts are. . . .

I hear now Mrs. Santomauro should have kept her kid out of school. That's what I just heard in my opponent's summation. So dangerous they should have kept the kid out of school.

Do you believe the gall, the gall? We're in the City here, we're paying taxes, we're not the slaves of the City, we have a right to live and to work and to be educated and she's supposed to keep her son at home because Sanitation doesn't want to clean the street? In a pig's eye. She's a casualty of war. I mean this is drama, this is drama. It's a fight: Sanitation against the elements. . . .

She's crossing the street, not running, she's walking. She's not at a crosswalk because the crosswalk you can't get to, the mounds are so high blocking the drains which would have let the water melt and, when it melted, go down the drains. . . .

What are they saying? They're saying she's at fault because she was on that street. She's at fault because she went on Reon. That street was so dangerous, so bad to go on it you've got to be stupid, you've got to be negligent, you've got to have no thought for your own safety or the safety of a child. . . .

I don't listen to my opponents' summations. I don't have to listen, but sometimes I do. I heard "she's a casualty of war," then I heard "negligence, she shouldn't have taken him to school that day." I guess they should have gone to Florida for the winter. Obviously, she now wishes she had.

That can't be the way you try a case. That can't be justice. That can't be. You create a terrible condition and you blame the person for going on it when they've got no other way to go. . . . When everyone does it, it's not wrong. Fifty million Frenchmen can't be wrong, as they said when I grew up. She wasn't the only one crossing Reon. . . .

This is not a case where you go to the beach, a storm comes up, the waves are high, they put the red flag up, the lifeguards leave, it's dangerous to go in the water, and you feel like taking a swim and you go in the water when you know it's dangerous, then you get hurt, then you've got no one to blame but yourself.

She didn't go there because she was looking for a thrill or danger.

She went there because she had to go there. She had to cross that street, and for the City to say she's at fault and thereby try to get some reduction in this case, comes with ill grace just as it's with ill grace, even though my opponent doesn't call the Santomauros liars, but instead says that "their memories have been enhanced," that's a lawyer's way of saying they're lying: their memories have been enhanced.

Calling that little boy a liar that's what it was, that's what he called him. "What happened when your mother fell?" "I slipped and fell too." That little boy, who said he wants to be a trial lawyer, obviously got affected and I doubt that it will affect his future, but it was traumatic for him.

Is there anyone here in the world who would think that little boy would say "I slipped and fell" when he didn't slip and fall? . . .

We know they didn't clear the street. We know Sanitation went on January 26th, the day before the accident and the street was still full of ice and snow. So what did they do when they were there?

And then in this day and age when we can go to the moon and we can go to Mars I've got to sit here and you've got to sit here and have both Mr. Caputo and the City's lawyer Mr. Ryan say you can't remove ice from the street. I must be living in another world.

You can't remove ice from the street? Think, if that was possible you would close down New York City in January 1994. . . . What do you mean you can't remove the ice, you go to the moon, make the atomic bomb, you can't remove ice from the street?

Can you remove ice from your sidewalk? Remove ice from your driveway? Of course you can. The whole world does it. They come and say that you can't remove ice and that's the defense. . . .

It's absurd and anyone who knows anything knows it's absurd. And it's an absurd defense because there is no defense.

The one question I asked – the one I should have done the summation with and sat down is the answer to the case: "Why did Sanitation permit an unusually dangerous accumulation of snow and ice to remain all month?"

Now you're going to have to decide certain things.

First, you're going to have to decide was it an unusually dangerous condition. You weren't there. How do you decide? . . . Is there any help? Yes. What's the help? Mrs. Santomauro, Mrs. Santomauro's mother Mrs. Gencarello, and the weather reports. . . .

Mrs. Gencarello, do you believe she was lying? Well, then there is nothing I can do. You believe she was truthful, the case is over.

What did she say about the unusually dangerous condition? "It was a nightmare." Remember I said at the beginning of the trial when the first word out of her mouth was "nightmare," I told her that is a conclusion, that's something that you have concluded based on certain things, give us the facts on which you base it. "It was treacherous, extremely slippery, mounds up high, ice up to the curb, extremely dangerous in walking. I'd rather do anything else, I dreaded going there." . . .

All right, in any event, you saw Mrs. Gencarello. You're going to hear how do you judge a person's demeanor. Observe them, how were they, how did she answer, did she seem to be hiding something, was she hemming and hawing, was she a wiseacre? Forget what I'm thinking, was she a wise guy? How did she appear? She appears honest or dishonest?

You judge in your whole life, you deal with people who are telling you the truth or not. If there is anyone here who will say in this case that Mrs. Gencarello was anything but sincere, truthful and honest, anyone felt differently I'll be totally shocked, totally shocked.

What did she say? "It was there all month and it got worse." She was afraid, she did everything she could to avoid that block but you couldn't avoid it.

Is that an unusually dangerous condition? It's worse – it was worse than an unusually dangerous condition, treacherous, hazardous, it's worse. . . .

She said it was like going into another world. It sounds to me, again, some of you may have seen it, most not, a movie when I was younger, a movie called "Shangri-La." I remember, it made a beautiful impression, it was in the Himalayas, all tremendous snow and ice and you went through an opening, there was a beautiful garden of flowers and trees and no one ever got old there. It was Utopia, you couldn't get old, you lived there in peace and harmony. This beautiful young woman who looked twenty wanted to see the outside world. They said don't go, you're not twenty, you're really a hundred, but she wanted to see the outside world. She went out and all of a sudden she left the garden, there is the blizzard, the snow and unfortunately she shriveled up and looked like she was one hundred. Beautiful story, but a sad story. But the example is extreme. We weren't going from a garden into the Tibetan highlands, but it was another world, that's her words, "another world."

You're going from streets that are cleaned of snow and ice into a street that's full of snow and ice.

Who else did we have on whether it's an unusual, dangerous condition? You had Mrs. Santomauro. . . .

I got to put myself as a juror and what would I think? If I just heard the person who is suing, and no other witnesses, come here and say "it was hazardous, it was treacherous, it was dangerous, it was like going into another world," I might think you're gilding the lily. . . . But you have to judge her, too, that's why we're allowed to go a little bit into who she is, what she is. You determine people's credibility and truthfulness in many ways by including their background. Twenty years old, she becomes a nurse. Everyone in the world loves firemen. Everyone in the world loves nurses. That I know, you never have to worry if you represent a fireman or a nurse. Represent a lawyer? I don't know. A politician?

Credibility. She's a nurse and she worked and she worked hard and she advanced and then she got married and like many nurses, she dreamed of marrying a doctor.

Unlike some who marry doctors she didn't now just say, "Now I get to live where I want and sit home." She continued to work. She then had a baby. Unlike many, where they have to take care of the baby, she was fortunate she had her mother. . . .

Now does that make her better than anybody else? No. Doesn't make her worse. It gives you some insight into her. You think she's here and her husband are here because this is a bumps and bruises case?

MR. RYAN: Objection, Your Honor.

THE COURT: Can't go into that.

MR. DeBLASIO: Okay, all right.

She's never been on the witness stand before, never sued anyone before. This is a serious matter. She was nervous on that stand and yet she answered every question if I say honestly, truthfully, I'm patting myself on the back because she's my client, but I can't see how anyone can say any differently.

MR. RYAN: Should not be permitted to bolster his own witness's credibility.

THE COURT: Is that so?

MR. RYAN: Right.

THE COURT: You're overruled.

You determine, you saw her, you see her, you're observing her. . . .

So the only question is: Is she truthful or not? . . .

Second, the next question is: Was the City negligent? . . . If they're putting salt down nineteen times on the rest of Staten Island with the salt spreaders, and they're doing only two times on this street, this isn't the Himalayas and Shangri-La, they're all the same, why did the others need nineteen days of having spreaders and their street only two?

The answer is this one needed nineteen also, but they didn't give it because it's only a block and a half long, and it's almost impossible to get there, only one way in through a little fork in the road, and those Sanitation trucks didn't go there. It was out of the way and they didn't go, they didn't care, primary no primary, school no school, they went two times. Then, the third time they went in and left the whole thing full of snow and ice. . . .

And the third thing you've got to decide is: Is it a "substantial factor"?

The judge will explain that. But, I like to think of it in relation to the movie "The Titanic." Everyone knows the ship hit an iceberg and people died. How did they die? They drowned or they froze to death in the water. Why? The ship sank.

Those who died by drowning or freezing to death in the water did so because there weren't enough life boats on that ship. The shipping company was negligent in not having enough lifeboats. The failure to have enough lifeboats caused the people to be in the water and drown. That is a "substantial factor" of their death.

But there isn't only one "substantial factor," there can be many:

> The ship hit the iceberg. Why? It was going too fast. Under the circumstances if it was going slowly, it could have turned in time and avoided the iceberg. That's a substantial factor, going too fast.
>
> The ship hit the iceberg. Why? Because the lookout didn't see it in time, they didn't have binoculars. Had they had binoculars they could have seen it in time, they could have turned the ship away from the iceberg. That's a substantial factor.

All "substantial factor" means is: it is a cause.

In this case, this is the most substantial factor case there ever was, it's the ice. The ice that was there is a substantial factor in the fall and in the injury and the City is responsible for it.

So those basically are the issues that you're going to have to decide. . . .

I end this summation with a line from a movie. When I heard it, it very much impressed me all my life, and I have ended with it in every case I ever tried, from the very first one, when I started out as a federal prosecutor. I never asked the jury to find anyone guilty. It wasn't for me to ask the jury to send someone to jail. I presented the facts. Right from that first trial, I ended my summation as Robert Donat said in the movie, because I always

> thought it was the right thing to do, he ended with four words: "Let justice be done." Thank you.

Mr. Ryan, defense counsel for the City, objected during my summation on 14 occasions, and each of his objections was overruled by Judge Leone. The jury found the City and the Department of Sanitation to be 100% at fault, and we tried the second half of the case in just two days. Excerpts from the second summation follow.

DAMAGES SUMMATION

> May it please the Court, Judge Leone, Mr. Ryan, ladies and gentlemen of the jury, today is July 14th, a holiday in France, it's Bastille Day and we all remember the uprising by the people from the tyranny of monarchy and the women holding the flags for liberty, equality and fraternity, those words were the credo of those people. They wanted liberty, they wanted equality, they wanted fraternity. They got that from our Declaration of Independence which talks of life, liberty and the pursuit of happiness.
>
> Life, of course. Of course we need liberty. Of course we need the pursuit of happiness. That's in our own Declaration of Independence. That comes from ancient Roman days, Cicero in the senate, life, liberty and the pursuit of happiness.
>
> Are these empty words? Certainly life is not. Certainly liberty is not. But what's life and liberty unless you can put aside the day's toils, the day's problems, the day's stresses and have some time for happiness?
>
> By the way, the Declaration of Independence . . . also said all men are created equal. Unfortunately we know that they didn't mean that *all* men are created equal, because right in our Declaration of Independence when they talk of getting away from the tyranny of King George they refer to Indians as barbaric savages. But they were men. They were women.
>
> You know, words sometimes say things but they don't always mean them. Life, liberty and the pursuit of happiness *for us*, but there's a lot of bias and a lot of prejudice. In life, there are a lot of subtleties to get people to become biased and become prejudiced.

We're all products, certainly I am, of our childhood.

And I remember growing up people were complaining about paying taxes and my mother always used to love to say: "I wish we could complain about paying taxes."

She couldn't complain about paying taxes. We didn't have to pay taxes.

I used to talk to my mother about my cases. All she had was me and my brother, and her whole life was waiting for our phone calls after we left the house. And I pictured her being on this jury and me talking to her about this case and I said and *she answered*:

> Momma, I represent a woman, she fell, she broke her ankle.
>
> *Oh, that's too bad.*
>
> She had an operation.
>
> *Oh, that's too bad.*
>
> She had pain.
>
> *Sad.*
>
> She had another operation.
>
> *That's too bad.*
>
> But she recovered, basically.
>
> *Well, good.*
>
> Still some pain but she's able to do almost everything she could do before.
>
> *Good.*
>
> Momma, she's a doctor's wife.
>
> *Oh.*
>
> She lives on Todt Hill.
>
> *Where's Todt Hill?*
>
> Todt Hill is a very fancy place in Staten Island.

Oh.

She played tennis.

Oh.

She played golf.

Oh.

She skied.

Ski?

Yes, skied.

Oh.

And I continued to picture my mother, and now she is asking me questions about the case:

I guess she had a telephone?

Yes, they had a telephone.

I guess they had a car?

Yes, they had a car.

Not like us, no phone, no car, no ski, no golf, no tennis, no Todt Hill, and they paid taxes, not like us. Oh, Peter, she has all those things, what's she complaining about?

Momma, she was also a nurse.

Oh.

She worked all her life.

Oh.

She married a doctor, but she didn't take the easy way. She didn't sit home nice and go to the country club all day and go play bridge and go play Mahjong, she continued to work as a nurse.

That's good.

She had a baby. She didn't stay home like a rich doctor's wife on Todt Hill would stay home. She continued to work as a nurse. A dedicated woman and not only that, took care of her husband, of her child, of her family, and worked night and day. But she lost certain things. She had a pursuit of happiness. The thing that made her most happy other than her child – and her husband may have been a child to her too – was she loved to ski. You never skied, momma.

Right.

Don't mean anything to you, does it, that she can't ski anymore?

Don't mean a thing to me, Peter. She's lucky she was able to ski as far as I'm concerned.

Momma, there are certain things that mean things to you though, and if they were taken away wouldn't it hurt you, wouldn't you feel bad?

What have I got except you boys?

(Momma used to love to smoke those Chesterfields.) Suppose they say you couldn't smoke those Chesterfields anymore?

Oh no. Oh no, that's one of my pleasures in life.

Momma, you got the TV, you sit alone and you watch the TV. Suppose they wouldn't let you watch the TV anymore?

Oh no. No, that's the pleasure of my life, I worked in the factory. I worked on piecework, I got to have some pleasure.

Momma, that's the whole point of the case, we're all the same but we're all different. Your pleasures are waiting for your boys' phone calls, watching your TV, smoking your cigarette. That's what makes you happy. Other people's pleasures are different, they're not less just because they're different. Her pleasures were like yours, her life, her husband, her family, but she loved to ski. Taking that away from her is like taking away the cigarettes or the TV from you. We're all different.

Me, my pleasures were sports. I never thought I was going to be a lawyer. I thought I was going to be a center fielder for the Yankees when Joe DiMaggio retired. That's childhood dreams, they're gone.

But also at eight years old I went to the Metropolitan with my brother. I love opera. I went to see Arturo Toscanini conduct at the New York Philharmonic as an eight-year-old boy. I loved to see him conduct. I loved it. If I lost my hearing I'd lose a big part of my love. I'd never be able to enjoy another opera again.

I'd never be able to enjoy Toscanini again. All of us have certain things that give us pleasure. I mean otherwise what's life all about. You know, people say, "You must love trying cases." I guess I'm stupid enough, I've done it for forty-four years. "You must love trying cases" people say to me at parties, and it reminds me of what they said to Toscanini, "Maestro, you must love conducting." He said: "Do you love dying every night?" He was such a perfectionist. He would die if it didn't come out right.

Do I love trying cases? You have no idea where I'd rather be right now. You think I love dying every trial waiting for the jury's verdict? That's not your problem. You've got no idea what it is.

You try cases to talk to people who don't want to be here, who are under an obligation, who have to listen to other people's problems when they got their own problems. Especially when they've got to listen to other people's problems, people who – like my mother would say – got a phone, they got a car, they're on Todt Hill, he's a doctor, they go to the country club. Not many people from Todt Hill are married to doctors. Not many people have all the benefits they have.

But they weren't born with a silver spoon.

I assume, even though the fatal mistake of a trial lawyer is to assume, but I assume a girl becomes, I'm brought up in a very -- basically I assume a girl becomes a nurse, a boy becomes a doctor. If a girl's lucky, if she's lucky, she becomes a nurse, and wants to marry a doctor.

I assume Mrs. Santomauro married her husband sure because she loved him, but she married him because he's a doctor and she wants all the benefits.

Now that I hear this case I'm wondering if she married him because he was an expert skier. Sounds like she loved to ski more than the benefits of a doctor's wife.

Now I think I know why she married him. She loved him. I am sure she loved him. Hey, there are a lot of guys to love. But the point of it all is like the opera, or like the symphonies meant to me, if I lost my hearing I'd be taking away all the things that I love, just like my mother and all things she loved.

And the point is it's not what I like that's important, it's not what my mother liked that's important, it's not, respectfully, what you like to do that is important, and what's alien to you is very difficult to understand and if no one here skies it may mean nothing to you. Being a juror, it's not easy. You've got to go beyond yourself.

You may remember in the selection of the jury I asked you certain things. I asked you two questions that form a trilogy of my asking questions: one, what are you proudest of; two, have you ever had any major disappointments? I didn't ask you the third question I always ask everybody, because I didn't want to take advantage in this case knowing what this case was about.

I ask questions for a reason. I want to know who I'm talking to. I want to know who's going to be able to understand, who is going to be able to go beyond themselves as a juror has to do.

What are you proudest of? I can go right down the line, right down: [pointing to Juror No. 1] you're proudest of your two-year-old son; [pointing to Juror No. 2] your school, your graduation; [Juror No. 3] your three kids; [Juror No. 4] your four children, son-in-law the fireman; [Juror No. 5] sure, the hard work you and your husband, the hard work and your children; [Juror No. 6] your hard work, your son the electrician, good, that's a good, hard-working family.

Any major disappointments?

I was surprised not one. That's fortunate. That's fortunate you've never been through anything like this.

What's the third thing I always ask that I didn't ask you purposely? "What do you like to do most in life?" I always want to know. I want to know who's there, you love to read, travel, love to go to the theater, love to play sports.

Everybody, almost everyone is the same, everybody who has children is proudest of their children, everybody. If I ask: "Who is the most important person in your life?" Almost everybody says, "My mother." Certain answers are always the same.

Pleasures of life: "What do you do?" Everyone is different and I didn't want to ask that question in this case . . . because I didn't want to be corrupted by your answers. I wanted to present this case as white as snow.

Me, to me athletics all my life. Skiing means nothing. I know people like it, I hear good things about it, but I haven't done every sport.

You may say why don't you ski? I'll tell you why I don't ski. I'm afraid to go on those things that you're in the air and you have to go up the mountain. I'm afraid of heights. Carrying a football I'm on the ground, playing baseball I'm on the ground. I'm afraid to go up there.

The one day I remember, never forget October 20th, 1986, fourteen years ago I went down like a tree at the New York Athletic Club in the handball championship in the nationals. I ruptured my Achilles tendon, worst sports injury there is.

I played handball three times a week, healthy exercise. Trying cases you need the release. I loved it. I loved it.

October 20th, 1986, I'd been playing since I was school-age, at school on a wall in Brooklyn. I never played again, never.

I can understand what it means that you can't do something you love. I never played again. My Achilles, it healed after a year. I'm afraid to go back on that court. I know what that pain was. I know what that injury did to me. I'm afraid it will happen again. That handball is a tough game.

My biggest disappointment in life, apart from losing my mother?

Never playing handball again. It's affected me health-wise, exercise-wise and pleasure-wise.

January 27th, 1994 what happened to me happened to her, although she was much younger. Could she go back on the slopes and ski? People can do anything. People can write with their toes when they have no arms. Helen Keller was blind and things. Of course, you can do something. But if you're afraid? If you're afraid, you can't do it.

Now she's skied since she's five, from a Norwegian skiing family. This was a skiing family, she skied all her life. She married a ski person. She went skiing on weekends. Every winter she loved skiing.

What must've happened to her to make her stop? She can't go down that slope, so she goes to the beginner slope. What must've happened? I can get on that handball court. You think I can't move a little bit? I'm afraid, can't rupture that Achilles again. She is afraid. That injury to her was so horrible, so painful, she heard the snap, she knew she broke her ankle.

You heard Dr. Bonamo . . . it was the one percent, the highest percent, the worst most severe injury in all of ankle fractures. . . .

She's never gone back to skiing.

You think I'm going to impress Staten Island jurors, half of you from Brooklyn, me from Brooklyn now Staten Island, you think I'm going to impress you when I'm going to say someone can't go skiing?

If I just told my mother that, she would have said, "Peter, what are you wasting your time?"

There is a point to all this. What does it matter if it's skiing, if it's the opera, if it's painting, whatever you like to do, if it's reading, ice skating. You can't read if you have no eyes. You can't hear if your ears are taken away. You can't walk if your legs are taken away.

What does it matter? It's not what matters to you, not me with my handball, it's her, she has had a big part of her life taken away and the injury is the reason, and that injury had to be so traumatic on her, so traumatic she won't even try to go back on the slopes. . . .

This case isn't about skiing, it's about a human being and it's about justice.

And the law doesn't say there is one justice for regular everyday people who live in Annadale or Great Kills, et cetera, and a different justice if you live on Todt Hill.

What's the big deal, we keep hearing about "Todt Hill." What do we have to hear this thing right now: "Oh the country club, they're rich, they don't need money. Give them less than you would if it was a poor person."

You think that's the law? You think that's the law? They live on Todt Hill they don't need as much, give them less. "She can still go to the country club, give them less."

There is all kinds of prejudice in this world. There are some good people who live on Todt Hill and not good people, some good people live in other places and not good. Don't take a broad brush, take the individual. . . .

Do not let bias or prejudice against the rich or against anything else sway you.

Lady Justice wears a blindfold. That means it doesn't matter how young, old, rich or poor, white or black, you're all treated the same, and you can't be treated the same if any bias or prejudice creeps into a trial.

It should not matter who broke their ankle, whether it was someone you knew or don't know, whether it was an American or not an American. It's who the person is and how did it affect them.

And certainly it does not matter who is being sued. There is no double standard of justice in this country.

Now that liability has been found, if it was on ITT property that she fell, or AT&T property that she fell, a jury and the law does not allow a different amount of money than if it was on John Jones's property, or if it was on the City of New York property.

Once there is liability, you cannot say "but it's the City, it's our City, it's our City, we can't hurt the City." There is no hurt, there is no punishment. You're not to consider where the money comes from. You're not to consider it. You cannot just think, common sense, if crossing the street and I'm hit by a car of a poor old person who's not working, and I break my leg, that leg is worth less money than if I were hit by IBM's truck.

I don't get more pain if it's IBM's truck and less because it's a poor person. I get whatever the injury is. She doesn't get more or less because it's the City. That goes without saying. . . .

One final quote and I'm about finished, reminds me about the bias and prejudice, one person likes and another one doesn't.

John Donne, English clergyman 1600s, again I learned about it from my love of movies. Once I saw the most beautiful girl I ever saw – Ingrid Bergman in "For Whom The Bell Tolls" – but John Donne wrote For Whom the Bell Tolls in the 1600s, it was an essay, a certain portion of it says: "No man is an island entire to itself, each person is part of the mainland; when a clod be washed away from the shore by the sea, Europe is the less. Every man's death diminishes me because I am part of mankind, so never send to know for whom the bell tolls, it tolls for thee."

And what he meant by that was in Old England, when people died and they had the procession, the church bells would ring, or as they said would "toll," and the farmer in the field would say to the other farmer: "There go the church bells again, who died?"

And John Donne is saying don't ask who died, a part of all of us died, we're all one. We're not an island even though we're here on Staten Island, we're all one.

Mrs. Santomauro happens to be the one who is the injured party in this case. Never ask to know for whom the bell tolls, her name doesn't matter. Her looks don't matter, her occupation doesn't matter, her place of residence doesn't matter. She's a person like we're people. She was hurt bad. It remains. It's going to get worse. She's entitled to justice.

> Justice is money damages and it doesn't matter whether it's her or me or anyone in this courtroom or our loved ones. Everyone is entitled to the same justice – we're not biased – without bias and without prejudice.
>
> So the final question: What's it worth, what she's gone through and what she's going to go through? Again, the law is based on reason. There are two parts: what is the amount of damages from January 27th, 1994 to today six and a half years for pain and suffering, for loss of enjoyment of life; and what is the amount of damages from today until however long she will live? . . .
>
> And I told you a little bit the other day, I'm basically a shy person except in a courtroom. I'm basically shy and I have never imposed on people. I never imposed on my children. I never impose on my wife. But I got to put away my shyness . . . because I voluntarily undertook a duty to represent people and to try to bring justice and I represent Mrs. Santomauro and I have to be, as I tried to be, an aid to you to bring out the facts, to bring out the truth of this case to aid you, not to hear me talk. . . . I'm going to mention to you what I believe the value of her case is. . . . For the six and a half years to today, I would say her injury, her damage is worth two hundred and fifty thousand dollars. For the 33 years of future worsening pain and worsening restriction, I would say her injury and her loss is worth five hundred thousand. . . .
>
> My opinion that's a fair and adequate verdict . . . seven hundred and fifty thousand dollars. I hope you understand although I'm an advocate, I'm trying to be as sincere with you as I can be as an aid to you, certainly as an aid to my clients.
>
> You know the ending, let justice be done.
>
> Thank you.

The jury awarded $225,000, which the City paid.

POSTSCRIPT: As I re-read my summations, I wondered why the City's contributory negligence defense – that Mrs. Santomauro should not have taken her son to school that day – wasn't instead that since she was such an expert skier, she should have skied down that street.

In any event, following the verdict the Santomauros met with Judge Leone and then they spoke with me. They said that the judge wished them well, and told them that they were lucky because "no other lawyer in New York City could have won this case." Very sadly, Judge Leone, like so many of my good friends, has passed on.

CHAPTER 46

What a Difference a Millimeter Makes

I remember when I was young there was a popular song called "What a Difference a Day Makes." I never spent much time listening to songs, and I'm sure I never learned the words which followed that opening line, and so it follows that I don't know what the songwriter had in mind or what the "difference" was.

But in 1993, in the malpractice trial of Johnson v. Schulster, tried in Nassau County before Judge Marvin Segal and a jury, I certainly learned what a difference a *millimeter* makes – a 25th of an inch – between life and death, breathing and suffocation. I learned that the diameter of a person's trachea (the windpipe) is roughly the same as their little finger, and that when a doctor places an instrument down a woman's throat that is off by a single millimeter, the legal maxim "de minimis non curat lex" (the law takes no notice of trifles) provides that doctor no defense.

Unlike many of my cases, the facts in Johnson were not so simple. One day in February 1986, Jean Marie Johnson, a lovely, petite (5'2", 105 lbs.), single, 28-year-old working woman, who lived at home with her parents, had a particularly bad asthma attack. She went to South Nassau Communities Hospital because of her difficulty breathing and, a little more than an hour after she was examined, a pulmonologist (a doctor specializing in the lower respiratory tract) intubated her, placing a breathing tube through her mouth and larynx down into the trachea to bring air into her lungs. The hospital record was sparse. Basically, all it said was that the pulmonologist Dr. Schulster (the only defendant in the case) intubated her, the intubation went smoothly, and the patient tolerated the procedure well.

Unfortunately for Ms. Johnson, she did not tolerate the procedure at all well; it was just the opposite. She had intense pain during the intubation, which was not done under anesthesia, and four or five people were called to come into the room to restrain her while she was on the operating table. She remained intubated for five days, in terrible pain, sedated with morphine and Valium, which was increased as she became more and more agitated, and uncontrollable.

After a one-week stay in the hospital, she returned home. Her throat hurt terribly, she was unable to eat solid foods, she had difficulty swallowing liquids, and she was not able to speak above a whisper. Two days later, she was readmitted to the hospital as she felt her throat closing up. Two days after that, she went into extreme respiratory distress, turned cyanotic (bluish) and needed a life-saving tracheotomy at her hospital bedside.

An otolaryngologist (an ear, nose and throat specialist), Dr. Michael Eden, performed the emergency surgery to bypass the swollen and obstructed larynx. (The larynx, which houses our vocal cords, is an organ we use for three critical functions: speech, breathing and swallowing. The glottis – the area of the larynx surrounding the vocal cords – when closed allows us to speak and to swallow, preventing food from entering the trachea and going into the lungs; when open, it allows us to breathe, permitting air to pass into the trachea.) Dr. Eden created a small hole in Ms. Johnson's neck – through the skin below the larynx – into which he passed a tube directly to her trachea allowing her to breathe.

Over the next four months, Dr. Eden's partner Dr. Dennis Draizin cared for Ms. Johnson and tried to remove the temporary tracheotomy tube. He both used medication and performed surgical procedures in an attempt to widen the larynx enough, just one to two millimeters, to enable Ms. Johnson to breathe normally again without the need for a permanent tracheostomy.[6] He was repeatedly unsuccessful.

Dr. Draizin recommended to the Johnson family that Jean Marie should follow up with Dr. Hugh Biller, a renowned otolaryngologist and an innovator in the field of laryngeal reconstruction. Dr. Draizin had great faith that Dr. Biller could succeed where he admittedly failed. In May 1986, Dr. Biller took over Ms. Johnson's care, and he was still treating her seven and a half years later, at the time of our November 1993 trial.

Dr. Biller performed several laser procedures and other operations on Ms. Johnson in the first seven months simply to be able to remove the tracheostomy tube; by the time of trial, he had performed a total of six reconstructive surgeries on her. He did the best that any surgeon could

---

[6] Dr. Draizin explained that while doctors use the terms interchangeably, a "tracheotomy" is more of a temporary opening, whereas a "tracheostomy" would involve suturing the lining of the trachea to the skin to permanently maintain an opening.

do, managing to reconstruct just enough of the larynx – now reduced in width by about 50% – to allow her to breathe on her own. But the stenosis (the narrowing) and the damage to her vocal cords were irreversible.

When working properly, our two vocal cords open like a "v" swinging outward toward the larynx walls, and they close swinging inward. This allows us alternately to inhale (cords, and glottis, open), and speak (cords, and glottis, closed). Ms. Johnson's vocal cords can no longer move, but are fixed in a position about half-way open, thus affecting both her ability to breathe and to speak.

When I met with Ms. Johnson, I found her to be very sweet and very sad. She told me how she could no longer do activities that required even modest exertion, certainly not tennis or dancing, and that she could barely make it up a flight of steps. As for speaking, she was not able to vocalize or project her voice beyond a breathy whisper. I told her I would do whatever I could.

After we obtained the pertinent medical records and had them reviewed by medical experts, we were in a quandary. Everyone agreed that the injury occurred when Dr. Schulster intubated her, but no one had a clue why anything went wrong. Everything was done according to Hoyle. The operative report was pristine – too pristine. Dr. Schulster did not write down a thing he did during the intubation, not even the size of the tube he used.

I decided to try to meet with Ms. Johnson's treating physician, Dr. Biller, to see if I could learn anything useful from him. Dr. Biller, Chief of Otolaryngology at Mt. Sinai Hospital in Manhattan, was one of the most revered otolaryngologists in the country. I have always been in awe when in the presence of people like him who have risen to the top in their field (except, of course, when I opposed and cross-examined them in a court of law). So I was pleasantly surprised when Dr. Biller readily agreed to meet with me at his office, and then turned out to be so kind and amiable.

It was only a few minutes into our discussion when he said to me: "I am getting to suspect something. I have a suspicion you would want me not as a fact witness, not simply to testify as her treating physician as you have said, but as an expert witness in regard to malpractice." I responded that I would not be so presumptuous to ask him to do that, unless he felt it the right thing to do. "It is the right thing," he said.

Dr. Biller then explained to me the mystery of Ms. Johnson's condition, making what had seemed so complex and obtuse sound so simple and clear. In intubating Ms. Johnson, Dr. Schulster had used a tube that was too large for her anatomy. He explained that the way to gauge the proper size tube for a patient's larynx is determined both by observation and sensation, if it feels too tight or too loose when trying to insert the tube. Ms. Johnson was petite and her airway was relatively narrow for a woman, but instead of removing the tube and trying the next size smaller, Dr. Schulster simply forced down Ms. Johnson's throat a tube that was too large for her. In so doing, Dr. Schulster irritated the lining of her larynx, which subsequently caused significant inflammation and the formation of scar tissue. After the extubation and her release from the hospital, her larynx continued to narrow at and below the vocal cord level, requiring the emergency tracheotomy less than two weeks later, which Dr. Draizin ultimately recommended that Dr. Biller repair.

I knew after speaking with this brilliant doctor that we would win the case. We filed a lawsuit against Dr. Schulster and prepared for the trial.

At trial, Dr. Schulster testified that he couldn't remember the size tube he used on Ms. Johnson, but she looked like an average-sized female, so he used either a size 7 or size 8 tube. (The number refers to the internal diameter of the tube measured in millimeters.) Probably, he said, he would have used the 8 – one millimeter larger – to allow more air to pass down her airway.

Dr. Schulster explained how he inserted a clear plastic PVC (polyvinylchloride) tube, a 7 or 8, with an attached balloon cuff, through her mouth and down into the trachea, a couple of centimeters past the vocal cords. He then inflated the balloon and, when he could no longer hear air between the cuff and the sides of the airway – indicating he had an airtight seal – he taped the tube to her mouth and lips. He then connected the tube to a ventilator.

We called two experts, Dr. Biller and Dr. Mark Johnson, an anesthesiologist who had intubated thousands of patients in his career. Dr. Johnson was a specialist in three areas of anesthesia (obstetrical, cardiac and respiratory ICU), and he had been my expert the year before on the Cotilletta case. (This was Dr. Johnson's fourth time testifying in a malpractice trial, twice for me on behalf of a plaintiff and twice on behalf of a defendant-doctor.)

Dr. Johnson testified that Dr. Schulster departed from accepted and proper practice in intubating Jean Marie without anesthesia, because asthmatics in particular have a hyperreactive gag reflex, and to avoid this reflex from closing the swollen airway even further, and causing injury in the process, the asthmatic patient must be sedated. The manner of the intubation, he testified, was a significant cause of the permanent damage she sustained.

Dr. Biller then testified that the size of the tube Dr. Schulster used during the intubation was too large for Jean Marie's throat and was a significant cause of her injuries.

Drs. Johnson and Biller explained that inserting a tube that was too large, and leaving it in place for five days – with the balloon pressing too tightly against the cartilage and the delicate lining of the trachea – had reduced the flow of blood in the area and caused more swelling which, in a vicious cycle, reduced the blood flow further and led to permanent damage to the organ (the larynx).

The defendant called two experts: Dr. Mattucci, a head and neck surgeon; and Dr. Rosen, a pulmonologist, whom defense counsel only managed to retain *after* our trial had started. Both testified that there was absolutely no malpractice.

I include part of my cross-examination of Dr. Mattucci to set the stage for my summation, which is to come:

> Q – Dr. Mattucci, did you meet with defense counsel Mr. Snyder this morning before testifying?
>
> A – Yes, I did.
>
> . . .
>
> Q – When was the last time before this morning?
>
> A – The last time was I believe Thursday or Friday of last week.
>
> . . .
>
> Q – Did you write a report in this case?
>
> A – No.
>
> . . .
>
> Q – Did you make any notes?
>
> A – I made summary notes of the chart as I read it.
>
> Q – First answer my question and then we will go to what they are. Did you make any notes?
>
> A – Yes.

Q – May I see them, please?

A – I don't have them with me.

Q – Where are they?

A – I don't have them. They were just notes I made during the review of all the charts.

Q – I understand that. Now I ask where are they?

A – I don't have them. I discarded them or don't have them.

Q – Discarded them when?

A – After I met with the attorney several days ago, because there was no need for them.

Q – The attorney said there was no need for the notes?

A – No. I had no need for them. They were my notes. They were my summary temporarily of the chart.

Q – You had them several days ago, Thursday or Friday?

A – Yes.

Q – You don't have them today?

A – No.

Q – After you met with the attorney, you threw them away?

A – I finished with them on Friday –

Q – No, please. Did you throw them away?

A – Sometime after meeting with the attorney.

Q – You threw them away?

A – Yes.

Q – Knowing you were going to testify in this case? You knew that? You knew that after you met with him.

A – Sure, yes.

. . .

Q – When for the first time did you make a note about anything to do with this case?

A – Many, many years ago, when I was sent the chart.

. . .

Q – Do you know who Biller is?

A – Sure.

. . .

Q – Do you recognize him as an authority?

A – I don't think there is anyone who is a single authority.

Q – I didn't say "single." Do you recognize him as an authority?

A – No.

. . .

Q – Now, if you can answer yes or no, you testified today it was not a departure for Dr. Schulster to use a size 8 endotracheal tube in Jean Marie Johnson? Did you testify about that today?

A – Yes, I did.

. . .

Q – Yes or no: you came to that opinion without ever seeing Jean Marie Johnson? Yes or no?

A – Yes.

. . .

Q – You came to that opinion without ever looking down her throat and seeing her larynx, correct?

A – Yes.

Q – You read Dr. Biller's testimony, correct?

A – Yes, I did.

Q – You know not only did he see her, he operated on her six times, right?

A – Yes.

. . .

Q – Do you know he has treated her for seven-and-a-half years?

A – I don't know how long he treated her, but --

. . .

Q – It's not only in his testimony, it's in the Mount Sinai records which you read? Correct?

A – Right.

Q – You would have made a note of that when you were reviewing the chart so you could be accurate, right? You would have recorded that, right?

A – In my notes, sure.

Q – That is one of the reasons you take notes? One of the reasons?

A – Sure.

Q – Because time and memory makes us forget. Normal people can, right?

A – Right.

Q – Okay. Did you read this from Dr. Biller's testimony: "It's my opinion that a size 8 tube in an individual of this size is too large and therefore would be a departure"?

A – Yes, I did.

Q – Do you agree with it or disagree with Dr. Biller?

A – I agree that is his opinion.

Q – Doctor --

A – I disagree --

Q – Excuse me, doctor. Please. Do you think I asked you, "Do you agree that that's his opinion"?

A – I disagree with Dr. Biller.

. . .

Q – Do you have an opinion with a reasonable degree of medical certainty of what the etiology, what the cause, of Jean Marie Johnson's glottic and subglottic stenosis [narrowing] was? Do you have an opinion?

A – No, I don't have any opinion.

. . .

Q – Was there any departure by Dr. Schulster from accepted and proper medical practice in this case?

A – No.

. . .

Q – Assume that Dr. Schulster did not write one word about his intubation in the hospital chart. Is that good practice?

A – Not the best practice.

Q – I didn't ask you if it was "the best." Is that good and accepted and proper medical practice?

A – It's not good practice.

. . .

Q – Do you disagree that she had laryngeal stenosis before the emergency tracheotomy? Do you disagree with that?

A – No, I agree.

Q – You don't disagree that the tube Dr. Schulster inserted caused that, do you?

A – The tube caused the stenosis most likely.

Q – What else caused it if not the tube? Tell us, what else?

A – That's probably the cause of the posterior stenosis as we discussed before.

Q – Doctor, you said the tube caused the stenosis "most likely." Not "absolutely," like Dr. Biller says, you said "most likely," so I asked you what else caused it if it wasn't absolutely the tube. Tell us.

A – I think it was the tube. . . . I can think of a lot of things that can cause laryngeal stenosis, but in this particular case I think it was the tube that caused that posterior stenosis.

Q – You are saying that with a reasonable degree of medical certainty?

A – Yes.

Q – Where you disagree with Dr. Biller is he says it was because the tube was too large, and you say, no, it wasn't because it was too large, right?

A – Yes.

. . .

Q – Would you agree that if a too large tube is used for the patient's airway that can be a cause of glottic and subglottic stenosis? Would you agree?

A – Yes.

Q – In your opinion with a reasonable degree of medical certainty, when did the first stenosis in this case occur, what day?

. . .

A – The groundwork that leads to the stenosis is inflammation and irritation. That was established during the intubation, yes.

. . .

> Q – Was there anything that could have been done for her, to prevent her stenosis, had she been treated in the first admission?
>
> A – One thing that you could do is extubate the patient as soon as possible. . . . The second thing is to place the patient on steroids.
>
> . . .
>
> Q – What caused her to almost die that night when Dr. Eden had to perform the emergency tracheotomy? What?
>
> A – Acute upper airway obstruction.
>
> Q – From what?
>
> . . .
>
> A – She possibly developed a cold, just a plain cold.
>
> . . .
>
> Q – Doctor, is there one word anywhere in all these records about a cold, one word?
>
> A – No.

When it came time for my summation, I didn't use any mirrors, or speak about my mother, or handball, or Toscanini. I focused on the experts, reprising much of Dr. Biller's testimony from my direct examination of him. And just as I did in the first Santomauro summation, I slashed and attacked, going after Defendant Schulster and his experts Drs. Mattucci and Rosen:

> May it please the Court, Mr. Justice Segal, Mr. Snyder, Mr. Foreman, ladies and gentlemen of the jury.
>
> When we started long ago, I apologized to you when we picked the jury, about the time it was taking, but I said I don't feel too bad because I know it will be an educational, learning experience to you for which we'll all be the better. I still apologize but I still believe it has been a learning experience for you which will do you for the rest of your lives, for you and your families. It can't help but do you in good stead.

Now what do you know about the events of life, events far and removed from all of us? Hospitals, doctors, intubations, glottis. Whoever heard of it before? Vocal cords open, close. Who knew these things? Intubation. A wrong size tube by a millimeter, by a millimeter. You can die. You can die. She almost died. You can die by a wrong size of one millimeter. Who in their right mind would have known it?

No one could have been expected to know it. Certainly she didn't know it. Certainly her family didn't know it. No one except your doctor. That's who was expected to know it. That's who should have known it. That's who has the obligation to treat you with reasonable care and prudence.

At the beginning I told you, in the opening, a trial is like a movie. I said I'd tell you what it is we expect to prove: the tube was too big; the intubation was done wrong; she was never examined, et cetera, et cetera. I told you so then. You are the truth finders, the fact finders. What I say is meaningless. It is not evidence. I'm put on this earth for one reason – if I say as a tool, as an instrument, as an instrument to try to help one who cannot speak for him or herself achieve justice. That's all I'm here for. I'm not justice. I'm not truth. I'm not evidence. It comes from the witness. I explained to you what the case was about, so you could focus on the witnesses.

And now the movie is almost over. And although I'm a lawyer, I'm also a person. My life isn't 24 hours a day in the courtroom. I live outside. Almost everybody I hang around with is not a lawyer – by choice. I like people who are regular people without airs. I try to think like people who are going to be on the jury, regular people, and if I were a juror here not only would I have learned a great deal about medicine, I would have learned a great deal about law. I would have had the privilege, as you've had, to sit before one of our eminent jurists. You've seen the trial conducted extremely fairly, extremely impartially, in the finest traditions of trials and I hope you realize now in sitting here that all these trials are not just a lot of mumbo jumbo. There's a reason for them.

And thinking about the movies, to me this trial seems like a movie I saw a long time ago. "Rashomon," Japanese movie, where they told about an event that occurred and you heard from, in that movie, four different versions and every version from the eyes of the beholder added or subtracted from the other. Here you've seen a movie where, in effect, you couldn't have a more complete divergence, a more complete who went east, who went west, who had the red light, who had the green light.

Mattucci and Rosen said everything done here was perfect, was good, accepted, proper medical practice. Not a departure at all. Not a hint of a departure. Good, reasonable accepted care. Nobody knows what happened. That's their doctors. Biller and Johnson said departures, absolutely, positively, without qualifications – intubation totally wrong, tube too big, no question.

This didn't come out of the air. This woman was caused to undergo the suffering she's undergone for one reason, the tube. For one reason, the tube was too big. From one person, the person who put the tube that was too big in her body, period. End of story.

But, you've heard two sides. Biller and Johnson, Rosen and Mattucci. Jones said the light was red for him. Smith said the light was red for him. You weren't there. How do you decide? That's why we had the opening statements at the beginning of this trial. So you could focus. You can use what God has given you to use in your everyday life to determine the truth. What rings true? What is the truth? What is the fact?

You look. You listen. You observe. You see who they are. You see how they respond. Are they trying to be for the right? Are they giving it to you without any mumbo jumbo? Who are they? Why are they here? Did God appoint them?

It's a movie, but a strange movie. The script was written before the actor was retained. Rosen. When we started this trial on October 27th, in the opening statement Mr. Snyder who told you what he was going to show, he told you all about it. He laid it out in the opening. There was only one thing wrong. He hadn't yet ever communicated or seen or gotten his witness, Rosen. Must be clairvoyant. The script was written.

Now they've got to find an actor who's going to read the lines. They then found Rosen. You heard him. Never contacted, never looked at a thing until November 11th. Remember I said, "Armistice Day"? Never looked at a thing. No opinion till the Sunday, November 15th. No final opinion till the night before he came here to testify.

Yet defense counsel, Mr. Snyder, told you what he was going to say before they had ever talked to Rosen. That's a learning experience. They know what a doctor is going to say before they get him. And he said it. He said everything they wanted him to say. No departures. No departures. No departures. If I'm a juror, I say to myself, who is he, where did he come from? Why him?

And I also say, November 11th, 1993, first time the defendant gets him. February 1st, 1986 this happened. February 17th, 1986, she's almost dead. February and March. She's already got three operations. She's got a tracheotomy in 1986. If I were a juror I'd say, why did they wait almost eight years till after the trial was begun to get a witness, to get an expert? Then I'd say maybe they didn't wait. Maybe they have been trying all along. Maybe they couldn't get any. Otherwise why? Otherwise why? An insult to your intelligence, a total insult. Eight years to get a man to say what they want him to say.

So how do you decide who's who and what's what? Mattucci – I guess you are getting to realize nobody comes with anything written down. Nobody comes with any notes. However, if I were a juror, I'd say I want to know if a person is telling me the truth. Mattucci, he says he was retained years ago. How do we know? We got to take his word. He's not bringing us his payment bill. He's not bringing us his report. He's not bringing us his notes. We got to take his word. All right. Not for me to call someone a liar. Initially.

Well, I ask him, "Did you have notes?" "Yes." "Made notes originally?" "Yes." "Where are they?" Do you know Clark Gable and Vivian Leigh? Gone with the wind, that's where his notes went.

"I threw them away."

> "When, Thursday or Friday? Today's Monday. You kept them all these years, you met with Mr. Snyder, on Thursday and Friday, you had the notes then. You knew you were going to come testify Monday. After you met with him, you threw the notes away? You kept them all these years, three, four, five years, to come here to tell this jury what the truth is, and yet you deprive us, deprive me of being able to question you about what you saw, what you decided, so we could see if you were changing your story to fit in what they wanted you to fit in now? You didn't think that would be something that we had a right to know, to know everything possible?"

If I were a juror I would say, there's got to be a reason. He kept those notes all the years he met with the lawyer and afterwards he threw them away. I don't think you got to go to Harvard to figure that one out. I don't think you got to go to Harvard to figure must be something in those notes they didn't want us to know about.

These are the little things about a trial. You are not professional jurors. You can't be focusing in on everything that goes on. Me? That's all I do. . . .

Now Dr. Biller, who is he? Where did *he* come from? Did I go searching the last minute to find somebody, a hack or a professional witness, a person to come in for a few dollars, to come here to make the case?

Remember I asked him: "Have you received any awards, any achievements, any honors in the field of medicine?" Biller's answer: "I've received some over the years." Period. End of story. That's like Einstein saying, "I received some over the years." It's like Thomas Edison saying, "I tinker a little bit with an electric light."

We only heard about one award – thanks to the defendant when they put Rosen on. They asked Rosen and he said his name was in a book that came out once, only in 1991, where doctors all voted for the best doctors in all of New York. Then I asked him, "Who was on the book's cover?" "Biller." Of the over one thousand doctors they picked as the best, the vote for number one was Biller. Of everyone, he's number one and he's on the cover.

Who's Biller? You know who Biller is. Just think, just think, voted number one, of every field. That's neurosurgery. That's heart doctors. That's everybody.

Biller, you saw him. The bigger they are, the nicer they are. The bigger they are, the more humble they are. . . .

He came 21 years ago from George Washington University in St. Louis to New York . . . to be a full professor . . . chairman, number one, of the entire Department of Otolaryngology of one of the greatest hospitals in the United States and the greatest medical schools in the United States, Mt. Sinai Hospital. . . . You have a right to say: "We saw a great man." And you did.

And what else makes him great? Who's he treating? The Maharajah of Jaipur? The wife of the Maharajah? If I say "plain," you know I don't mean she's plain. Plain, sweet, innocent, young Jean Marie Johnson. . . . He's treating her seven and a half years. Ordinary family. High school girl. Nothing special. Regular, typical person. That's Biller. Don't you think he could select the princesses and queens, especially if he's in it to make money?

She's sent to him because she had a problem that could not be taken care of by Dr. Draizin, who himself was a Diplomate in Otolaryngology. Could not. Tried three times. You heard him, honest: "You feel bad when you fail and I failed. So, I sent her to the man I had respect for." And you heard Biller: "She's sent to me to make her able to breathe without that tracheotomy tube." And he did that outside operation, which added to the scar of the trach tube, and reconstructed and then did another surgery, and finally, seven months later, was able to give her enough of an airway to get rid of that ugly tube and not have it the rest of her life.

He couldn't cure her. No one could. Once that airway is destroyed, like hers was destroyed, there's just so much you can do. You could keep lasering and removing and removing and removing, but there's a limit. There's a limit to what you can do. He couldn't give her a voice back. He couldn't give her better than 40%, maybe 50% of her normal airway. This is after ten operations. All general anesthesia. After seven and a half years.

You think Biller's a fool? You know what it means for the chairman of the department, full professor at Mt. Sinai here in this city, the man looked up to and respected by all, selected as number one? Do you know what it means for him to get on the witness stand, swear, testify in a malpractice case against another doctor? Do you think he's got to do that? Do you think you can force him? No way. . . .

Biller testified that malpractice was committed by Dr. Schulster. . . . Remember what defense counsel Mr. Snyder asked him: "You didn't see what Dr. Schulster did, how can you say malpractice?" Do you think Biller's stupid? He knows he didn't see it. . . . Biller doesn't have to be there when she's intubated. Biller for seven and a half years has been inside her mouth and inside her throat and knows more about her glottis and more about the passageway than the man in the moon. What's he say about Jean Marie Johnson's throat and what Dr. Schulster did? "You couldn't put an 8 down there *unless you forced it*. Impossible."

Mr. Snyder tried to challenge him: "But Dr. Biller, Dr. Schulster didn't write the size down." Mr. Snyder wants to reward him for being negligent. . . . He puts on Mattucci and Rosen, they say, "yeah, that's good practice not to write it down." Anyone believes that believes in the Tooth Fairy.

You do a procedure like this, you intubate, these things got all numbers, all calibrations, you are supposed to record what size, what name, how far you put it, write it all down there in centimeters, in millimeters. How many times you tried it, how was the passageway. . . .

When I think no matter how hard I tried, how dedicated I wanted to be, when I'm dealing with no records, missing notes, no 7, no 8, no this, no that, and I've got to deal with things like that, and I think how thankful Jean Marie Johnson has to be that there was, and is still living, Dr. Hugh Biller. Not only to be able to give her as much comfort as possible medically but to come in and do the right thing legally. Dr. Biller is the difference in this case. Not me, not anyone else, not you either.

Believe him or you don't. He said the tube was too big. He's the treating doctor. . . . He says, "Absolutely." If he says that tube was too big, it was too big. He says the tube did it, the tube did it. He says it was a departure from good and accepted practice, it was a departure. He says an 8 is too big, an 8 is too big. He says a 7 was too big. He said whatever they put down her throat – he doesn't know what they put down – whatever they put he knows the damage that was done by a tube too big, period.

Or do you want to believe in the Tooth Fairy of Mattucci, who says "could have been a cold"? Insanity. This has to be insanity. His last words, "it could have been a cold." That's the straw that broke the camel's back. I mean really.

I always amaze myself at the restraint and patience of jurors. I can't restrain myself. I can't. But you were great, you were great. And I wish I was born – next time I want to be born that way. I can't – "a cold." A cold? Not the tube, a cold? What are you going to do. Am I going to insult your intelligence anymore? Keep Mattucci up there any longer on the witness stand? . . .

I ask Rosen: "How is that injury? Tell us what kind of injury is that?" Do you remember Rosen's answer? "Mild, mild." Unbelievable. "Mild"! Goes up one flight of stairs to her sister's, out of breath, one flight, no dancing, no bowling, no tennis, at the prime of her life, 28, 29, 30, 31, prime of her life. "Mild"? You are going to keep questioning a person like that? I wouldn't honor him. You know what I would do with a person like that, that they get only after the trial has started? . . . He tells us that the injury, which to the whole world is horrible, he tells us is "mild." Me? I throw him in the wastebasket.

The other guy, Mattucci, an expert doctor who throws his notes away? Who won't recognize Biller as an authority? Yeah, no authority, no authority. He disagrees with Biller? Biller who's there seven and a half years? Mattucci never saw the pictures . . . never looked at her, never looked down her throat, never looked inside her: "An 8 is perfectly fine, that's what women use." Yeah, women six feet, five ten, five eight. But according to him: "She's a woman, she uses an 8." He disagrees with Biller.

I'm not going to ask him the most ludicrous question in the world: "Who should have a better idea of knowing such and such, the doctor who's treating the patient, or you, who never saw her?"

Ridiculous. I've got to tell that to you jurors? You can't figure it out? Biller's seven and a half years, this guy just retained to come here to say "no, no, no, no." Ridiculous. Mattucci, he threw his notes in the basket. I throw him in the basket. . . .

So what do we have? We have what I told you at the beginning.

The intubation was done wrong. The tube caused the injury. The tube caused the injury because the tube was too big. The person responsible who departed from good, accepted and proper medical practice, Dr. Schulster.

No emotion.

No crying.

No sympathy.

Pure hard fact.

It's taken us almost eight years to be able to present this case.

I said to myself and to the judge even, I was going to finish in less than an hour and I see there may be six, seven minutes left. I'm not even going to take that. Why are we really here?

For justice, sure.

For truth, sure.

For education, sure.

Do you know what one of the crimes is? These doctors don't learn. We think we are doing such good opening their eyes. They have on blinders.

"Dr. Schulster, why did this happen to Jean Marie Johnson?"

"I don't know."

"Was it the tube?"

"I don't know."

"Was it the size 8?"

"I don't know."

> Where have we gotten all these years? Where have we gotten?
>
> Have we improved medicine? I won't say, "I don't know." I do know. You want to have blinders? You don't want to face up and say, "Look, Jean Marie, I'm sorry, I'm sorry. I realized I was wrong. I realized I caused you harm. Please forgive me." No. Instead: "I didn't do anything wrong. Nothing wrong. Nothing wrong. Nothing wrong." And they retain two doctors to come in and say the same thing. And if the jury doesn't buy it, so what. They've got nothing to lose, because they were wrong the day he first treated Jean Marie Johnson.
>
> It has taken seven and a half years. The only issue, the only issue, where you are going to have to come together and put all the brain power of each and every one of you – damages. What's fair, adequate and just? Not easy. You have to determine the truth and the facts there, too. . . .
>
> All that I ask you is one thing I've never varied from in any case for anybody, do one thing: to yourselves be true – to the law be true – and let justice be done.
>
> Thank you.

The jury verdict was $2,500,000, and the case was not appealed. There may not have been any shouts of joy from Jean Marie, but her whispered "thank you," plain and sweet, 'twas enough.

CHAPTER 47

An Angel Too Soon

The most difficult thing for me to do in my career was to meet with a prospective client who I knew would be dead before a possible trial. In 1989, I met with such a client. Her name was Dorothy Kaffka and her story was heart-rending.

The negligence committed on her was clear and so was the fact that she would soon die. The issue before me was one of proximate cause: was she to die because of the negligence or, even more fine-tuned, did the negligence shorten her life span? Her sad story is as follows.

Ms. Kaffka, Norwegian-born and then educated in the United States, became a cloistered nun at age 19. While a nun, she was permitted to speak only five hours a year.

She left the nunnery at age 21 and worked for an insurance company and then in her father's business. Shortly after she married at age 41, she became pregnant and, on October 21, 1988 she gave birth to a daughter, Annie.

I interviewed Ms. Kaffka in the summer of 1989 and she died a few months later on October 3, at age 42. The cause of her death was a cancer of her left breast, which had metastasized to her spine, hip and liver.

In July 1988, when she was six months pregnant, she noticed a swelling in her left armpit (the axilla and tail of the breast). At her monthly visit with her obstetrician Dr. Degann, Ms. Kaffka told her of the swelling. Dr. Degann examined it and told Ms. Kaffka it was a normal condition in pregnancy and they would do a baseline mammography after the birth. Dr. Degann did not examine Ms. Kaffka's breasts thereafter during the pregnancy.

In October and November 1988, following the delivery, Ms. Kaffka developed a mastitis infection of her left breast, which Dr. Degann treated with antibiotics for a month until she sent her to a breast surgeon for an incision and drainage. On November 29, the surgeon, Dr. Eugene Nowak, upon examination of the left breast, found it to be red, swollen, hardened and with a peau d'orange (skin of an orange) appearance. He believed Ms. Kaffka had an advanced cancer and ordered immediate biopsy and drainage, which Ms. Kaffka had on December 1.

On December 2, 1988, Dr. Minick, Chief of Pathology of New York Hospital, examined the biopsy tissue and diagnosed "acute and chronic inflammation, focal fat necrosis" (benign and not cancer). Ms. Kaffka was particularly relieved because at the time she was focusing all of her attention on her newborn Annie, who was then undergoing a series of procedures for a heart condition.

One month later, however, Ms. Kaffka went to her primary physician, Dr. Louis J. Vorhaus, because she had developed severe back and hip pain since the delivery. Dr. Vorhaus, an eminent physician who had been an expert witness on some of my trials, suspected cancer and ordered X-rays, CT scans, bone scans, MRIs and biopsies. During this time, he also spoke with Dr. Nowak and asked him to have NY Hospital reexamine the pathology slides because he felt sure that Ms. Kaffka had metastatic cancer and believed the primary site had to be the left breast. (If I remember correctly, it was probably Dr. Vorhaus who referred Ms. Kaffka to our office to pursue the lawsuit.)

Dr. Nowak spoke to Dr. Minick, who reexamined the biopsy slides of 12/1/88 and this time he saw and diagnosed an intraductal and microinvasive duct carcinoma. It was now March, more than 90 days after the cancer was missed on Dr. Minick's original reading.

In the meantime, the doctors at Lenox Hill Hospital where Dr. Vorhaus was treating Ms. Kaffka found that the cancer had metastasized to Ms. Kaffka's spine, hip and liver with the left breast being the primary site. Chemo, radiation and a mastectomy were performed. Tests were done to determine Ms. Kaffka's estrogen and progesterone receptors and unfortunately they were negative and thus, Ms. Kaffka's last chance for a cure or longer survival was markedly decreased.

We started a lawsuit against Dr. Minick and Dr. Degann in the summer of 1989, and in September, two weeks before she died, we held an EBT to preserve Ms. Kaffka's testimony. Five years later, in 1994, we went to trial in Supreme Court, NY County, before Judge Elliott Wilk, a brilliant witty judge in the style of Judge Gammerman on the Crabbe case.

Our malpractice claim against Defendant Minick (and his employer New York Hospital) was basically: 1) he departed from good pathology practice in failing to see and report that the 12/1/88 biopsy showed cancer; and 2) his departure led to a three-month delay in the diagnosis and prompt treatment for the cancer, and thus was a proximate cause and a substantial factor in decreasing Ms. Kaffka's life expectancy.

Our malpractice claim against Defendant Degann was basically: 1) she departed from accepted obstetrical practice in failing to suspect cancer in July 1988, in failing to follow up with breast exams up to delivery, and in failing to refer Ms. Kaffka to a breast surgeon during the pregnancy and immediately following delivery; and 2) her departure led to months of delay in diagnosis and treatment, and was a proximate cause and substantial factor in the untimely death.

One might have thought that Defendant Minick would concede that missing the cancer that was on the slides he examined was a departure, but that was not to be. He fought against it tooth and nail, and I believe that such a course played a large part in his downfall. His other claim was the common "so-what defense": *If I did depart (which I deny) "so what?" – it made no difference – she was doomed on December 1 when the biopsy was taken because her cancer was Stage 4 – it had metastasized – it was incurable. She would've died when she did even if I correctly read the biopsy slide and found the cancer.*

I do not object when defendants use the "so-what defense" on a trial, because it sounds too harsh, too authoritative, too cavalier. I have found that jurors do not like to have their decision-making and fact-finding power taken away from them in this way, and that typically they reject such a defense. (On appeal, however, the impact of the "so-what defense" is a different story. Unlike the jurors, who live the drama of the trial and observe the experts first-hand, making credibility determinations in large part based on demeanor, the appellate judges rely only on dry transcripts devoid of the experts' tone and manner. What jurors reject in a witness, the appellate judges may override; and thus, the "so-what defense" rejected at trial is often a winner on appeal.)

At trial, the defendants called eight expert witnesses, including the two defendant doctors themselves, and together as a team they testified in unison that there was no malpractice. But even if there was, it did not matter, they all said, because six months before Defendant Minick read the 12/1/88 biopsy – back in June and July 1988 when Defendant Degann saw the swelling of the tail of her breast – Ms. Kaffka's inflammatory breast cancer was already Stage 4 (the highest stage and incurable) and already had metastasized (been carried by the blood from the original site in the left breast). Therefore, any departures by Defendants Minick and Degann caused no harm.

We had two experts to prove our claim: one was a pathologist at Mt. Sinai Hospital, the other was a retired breast cancer surgeon whose 50-year career and approximately 10,000 breast surgeries, the majority on cancerous breasts, had been at Memorial Sloan Kettering Cancer Center in Manhattan. Dr. Steven Dikman, our pathologist, testified that Defendant Minick departed in not seeing the cancer on the biopsy slides. Dr. Guy F. Robbins, our surgeon, testified that Defendant Degann departed in failing to do follow-up breast exams after July 1988.

Both Drs. Dikman and Robbins testified that the defendants' departures were a proximate cause and substantial factor in reducing Ms. Kaffka's lifespan. In partial response to the defendants' so-what defense, Dr. Robbins's trial testimony was that but for the malpractice "she would have had a much better chance of survival, at least of long-term survival," and that the malpractice "certainly decreased her longevity."

The jurors and I learned a lot about inflammatory breast cancer in this case. It is a terrible cancer, one reason being it does not form a lump and without a lump the doctor and patient cannot see or feel something that might be cancer. Instead, little spots in the cells of the breast are the cancer. As a result, the diagnosis of the cancer is delayed until either the person feels pain in the breast or elsewhere, or sees a change in the breast such as redness, swelling, hardness, or a peau d'orange appearance of the skin.

By the time the pain is felt or the changes seen, and a biopsy done, however, it is almost invariably true that the cancer cells have entered the patient's bloodstream and been carried to other parts of the body where they sometimes nest in narrow spaces such as the hip, the spine and liver. Once this happens, the patient has a Stage 4 cancer that is deemed incurable.

The statistics are maybe 20% to 30% of the patients with inflammatory breast cancer survive for five years, but only if the cancer is estrogen and progesterone positive and can be successfully treated with chemotherapy and radiation, and hopefully before metastasis has occurred. Unfortunately, Ms. Kaffka's cancer was in the vascular channels (in the bloodstream) at the time of the 12/1/88 biopsy, as testified to by both plaintiff's and defendants' pathologist experts. She was doomed.

We got a big break on trial, though, when the defendants' expert pathologist Dr. Alan Schiller was called by Defendant Minick's lawyer Peter Crean (a good friend of mine and an excellent lawyer). Although I called Dr. Schiller an "egomaniac" on my summation, he was very well educated and very smart, and he held a very high position as Chief of

Pathology at Mt. Sinai Hospital, which he assumed when he replaced our expert (Dr. Dikman) as Chief. As a prelude to Dr. Schiller's testimony and to put into context our big break, I have to say a few words about my cross-examination of Defendant Minick.

Defendant Minick's defense to not seeing the cancer on the 12/1/88 biopsy the first time he examined it (on 12/2) was that it was extremely difficult to see because 99% of the slide showed inflammation from the mastitis Ms. Kaffka had. This inflammation, he testified, "obscured" the very few cancer cells that were present and thus his failure to see the cancer was not a departure from accepted practice. By the word "obscured" he testified that he meant "rendered difficult to see."

At that time, in my mind, I thought by his use of the word "obscured" he meant to imply the cancer cells were behind and blocked by the intense inflammation, so to clarify I asked him:

> Q – If you look in the sky – you don't have to look there, that's not the sky [he had looked up at the ceiling of the courtroom] – if you look in the sky and you see clouds, you see a whole row of clouds, you can't see anything but clouds, this is the nighttime, there are times when the stars above the clouds can't be seen by us, right?
>
> A – Correct.
>
> Q – The clouds could block our view?
>
> A – Yes.
>
> Q – But we know the stars are behind them, right?
>
> A – Correct.
>
> Q – Now, in looking at these slides, with all those inflammatory cells, in your opinion, are there cancer cells behind them that are being blocked, so like the clouds block the stars, are the cancer cells behind?
>
> A – No.
>
> Q – They are alongside?
>
> A – Yes.

Those admissions by Defendant Minick, that the cancer was there to be seen, greatly watered down his defense. And then his rationale for not seeing what was admittedly observable – "it was difficult" – well, that did not stand up for long either. I asked him:

> Q – So when you say, "they were obscured," what are you saying?
>
> A – It makes it more difficult for them to be seen.
>
> Q – "More difficult." Doctor, you were the director of surgical pathology at New York Hospital at that time, right?
>
> A – Yes.
>
> Q – You're used to dealing with difficulties, in looking at slides, aren't you?
>
> A – Certainly in the past, yes. Absolutely.
>
> Q – That may be one of the reasons, one, why you are the director, you're able to handle difficult circumstances well, usually?
>
> A – Possibly, yes.
>
> Q – Is "difficulty" that which makes you say it's not a departure from good and accepted practice, that you didn't see the cells? Is it because of difficulty?
>
> A – Yes.

A very weakened defense indeed.

Defendants' expert pathologist Dr. Schiller then put the lie to Dr. Minick's testimony in every way possible. Dr. Schiller was the last witness in the trial and our big break came when he projected the biopsy slides on a large screen for the jurors and all others in the courtroom to see. I can still see those pictures in my mind today – the cancer cells looked like large purple grapes in the shape of the Big Dipper – and to any lay person they were clearly and obviously different from the adjacent inflammatory mastitis cells. For a trained pathologist such as Defendant Minick to fail to at least suspect that they were cancer cells bordered on the incredible.

Dr. Schiller testified that there were three reasons why someone, with a trained eye and experience such as his, would know that cancer was present: 1) the nuclei of the eight cancer cells, in the particular field of tissue on the slide he projected, were much larger and much darker than the adjacent inflammatory cells; 2) the eight cancer cells were in a group – a small clump; and 3) their nuclei were much larger in proportion to the cytoplasm (the body of the cell) than were the nuclei in the adjacent inflammatory cells. These, he said, were classic signs of cancer.

In finding the cancer, Dr. Schiller used a standard microscope with three levels: low, medium and high power. It was when we reached high power on the projected biopsy slides that the cancer cells were identified. Dr. Schiller said that he did not know if Defendant Minick was unable to see the cancer cells, or if he saw them but did not recognize them for what they were, but whichever the reason, Defendant Minick made a *mistake*. However, he dutifully excused Defendant Minick, sticking to his guns as a tried-and-true defense witness, stating his opinion that Defendant Minick *did not depart* from accepted medical practice in misdiagnosing the biopsy tissue as benign and not cancer.

What his opinion was didn't really matter though, because what Dr. Schiller did not realize was that he had already told the jury that Defendant Minick did indeed commit malpractice. Because earlier I had asked him: "If the pathologist were *not* to use high-power, for whatever reason, in examining slides like this, I take it that would be a departure from accepted and proper medical practice?" And he had replied: "Yes."

Why do I say that Dr. Schiller's "yes" was confirmation that Defendant Minick was guilty of malpractice? Because Defendant Minick had testified earlier in the trial, and outside of the presence of Dr. Schiller, that he had *not* used high power in examining those slides. Defendant Minick had explained to the jury that "you only go to the highest power when you see something you are suspicious of on low or medium power," and as he hadn't seen anything suspicious on these slides he didn't use high power. Thus, Drs. Minick and Schiller were in total disagreement about whether for these slides high power should have been used, and it didn't take the jury much effort to decide who was right, Dr. Schiller the expert, and a proud one at that, or Defendant Minick whose career was on the line.

Dr. Schiller seemed to revel in his time on the witness stand, especially when he was pointing out the large purple grapes and telling the jurors how he discovered them thanks to his special gifts, which few others possessed. So, I couldn't resist bringing him down a notch with one last, essentially rhetorical question, forcing him to give an answer I knew would get caught in his throat:

> Q – Are you saying, with a reasonable degree of medical certainty, that a competent pathologist, in this community, at that time, who sees these cancer cells, which you showed us, who sees the color

of the nuclei, who sees the size of the nuclei, who sees the pattern of the nuclei of the cells, and who sees the proportion of the nuclei in the cytoplasm, seeing all that, are you telling us that a competent pathologist in this community, who doesn't recognize it's cancer, isn't departing from good practice? Is that what you are saying?

A – Yes.

Mr. DeBLASIO: That's all.

What baloney and he knew it. So, too, did the jury.

I liked Dr. Schiller. I thought he was straightforward, and although he wasn't forthright and honest in his answers about the departure of Defendant Minick, he and I both knew that he was boxed in by my final question. I am sure he would have liked to have answered truthfully ("no"), but that he felt he would be a pariah in the medical community if he did so. (Following the trial, Dr. Schiller and I would meet again, when he asked me to represent a family member in a possible medical malpractice lawsuit.)

I believe a final epitaph for Dorothy Kaffka is in order and so I relate some of my remarks in my summation to the jury of March 22, 1994:

Mr. Justice Wilk, Ms. Rabar, Mr. Crean, members of the jury.

Certainly, we started a long time ago. Certainly, although it's not good form to curry favor with those whom you're asking for something, I'd like to say, I think it was Abe Lincoln who said, "These words won't be remembered long, but it would be bad form not to thank you for your extreme attentiveness."

Now, why are we here? Why have you devoted a great part of your lives, recent lives, to spend time with us?

We are here trying a lawsuit. We're here for truth because by your verdict, under the Latin veritas dictum, truly said, we are here for the truth. We are here to right a wrong, we are here for justice.

We are here for someone whom you've never seen, Annie. This is her lawsuit. I haven't paraded her here in Court, in any way, to distract you from your function as fact finders. . . .

And we are here because this is the last act of a very fine person, the last act of Dorothy Kaffka, the last event over which she can, in any way, play any part. It's all over for her, we know that, but her words do live on, and this is her case.

And you haven't seen Dorothy Kaffka, although I did submit some photographs. And I realize not everyone wanted to see them. I understand it. I didn't submit any photographs when she was ill. That, I didn't do.

I submitted photographs when she was happy, when she was happy with her baby, and with her husband.

It's her last act. And why is her last act important?

Well, it's her story, in a sense a legacy by her, to us, to mankind.

John Donne, the famous, great English clergyman, essayist, over 300 years ago, told us, in effect, what this case is all about, what Dorothy Kaffka's death means, when he wrote, in part, "No man is an island entire of itself. Every man is a piece of the continent, a part of the main. If a clod be washed away by the sea, Europe is the less. Any man's death diminishes me, because I am involved in mankind, and therefore, never send to know for whom the bell tolls, it tolls for thee." . . .

To bring it down to modern times, over 350 years later, Tom Hanks said, in effect, last night, something very close when he accepted the best actor Oscar award for "Philadelphia" [a movie about the early years of the AIDS epidemic]: "The streets of heaven are too crowded with angels."

He was emotional.

So it's easy for me to be a Monday-morning quarterback.

I would have added just two words to "the streets of heaven are too crowded with angels," but I wasn't getting any awards so I could still think: "too soon."

"The streets of heaven are too crowded with angels *too soon.*" That's what he meant.

We know there's an angel in heaven, named Dorothy Kaffka. Too soon, too soon. Why?

Because her biopsy result, she took it for granted. I don't know anyone in the world who gets a biopsy and isn't as nervous as you can be, you don't want to hear from the doctor, you don't want that phone call, you don't want to hear what it was. And when they call, you wait with bated breath. What are they going to say? Because that's life and death to you. A few words from a doctor could be life and death, it's cancer, or it could be hope, it's not cancer.

Who in their right mind challenges a biopsy? . . .

Who in their right mind would feel anything except reassured, happy, pleased, thankful, that a biopsy showed no cancer? . . . If that's not malpractice, they may as well take the sign down on the wall, close the courthouses, because there will never be malpractice, never. The most flagrant malpractice you can have is in this case. . . .

Well, the purpose of a summation is to review what has occurred, to review what's been put in evidence, and to aid you in making legal conclusions, rational conclusions, logical conclusions about what's in evidence. . . .

What are some of the facts? . . .

Now, facts: Before Ms. Kaffka died, you heard a little bit about her. . . . Magnificent courage. . . . Here is the examination before trial, September 19th, two weeks before she died and you saw, it was a six-hour exam.

What did she say about Dr. Degann? I read this, and I want to read it again for a reason [reading from the EBT]:

> My belief was, I think something should have happened, something should have been done to try and prevent this from happening. And I said I liked Dr. Degann as a person, but somehow, this should not have happened. And I think it hurt me doubly, you see, because I did like her, and I do like her. I think she is a fine doctor.

Two weeks before she died, and she knew she was dying. You know what she did, what Dorothy Kaffka did? She gave Dr. Degann spiritual forgiveness. She forgave her. She forgave her. She knew Dr. Degann had a long life ahead of her, she knew she had a long career ahead of her.

Dorothy Kaffka was going to meet her Maker. She gave Dr. Degann spiritual forgiveness, maybe as she did when she was a nun in the most cloistered of settings, ten times a year, a half hour is all they could speak. That's five hours in the year. You can't see anybody except through a – I don't even know what they call it – a grill, for two years.

She gave her spiritual forgiveness, but you know what she didn't give her, and what she couldn't give her? (Oh, she could have, she could have, she started the suit, she was suing her for malpractice.) She couldn't give her legal forgiveness. Why not? What good is a lawsuit going to benefit Dorothy Kaffka? She is going to be dead in two weeks. Why not? Because that was her legacy and her heritage to her beloved Annie.

This lawsuit is Annie's life. This lawsuit is for Annie. Dorothy Kaffka could forgive Dr. Degann for herself, but she couldn't give away Annie's heritage. She could have stopped this lawsuit, then and there at the EBT. She liked Dr. Degann. She said she liked her. But she knew. . . .

Dorothy Kaffka forgave Dr. Degann spiritually. God bless her, Dorothy Kaffka. Legally, she didn't, and neither can we.

So now we get to the point, why are we really here? What's your real function? How can we, how can you, how can the law compensate her?

Dorothy Kaffka is gone. She can't be compensated.

Who does she want compensated? Who does the law permit to be compensated? Her husband. And you heard what she said about him, and how she felt, and most, most, most important, because, to me, he's a man, he's a middle-aged man, he can take care of himself. That little baby cannot.

What does a mother mean?

Well, we got a little taste of it when we saw that 82-year-old medical expert [Dr. Guy Robbins]. . . . That man, for the last half of this century, is one of the greatest breast cancer people in the world. . . . He's written more books and more articles on cancer, survivability, inflammatory breast cancer, lectured all over the world. . . . What did he say that struck me? "When I was 14, my mother died of breast cancer."

And that's why he became a breast cancer surgeon, out of homage to his mother. How wonderful that mother must have been to him in those 14 years. And what is it? It's like a little pebble into the pond, the ripple, the goodness of that mother to this little boy, made that little boy grow into a great surgeon, and dedicate his life to helping and saving, when he could, mothers and women, all, according to him, because of his mother.

No one in their right mind can . . . go against what it means for a baby to have a mother.

You heard Dorothy Kaffka, you heard what she said about her own mother . . . and about her mother taking care of her baby.

You saw Gudrun Orban, the mother of Dorothy Kaffka, you saw her on the witness stand. Did you see any tears? Did you see any wailing? Did you see any requests for sympathy? . . .

We can't see Dorothy Kaffka, but we see her noble mother. We can't see Annie, but we can imagine how she is.

I just want to read a few . . . words from the Nurses Notes, and I'm just about finished. You haven't heard these. These are from the Phelps Hospital record in evidence. I know you remember Dorothy Kaffka died October 3rd. September 20th, two days after the examination before trial, she cried about her condition [reading from the Nurses Notes]:

> "I am going to die. It's unfair. I want to see Annie grow. Why me? I never did anything to deserve this." The patient feels no one will love her husband Bill like she has. Annie should have Gudrun as a surrogate mother, because she has the strength to see Annie's heart surgeries through. . . . The patient wants to

> be held, and cries with dismay about the tragedy of her illness and Annie's.

Am I reading this to make you sway and give her a verdict, when she doesn't deserve it? Anyone could think whatever they want. I'm reading this because these are facts, because your verdict has got to be what's fair and just compensation for Dorothy Kaffka's pain and suffering, and these are facts.

That was pain. That was suffering.

And when she told you on the EBT how terrified she was, so was that. So it may be sympathetic, but it's also a fact.

The next day, September 21st [reading from the Nurses Notes]:

> "It's so unfair. I don't want to die. I decided I am going to fight this thing." Patient in bed with mother present, tearful, wanting to verbalize. Mother physically comforting patient.

The next day, September 22nd [reading from the Nurses Notes]:

> Pain has increased. . . . She has terrible pain.

Two days later, September 24th [reading from the Nurses Notes]:

> "I want this pain to stop. I am so tired of the pain. I want it over."

September 27th [reading from the Nurses Notes]:

> Patient visited with her minister last night, and has planned her service. Has also said her good-byes to her family and to her friends.

The next day [reading from the Nurses Notes]:

> "I thought I was going to die this a.m." Patient reports loss of eyesight and hearing this a.m. with a vision of "people calling me there."

Sure, many people die of cancer, many people suffer. That's a tragedy, to die needlessly, to die before your time. Who's Tom Hanks? But he said it. "It's too crowded up there."

Had she received what she's entitled to, good, accepted, proper medical care, this would not have happened. People can be, can and are saved, who have cancer.

So what's the value of this case? I'm going to tell you what I think. . . . What I think doesn't matter, it's not evidence, it's coming from an advocate. I use it as an aid. Accept it, reject it completely. You're entitled to give less, you're entitled to give more, you're entitled to do whatever you want.

It has to be broken down in different parts.

You've heard, and I haven't gone into it, about Dorothy Kaffka's personality, character, with all this pain, with a baby just born.

She went back to work, she has worked all her life.

You heard the kind of person she was, she was helping her hospital roommate while she was dying. She went to her husband's mother's grave for a funeral two and a half months before she herself died. What thoughts must have been going in her mind of how soon she was going to be there too? She was a courageous, brave woman, not because I say it, because of the record, dearly loving to her family, and most of all, to her baby.

The loss to this baby is insurmountable, insurmountable. You can't even conceive of it. And frankly, when this case is over, with all my heart, I wish you take from it, the good you take from it, the education you take, that which you can do to help your own lives, and the lives of your loved ones, when they come up with certain conditions which, God forbid, will ever appear. You'll know what to do. You'll know your rights. You'll know what you should question.

But the rest of the case, forget it. Dorothy Kaffka's family will remember her. Annie will get to know who she is and remember her. But right now, you *must* think of her.

I submit, a fair and just and adequate amount, under the law for Annie, for the loss forever of her mother, the sum of three million dollars.

I submit, fair, just, adequate amount of money for what Dorothy Kaffka went through in those last horrible, horrible days, when,

> no matter how she tried, she couldn't fight, it was stripped away from her, two and a half million dollars.
>
> I submit that the man she loves so much, and who lost more than almost anyone can lose, in losing a person such as she, two million dollars.
>
> For a total of about seven and a half million dollars.
>
> I've gone over the facts, as I remember them, of liability, and of injury. I've given you my opinion in regard to damages.
>
> But I intend to be true to myself. I will not vary.
>
> No matter how serious this case is, how significant, and how powerful, I never, ever, ever asked a jury for a verdict on behalf of my client. When I was a little boy, I had seen Robert Donat in a movie, and I was very impressed. He was a lawyer, and he ended up with the words, "Let Justice Be Done."
>
> And I thought, what better, what better thing to happen, than having justice done. And I grew up in a time when there was a lot of injustice to a lot of people, a lot of people.
>
> And so I say to you, as I say in every case I ever tried, no matter how strongly I believe in it, give a verdict under the true meaning of it, veritas dictum, truly said. Say the truth. Say the facts. Do justice. And no one can complain. Let Justice Be Done.
>
> Thank you.

The jury's verdict was in favor of the plaintiff, finding that Ms. Kaffka's life expectancy was shortened *by five years* due to the defendants' malpractice. Defendant Degann's share of the liability was 55%, Defendant Minick's and New York Hospital's share was 45%.

The jury awarded $6,000,000: $3,000,000 for Ms. Kaffka; $2,000,000 for her daughter Annie; and $1,000,000 for her husband. In his post-trial decision, Judge Wilk reduced the award to $2,400,000. He allowed only $250,000 for Ms. Kaffka and $150,000 for Mr. Kaffka. Judge Wilk explained that he reduced the awards to Mr. and Ms. Kaffka because her death from the cancer was unavoidable, and thus most of her pain and suffering and most of his loss of services was inevitable and due to the underlying cancer, not the malpractice.

Judge Wilk did not disturb the $2,000,000 award for little Annie. He agreed with the jury that the malpractice shortened Ms. Kaffka's lifespan and inalterably affected Annie's life. In his decision, Judge Wilk said that he was in no better position to assess that value than was the jury, and he declined to interfere with their judgment.

*****

Unfortunately, in 1996, the Appellate Division, First Department, reversed the verdict. Ms. Kaffka's family received nothing.

The Appellate Division dismissed the Complaint in its entirety against Defendant Minick on legal grounds, and set aside the verdict against Defendant Degann as against the weight of the evidence, and sent the case back for re-trial. The Appellate Division stated in part:

> No rational view of the evidence can support a finding that Dr. Minick's misdiagnosis on 12/2/88 proximately caused a diminution of Dorothy Kaffka's life expectancy. . . . By the time of his exam, Mrs. Kaffka's cancer had already metastasized to the bone and liver, tragically sealing her fate. . . . A finding of proximate cause can only be seen as speculation. . . . The jury's determination that, in the absence of negligence Mrs. Kaffka would have lived for five more years was impermissibly speculative. . . . The cancer had reached the patient's spine and had become resistant to chemo.

I take issue with the Appellate Court's reversal because I believe that the judges improperly invaded the jury's fact-finding function. Our expert, as previously stated, testified that had the negligence not occurred, the probability of long-term survival existed. The appellate judges made it clear in their questioning of me at oral argument that our expert's failure to state a specific number of years Ms. Kaffka would have lived made his testimony worthless and the jury's determination of five years unsupported by expert opinion.

I believe that was error because the number of years was a question of fact for the jury to determine and not a question of law for the appellate court. I believe Judge Wilk correctly stated what the applicable law was when, in his post-trial order reducing the damages award, he stated: "Where the issue to be considered is plaintiff's opportunity for extended life, plaintiff must prove that the malpractice more probably than not deprived her of a 'substantial possibility' of longer survival." Longer survival – not specifically how long – was what we had to and did prove through our expert.

*****

I tried the case again in November 1998, but only against Dr. Degann as the Appellate Division had dismissed the case against Dr. Minick.

I lost.

I am violently against excuses so what I say here is not meant to excuse my loss, but explain it, to maybe help those coming after me.

I never liked trying a case a second time. Toscanini may have conducted the same symphony many times, but no two times were ever the same; they could not be. Nor would a second Mona Lisa be the same as the original if Da Vinci had been directed to paint it again. I do not compare myself to these men, but trials too are an art, a form unto their own. Each one unique.

Very occasionally, trying a case a second time can turn out well for a plaintiff, as in Ferdon v. Stamm, but that was after a hung jury, a mistrial, and I had a second chance to discover something the defendants had been hiding (the 10 cc of Lidocaine changed to 7.5 in the hospital record). A second trial after a win is completely different, for many reasons. Chief among them, the *plaintiff's* evidence doesn't change, it is the same the second time around. By the re-trial, the defendants and their lawyers know everything in the plaintiff's arsenal, and they have seen how the plaintiff played his hand. They know everything in store for them, all element of surprise removed, all booby traps exposed, and they've had years to prepare for the inevitable. For the plaintiff's attorney, the spontaneity and novelty – such strong weapons – have been spent. Boxing in a witness or catching a defendant doctor in an untruth on cross-examination is more difficult. And sometimes you lose a witness, as we did in Kaffka, our elderly expert surgeon no longer available.

At the re-trial, our task was made tougher still with the pathology expert who misdiagnosed the condition as benign, Dr. Minick, now absolved of all blame – absent and untouchable. The obstetrician was left holding the bag, and the jury was unwilling to find her negligent for having missed a cancer diagnosis that six months later the pathologist, whose sole role was diagnosis, wasn't even able to see.

It was a devastating loss, the second trial. I felt that justice had not be done.

The day after the verdict, I received a letter. It was from Dorothy's mother Gudrun - but really it was from Dorothy, "Dody" as her mother called her. And just as she had done for Dr. Degann, whom she so liked and admired, Dorothy forgave me. Even more, she allowed me to forgive myself the loss.

Dec. 2. 1988.

Dear Peter DeBlasio - Dorothy's Friend and worthy spokesman,

Last night - after Mary's call I sat alone in my favorite chair. Annie had her ice cream, was busy with homework. It was all quiet. So very, very quiet.

It was over.

I remembered so many years ago. I came from the north, from silent, sturdy, patient people, who learned to live under a difficult climate, learned to battle their friend and enemy: the sea. They learned to watch the magic of the Northern Lights and keep alive with a passion living in their heart.

I met my husband in the south. Alive, talented, joyful with exquisite taste and tremendous charm. Budapest, Vienna with its lovely music and waltz.

And a little girl was born, I named her Dorothy - the gift of God. She took the best from both of us.

It is so typical of Dody that she kept fighting even from beyond the grave. She found in you a magnificent spokesman. Two of you kept saying the same words, battled honorably, fought for justice.

You - together won. You got justice. The one who was negligent and because of that she deprived Dody from the chance, the only chance she had, was found guilty.

There is a delicate border between justice and human law. The law prevailed but justice was done. The punishment will wait for the Youngest Day.

So – I sat in silence and quiet. My tears were flowing inside and outside of me. They still flow but now only inside. Last night I talked to Dody:

> "My darling, it is over now. It is time to rest. You said that the words 'with a song in her heart' should be written on your stone. They are there, but you kept singing for ten more years through your spokesman. It was a magnificent song beautifully performed. You wished so much to be happy, still, you did not quite succeed. Now you are in a different world. Your Swan Song has ended, fly away my darling, to the place where complete happiness exists and is within your reach. So long my dear – farewell."

Dorothy's spirit, dignity and nobility was represented in style by you. You should be proud of yourself just as we – the living – are proud of you.

We all need money. But there are values way beyond what money can buy.

Yes, there was a John Donne, Augustine, Thomas Aquinas, John of the Cross, Plato and Sophocles and many, many more. And their values last centuries beyond them because of the memory in people's minds of them. Somewhere among them are you. Because you leave a memory behind, which will live for a very long time.

Dorothy's life's testament is living with me now. Her name is Annie. She is continuing where Dorothy stopped. And I will guard her integrity and dignity.

Thank you dear Friend – more than words can express. And I thank Mary, who was a Rock of strength, gentleness, consolation and warmth.

Your Gudrun Johnson Orban

POSTSCRIPT: Gudrun wrote the letter in 1998, after the second trial, but misdated it December 2, 1988. A Freudian slip. On December 2, 1988, Dorothy was still alive. It was in fact the very day that Dr. Minick misread the biopsy slides as benign. It was a time when the two women, mother and daughter, still thought Dorothy had a long life ahead of her. (And so I say, in a way, it was as if Dorothy herself, still alive, were writing the letter to me.)

The Mary of the letter was Mary McDermott, our investigator who attended the trials every day, in part to look after Dorothy's mother.

The "Youngest Day" to which Gudrun Orban refers is what follows "Doomsday," known in the Norse mythology of Gudrun's native country as "Ragnarok," the end of the world of gods and men, after which the world will renew and repopulate. A few years before the trial, a popular American Episcopal priest, Robert Farrar Capon, wrote THE YOUNGEST DAY, a book with which Gudrun likely was familiar. Capon wrote metaphorically of the four seasons - pairing winter and death, spring and judgment, summer and hell, and autumn and heaven - and took his book title from the spring and judgment chapter where he wrote that the spring-like "Doomsday" was the "youngest, freshest day of the world."

Gudrun seemed to believe that Dr. Degann had been absolved by human law, but that she would be judged and punished, in the future, on the Youngest Day, by her Maker. I prefer to think that the jury, both juries, each had the final say in the matter, which seems to me appropriate as life is full of contradictions and we all make mistakes.

CHAPTER 48

Perpetual Infancy

On May 7, 1990, I summed up in Braun v. Shaki and GMAC, the case where we had that lucky break at the EBT and discovered we could add a second defendant with a significant insurance policy. The accident that David Braun suffered was catastrophic, but he survived and, on account of his strong will and the total sacrifice and devotion of his family, he thrived. It is as bittersweet a case as any I ever tried.

I include the summation here, toward the end of my stories, after the other summations, because in this one I did one thing that I never did any other time in my life: I didn't end with the words "let justice be done." I had already won the liability in this bifurcated case - justice had already been done - so I broke my rule and said something completely different and totally out of character for me.

> May it please the Court, Mr. Justice Stolarik, Mr. Kelly, Mr. Lewis, Madam Forelady, ladies and gentlemen of the jury. I have put you through a great deal above and beyond the call of duty to sit and to have to listen to the problems of the Braun family. You have done it with the greatest of attention. For this, naturally, we thank you. I am going to sound somewhat cruel in this summation. The last thing I want to be is cruel. I am going to have to tell the facts and the truth as I see it, and very often the truth is very cruel to us.
>
> One week ago, David Braun became a grandfather. His son had a baby girl. The treatment for the baby girl and David Braun is the same. She is bathed; she is washed; she has no control over her bowels; she has no control over her urine. She cannot do anything whatsoever for herself. She is totally dependent, 24 hours a day, on her mother, needs all the loving care, all the watching, all the attention that every little baby should receive and needs to receive to live. Now, take away the baby girl, and substitute David Braun.

No control over his bowels; no control over his urine; needs 24 hours a day of loving care; needs to be washed; needs to be fed; needs to be turned; cannot move; cannot do anything whatsoever for himself. These defendants, through their adjudged wrongdoing, have doomed David Braun to perpetual infancy.

The difference between him and that baby girl is she is not going to have to be a baby for very long. She is going to grow. She is going to be able to take care of herself. David Braun, never. There is another difference. She is in no pain. David Braun is in constant pain.

There is another difference. She has no memory. She doesn't know what life is about. David Braun, in body, is and always will be a baby boy, an infant, one totally dependent on others. But he has got a mind. He has got a brain. He has got feelings. He can think. He knows what life is. He knows what he had.

He knows all the beauties of nature, of being a living human being, of being healthy, of having a devoted wife and family, of being a father. He knows the pleasures of life, which I need not go into. And on December 24th, 1987, they were forever taken away. So, while he is going to live in perpetual infancy, he is going to live with an adult's brain and an adult's knowledge and an adult's memory. He is entombed in his own body.

And yet, you look at him. Did you ever see a nicer man? Did you ever see a more uncomplaining person? From all the records, all the hospital records, pleasant, compliant, motivated, positive. Have you seen any tears in this courtroom from him?

You have seen one thing. You have seen the spasm attacks, which cannot be controlled. Cannot. Involuntary. That, you have seen.

A finer adult is hard to conceive. He looks good. He looks very good sitting there. Why?

Because of that wonderful, wonderful, wonderful registered nurse, Patricia Ryan, the wonderful nurse who is with him now, and the other wonderful nurses who have dedicated their time to giving him the best. . . . [And defendants'] paid professional witness, Dr. Carle, stated that . . . it was detrimental, harmful, bad, wrong, for David Braun to have the registered nurse.

In all my years in court, I have heard fakers, I have heard liars, I have heard connivers on a witness stand. I have never heard the inane, ridiculous testimony that the reason he should not have Patricia Ryan is because she is over-caring, she is smothering, she is interfering with his quality of life.

Over-caring, smothering, interfering with the quality of life. I guess you can say that about the little baby. I guess you can say that about the mother. I guess you can say that about all mothers: they are over-caring. I guess you can say they are smothering, smothering with love, smothering with attention, interfering with the quality of life. Beyond reason.

Patricia Ryan. Because of her, he is here today. Because of her, he looks so good. She is interfering with his quality of life? . . .

Now, counsel, Mr. Lewis, made certain statements to you in his summation. "How would you feel to pay $48.00 an hour to have a nurse sit around? Would you pay $48.00 an hour?"

That was directly addressed to you, to you, the jury, the people he is asking to keep these damages down. "How would you feel?" I have never asked a juror how would you feel about such and such. I think it is an invasion. Would I ask how would you feel to be David Braun, to be quadriplegic, to be paralyzed, have your life over? No. No. It is not how you would feel. It is how he is, how he feels and what the facts are. That is too invasive to ask you how you feel. What can you answer? What can you answer? What can anyone answer?

Talking about money, you are going to decide, you are supreme in that. I will say one thing, and it is not because I am a smart aleck, and it is not because I think I know more than anyone else. I will say one thing, which is as true as anything. No matter what amount you give him, it will not be enough. No matter what amount you give him, I do not care what amount, you cannot give enough. Do you think he would have sold his soul to the devil, made a trade? Is there anyone, you or anyone else, who could believe that on December 24th, if David Braun were to make such a contract for the sum of one hundred million dollars to be left this way, is there anyone, who is not in an insane asylum, who would believe he would have taken it? No way in life. No way any sane person would give up their life and live the rest of their life like this for one hundred million dollars. No way.

You are not going to give one hundred million dollars. No money, no money, you give is going to be enough. But, we have to go by the law. We have to go by reason. We have to go by fairness. We have to go by justness. What money is just, reasonable, and fair to David Braun and for his devoted, lovely wife, when, from the facts, this accident has destroyed as much as possible, as much as can be?

You saw the lovely young girl, Chava, who is getting married next month. She is as nice a young girl as you could want, just by looking at her, just by hearing her. She is a teacher. She is at a time of life when she should be the happiest; and with marriage next month, her life should be blossoming out.

I brought her here to have you see her for several reasons. Number one, I have always been taught the apple doesn't fall far from the tree. You do not get lovely children most of the time unless you have got very fine parents. Lovely, lovely, lovely young girl. I also wanted her to tell you how her father was to her, her sister and her mother, what kind of a man he was. We never got the answer. This, I guarantee you, is not a family of actors and actresses. These are people who can bear anything as well as anybody. That young girl emotionally broke down.

Can you imagine, can you imagine, what it has been for her sister, her mother, her father, his mother, his father? I did not bring his mother and father here. There is a lot more I could have done, a lot, lot, lot more. I could have had motion pictures taken. I could have had videos taken of all the things that are done for him every day. Because all that I am doing and all that we are doing by listening to the evidence is using words.

Clarence Darrow as great as he was, with his unlimited words, could not express to you one one-millionth of the life of David Braun. We have just touched the surface. You haven't seen pictures of the scars he has got all over his body, his chest, his abdomen, his groin, his neck, in the head, where they put in the pins. You haven't seen what the catheterization is. You have heard it, catheterization. You can picture it but you do not want to picture it too much. But you have not seen it. You have not seen the evacuations. To me, it is above and beyond the call of duty for you. I do not have to do it. To me, it is too disgusting. It is too gruesome. It is too embarrassing. It is too degrading. We do not need it.

You know enough, by knowing one millionth of what he goes through, one millionth. There is no way in the world he or I can describe everything. He is in the hospital nine months. It took me one, two seconds to say that. Nine months. It wasn't one or two seconds though. It was nine months. And you heard he had the open-heart surgery. He had the neck. You know it better than I do.

I know, it is getting too much for me too. You know as much as I do, six surgeries, the Gardner-Wells tongs, these things he had in this picture. But really, when I just show you these pictures, that is a lot different than saying a person that is in the hospital – with all tubes in him, with those tongs in his skull, tightened down – cannot move an inch, 24 hours a day, for months and months and months. One picture, as the Chinese say, is worth one thousand words, a million words.

With one picture, you get some idea, by just seeing the picture, what we have described in words. They are a tool, but not an effective one. But you know enough. You know enough from common sense. You know enough from reason. You know enough from seeing him. You know enough of what life is. You know enough of what the pleasures are. You know what we look forward to.

What is the worst thing about David Braun and his condition in my mind? To realize that, I have to think what is life all about. What is he being deprived of, and then in my mind, that is what the worst thing is. The obvious things we know. Cannot walk, cannot do this, cannot do that, pain all the time, dependent. Those are obvious. You have heard it time and time again. To me, when I look and see old, old people, and I see how depressed they look, and I see how sad they look, it saddens me because I know I am going to get that way some day.

But I realize why they are that way. They have no anticipation of beauties of life occurring to them anymore. It is over. They have nothing to look forward to. They have no hope. Nothing good is going to happen. They are not going to go out and have a wonderful time playing ball or dancing or meeting a person they are going to fall in love with or getting a promotion or doing anything great. They have lost the anticipation of anything good ever happening again. That is what leads to depression. That is what leads to life just hemming away.

David Braun has had that taken away from him. He has got faith. He prays every day. But what does he have to look forward to? What good can possibly happen to him? The essence of life has been taken away. He is existing. He is being spoon-fed.

He has one more thing in life, one more thing, a sure thing as things are sure, that he can look forward to. Just one. And that one thing will determine the rest of his life. You know what that one thing is? Your verdict. This is the last thing left. Your verdict tomorrow. May the 8th, 1990.

By your verdict, under the law and the truth and the facts, you control his life for the next thirty years, because you are going to award him money. That, you must do. The amount is the question.

He is hoping, and in anticipation, that you are going to award him so much that all the exigencies of life, all the unknowns that are going to come up, can be countered when there is enough money available. Money is power. Money used in the right way is good power.

He is praying, and has a right to pray, that he, at your hands, will receive enough money to take away the worries of not having money, which afflict all of us. Take those worries away from him. Let him have something we do not have. We have to worry about money and about the future and about how we will be when we are old and are we going to be healthy, and am I going to be able to try cases, and are you going to be able to do what you have to do. Everything else has been taken away from him. Let's give him that.

Let's give him the right not to have to worry about money. Not out of sympathy, not out of emotion, not out of anything else, but because it is just, because it is what justice is all about. He deserves it.

What does he deserve? You are going to get a jury sheet, and on that jury sheet, there are going to be different sections relating to questions like how much for past pain and suffering up to today. . . . That includes pain, suffering, the hospitalization time, the six operations, the scars on his body, and everything else in the case without my repeating it. The bowels, et cetera, et cetera, et cetera. My repeating it doesn't change it. You know it by heart. From the day of the accident to today.

Also, the lost earnings to today, and then there will be another section regarding how much in the future for pain and suffering. Naturally, it will not say it on the sheet, but in pain and suffering, inherent in it, is loss of enjoyment of life, loss of everything we enjoy, everything we hold dear, totally gone. That is part of pain and suffering.

It will be for the future pain and suffering, future medical expenses, future equipment expenses, future custodial care, which are the nurses, and future loss of earnings, and the first question that you are asked is give the total amount. . . .

I am an advocate. I have been fortunate to be asked to be David Braun's lawyer, fortunate in many, many, many, many ways. One way, and, naturally, I am selfish like many of us, I have learned a lot. I have made a promise to myself. Unless I am told I have a fatal illness or my children do, or my wife, I am not going to complain again. My mother used to tell me what a complainer I was. And my wife took over after my mother was gone.

How can I complain again after being with this man for so long? How could I complain? I have learned a lot. I hope it lasts with me. I am sure you have learned a lot, too.

Just one final word before I get into what I believe a fair, just and adequate award should be. Defense counsel has told us a little bit about himself. I do not want to dwell on it, but we have to think of ourselves in order to express ourselves. I remember when I was a little boy, growing up in Brooklyn, ordinary, everyday little boy, no better, no worse, no smarter, no dumber than the others, but my beautiful mother used to ask me, "Peter how much do you love me?" A thousand times maybe she asked, a thousand times I told her, "Momma, I love you all the money in the world." A little Brooklyn boy, I did not know any better. To me, that is the most,

> most, most there is, the most you can love: all the money in the world. I wanted her to be happy. I wanted her to stop working in the factory as a piece worker for $20 a week. I wanted her to have everything. I have never changed. It is a long time since I can say it to her any more.
>
> I want David Braun to have all the money in the world. He cannot, but I want him to have enough. Under the law, it says he is entitled to enough. . . .
>
> I am going to close this summation by saying something that in all the years since I was twenty-four, when I started trying cases, representing people in all walks of life, with all disabilities, I have never said to any client of mine. I mean it as truly as anything I have meant in my life. Having been with and having known David Braun: David, I love you, and you, Mrs. Braun.

POSTSCRIPT: On the verdict sheet, a few lines below the $20,110,500 award, and below the itemization sections, the jurors were asked to give the period of years over which such amounts should last. In other words, how long they thought David Braun would survive. On the verdict sheet they wrote "30 years" – to May 9, 2020.

As of this writing in May 2020, those 30 years have passed and David is still among us – I heard from him as recently as February – cared for by his children and his children's children, his wife Esther sadly having passed away.

From left to right: Dominic's wife Liz, his choirboy son who testified at trial, his daughter who went to fetch the police, and Dominic turning around to wave at them before the summations begin.

The son, Sam.

The father, Edgar.

CHAPTER 49

FATHERS AND SONS

On Monday December 6, 1976, we summed up on the Bronfman trial. I went first and so was able to set the tone and lay out the issue the way I wanted the jury to hear it: Was Sam Bronfman kidnapped, or was this a sick scheme a son dreamed up to extort millions of dollars from his father?

If a real kidnapping, how could it be that Sam, 21 years old, 6'3", 180 lbs. would not have tried to escape when Dominic, 53 years old, 5'2", 125 lbs., "the little guy" as Sam referred to him, was there alone with him? (I knew why: Sam was extremely frightened; he didn't know where he was; he knew there was a gun in the apartment; he didn't know if there were others nearby, in addition to Dominic, guarding him; and he believed his best chance to survive was to wait for his father. But I kept these thoughts to myself.) Impossible, I told the jurors. Inconceivable that Sam would not try to escape. That is why we know this was no kidnapping.

Then, in every way I knew how, I asked the jury again and again if there was anyone less likely in the world to abduct a person and hold him against his will than Dominic Byrne? Anyone? And I answered my own rhetorical question over and over throughout the summation.

If Dominic was to go free, the jury had to believe this was no kidnapping, that the victim was really the victimizer, and to convince them of this I had to explain how a son's mind could become so twisted as to think of and perpetrate this dreadful deed upon his father. The answer, like so many answers, was simple, a tale as old as time - fathers and sons, sons and mothers, sons vs. fathers. Everyone has told it in their own fashion, the Ancient Greeks had their prophecies, the Elizabethan English their dramas and the 19th Century Russians their novels. Love and hate, betrayal and revenge. Fathers and sons.

I soaked in my tub a long time that Sunday before the summation. The theme I knew - Sam's love for his mother and hate for his father - and had known it ever since Lynch concocted his cock-and-bull fairytale and then delivered it up so flawlessly. Sam disappointed Edgar by not immediately joining the family business but choosing to pursue a career at Sports Illustrated; Edgar devastated Sam by divorcing his mother for a younger lady, and then again for a third and even younger wife. Both men betrayed, but the son – who so loved his mother – was the one to seek revenge and literal payback.

What, though, more fundamental or far-reaching even than love and hate would be the Key that would allow me to bring Dominic into the summation as well? And what hook could I use at the outset to lure and compel the jurors forward with me?

After a long time soaking, letting my mind wander, thinking of love and hate, of fathers and sons and mothers, of oracles and ancient Greeks, of my Greek friends, of my best friend Nick Coffinas – of his name-day we were about to celebrate that next day as we did every year on December 6 in honor of Saint Nicholas the patron saint of children – and then it came to me, the Key to my kidnapping summation. It was so simple. It would be *kids*: Sam, the man-child Dominic, and even Dominic's son. And the hook? St. Nick, Santa Claus.

The next morning, I stepped up to the podium, now placed in front of the jury box for our summations, and on the evidence table there alongside, I noticed a photograph. I picked it up, held the photo of Sam's mother's estate house for all the jurors to see, and when I had all eyes focused on me, I began with a quip:

> It's not much, but I guess it's home.
>
> May it please the Court, Mr. Justice Beisheim, Mr. Orlando, Mr. Higgins, Madam Forelady, ladies and gentlemen: Today is December 6, 1976. December 6th is a day that is still celebrated in Europe. It's the Feast of St. Nicholas, and over 300 years ago when the Dutch were here, St. Nicholas, to them, was Santa Claus. And they celebrated with an exchange of gifts, back in the 1600s.
>
> And I think, in a way, it is fitting that in my summing up, in my representing Dominic Byrne, it comes on this day of the Feast of St. Nicholas, the patron saint of children.
>
> A man who we all know was always smiling. The man who we all know was always good, kind-hearted, generous, giving of himself, and I know that, as Mr. Orlando said, this is not a breach of promise trial, and I certainly know it's not a trial of canonization

of Dominic Byrne. It's a kidnapping trial. It's a trial of a person who would have to be the exact and complete antithesis and opposite of St. Nicholas.

It's the trial of a person who would have to be the most despicable human being, the most antisocial human being to kidnap somebody, no matter who that person is.

Can you really imagine what it means to kidnap someone, to take away a person's liberty, to put a person in fear of death, to make a person go through a living nightmare, and beyond, not only the person, the parents, the loved ones?

What kind of a despicable, base human being would inflict that most cruel punishment on anyone else? For what? For money? This is what Dominic Byrne is accused of being? This is what Dominic Byrne is accused of having done?

He is accused of having destroyed the life of a young man, having put that young man's parents and loved ones in the most outrageous and terrifying fear? And why?

Well, you heard, in the opening, the motive. Cherchez la femme – find the woman. There must be a motive. What is the motive in this case?

The District Attorney told you. He wanted to make easy money without working. The only motive you were told at the beginning of the case. No other motive. Not that he was in debt; not that he was without a job, without a family, without friends, without home; not that he is a man of criminal activity all of his life, or that the Bronfmans did something to him.

Not one reason, not one reason whatsoever why this man is supposed to have taken part in the most despicable act a human being could do to another except he wanted money.

And you have to ask yourselves why. Why is there no motive? Why is there no reason? When you ask why, the answers usually come. Because there was no kidnapping.

Dominic Byrne could not – he is incapable of – it's inconceivable to any person that Dominic Byrne ever could, or did, or would do the slightest bit of violence to anyone. To kidnap someone? Absurd.

Why is it absurd? Because of what I say? Will Rogers is supposed to have said, "I love to hear a man talk about himself. I know I will only hear good." Dominic Byrne didn't talk about himself, but his neighbors did. . . .

Everybody knew this 55-year-old man as "Dominic." And I told you at the very beginning, going back to St. Nicholas, going back to the day that we are celebrating, or certainly, some people celebrate today, Dominic Byrne, in one sense, is a child, but in the nicest sense. I don't mean in any way to imply that he is a dummy, that he lacks wits, that he lacks reason.

No, really, when you look at it, he is abnormal, he is abnormal, no one can be that happy.

Dominic Byrne is away from the normal, from the ordinary person, in the best sense of the word. He only thinks as a child thinks in some matters: pleasantness to all; good will to all; life is good. You know who can think that way? The pure of heart. We're a little cynical; we're a little skeptical.

Dominic Byrne has as pure a heart as anyone you will ever get to meet. His neighbors know it; his friends know it. . . .

And just to remind you of some of the things that were said of Dominic Byrne, I would like to read a few portions of what's in evidence. This is from Mr. Greenberger. He is the gent, as you remember, who was called to the stand by the District Attorney, and in whose apartment the money was found. . . . "He fed me, he dressed me, he was better than a father or mother could be." . . .

Can you imagine, can you imagine Dominic Byrne being on trial in his Brooklyn neighborhood of Flatbush? Could you imagine him on trial in front of his neighbors? This case would be laughed out of court. And I will tell you, I have done more laughing in this case than I have done in any. And I don't want you to think really – and I am sorry I have laughed so much, it's not a laughing matter. . . .

Let me continue a little with what has been said not by him about himself, but by others based on his actions for his whole life.

Continuing with Mr. Greenberger:

> Q – Dominic had the key to your apartment?
>
> A – All the time.
>
> Q – How did he get the key to your apartment?
>
> A – I gave it to him because if he rang the bell, sometimes I couldn't walk to the door to answer the bell. And he used to come, when I was sick, he used to come three times a day, middle of the night, 3:00 o'clock, 4:00 o'clock, and if I was sleeping, he just turned around the chair to show that he was there.

Why? Why did Dominic Byrne do that? Because he's the type of person who wants to inflict harm on people? Because he's vicious, because he's despicable?

You remember Father Neufeld? . . . I quote exactly as was testified to by him: "Violence is the farthest thing removed from Dominic Byrne as far as I knew him." . . .

Could you imagine or conceive Dominic Byrne in a fight? Could you imagine or conceive Dominic Byrne restraining anyone against his or her will in any way, in any way? . . .

Each and every FBI agent who met Dominic, I asked the same questions:

> Q – Was he polite?
>
> A – Yes.
>
> Q – Was he respectful?
>
> A – Yes.
>
> Q – Was he cooperative?
>
> A – Yes.
>
> Q – Did he respond to every question?
>
> A – Yes.
>
> Q – Did he seem to try to help?

A – Yes.

Q – Was he a wise-guy?

A – No.

Q – Was he antisocial?

A – No.

Q – Was he in any way violent?

A – No.

And you may say to yourselves, he may be a very, very clever fellow. And true those FBI agents are smart and, true, they're trained, but they can be fooled and he may very well have fooled ten or twelve of them, from McGillicuddy to McCarthy. . . .

Now, you say to yourselves, was he acting to the FBI? Was he fooling the FBI, or was everything he did the only way he could do it? Only one way: in one sense, he's as simple and as naïve as a child. He cannot be any other type of person and he never was.

And, speaking of being simple as a child, and I say it in the nicest way, it's an old saying, "The apple does not fall far from the tree."

You have seen here, I need not say, a very lovely, fine, seemingly nice young boy. . . . That little boy, Dominic's son, wasn't putting on any act. . . .

I brought to you what I could, as a representative group, for one reason: to aid you in deciding why, why would he kidnap anyone? Why would he be the most violent person in the history of mankind, when for 55 years his life is the exact opposite? Why? It is impossible. It's inconceivable, and in a moment you'll hear it again from the lips of the person who certainly knew best – Sam Bronfman.

When Sam Bronfman told you, and I will read it back to you again, he told the FBI two days after the arrest, August 19th, 1975, "To me, Dominic Byrne was innocent." Two days after. It's now 15 months later, and now Dominic needs not only Sam Bronfman to say it, he now needs you. Why? Because in 15 months they haven't come up with one iota of evidence against him. Not one, and you think about it.

You know this case, 53 witnesses, 53. Forty out of 53 are FBI agents. The biggest cover-up you'll ever be a witness to. The biggest bungling job there ever was, and I'll prove it.

You know why they had so many witnesses? Because they didn't have a case. And you know why else they had so many witnesses? So they could leave off the important witnesses, and you'd just think, "well, they had so many."

They brought in to you – just think about it – three FBI agents who did nothing but say they went to the newspapers and put in the ad the ransom note told them to. . . . They had five come in and say they delivered and received a letter at 740 Park Avenue. . . .

They brought in 40 FBI. But who didn't they bring? . . . The agent in charge of the entire case, whom you have been deprived of ever seeing or hearing. But it was important for you to see the fellow who counted the stamps? That was important? The fellow who was in charge of the whole case bungled it. They lost the car. They lost the car with the two million dollars in it, with a hundred agents there; with women in taxicabs and men on motorcycles and helicopters, they lost the car. How could it be?

Do you know what must have happened to the FBI when they checked the license plate and they saw some dummy didn't steal a car, he is using his own car? What kind of a kidnapper is this? What kind of a kidnapper uses his own car? They lost the car. They only got him because he used his own car.

And you say to yourselves, why? What kind of kidnapper plans for three years and uses his own car to pick up the money? Do you believe that is kidnapping? The most botched up, most botched up investigation there ever was. And the man in charge wouldn't even come on the witness stand and testify. . . .

Bronfman is missing nine days. Twenty-four hours – from the ransom pick-up until Dominic contacts the NYPD – the FBI is outside that apartment wondering, "How are we going to get in?" There, at four in the morning, only until Dominic Byrne comes, after 24 hours, and who knows what could have happened to Bronfman, they have Dominic putting the key in. Couldn't get a key from the super, big apartment house? I can't understand it. Twenty-four hours; they needed Dominic. . . .

Cerbone, the big detective was right, when they had Dominic call Lynch, forewarned is forearmed. If that was a real kidnapper there, that boy Sam wouldn't be here today. . . .

But, as usual, I got off the point. Still talking about Dominic Byrne's neighbors. . . . What did Mr. Arrington say about Dominic? "Nicest man you would ever meet."

That is not Dominic Byrne after he is arrested. That is not Dominic Byrne trying to fool you. That is not Dominic Byrne trying to fool the FBI. That's Dominic Byrne, the person.

And one thing I learned from the very old, great trial lawyer [John Reilly], whom it was my privilege to be under, people are as constant as the stars. They never change. They never change. Good is good, and good cannot become bad. And good is what Dominic Byrne has been all his life.

Let's talk, now, about, well, why are we here? We are here for a reason. We don't have Dominic's son on trial. They have Dominic on trial; he must have done something. Yes, but I want you to think about that for a moment. It would be inconceivable if they had a 14-year-old boy on trial, about the same height as his father, about the same weight as his father, same kind of smile as his father, same religious training as his father; inconceivable, inconceivable.

Assume arguendo, assume for argument, Dominic's son was asked, "Mail this letter for me." He mailed the letter, and it was going to Edgar Bronfman. Assume the son was asked: "Do you have a tape recorder? Bring your tape recorder over for me." Brought his tape recorder. Assume the son was asked, "Make a phone call for me. Dial this number." The boy dialed the number. "Bring some food in, I have someone in my apartment. Bring some food in." The boy brought some food in. Assume there was a real kidnapping. Would that not be an aid to the kidnapper?

Mailing a letter; didn't read it. Dominic Byrne didn't read it either. Mailing a letter, bringing over a tape recorder; didn't hear what was made, what was done. Dominic Byrne wasn't there either. He didn't hear what was made or what was done.

Dialing a phone, all those things are aids to a kidnapper. But would you ever conceivably say that that boy should be on trial for kidnapping, as an abettor, as an accomplice, as an aider? Absurd. Why? Because he did not share in the interest and have the criminal intent of aiding someone criminally. That's why it's absurd.

And you remember that word, please, intent, criminal intent. What has been shown? One word of Dominic Byrne having a criminal intent?

Yes, he aided. He mailed the letter; he drove a car; he dialed the telephone; he brought a tape recorder over; he mailed another letter; he brought food. Yes, those are aids, but that is not grounds on which a person should be convicted of a crime of kidnapping. You must have more, or the law is meaningless, or you can just as well indict the son. . . .

By the way . . . did you ever hear a kidnapper plan a kidnapping for three years and go without money and make a collect call, which would pinpoint where he is? On the Belt Parkway, right near his residence in Brooklyn. Collect call; they would know within hours where it is.

How could they do it? How could they plan and do that? Did they know the FBI wasn't going to check it? Could you believe that? The FBI, in nine days, never checked where this collect call came from. Inconceivable, inconceivable. Right near their apartment in Brooklyn. They could have narrowed in like that – never checked.

They make a collect call, the FBI doesn't check. The whole thing is too strange, and you may say to yourself: "How could the FBI really, we know the FBI, how could they really be so bad? How could they really botch it up so much?" . . .

But you know what the most important thing in the case is, to me? The best thing the FBI did, when they took a taped interview, two days later of Sam Bronfman, the best thing in the case. You know why?

Number one, Sam Bronfman was committed before the million dollar Wall Street firm came in preparing him. . . . Two days after, on tape, in his own voice for over an hour, you heard . . . "Dominic Byrne was innocent," or "Dominic Byrne was the nicest thing that ever wore shoe leather," or "Dominic Byrne looked out for every comfort of mine."

But even more, more important, what does it mean that they taped Sam Bronfman? What does the FBI have at their disposal if they want to give you the truth? A tape recorder. . . . Why didn't they keep a tape recorder running when they were questioning Dominic Byrne? Why didn't they have a tape recorder when they were questioning Mel Lynch?

So you could hear everything, there it is on tape. Dominic, what did you do? Why did you do it? Why? Then we wouldn't have to worry – the agents saying "I don't remember. I think he said this, but that's not the gist of it." Ask yourself and I wish, really, any reasonable person would: Why?

Why a tape recorder to record what Sam Bronfman says . . . and not what the two defendants say? Because they want to give you a one-sided picture. That's why. That's why. Go through all the testimony, if you need to, of Mr. McGonigel and Mr. Fuller who questioned Dominic. . . .

What else did Sam Bronfman say? . . . What else? What about Dominic's personality?

> "He seemed to be so much of a, sort of a flighty guy, a guy that was scared of the big guy, as I was, and that he really wouldn't do anything to cross him. And that told me how scared he was of the whole thing, how he thought he made a big mistake and never wanted to get into it but he was forced to, and the fact he was such a nice guy, and such a considerate guy to me when I was kidnapped. All that led me to believe what he told me was true. He was forced to do it, and I believed him." . . .

What did the FBI, Mr. McGonigel and Fuller who questioned Dominic say? . . . Oh, they didn't need psychology on Dominic Byrne. Dominic Byrne would tell them anything no matter what they did. Get him a lollipop, he would tell you, he didn't care what it was. . . . Now, the final thing which I would like to discuss about the questioning is Mr. McGonigel, because that is, as I see it, the entire case against Dominic Byrne, the entire case:

> Q – Did Dominic Byrne ever say "I intended to kidnap somebody"? Did he ever say that during all the time you questioned him?
>
> A – No, sir.
>
> Q –Did he ever say, "I planned to kidnap anybody"?
>
> A – No, sir.
>
> Q – Did Dominic Byrne say he wrote the letter?
>
> A – The best I can remember, he did not say that he wrote the letter.
>
> Q – He told you he didn't read the ransom letter. He told you he didn't write the ransom letter. Did he tell you if he is the one who made the original demand of $4,600,000, or if he is the one who reduced it? Did he tell you that?
>
> A – I don't remember him telling me that, sir.
>
> Q – Did you ask him, "Dominic, did you have anything to do with the reduction?"
>
> A – I don't remember if I asked him that, sir.
>
> Q – Did you ask him, "Were you consulted?"
>
> A – Again, sir, I have no recollection of that.
>
> Q – Did you ask Dominic about the tapes that Sam Bronfman had made?
>
> A – I don't remember if I asked him about any tapes.
>
> Q – Did you ask Dominic if he heard the tapes?

> A – I don't remember that.
>
> Q – Did you ask him if he was present when the tapes were made?
>
> A – I don't remember anything about tapes.

This is the agent of one thousand, of one thousand selected to question this man. This is the agent of the entire case who is supposed to testify about Dominic and what he said. Can you possibly conceive, can you possibly conceive that an agent who spent all this time interrogating Dominic Byrne would not know about asking him about the tapes, wouldn't know about asking him about the letter, wouldn't know about asking him about the ransom?

What was he asking him about? What was he asking him about? The simplest question, to me, is "You want to tell the truth? You did it? Good. Why did you do it? What were you going to get for doing it? What part did you play?"

Do you think you have to be a genius to ask those questions? But they don't ask any of them. They don't ask any of them. We would have not had to rely on his non-recollection if he had tapes made.

Let's continue with him, please:

> Q – Did Dominic Byrne tell you, during all this time, he ever threatened Sam Bronfman or anyone else?
>
> A – I don't remember him telling me that, no, sir.
>
> Q – Did you ask Dominic if he had a gun?
>
> A – My best recollection was that I did and he said that he didn't.
>
> Q – Did you ask him if he ever touched a gun in his life or held a gun in his hand?
>
> A – My best recollection was that he said he didn't like firearms. I don't know if it was exactly the way he said it.
>
> Q – Finally, Mr. McGonigel, did Dominic Byrne say he ever gave any order, any direction, any instruction in regard to

> anything in the entire kidnapping case.
>
> A – I don't remember him ever saying that he gave anyone a direction in the case to do anything.
>
> Q – I asked you three things.
>
> A – Can I have them again?
>
> Q – Order, direction, instruction.
>
> A – My best recollection is that he never told me anything that would indicate he gave anybody an order. What was the other one? . . .

Really, I am not making fun of him. You don't have to have a great memory in life to be good and decent. But if you are going to be chosen out of a thousand agents to question somebody, and to have everything uttered by him staked on your word, how can you disremember what was just said to you two seconds ago? How was he able to get down what Dominic Byrne was saying to him? He can't remember when I am asking him a simple question. . . .

The whole thing, really, you know why it makes no sense? Because there was no kidnapping. Because it couldn't be. Because Mel Lynch got himself involved where he shouldn't. Kidnapping? Do you remember what Sam Bronfman said:

> "At all times when Dominic Byrne was there I was in control. I could have escaped when I wanted to. I knew he was middle aged. I knew he had a family. I knew he was religious. I knew he was a foot shorter than me. I knew he was crying. I knew he was praying." . . .

And I am getting to the point. You heard when his father was testifying. What was he calling Mel Lynch? "The opposition." The opposition. The father knows life is a war. And that's what sports are. Sports are war. It's you and them, and you don't just play sports, you know, just to play sports. It's good; it's good for the heart; increases the flow of blood. But it also is supposed to train you. Trains you for meeting obstacles. For meeting things in life.

Sam Bronfman, a big athlete. Great, great. Put it to use! If his father was there, he would run away. No one would have kept him, and you think of anyone else, who would have remained there? The first instinct, escape, anyone, any prisoner, anywhere – escape.

My God, when it's offered to you, as Dominic offered to let Sam go that one instance? When it's offered to you and you don't go? You must say: "Why not?"

But if he wanted to go, even if Dominic didn't offer him, he is in the bathroom, what does it take? Take off the blindfold. Just put his arm right around Dominic's neck. Now, he doesn't want to go outside; he's afraid there's someone outside with a tommy gun or something. Go right over to the phone. There's no lock on that phone. There's a phone right over there. "Okay, where are we, Dominic?" Dominic will tell you faster than that. If Dominic didn't tell him, fine. "Hello, operator? I'm at ###-####. Where is it? I am kidnapped. Get the FBI. Trace where it is. Come right over." If he doesn't want to go right out the window on the ground floor in the back, or he doesn't want to go out the door, that is all he has to do. That is all he has to do. Never tried it. Why not? Because he was never kidnapped, that is why not. . . .

I could see reasons why, if you are a billionaire's son, you might be upset at your father: you don't match up. You can see. Just look at them. What is Sam Bronfman? Born with all the advantages in life.

In 1942, when the father is only 13 years old, three quarters of a billion dollars. That is in '42, during the War. Forget what has come since. His other son, Edgar Jr., didn't go to college. His daughter didn't go to college. Sam went to college, what is he going to do with all these opportunities? Is he going to be a scientist? Is he going to be a doctor? Is he going to be a professor? Is he going to be something, you know, to take what God has given you and advance mankind? He is going to be a sportswriter at Sports Illustrated.

I don't quarrel with what anyone does if it's honest work, but I can see how a father, you saw the Who's Who, in his 20s, in his 20s, that man was in charge of a billion-dollar empire. In his 20s.

You know, our children are our children. Do you think this boy has grown up the way the father wanted him? I don't care who you are and what you are, you call up: "Pop, I'm kidnapped." And for your father to curse at you? I don't know anyone's father would do that. Call up and say: "Pop, I'm on the moon; Pop, I'm on Mars." The father said – what did he say? Then, Sam curses back at him. Then he curses all over that tape. *I* was mad at him.

I didn't ask Edgar a question on cross-examination. Don't you think I knew all these things that could possibly have gone in? Mr. Orlando brought it out, not I: married a lovely young lady, the mother of this boy, five children. Divorced her and the five children. Two months later, bought or wanted to buy, for a million dollars, a title. That's love. That's love. Gave her a million dollars and a mansion, Lady Caroline Townshend. See how you can go so far with money? You want to buy titles, too.

Two months after he divorces the mother of the five children – I didn't bring that out, they wanted to put it in – "marriage not consummated." Imagine, putting these things in the paper. Consummated before, but not after. Then, marries when all this occurred. First wife, now in her 40s, now we have the second one in her 30s, now he is marrying someone his son's age. Strange this kidnapping occurred right at the time of the wedding, very strange.

Why didn't I ask the father anything? I will tell you why. I could have gone into this motive: "Oh yes, really? The greatest relationship? Your son Sam is exactly what you wanted?" I didn't ask him anything because I don't care who he is or how rich he is or how powerful he is: this man had to have suffered. Whether that son committed a hoax or was kidnapped, that man had to have suffered because, you know, the "golden Rooster," or so the FBI called him, we all have blood in our veins. And I don't care who our children are, or what they are: you harm our children, you harm us. I am not here in any way to degrade or downgrade that man, he suffered enough. And that is why I didn't ask him a question. If they wanted to start bringing dirt in, that was up to them. . . .

Now, you say, well, all right, what about Dominic Byrne – well, I know when I didn't put Dominic Byrne on the stand, I wasn't going to win any popularity contests. Because if I was a juror, all I would be waiting for the whole trial is to hear that one, Dominic Byrne.

But, I will tell you this. Everything that has occurred, you know, Dominic Byrne, no matter what happened, was the driver. All he did was do things that he was told; never did anything else.

And the judge is going to tell you what the law is, at the end of this case, and I am not going to trespass in the judge's area, but he will tell you about intent and criminal intent. And I haven't said one word, throughout this, about beyond a reasonable doubt, but wait until the judge does.

To me, there is no proof of anything beyond a reasonable doubt. Inconceivable. My God, inconceivable, but the judge will tell you the law. He'll tell you the law of the rights of every defendant, no matter who you are, to have them prove the case against you. And if you think they haven't proved a case against you, what your perfect right is.

I am not here to win popularity contests. I am not here to prolong, I am not here to have a good time, listen to Dominic Byrne. I make the decisions throughout, on what I think is a legally proper – I will fight as legally and legitimately, and as hard as I can for Dominic Byrne, or anybody else, to protect his rights, and it's my decision, it's my decision.

Dominic Byrne sits there like anyone else with that same presumption of innocence, and I know you have to be upset. And I'm surprised I didn't see things thrown at me, when I said I rested without calling him to the stand. But I realize, I saw a few people almost fall out of their chairs. I am sorry, but it's my decision.

And in closing, all I want to say is this: There has been a lot of talk here – wait, I just thought of Mr. Cokley. Just before I close, Mr. Cokley testified. . . .

Now, to the end, two things: Number one, I started this off by saying anyone who commits a kidnapping is a monster, I don't care who they are, anyone. And there's only one thing that makes them worse than a monster: if Mel Lynch kidnapped Sam Bronfman . . . and he brought in his friend Dominic Byrne. . . .

After knowing Dominic's son, that lovely boy, for ten years, and that boy idolizing Mel Lynch as you heard the boy testify. And after knowing this lovely girl, Dominic's daughter, for ten years.

After knowing them, and after them taking him in as a second member of the family, for him to go to kidnap someone – why that is disgusting in itself.

But for Mel Lynch to go and take their father, and take her husband, whom he knows is an innocent man all his life for 55 years, to take him and to bring him along, force him or otherwise, to bring him along on a kidnapping, where they must be caught, they must be caught – the least is they're caught. Dominic could have died. They could have got shot. They could have gotten killed.

Dominic could have gotten killed leading the FBI in there. That's not a monster, that's someone unheard of. That's the vilest, worst human being in the world.

You want to do something, and you involve yourself, that is terrible. You want to do something and involve Dominic Byrne – Lynch who is a bachelor and all, that is worse. Do you want to bring Dominic Byrne and ruin Dominic Byrne, and ruin him, and ruin his wife, and ruin his daughter, and ruin his son for the rest of their lives and bring him in on a kidnapping?

Bring him in on a little hanky-panky with Sam's father, and Dominic doesn't know about it. But bring him in on a real-life kidnapping, where he can get killed, and if they don't get killed, they got to get caught? We are not born yesterday. We know what happens when you get caught. He can't eat a piece of candy in prison without somebody opening the box.

To that family, that is the worst monster you have heard in your life. No one is that bad, and Mel Lynch isn't.

Everything to the contrary. Inconceivable that he kidnapped somebody, and bring Dominic Byrne along and ruin that family. Inconceivable. And I don't care what the proof was. In this case, it's an outrage to justice.

There has been no proof. We've heard of Dominic being tiny and being small, and to some of us it means nothing, and to others it means more. Anyway, I'm partial to that sort of thing, and also a little sensitive to it. And also to, what had to come up with Mr. Cokley about, not reading and writing.

The only grandparent I ever knew couldn't read or write, and that's not only in English, that is in Italian. I don't think the others could either, and they were all small or smaller than Dominic Byrne.

Size, in life, shouldn't mean anything, but, unfortunately, like a lot of things that shouldn't be, we do know they mean things to other people: oh, he is big and tall; oh, he is handsome; oh, he is this; oh, he's that.

The fact is the fact. Dominic is small, and Dominic is tiny. But I say it without equivocation, without fear of contradiction, where it really counts, when life is over, and we are judged by the final Judge, no one will have a bigger soul than Dominic Byrne.

And all I ask for Dominic Byrne is what I have asked throughout my life. When I was much younger than Mr. Orlando and Mr. Higgins, in fact when I was about Sam Bronfman's age, as an Assistant United States Attorney, I prosecuted many of these cases. I never asked a jury to find anyone guilty.

I presented the facts as I thought, as honestly and as objectively as possible. And I didn't care who the person was, most despicable crime or person involved, everyone to me is a human being. They all have their rights.

If a jury found them guilty, they found them guilty under the law and the facts and not because I told them.

I would end every case, every case with the words "let justice be done." And, obviously, if justice is innocence, that's justice. I have defended a few cases since then and I never asked anyone to find anyone innocent. I still thought I should leave it to the jury, to let justice be done.

And I have had to think here, am I going to change 20 some-odd years of my thinking and my body and my way of life for Dominic? Because, Dominic, I have never seen anyone like him.

And the answer is, no. I am going to ask you for Dominic, like I ask for everybody else – and I am sure that that is what Dominic wants – I am going to ask you to do for Dominic what he, all his life, this case notwithstanding, has done. He has given justice to everyone, regardless of race, creed, color or religion. They are all neighbors, they are all human beings.

And we have a jury here not of neighbors, but a jury that makes up this county. We spent a lot of time picking you. I am not going to curry favor with you and say you are the best jury, the nicest jury, I have ever had. Easy to say. I can say the truth – you are the healthiest jury I ever saw.

I am going to say this, and I am going to ask you with all the sincerity I have, treat him like everybody else. Let justice be done for him, too. Thank you.

THE COURT: Madam Forelady, ladies and gentlemen: We will recess for lunch until 2:25. I guess that is an hour-and-a-half.

Don't talk about the case during the lunch, don't start to do any deliberations yet. You still have to hear two more summations and the Court's charge.

Higgins summed up that afternoon, and Orlando the following morning.

On that next day, in THE NEW YORK TIMES, M.A. Farber summed up my summation:

Defense lawyers, in detailed, often emotional, summations to the jury in the Bronfman kidnapping trial, said today that neither of the two defendants had any motive to kidnap Samuel Bronfman 2d and that the facts in the case "cry out with reasonable doubt" as to the defendants' guilt. . . .

Peter E. DeBlasio, the lawyer for Dominic P. Byrne, said the prosecution had failed to prove any "criminal intent or interest" on the part of his client, a 55-year-old operator of a limousine service.

"The proof here is an outrage to justice," Mr. DeBlasio said in a voice that rose and fell from a shout to a whisper. "There is no proof. This is the most botched-up investigation there ever was."

Throughout the trial it was Mr. Lynch who maintained that Mr. Bronfman was a homosexual who had conspired with him to extort money from the Bronfman family – without Mr. Byrne's really knowing what was going on. But today it was Mr. Byrne's lawyer who was most explicit in his assertions that the 21-year-old heir to the Seagram liquor fortune had been engaged in a "phony" abduction.

The prosecution was pointing to "the wrong person" in accusing Mr. Byrne, Mr. DeBlasio told the jury of seven women and five men. "They should have been looking into Sam Bronfman." Mr. Bronfman, he continued, did not try to escape from his alleged kidnappers in August 1975 "because he was never kidnapped."

With Samuel Bronfman's wife, Melanie, sitting in the courtroom near the alleged victim's divorced parents, Ann Loeb Bronfman and Edgar M. Bronfman, Mr. DeBlasio suggested that personal and financial relations within the Bronfman family might have created a climate in which Samuel Bronfman would have wanted to stage his own abduction.

Edgar Bronfman, Mr. DeBlasio said, may have been disappointed in his son's ambition to be a sports writer, while his son may have been upset at his father's intention, around the time of the alleged abduction, to marry a woman only several years older than Samuel. The woman, Mr. Bronfman's third wife, sat next to him today, while Mr. DeBlasio said that Mr. Bronfman had married his second wife "to buy a title only two months after divorcing a woman with five children." Mr. Bronfman's second marriage, to an English noblewoman, was annulled in 1974.

M.A. Farber, THE NEW YORK TIMES, "Defense in Bronfman Case Offers Summations, Citing Lack of Motive," December 7, 1976.

Waiting three days for the verdict (left to right): an officer to guard the defendants, Dominic, me, Lynch and Walter J. Higgins, Lynch's attorney.

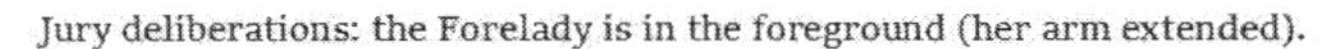

Jury deliberations: the Forelady is in the foreground (her arm extended).

The Forelady announcing the jury's verdict in the Bronfman trial on Friday, December 10, 1976.

After reluctantly convicting both defendants on the extortion count, some of the jurors came to the sentencing on January 6, 1977. Judge Beisheim sentenced Mel Lynch to four years and Dominic Byrne to three years in prison.

THE AFTERMATH

On Friday, December 10, 1976, after three months of trial testimony and three days of deliberation, the jurors in effect spat back at Edgar the prophetic word he uttered a year and a half earlier – "Bullshit" – when they brought in a not guilty verdict on the charges of kidnapping and possession of a loaded gun.

Unfortunately, though, the jury found both Lynch and Dominic guilty of grand larceny (the extortion). Immediately after the verdict, while the jurors were congratulating us on our victory, I asked some of them why, after acquitting on the kidnapping and the gun charges, they found them guilty of extortion. Their answer: "What did you want us to do – call Lynch a liar? He admitted it on the stand."

I am still furious about it 40 years later. On direct examination, Higgins had asked Lynch point blank if he was guilty of extorting Edgar, albeit at Sam's direction. The way Higgins asked him, Lynch had to admit it. Had I been told Higgins was planning to do this, I would have done all in my power to prevent it, and I am sure I would have succeeded.

Why did Higgins do it? I never asked, but the reason was obvious to me. Higgins was not as confident of victory as I. He knew that Lynch had a tall tale to tell. He decided it was best to hedge his bets. Give a little to get a lot in return. Have Lynch show he was an honest person. Have him admit he had done some wrong, namely the extortion, so that the jury would be able to trust he was telling the truth on the important matter – that it was all a hoax and not a kidnapping. Some might consider that Higgins made a good trade. I am sure he felt that way, but I will never be convinced of it.

Having been convicted on the extortion charge, Lynch and Dominic returned to jail that afternoon to await sentencing.

Sam, who was not in the courtroom for the verdict, gave a press conference after it was announced. Pete Axthelm, who was in attendance at the conference, wrote about Sam's reaction to the verdict in his NEWSWEEK article "The Bronfman Verdict," on December 20, 1976:

> Sam heard the verdict on a radio in his father's office in the Seagram Building in mid-Manhattan. "I was shocked and stunned," he said. "I was furious that people could believe that I was a homosexual or an extortionist." Later, he held a bitter news conference. Then he settled back into his father's inner sanctum, surrounded by Rodin sculptures and a Miró tapestry, and talked.

> "I've had everything I've ever wanted," he said. "Where's my motive for a crime against my dad? Look around me – I'm rich and happy. If that jury didn't believe I got kidnapped, I wonder if they can imagine what being kidnapped was like."
>
> Bryne's brilliant attorney, Peter DeBlasio, had apparently stirred jurors in his summation by questioning Sam for not trying to escape. "When your life's at stake," said Bronfman, "you tend to place surviving above escaping. I don't want to sound like a martyr, but until you've been in certain situations, you can't judge what you would do. I was forced into a new world, far away from Williams College and Deerfield Academy and the hallowed halls of the Seagram Building. And I thought my best bet for survival was to stay put and wait for the ransom to be paid." Sam's voice rose suddenly. "And goddam it, whatever the jury said, I played it right. I'm alive today, aren't I?"

As for myself? The day after the verdict, I returned to my usual Saturday routine and went to the racetrack (that season, Aqueduct) with Nick Coffinas. That Saturday evening, my wife Jo and I went to the great French restaurant La Caravelle to celebrate with Mr. Reilly and his wife. That Sunday, I was exhausted and stayed in bed all day, but in the evening I went out with my family for dinner at the PEA.

Though still exhausted on Monday, I went to work and out for a celebratory lunch at Sweet's, the great long-gone fish restaurant down by Fulton Market, again with Mr. Reilly and this time with his daughter (who was also his law partner), as well as with my office manager Joyce (who is now my wife). On Tuesday, feeling no better, I went into the office anyway and that evening, as on all Tuesdays, I went to the PEA for dinner and to play cards. I gave in to exhaustion and stayed home on Wednesday, but on Thursday I was back at work and again at Sweet's for lunch, this time with my law partner Tom Meagher. Friday I went to lunch to celebrate with my staff at Miller's, a restaurant on the ground floor of the Woolworth Building, where we had our office. A full week of celebrations.

On Monday, December 20, I was back in court seeking bail for Dominic, so he could be at home with his family through the Christmas holidays until his sentencing. My request was denied. On Tuesday, I went to Sweet's for lunch, again with Mr. Reilly, his daughter and Joy, and to the PEA for dinner and cards. Thursday I went to lunch with Nick and his brothers Gus and Teddy, and that evening was our office holiday party at the PEA. On Saturday, my family and I went for Christmas dinner at the home of our great friends Bob and Missy Pinckert who lived across the Hudson River from us in Upper Nyack.

On Monday, December 27, my daughters and I went off to Puerto Rico, to the Dorado Beach Hotel. We returned to New York on New Year's Eve, and 1977 began with me back in court on Thursday, January 6, for Mel and Dominic's sentencing.

Judge Beisheim sentenced Lynch to four years of imprisonment, and Dominic to three. Orlando's boss, District Attorney Carl Vergari, had demanded that Judge Beisheim impose the maximum penalty of 15 years. The judge ignored him. As they had already spent 18 months in jail, Dominic had just 18 months more to serve before he was released, and Mel had another 30 months.

After all was said and done, I spoke a bit with Judge Beisheim, as we were now fairly friendly. I thanked him for his kindness toward me throughout the trial, for which I was then and am today still grateful. His last words to me, as I remember them, were: "You know, Peter, this would have been a good trial if it were limited to Orlando against Higgins."

I knew that the judge would not have been disappointed if the verdict had turned out differently. And my last words to him? "Respectfully, Judge, this would have been a better trial you against me." And I meant it, just as I mean I am sorry I never again had the opportunity to appear before him. He was an exceptional judge.

THE EPILOGUE

Whether justice was done in this case may not be for me to say. I did what I had to do for Dominic, which meant not helping to convict Lynch.

As for what became of everyone, I'll start with Dominic, and end with myself.

Of all my thousands of clients, Dominic in the end was one of my least favorites. Dominic died only a few years ago, but I hadn't spoken to him in decades. During a phone conversation a few years after the trial, Dominic said something that caused me to become annoyed. I no longer remember what it was that he said, but I very clearly remember my retort: "Dominic, if it wasn't for me, you would have spent the rest of your life in jail." Dominic replied, "I'm not so sure of that." To me that was the least respectful remark I had ever received from a client and I don't remember ever speaking to Dominic again.

As for Mel, well, he got away with the crime of the century. And he damaged, if not destroyed, another man's life (Sam's, not Dominic's) in doing so. But, I grew to like Mel. I never knew him or spoke a word to him during the trial. Afterward, though, after he was released from prison, Mel would call me from time to time, usually when he had a friend's personal injury case to refer to me. During these calls, he always thanked me and said: "I pray for you each and every night." I know he meant it. I know he told me that because he was grateful for what I had done for him, and what I did not do to harm him, as we both knew I could have torn his story to pieces. On one of our last phone calls, sometime in the mid-1990s, he told me something that would have surprised our jurors, but did not surprise me a bit: he had gotten married. I never had the opportunity to meet his wife, but I imagine she was a lot like Dominic's wife Liz, both his intimate and his confidante.

About Sam. I have always felt sorry for him even though he was and is a millionaire a hundred times over. Nobody should have to suffer and endure what he did. But it was not my place to win the government's case for them, or to protect Sam and rehabilitate his reputation after Lynch did his damage. *But that was then.* Now, with all the other major players dead (first Lynch, then Edgar, and most recently Dominic), and before it's too late for me, I want it to be clear to all who may ever read these pages that Samuel Bronfman was not a part of the kidnapping, he never met Lynch and Byrne before they abducted him, he played no role in their extorting his father, neither he nor Lynch were gay as far as anyone ever knew and certainly they were not lovers. I was sorry to hear some years after the trial that Edgar passed over Sam – who was his eldest and who was the one he had been grooming to take the helm at Seagram, the only one of his older children who ever bothered to attend college – and anointed his second son Edgar Jr. as the heir-successor. It was never stated publicly, but the damage done by the trial must have weighed heavily in Edgar Sr.'s calculations. And so I say, even with his great fortune, Sam Bronfman was among the unluckiest of men.

As for Edgar, of course I never saw or heard from him after the verdict. Except once, in an offhanded sort of way, about 19 years after the trial. In 1995, I fired a junior partner and had to dissolve our partnership, for which each of us would need an attorney. My good friend Tom Moore referred me to a top-notch Wall Street lawyer who handled just such matters. He was a partner at Simpson Thacher – Seagram's law firm – but I figured so much time having passed, my former relationship to the Bronfman family should no longer make any difference, particularly in this instance given the minor nature of the case, a law firm dissolution. The lawyer and I met, we spoke about the matter, and he said he would be pleased to handle it on my behalf. Before we parted, however, I mentioned the Bronfman kidnapping trial and said I thought he should probably check with Simpson's managing partner just to be sure they had permission to take me on as a client. The very nice fellow, Reardon as I remember his name, called me within days both to sincerely thank me for giving him the heads-up and to let me know that all was not forgotten and that, as he phrased it, "still waters run deep." Edgar was still mad, and still all-powerful. But Reardon gave me the name of an attorney at a different firm, an Italian-American fellow, and all went smoothly with the partnership dissolution.

As for the lawyers, Geoffrey Orlando eventually left the District Attorney's Office and, as it happened, he followed my path and went to work as a personal injury plaintiff's attorney.

Wally Higgins, on the other hand, left the practice of law altogether, a year or so after our trial. From what I understood back around that time, he went to work on the corporate side of the food services industry.

I returned to my personal injury plaintiff's practice and went on to try hundreds more cases until my retirement exactly 30 years later. The Bronfman kidnapping was my last criminal trial, for the simple reason that nobody else ever asked me to defend them.

CHAPTER 50

The End of an Era

Looking back now over journals I kept throughout my career, I am only a little surprised to see how many evenings a week I spent playing handball at the New York Athletic Club (the AC) and playing cards at the Progressive Era Association (the PEA). Back in the 1960s, 70s and 80s, I could be at the AC and the PEA four evenings a week, leaving a single weeknight to have dinner at home with my family. I would then spend all day Saturday and Sunday at the racetrack, Aqueduct and Belmont during most of the year, and a week or so during the summer up at the track in Saratoga with my best friend Nick Coffinas and his brothers Gus and Teddy.

Handball and cards and the racetrack provided relief from the pressure and pace of being a trial lawyer. Pressure because as a plaintiff's personal injury lawyer, working on contingency, if I lost a trial, not only did I not make money, but I was out tens of thousands of dollars in case expenses. And the pace in those days was unrelenting. So often I was waiting on the verdict in one trial as I was picking a jury for my next trial. As an outlet, I played sports competitively into my fifties – I have always believed that to be a great trial lawyer you have to be in great physical shape – and spent leisure time with friends out at restaurants eating, drinking, smoking cigars, and then playing cards. Mostly I alternated between the AC and the PEA, on my own without my wife Jo, though a few times a month she and I would go out together with friends. In the 1950s and early 60s we'd often go for dinner and drinks after art openings at the galleries on East 9th and 10th Streets, which were popular back then in the days of Abstract Expressionism, and I'd always try to pick up the check as times were tough for my wife's artist friends. From the 1970s on, we went out with close friends to the great French restaurants of New York: Lutèce, La Caravelle, La Côte Basque, La Grenouille.

In 1971, in celebration of Jo's 40th birthday, I threw a party at Lutèce for 16 people, which was quite extravagant back then (the bill came to

$832 and I left $240 in tips), and from that day onward I became friends with the extraordinary chef and owner André Soltner. He always found a table for us when we wanted to have dinner, and he always let me smoke my cigars in his restaurant. Exactly 35 years later, Lutèce having closed, my daughter Alessandra arranged with Soltner (then affiliated with the French Culinary Institute) to hold a retirement party for me. Over cocktails we watched Soltner, the master, prepare a dish of his own choosing (saumon en croûte) for our main course. Among the 50 guests were several whose names appear in these pages: Peter Johnson, Peter Crean, Peter Kopff, Tom Moore, Dr. Bernie Ackerman, Dr. Armen Haig, Dr. Louis Vorhaus and Judge Ira Gammerman.

The New York Athletic Club back in 1959 – when I joined at the invitation of Mr. Reilly's great friend Judge Ughetta – was, and still is, the city's premier athletic club. Only men could be members of the AC. At its main West 59th Street location, the swimming pool (where it was de rigueur to swim naked), and the handball, squash and racquetball courts were all off-limits to women. During the year, wives and children were permitted on the premises only to dine; in the summertime, they were allowed to play golf and tennis at the AC's Travers Island location in Westchester, but only at restricted times.

I played handball at the AC, often followed by dinner, three nights a week for decades. I had grown up playing one-wall handball on the streets of Brooklyn, but at the AC they only had four-wall handball, which as it sounds means the players hit the ball against the four walls of an enclosed court as well as off the ceiling.

The greatest handball players in the world in those days were the Obert brothers from Queens, Oscar (the acknowledged best), Rubrecht and Carl. Among them they had 85 national championship medals. They were unrivalled. They routinely did what I never saw any other player ever do: they returned what was known as "the killer shot," which was a perfectly hit ball to the bottom of the wall that would roll along the floor, unreturnable, except by the Obert brothers who somehow, someway managed to get at the ball when barely an eighth of an inch off the floor. Rubrecht, known as "Ruby," would play at the AC from time to time, and he would spot me 19 points and still beat me 21-20. Usually, though, I played with Jim Fauci and Andy Romeo, who was my partner one year in the quarter-finals at the national championships.

I played handball for the last time in my life on October 20, 1986, in a Masters doubles match against Andy. The score was 30/30, where 31 wins, and as I was going for a final shot, pain ripped through my calf and

I fell unconscious, my Achilles tendon ruptured. I was lucky that Richard McCarthy – coincidentally one of the FBI agents from the Bronfman trial whom I cross-examined mercilessly but later became good handball friends with – happened to be passing by the court and saw me go down. He rushed to my aid, getting smelling salts to bring me to, and called an ambulance.

I was in a cast for six months following the surgery to repair the tear, perfectly done by my great friend Dr. Armen Haig, but I never again wanted to return to the handball court. Nor did I go to the AC much after that, in part because I moved with Joy from Manhattan to Staten Island in August 1986 when we married.

But I was back at the AC one evening in the spring of 1988, for the annual handball roast where I was lambasted. The evening was memorialized in the AC's June 1988 Winged Foot Magazine:

> Once again, the perceptibly aging core section of the Killers Handball Group met to roast Tommy Hamm and Peter DeBlasio. Whoever makes the annual selection of the "Roastees" seems to pick sharply contrasting types. Last year we had a Polish Nobelman [sic] and an Irish Banker. This year we have Hamm and Provolone.
>
> Tommy Hamm is a friendly, gregarious type who belongs to over 20 of NYAC's outstanding Intramural Clubs, including the Killers Club. . . .
>
> The other roastee is, as Winston Churchill might put it, "a conundrum wrapped in an enigma and enveloped in mystery." Peter DeBlasio is a savvy, articulate lawyer who has achieved an enviable record in his profession. He is esteemed and admired in legal circles. Indeed, a judge graced our roast with his presence as a tribute to Peter.
>
> On the handball court he becomes a different person. He is first of all a Class A player. But, where I have been compared to Dorian Gray, growing old before everyone's eyes, Peter changes from the very proper Dr. Jekyll to the unpredictable Mr. Hyde.
>
> He may be the victim of a bum rap – but on the court he has been described as having the stiletto mentality of a Renaissance assassin.
>
> He becomes so involved emotionally in the game that he can become enraged when he perceives an unfair call, or an unpunished block by an opponent. I don't know which is worse, playing against him or with him. He treats all with equal contempt and disdain in his desire for perfection.

> Yet when the game is over and "Melt Down" begins, he is once more the quiet, reserved gentleman and the frenzy of the game is forgotten.
>
> Peter and Andy Romeo have two different approaches to the calls of referees. If DeBlasio feels he has been wronged, he will argue "usque ad mortem" to correct the call. . . .
>
> However, the other night Peter unraveled the mystery. He agreed he was misunderstood and explained that it was all due to his *shyness* and his *desire to win*. There wasn't a dry eye in the house.
>
> Whatever the histrionics, you know you have been in a handball game when you play against Peter DeBlasio.

Many a truth, I know, is said in jest. They knew me well at the AC, I did fight to the death, both on the court and in the courthouse.

Even more though than the AC, I miss the PEA. The PEA was an Italian-American social club founded in 1929 and located in a brownstone in the heart of Greenwich Village next to Washington Square Park, at 73 Washington Place. The club was founded with the purpose of advancing men of Italian heritage and promoting the common good – primarily for Italian-Americans. The founders did not set such a good example at the beginning though, because membership was restricted to "white Italian-American men," which meant that had legendary football great Franco Harris wanted to join, his membership application would have been denied. (Although Franco's mother was a native-born Italian, his father – a soldier during WWII stationed for a time in Italy – was Black.) I am not sure the founders were really racists or if it was just that they thought all Italians were white. In any event, the "white" was removed from the qualifications before I joined, but membership remained restricted to Italian-Americans, men only.

I became a member in 1954, just when I was hired as an Assistant U.S. Attorney. Joe Parisi, whom I met when I dutifully went to register as a Republican, introduced me to many prominent Italian-Americans and among them was Mike Russo, who sponsored me for membership in the PEA. Mike was a savvy and well-connected individual who was then the chief assistant to Judge Edward Re, a highly respected and decorated Italian-born lawyer nominated by Presidents Kennedy, Johnson and Carter to various federal judicial posts. Mike and I became life-long friends, and among the very many people he knew back then was a young opera aficionada Irene Maruzzella whom he introduced to my brother Edward. They married in 1957 and were together until Ed's death in 2015.

For more than 50 years, I had dinner and played cards – an Italian tradition brought over from the old country – at the PEA every Tuesday night. On weekends, many members brought their families and friends for dinner. From the time my daughters were born in the mid-1960s, we ate at the PEA every other Sunday night as a family. We were always accompanied by my brother and Irene and their two girls, until they moved in 1971 to Los Angeles, and by my father up until his death in 1976. My mother's sisters Isabel (her husband Pete Cataldi) and Jean joined us on occasion, as did her brothers Jimmy (his wife Kaye and son James), Danny, and Kelly (his wife Marie and children Janice and Robert) Rubertone; and my father's sister Irene (her life partner Jo) came as well.

We also celebrated many birthdays at the PEA, one of the most memorable being a Saturday afternoon party when my daughter Alessandra turned eight. Memorable because just as they were bringing out the chocolate cake Jo made for the assembled 11 children and 7 adults, my great friend Pinky (Bob Pinckert), who was there with his young son Eric, got an emergency call from the hospital and rushed off, his wife Missy having just gone into labor with their second child Miranda.

We continued to go to the PEA regularly until my daughters went off to college, Alessandra to Princeton and Caralee to Columbia. (The PEA's greatest chef ever, a Sicilian-born immigrant named Giovanni who arrived in the United States virtually penniless, sent his daughter off to Princeton as well, three years after my daughter.) The fried shrimp, mussels posillipo (in marinara sauce), manicotti with tomato sauce, fusilli with meat sauce, veal francese, veal parmigiano and osso buco were unrivaled anywhere in the city, as was the bread from the famed but long-gone Zito's bakery on Bleecker Street.

Over the years, I was alternately a board member and president of the PEA, and eventually I oversaw the opening of its membership to non-Italians, and finally to women. In fact, the first woman to become a member was my younger daughter Caralee. I am happy to have lived long enough to see times change.

After my retirement from work in 2006, though, I rarely came into the city (Manhattan) from Staten Island and no longer went to the PEA regularly. The last great event we held there was in 2007, when Alessandra married Allan (Haynes). They had met back in the third grade at the Ethical Culture Fieldston School, and their wedding reception was a reunion of sorts for their many Ethical-Fieldston friends, most of whom had been to the PEA with us at one time or another over the years.

So many wonderful things from my past have come to an end. By the time the PEA closed its doors in 2014, it had long since gone down in quality and membership, which I imagine had a lot to do with the turnover in chefs and the first generation of Italian-Americans (my parents' generation) dying off and the younger generations becoming more assimilated.

When the PEA was dissolved, according to the club's charter the then-surviving members were to get a share in the proceeds from the sale of the brownstone, which was prime Greenwich Village real estate. The percentage allocated to each surviving member was to be determined according to the length of their membership in the club. I was one of the longest-serving members – if not *the* longest with my 60 years of dues paying – and so I was due to receive a substantial percentage of the building's more than $10 million sale price. Not only did I not receive notice of the sale, but I did not receive a cent.

The reason? Oscar Ianniello, the head of the family that was in nearly full control of the PEA by 2014, had presumed me dead. When news of the sale eventually did reach me, still very much alive, I made an inquiring phone call to Oscar. "Well, Peter, we hadn't seen you at the PEA in a while," was the best he could come up with. His lack of due diligence in searching me out – my home phone number had not changed in nearly 30 years – may have had something to do with the fact that in the months leading up to the PEA's dissolution, he had seen to it that all his children, nieces, nephews and grandchildren were inducted as members. The spoils, I learned, had been evenly distributed among any PEA members they could find, in other words, among the Ianniellos themselves.

A week or so after I spoke with him, Oscar called me back to say he had gotten everyone to agree to chip in and he hoped I would accept their apologies together with $250,000. Far less than I was due, I considered myself lucky to get it, as it was well known that some among the extended Ianniello family were associated with the Genovese crime syndicate.

The Ianniellos were not alone in their ties to underworld figures. Many Italians in my lifetime had at least one distant (or not-so-distant) relative involved with the Mafia. My father's older sister Anna Di Blasio, born in 1898 in Italy, a Neapolitan beauty who looked just like Gina Lollobrigida, married into the now-infamous Gallo family. One of my Aunt Anna's sons, Lawrence, who everyone called "Bellil" and eventually simply "Billy" (from *bello*, Italian for beautiful), was the handsomest of all my hundreds of relatives, and probably the handsomest man I ever saw in my life. Another one of her sons, Mario Gallo, an ordinary looking guy, became a Hollywood character actor, often playing Italian gangsters in the movies, the best-known being Martin Scorsese's "Raging Bull."

But the real gangsters in the family were my Aunt Anna Gallo's nephews – and I don't mean me and my brother – the ones on her husband Ralph's side. They were "made men," mobsters whose exploits, none of them honorable, would be depicted in the 1974 Mafia movie "Crazy Joey." (I never once met or even saw Joey Gallo, even though he was my age, and lived close to my Aunt Anna. I did occasionally hear stories about him when we were young, like the time our Aunt Anna refused to take Joey and his two brothers to Coney Island, and so the three of them stood outside her house and threw rocks at the windows, one after the other, breaking all the glass. From what I heard about them when I was growing up, it was clear to me that Joey and his brothers were crazy, and I mean sociopaths, from a very young age.)

Eddie and I never met that side of the Gallo family because my father rarely took us to Aunt Anna's, she had to visit us. My father didn't survive near death in World War I to have gangsters for children. He kept us away from that crowd and devoted his life to our lessons and education. I don't know how he did it; he was a man a hundred years ahead of his time.

A "100A" my mother always wished me and in return I wished her all the money in the world. "Cent' anni" was another Italian wish I heard often in my childhood – that one should live to be a hundred years old – as nearly unobtainable and unlikely as a lifetime of 100A.

I am now 90. I have lived through the Crash of 1929, the Great Depression, World War II, 9/11 and the onset of COVID-19. I have had my foot in 11 decades. 'Tis enough. All my great friends are gone, as are all the judges and doctors I knew and respected, and almost all of my lawyer colleagues with the exception of a few of the younger ones. My mother died more than a half century ago, at the age of 60. An angel too soon. My father, my brother, my former wife, all have passed on. When I was 57, I was lucky to marry Joy, the love of my life, and she is with me to this day. She and my two children and my grandson are the only ones left to me.

I never did get to be a juror on a trial. But if I were to voir dire myself, I'd say that my proudest achievement apart from my children was my success as a trial lawyer; and my greatest disappointment was not being a professional baseball player. When I think of career highlights and what someone might say about me, I think back to what my great friend Bernie Ackerman said at our long-ago EBT, that we had exactness and precision in common. And I think too about what he said of himself and I'd like to believe we had that in common as well: we took our life's work seriously, we went beyond the outer limits of our possibilities, we played no political games, we were honest, and we brought imagination and creativity and iconoclasm to our respective fields. I would add if I might, and I can as these are my memoirs, that I hope those left to remember me will also say that I was generous, I tried my best to help others, I was gracious to all, and I was never envious.

I was not born to privilege, but the Fates bestowed on me great luck and I tried to use it to "Do Good." I tried to see justice done for all, no matter who it was seeking my help, rich or poor, Black or White, man or woman, young or old, Catholic or Hasidic, foreign or American, guilty or innocent. All deserved their day in court, the respect of the judge and jury, and an honest hard-fought true verdict.

Me and Joy with our grandson Allan after his graduation from pre-kindergarten, New Jersey, June 2013.

The Coda: Passing the Baton

My grandson has been to court once, federal court in Brooklyn, where I began my career as an Assistant U.S. Attorney. He went with his mother, a former Assistant U.S. Attorney herself and now a federal criminal defense attorney. She had a short status conference on a case and could not find a babysitter on a day when the schools were closed. So she brought him along. A good experience, she thought, for him.

Judge Sterling Johnson, Jr., then in his 80s, a former Marine, police detective, prosecutor, and federal judge of more than 20 years, was presiding. According to my daughter the courtroom, atypically, was packed. He had scheduled several cases, some with many defense counsel, all for the same time, 9:30 a.m. His courtroom deputy, Ana Rodriguez, seeing my daughter with a very young child motioned her into the well of the courtroom before His Honor took the bench. She would call my daughter's case first because she knew children could quickly become bored, and perhaps she feared a minor disruption.

While quite imposing, the judge could not have been nicer when he entered the courtroom and his deputy alerted him to my grandson. Before calling my daughter's case, he asked my grandson to approach – on his own. My grandson walked into the well and all the way to the front of the courtroom, where he looked up to His Honor. But Judge Johnson had something else in mind and invited him up farther still, past the deputy and around the court stenographer, and up the final few steps to the judge's bench. There, "holding court" before the roomful of lawyers, he asked my grandson his name. "Allan Haynes, Jr.," he answered. Speak up, said the judge, who then asked him his age. "Six years old," boomed my grandson. What grade, young man? "First grade," he declared. And do you know what you want to be when you grow up? "Yes," he replied firmly. Well, tell us, are you going to be a lawyer like your mother? "NO," he shouted.

As I understand from my daughter, when the laughter had finally died down and the judge regained control of his courtroom, he asked perhaps one question too many. "What, then, do you want to be when you grow up?" Without missing a beat, and with the judge right where my six-year-old grandson wanted him, he replied: "A comedian." He brought down the house.

Hope is eternal and I hope to see my grandson try his first case. But I have done the math and I am 78 years older than he is, so by the time he graduates from Columbia Law School, or even from Yale, I shall likely be a grave man for whom the bells have tolled. But 'twill serve, 'tis enough, what I know of my grandson already. He, I believe, will be the one to surpass my father's idol, Bill Fallon, and become this century's "Great Mouthpiece."

In my book, he already has.

ACKNOWLEDGMENTS

My wife Joyce, who was my Office Manager from the 1960s to my retirement in 2006 and kept the firm at peak performance over the course of 45 years. She has remained at my side through today and is the reason I was able to turn to my trial memoirs these last few years. I am a man of words who finds himself incapable of calling forth those that could do justice to her lifelong endeavors in the legal profession. If it were within my powers, I would long ago have awarded her an honorary law degree.

My daughter Alessandra, who attended many of my trials as a child during school holidays and went on to law school herself. She, too, became an Assistant U.S. Attorney – playing a lead role in the only federal criminal prosecution against the perpetrators of the 9/11 terrorist attacks on the United States – and now has a federal trial and appellate practice. I am exceedingly grateful to her for compiling these stories, assisting in drafting the Bronfman chapters, editing the manuscript, and preparing the book for publication. (My thanks as well to Debbie Burke who assisted her at the end in getting it to press.) Also, I have insufficient words to thank Alessandra for finally locating the Bronfman trial transcript, which I had wanted to read for more than 40 years, and for copying its nearly 6,000 pages at the courthouse copier with the assistance of her sister-in-law Alice Haynes, whom I also thank.

My daughter Caralee (Cari, as she is known) and my former wife Jo Warner, who came often to watch me in court, regardless of the time of year, and who for decades put up with a trial lawyer's temperament, which I know was no easy feat. I owe them a special debt of gratitude for helping to sustain my career, in part at the expense of their own.

My alma mater Columbia College and Columbia Law School.

My esteemed colleagues along the way, John G. Reilly, Peter James Johnson, Charlie Kramer, Tom Meagher, Thomas A. Moore, Emmett Agoglia, Henry G. Miller, Bob Bell, Frank Bensel, Peter Crean, Jack Downing, Peter Kopff, and my Inner Circle friends Jack Mullen, Jim Butler, Sal Liccardo, Stu Schlesinger, Bill Sneed and Lantz Welch.

My good friends, the Hon. Nicholas Coffinas (whom I met at the U.S. Attorney's Office in 1956) and his brother, attorney Gus Coffinas (we three played pinochle together weekly for decades), and their lovely wives Dolly and Angie, and their children George, Maria, Eleni, Gigi and Ethel; Prof. Robert "Pinky" Pinckert (whom I met in college on the varsity golf team), his wife Missy and their children Eric and Miranda; Gene Rossides (whom I met in college on the varsity football team); Aldan Markson (my law school roommate); Mike Russo; Frank Amendola; Nick Christy; Jim Fauci; Andy Romeo; Dom Ciucci; Rubrecht "Ruby" Obert; Chef André Soltner; Andy Gerzel (owner of Sweet's Restaurant); John Erb and Phyllis Skelton Erb (Idaho and Montana cattle ranchers, who hosted me, Jo and the girls on our trips out West and took a Brooklyn boy trout fishing); Tony and Carolyn Soglio; Joe and Alice Foreman; Sabine Mueller; Glenda Robinson; Carl and Frances Tavolacci; John and Connie Profaci; John and Mary Ann Pitera; John and Maryann Saraceno; Frank and Pat LaRocca; Vito and Patrice Cannavo; Vicky Lombardi; Dr. A. Bernard Ackerman; Dr. Joseph Mormino; Dr. Louis Vorhaus; Dr. Armen Haig and his wife Johanna; Dr. Bill Sykes and his wife Joyce; Dr. Norton Spritz and Dr. Marilyn Karmason; Dr. William Schaffner and Lois Knight; Dr. Jonathan Mauser and Ivy (an excellent attorney who worked in our office); Dr. Norman Canter; and my wonderful cardiologist friends who have kept me ticking all these years, Dr. Lucien Arditi, Dr. Jay Meltzer and Dr. David Sherman. A special thanks as well to my newest friend Richy Russo, who has become my right-hand man these past months, helping me to get back and forth to the hospital three times a week and brightening the otherwise miserable hours spent there.

My great office staff: Joyce, then Marruso, my office manager from 1962 through to the end; Rosalyn Trapani Palladino and Louise Fiorello Canale, secretaries extraordinaire, who joined early on and stayed with me through to the end; Kristy Amador, our magnificent receptionist and deposition clerk, who started when still a teenager and stayed on for decades, transferring to Kramer, Dillof, Livingston & Moore when we closed our doors; and all of our other wonderful and irreplaceable secretaries, bookkeepers, investigators and file clerks - Mary Bonadies, Peter Christy, Tony D'Antuono, Dominick Eastham, Vivian Hagel, George Kast, Danny Liu, Anita Lombardo, Mark Marino, Phil Massaro, Mary McDermott, Frank Minucci, Brian O'Connor, Carmine Russo, Carolyn Scarimbolo, Mitchell Seda, Kevin Tang and Betty Thurman. Thank you as well to Joyce's children Lisa and Steven Marruso, Lisa's son Danny

Bowman, and my third-cousin Stephen "Rocky" LaRocca (his mother and aunt, Jean and Dorothy Tricarico, were Eddie's and my closest playmates when we were very young children), himself a fine lawyer, all four of whom worked at one time or another at our office; and to Lisa's other two children, Christopher and Brianna, an integral part of my family for many decades. And my apologies to Sam Soo Yi, a great young lawyer, for not being able to keep my promise to train him, on account of my retirement not long after he joined our firm.

My extended family past and future:

Everything I achieved was on account of my ancestors – Di Blasio, Colamarino, D'Alesio, Dolcimele, Gargiulo, Roccanova, Rubertone and Spera – and my father Amerigo and most beloved mother Lena. I honor you always.

I thank as well my aunts and uncles and cousins – Brancaccio, Cataldi, Di Blasio, Entico, Gallo, Izzo, Lo Freddo, Lubrano, Rubertone, Sinisgalli, Spero, Stuster, Terranova, Tricarico, Zito – who supported me and my brother and kept us in their hearts always.

My abiding love to my brother Edward, who passed away in 2015 and whom I miss deeply; my sisters-in-law Irene Maruzzella DeBlasio and Jan Warner George; my brother-in-law Pat George; my four nieces Michelle DeBlasio, Gioia DeBlasio, Rikki George and Andrea George, and their spouses and children; and my son-in-law Allan Haynes, Sr.

My only grandchild, Allan Haynes, Jr., of whom I am infinitely proud, already a scholar, an athlete, and an actor, singer and comedian, to whom I hand off the baton, wishing him "100A" and "cent' anni" of great and good luck.

I would be remiss if I did not acknowledge here as well my immense gratitude to my grandson Allan's other grandparents, those who did not live long enough to know him. Only Joy and I were the lucky ones. Allan carries them forward within him, their wealth of diversity having made him a great and remarkable young man:

> Allan's maternal grandmother, my former wife Jo Warner, was the daughter of college-educated parents, one an osteopath, the other a school teacher, both of whom were descended from German, English, Irish and Scottish immigrants who arrived in

this country in the mid to late 1800s, and moved westward from Indiana, Illinois and Iowa to Idaho, homesteading along the way in Minnesota, Nebraska and South Dakota. Jo herself was born in New Mexico, spent her first three years in Texas, grew up in Idaho, earned her college degree in Colorado, and moved to New York to study painting at the Art Students League from 1953 to 1955. She was an all-American in the truest sense of the word and, at the same time, a New Yorker through and through. As an artist, Jo showed her work first at the 10th Street Camino Gallery and from the 1970s onward at the Phoenix Gallery, which was the first artists' cooperative in New York City. She had paintings at several museums and galleries around the country, best known among them the Museum of Modern Art in New York. But she was an artist at a time when virtually the only women artists recognized, and whose work was collected, were those married to famous artist husbands. Jo persevered in an extremely difficult professional environment from the 1950s until her early death from cancer in 1999.

My grandson's paternal grandparents were equally impressive. Allan's grandfather Frank Haynes immigrated to this country from Barbados barely a teenager, his ancestors having been brought as slaves from Africa. Frank, whom I never met, earned his college degree from New York University and then fought in World War II. He spent his career as a Navy draftsman – many other avenues having been denied him as a Black man in America – and was a fine craftsman and much beloved father. Allan's paternal grandmother Carrie Stewart Haynes, whom I also never met, was born in Rhode Island to parents who had moved north from the Gullah Islands off South Carolina, their people having been brought as slaves from Africa. Carrie worked for the New York City Department of Education and, after she had seen all eight of her children off to college, she went back to school to earn her college degree in education.

Frank and Carrie Haynes, like my father Amerigo, understood that education offered the greatest chance to overcome historic and daunting social disparity. Like so many Black families in mid-twentieth century New York, Frank and Carrie were relegated to living in a neglected housing project, theirs in the Bronx.

Nevertheless, they sent their eldest son Frank Haynes, Jr., to the private Horace Mann School on full scholarship, from where he went on to Yale University for both undergraduate and Law School degrees, one of the first African-Americans to achieve such a feat in the 1960s. Frank and Carrie's next four children attended among the best public high schools in the city - Bronx Science, Dewitt Clinton, and Music and Art - and went on to top colleges, among them Smith and Wesleyan. They sent their final three children on full scholarships to the private New Lincoln School and the Ethical Culture Fieldston School, from which they went on to the University of Michigan, the University of Pennsylvania and Yale University. Their seventh child, my son-in-law Allan, continued on to earn a Master's degree in architecture at the University of Pennsylvania and is a practicing architect today.

My girls, Alessandra and Caralee, you are the pride of my life.

My final words I save for my wife Joy. It would take me another book of even greater length to express my love and devotion and appreciation and thankfulness to my best friend, my Michelin chef, my caregiver and my protector. Grazie for everything, my dearest and my greatest love.

INDEX

ABOUT THE AUTHOR

Peter DeBlasio led a storied career as one of the greatest trial lawyers in American history. By the time of his retirement in 2006 after 50 years of practice, he had tried 600 cases, taking 500 to verdict and favorably settling another 100 during trial - undoubtedly more than any living lawyer, and likely more than any lawyer of old.

Fiercely competitive and in full command of the courtroom, he was revered by the bench, fellow trial lawyers and grateful clients alike. In 1973, he was among the first to be inducted into the Inner Circle of Advocates, an organization of the top 100 plaintiff's trial lawyers in the country, and thereafter he was admitted into the International Academy of Trial Lawyers, an association of the 500 best trial lawyers in the world.

Although virtually unknown to the general public in an era before social media and cameras in the courtroom, thousands nevertheless thrilled to his performances - full of wit, wry humor, rapid-fire questioning and heart-rending summations - from their front row jury box seats.

Peter was a marvel to behold. A genius in the courtroom.

Made in the USA
Middletown, DE
21 May 2021